THE MEMETICS OF MUSIC

In Loving Memory of my Grandparents

George Bradley Bateman

1911–1981

Grace Marion Bateman

1914–2005

The Memetics of Music

A Neo-Darwinian View of Musical Structure and Culture

STEVEN JAN
University of Huddersfield, UK

ASHGATE

Published by
Ashgate Publishing Limited
Gower House
Croft Road
Aldershot
Hants GU11 3HR
England

Ashgate Publishing Company
Suite 420
101 Cherry Street
Burlington, VT 05401-4405
USA

Ashgate website: http://www.ashgate.com

British Library Cataloguing in Publication Data
Jan, Steven B., 1965–
The memetics of music : a neo-Darwinian view of musical structure and culture
1. Music theory 2. Memetics I. Title
781

Library of Congress Cataloging-in-Publication Data
Jan, Steven B., 1965-
The memetics of music : a neo-Darwinian view of musical structure and culture / Steven Jan.
p. cm.
Includes bibliographical references and index.
ISBN 978-0-7546-5594-7 (alk. paper)
1. Music–Psychological aspects. 2. Music–Social aspects. 3. Memetics. I. Title.
ML3830.J36 2007
781'.1–dc22

2006101545

ISBN 978-0-7546-5594-7

Printed and bound in Great Britain by TJ International Ltd, Padstow, Cornwall.

Contents

List of Figures

List of Tables

List of Music Examples

Preface

> There is grandeur in this view of life, with its several powers, having been originally breathed by the Creator into a few forms or into one; and that, whilst this planet has gone cycling on according to the fixed law of gravity, from so simple a beginning endless forms most beautiful and most wonderful have been, and are being, evolved.
>
> (Darwin 1996: 396; 'by the Creator' not in the first (1859) edition)

Since at least the middle of the eighteenth century, the relationship between the living world and the products of human intelligence has stimulated and challenged many writers. Parallels drawn between nature and culture since the time of Darwin have tended to see changes in socio-cultural products in terms of similarities with biological evolution, but before Darwin, the opposite was the case: the ebb and flow of culture, specifically the structure, development and transmission of language, was used as a weapon in the debate between creationists, with their static view of the universal order, and those advocating the dynamic mutability – the evolution – of species.

Organicism – the conception of cultural products in terms of ideas derived from the biological sciences – reached its height in the nineteenth century and its incorporation into discourse on music coincided with, and nourished, the growing discipline of musical analysis, which had by this time become distinct from its *alter ego*, music theory. After the high tide of organicism had receded, some theorists, notably Réti and Schenker, continued the tradition well into the twentieth century with analytical systems which were predicated on (and developed in order to demonstrate) an assumed organic unity in their objects of study. It is clear that the reverberations of organicism, albeit more subtly expressed, still affect our thinking about music today, despite the apparent triumph of postmodernism, with its celebration of fragmentation, multiple readings and the anti-structural and anti-hierarchic.

This book reconceives organicism, not in an endeavour to rehash long-spent notions of high romanticism and German Idealism, but as a consequence of its focus on the *meme* concept formulated by the ethologist Richard Dawkins. This idea sees human culture as comprised of a near infinity of independent, selfish *replicators* analogous to the genes of biological evolution. In this work, tangential to his main concerns with biological replicators and their effects on animal behaviour, Dawkins has powerfully reinvigorated an idea which has its roots in the work of many earlier writers, some dating back to the ancient world. Thirty years after its initial presentation in the first edition of *The Selfish Gene*, the idea of memes has spread widely in human culture – it is clearly a successful replicator. While the reproductive success of a replicator is no guarantee of the veracity of the ideas it encapsulates (popularity, in other words, does not signify truth), the *meme meme* (Ball 1984: 146; Costall 1991) has, nevertheless, shown itself to be a powerful tool for understanding human behaviour and the artefacts it gives rise to. The time is ripe to apply the meme concept systematically to music, to develop a *memetics of music*.

The purpose of this book, therefore, is to show that memetics offers a new perspective on musical structure – which can be conceived as the disposition of memes within a work, at various hierarchical levels; musical style – the nature of memes within a single work, within the output of a composer, or within the output of an historically or geographically discrete group of composers; and musical style change – the transformations occurring in memes at these three 'levels of stylistic relevance' (Nattiez 1990: 135–6) over a given time span. To this end, the book is organized as follows.

Chapter 1 provides a context for the book's central ideas by reviewing conceptions of biological evolution before and after Darwin's revolutionary idea – his 'Dangerous Idea', as the philosopher Daniel Dennett has described it (1995: 21) – including the *selfish gene* perspective advocated by Dawkins and fundamental to this study. After consideration of the scope of nature-culture analogies, a brief initial overview of memetics sets the scene for its more detailed treatment in subsequent chapters. The chapter concludes with reflections on some philosophical issues pertinent to developing a memetics of music.

Chapter 2 and Chapter 3 offer an introduction to what might be regarded as the 'static' aspects of memetics. Chapter 2 starts with a discussion of the nature, ontology and basic attributes of memes in general. After considering some issues concerning style analysis which offer a useful bridge between more conventional musicological concerns and the less familiar standpoint of memetics, it concludes by suggesting some ways in which memes might exist in its various parameters.

Chapter 3 continues the definition of musical memes, introducing an analytical symbology for their representation and discussion. After discussing the central issues of particulateness, segmentation and coindexation, it goes on to examine ways in which musical memes combine to form complexes and how such complexes are hierarchically structured. It concludes with a consideration of how memetic-structural and memetic-cultural hierarchies might be analogically related to those of nature.

Chapter 4 turns to the 'dynamic' aspects of memetics, the propagation and evolution of memes, by examining the mechanisms by which memes are transmitted in the environment of human culture. It considers how memetic mutation and differential selection is the driving force of socio-cultural evolution and, therefore, of musical style.

Chapter 5 looks at the origin of large-scale musical structures – especially the complex formal archetypes of eighteenth- and nineteenth-century music – in terms of the replication and evolution of *structural memes* originating in the music of earlier periods. This concept allows the ontogeny of a musical work, its individual genesis by means of memetic conglomeration, to be related to the phylogeny, the 'species-history', of the structural meme of which the work is an instantiation.

Chapter 6 moves from the theoretical to the practical in considering how musical analysis might be conducted in the light of the meme concept. After a discussion of the memetic nature of theoretical frameworks and analytical systems and a consideration of methodologies in memetic analysis, it discusses ways in which computer resources, in particular David Huron's *Humdrum Toolkit* software, may be used to expedite the theoretical development of memetics and to facilitate the practice of memetic analysis. A short case study illustrates the mechanics of using *Humdrum* for the latter purpose.

Chapter 7 begins with a formal summary of the meme concept as it applies to music. After reviewing some of the central problems and prospects for musical memetics, it briefly explores some other ways in which memetics impinges upon music, including the issue of animal culture and musicality. In the light of recent research in neuropsychology, it concludes by offering a critique of the notion of the conscious intentionality or agency of the composer, replacing it by a view of consciousness as the consequence of vast meme-complexes running like software on the physical platform of the human brain.

The present study is interdisciplinary in nature. Taking as its basis ideas from contemporary science, it attempts to apply a scientific perspective to the realm of music in the wider aim of fostering a more unified approach to the spheres of nature and culture. It seeks to do this using the tools of musicology, music analysis and music psychology, and is both qualitative and quantitative, critical and technical, in its scope. It also draws upon, and adapts, the somewhat arcane language of evolutionary biology and (especially) memetics. The use of such terms here ('phmnemotype', of my own coining, is perhaps the most extreme) is not motivated by a fondness for jargon: rather, one might justify this terminological expansion by an appeal to Gould and Vrba's observation that 'unnamed ideas generally remain unconsidered' (1982: 4). Nevertheless, the book avoids the explicitly mathematical formulation of its subject matter found in some sources on evolution and memetics; and the tone is at times rather more humanistic than is perhaps the norm in most current work in music psychology.

To a large extent, therefore, a good deal of the book is concerned with developing hypotheses which might act as stimuli for, and which might be refined by, later empirical research. More broadly, it is a work of theory; and like many scientific theories, it is speculative (even improvisatory), hunch-driven and often provocative. As with much speculation in this broad tradition, it does not claim to offer proof for all of its claims; yet while I do not claim to offer a complete confirmation, I hope to have provided some useful concepts, frameworks and methodologies for future research to do so. Moreover, it does not always take an orthodox line on certain controversial issues in memetics – even where orthodoxy is established in such a new and often turbulent discipline.

I largely focus in this study on the music of Haydn, Mozart and Beethoven and, more broadly, on the 'common-practice' era of J.S. Bach to Brahms of which the classical trinity are a central part. Yet, in the process of examining memetics using this time frame and these composers as my 'home base', I shall introduce concepts that have far wider resonance, with applicability to musics of all styles, times and places; and I shall aim to demonstrate this applicability by reference, albeit somewhat limited, to such musics. It is typical of the boldness – some would say the recklessness – of memetics that its claims are not chronologically or geographically circumscribed, but are argued to be of universal applicability to all ages and all cultures. Therefore a theory of *musical memetics* – stimulating the development within musicology of such a sub-discipline being one of the principal aims of this book – must embrace the same ambitious claims to universality and it will be judged to have failed if it cannot substantiate them.

I embarked upon this book because, having written several articles on musical memetics, I felt that only a book-length study could do the subject full justice. Having now written such a study, I have now come to the conclusion that one book is insufficient for the task – I have merely scratched the surface of an immense field here – and that several books are necessary to deal with all the implications for music of this powerful and wide ranging theory. As a result, I have had to omit discussion of many interesting and provocative topics, such as the relationship between memetics and chaos theory and memetics and information theory, cultural-taxonomic questions in memetics, and the concept of evolutionarily stable strategies. I hope to consider these subjects in future publications, as well as developing further the issues covered here.

Steven Jan
Didsbury, Manchester, July 2006.

Acknowledgements

In part because this book has had a relatively long gestation – my first ideas on musical memetics date from the mid 1990s – I am indebted to numerous people for their help and support in its writing.

My former colleagues at the Royal Northern College of Music in Manchester Douglas Jarman, David Ledbetter and Charles Bodman Rae read some of my earlier work and provided helpful feedback. Douglas, in particular, was instrumental in the genesis of one of my first articles on memetics (Jan 2002), which represents the source, in embryonic form, for several of the ideas in this book.

My colleagues at Huddersfield have provided a supportive and fertile intellectual environment in which to work. In particular, Mathew Adkins, John Bryan, Michael Clarke, Lisa Colton and William Stafford have made valuable suggestions or provided information from their own fields of expertise. Of all my colleagues, however, I am most deeply indebted to Michael Russ, who carefully read the manuscript and suggested numerous improvements. Without his intelligence and wisdom, this book would be very much poorer.

Elliott Antokoletz, Nicholas Bannan, William Caplin, Tim Carter, Eric Clarke, Nicholas Cook, Benjamin Davies, Kate Distin, Jonathan Dunsby, Margaret Kartomi, Adam Ockelford, John Sloboda, Hans-Cees Speel and Robert Walker have all, in various ways, encouraged or helped refine my ideas at various stages. Having kindly read some of my preliminary thoughts, Eugene Narmour's helpful comments stimulated me to develop some of the ideas in Chapter 4 based on his own seminal work. Charles Heller has given me long-distance encouragement with his enthusiasm for all things memetic.

In addition to the constructive comments of the two anonymous reviewers, the staff at Ashgate, especially my Commissioning Editor Heidi May, Editorial Manager Ann Newell and Commissioning and Contract Administrator Anne Keirby, have been most helpful. I am also grateful to Yo Tomita for the use of his *Bach* musicological font, which renders note symbols, sharps, flats and Schenkerian carets so elegantly.

Of course, for all their help and support, these kind people are in no way responsible for the errors, omissions and infelicities that remain.

My family and friends have provided constant encouragement, especially my mother, Maureen Jan, who made many sacrifices for my education; and Connie Bateman, whose love of knowledge and learning has been an inspiration since my childhood. Finally, and most importantly, for his limitless reserves of patience and understanding, this book would not have seen the light of day without Philip Partridge.

Some material in this study is adapted and developed from earlier published work (Jan 2000a, 2000b, 2001, 2002, 2003, 2004). I am grateful to the Evolution, Complexity and Cognition Group, Vrije Universiteit Brussel, for permission to adapt material originally published in the *Journal of Memetics: Evolutionary Models of Information Transmission*; to Peter Lang GmbH for permission to adapt material originally published in the *International Journal of Musicology*; and to the MIT Press for permission to adapt material originally published in the *Computer Music Journal*.

Chapter 1

Introduction: Biological and Socio-Cultural Evolution

1.1. Prologue: Why a Memetics of Music?

> Nothing in biology makes sense except in the light of evolution.
>
> (Dobzhansky 1973)

Much theoretical and analytical musicology of the past two hundred years has devoted itself to the detection and discussion of patterns in music, from small fragments of musical information to large-scale formal archetypes. A pattern normally only attains significance if it occurs in more than one context. Ways of conceiving and representing such recurrences have changed significantly over time, but they are now often considered under the aegis of the notion of intertextuality. From the point of view of the listener, their recurrence in different contexts facilitates perception and cognition of the music, giving a frame of reference with which to negotiate the work, to predict its unfolding processes, and to manage its novelties and unpredictabilities. From the point of view of the composer, learning the craft of composition generally involves learning how to manipulate such standard patterns and figures; and even when the composer discovers his or her distinctive 'voice', there is perhaps more that is borrowed (albeit transformed) than is genuinely new in his or her style.

To take a simple and clear-cut example of pattern recurrence, the passages in Example 1.1 below show a direct and unequivocal morphological relationship – the patterning is essentially 'the same'. Because of the close conformance, because Mozart was known to admire and respect J.C. Bach as a person and as a composer and because *Die Entführung* was written around a decade after Bach's concerto, we are strongly inclined to say that Mozart copied this pattern from J.C. Bach – or copied another example (or 'instantiation') of it from J.C. Bach or another composer. Throughout his life Mozart assimilated the styles of composers whom he respected and this often took the form of copying such style-defining patterns – a receptivity which is probably true of most composers.

Example 1.1: Replicated Patterns in Works of J.C. Bach and Mozart

i) J.C. Bach: Keyboard Concerto in E♭ major op. 7 no. 5 (C 59) (1770), I, bb. 52–5

ii) Mozart: *Die Entführung aus dem Serail* K. 384 (1782), no. 11, 'Martern aller Arten', bb. 13–15

From the listener's perspective, such connections are often very striking and, provided we are familiar with both contexts, hearing one of the passages tends to interrupt our intra-work processing and jolts us to an inter-work perspective, rather like clicking on a hyperlink and moving to another, related, page on the internet. By virtue of our exposure to myriad other such connections, we assimilate a deep-level stylistic knowledge: we form 'top-down' cognitive schemata which structure our 'bottom-up' perception of a style and which provide predictions as to how an incoming sequence of musical information might unfold over time (Bharucha 1987: 2–3). Even if we get the relationship of precedence the wrong way around – if we think, on hearing the Bach concerto, that it is 'by Mozart' or 'sounds like Mozart' – we make a diachronic error which does not necessarily undermine our synchronic perspective on the style: both hearings contribute to our formation of a mental representation of the style.

We have so far invoked the two clear points of view of the listener and the composer – Nattiez's esthesic and poietic poles respectively (1990: 10–16) – but are these the only points of view which matter in such cases? The purpose of this book is to argue for a distinct and illuminating third perspective. This point of view is metaphorical and anthropomorphic and the metaphor is challenging and controversial, but the way of thinking I aim to outline here derives from a fundamental reality which has its basis in well-established scientific principles. The point of view I am referring to is that of the recurrent, or replicated, pattern itself, which is the central standpoint of memetics. Dennett states the issue clearly when he argues that

> In the beginning, there were no reasons; there were only causes. Nothing had a purpose, nothing had so much as a function; there was no teleology in the world at all. The explanation for this is simple: There was nothing that had interests. But after millennia there happened to emerge simple *replicators* .... While *they* had no inkling of their interests, and perhaps properly speaking had no interests, we, peering back from our godlike vantage point at their early days, can nonarbitrarily assign them certain interests – generated by their defining 'interest' in self-replication.... Put more anthropomorphically, if these simple replicators want to continue to replicate, they should hope and strive for various things; they should avoid the 'bad' things and seek the 'good' things. When an entity arrives on the scene capable of behavior that staves off, however primitively, its own dissolution and decomposition, it brings with it into the world its 'good'. That is to say, it creates a point of view from which the world's events can be roughly partitioned into the favorable, the unfavorable, and the neutral. And its own innate proclivities to seek the first, shun the second, and ignore the third contribute essentially to the definition of the three classes.
>
> (1993: 173–4; his emphases)

As the keystone of all Dawkins's work on evolution, the consequences of this argument is that a replicator will be selfish (1989). I will consider in detail later what a replicator is, how it might be said to be selfish and how music might engender and sustain replicators, but for the moment my three basic contentions are that patterns such as those shown in Example 1.1 are replicators – specifically, they are musical memes – that music is largely made up of such replicated patterns transmitted from generation to generation of composers, and that the synchronic (structural-hierarchic) and diachronic (historical-developmental) dimensions of music may be understood in terms of their transmission and evolution. In short, I aim here to advocate a (neo-) Darwinian perspective on music. If this viewpoint is legitimate, then Dobzhansky's maxim cited at the head of this section will also apply to music and indeed to all the products of human culture.

While the detailed definition of what constitutes a musical meme will need to be developed over the course of several chapters, it is useful to have a provisional working definition in mind until we are ready to turn to detailed musical considerations towards the end of Chapter 2. (This may seem a long wait, but it is important to outline a number of foundation concepts in memetics in order to provide a clear context for the main, specifically musical, discussions.) To this end, we might regard the musical meme as a discrete 'packet' of musical information, demarcated from neighbouring material by various kinds of articulation and consisting of a relatively small number of uni- or multi-parametric elements – a collection of pitches in a distinctive rhythmic garb, for instance, as in Example 1.1.

What are the advantages of this way of thinking about music? Why adopt the new and contentious point of view of the selfish replicator as against the established perspectives of the composer or the listener? While these advantages will emerge, and be justified, over the course of this book, the advantages of a memetic view of music might initially be summarized as follows:

- As a metatheory, it links theoretical, analytical and historical perspectives on music with those of psychology, showing how musical patterns and structures, and the processes by which they alter over time, have their roots in perceptual and cognitive processes.
- It motivates systematic empirical testing of its hypotheses.
- It is elegantly compatible with applications of Darwinian thought to other realms and other substrates, such as evolutionary perspectives on the transmission and transformation of languages.
- It allows us to address a number of issues in musicology and music theory and analysis more satisfactorily than other perspectives. These include the questions of why certain musical patterns and procedures are more common than others at certain times, how ways of organizing musical structures change over time, and even how trends and traditions in discourses about music arise and develop.

Because adopting the viewpoint of the selfish replicator requires one to follow a Darwinian path, this first chapter is a necessary (and necessarily concise) summary of the development of views on biological evolution and their extension, since the eighteenth century, to the realm of human culture (for comprehensive accounts of the theory of evolution, see Maynard Smith 1993 and Jones 1999). Having covered these issues at the outset, the parallels drawn between nature and (musical) culture in subsequent chapters – and the sometimes esoteric terminology used in drawing them – will then hopefully be clearer.

In this chapter, after a review of the development of evolutionary thought from the eighteenth to the twentieth centuries, culminating in the acceptance of the Darwinian model of natural selection, I turn to Dawkins's reinvigoration of Darwinism by means of the powerful 'selfish gene' model. As a prelude to a brief history and overview of memetics, I consider the extension of evolutionary thinking to culture and the central notion of universal Darwinism. I conclude with a consideration of the methodological and conceptual issues underpinning the theorization of the memetics of music.

1.2. Theories of Biological Evolution from Lamarck to Dawkins

1.2.1. *Pre-Darwinian Theories and Creationism*

'When Darwin's friend and colleague T.H. Huxley first read [*On*] *The Origin of Species* [*By Means of Natural Selection*] in 1859', Miller recalls, 'he said to himself "how stupid not to have thought of it before!"' (1992: 3). With the benefit of hindsight, all the evidence for Charles Darwin's theory of evolution – 'by means of natural selection' is the most important phrase – was in place by the early years of the nineteenth century. The reason this evidence was misinterpreted by most thinkers before Darwin was that commentators of the eighteenth and early nineteenth centuries had clear, but incorrect, views about the patterns of evidence they saw. As Miller notes,

> a strong preconception about what a pattern *means*, what it represents, can stop you seeing it in any other way. Presumably this happened to Darwin's predecessors and some of his contemporaries as well. They failed to 'see' what Darwin 'saw', not because they were short of facts, but because they had reasons for 'seeing' the facts in a different way.
>
> (1992: 9; his emphasis)

In the eighteenth century the very notion of evolution[1] itself – in the sense of gradual mutational change in the morphologies of living organisms over time, the transmutation of species – was fiercely disputed as a result of adherence to two of these 'strong preconceptions': the Biblical account of creation given in the book of Genesis and the Platonic notion of Ideal Forms (Essentialism) (Miller 1992: 9). The first of these, Creationism, argued that the earth was created relatively recently (all estimates fell far short of the now widely accepted figure of *c.* four billion years), fabricated over a short space of time and then filled with a plethora of flora and fauna which maintained a constant form over time by means of true breeding. The earth itself was believed to be inert, the only differences between its present form and that of the creation having been caused by the flood described in Genesis 6–8 (: 10–13).

---

[1] The *Oxford English Dictionary* offers diverse definitions of 'evolution' arranged in twelve distinct categories (Simpson and Weiner 1989: Vol. 5, 476–7). The sense in which it is understood here – one of the earliest instances of which appears in Charles Lyell's *Principles of Geology* of 1832 – is as '[t]he origination of species of animals and plants, as conceived by those who attribute it to a process of development from earlier forms, and not to a process of "special creation"'. This is closely allied to '[t]he development or growth, according to its inherent tendencies, of anything that may be compared to a living organism (e.g. of a political constitution, science, language, etc.) …. the rise or origination of anything by natural development, as distinguished from its production by a specific act; "growing" as opposed to "being made"' (: 477).

Logical support for creationism seemed to come from the 'Argument from Design', expressed most clearly in William Paley's *Natural Theology* of 1803. Paley believed that the rich complexity of biological forms – the perfection of design manifested by the eye, the wing and the hand – could not have arisen in any way other than through the actions of an intelligent designer. The existence of God, it seemed to Paley, could easily be proved merely by casual observation of the natural world, in all its wonder and diversity, around us (Miller 1992: 17–19).

The first evidence to undermine these views of a static, immutable creation, and therefore to admit the possibility of some kind of evolution, came in the form of fossils. When it was finally acknowledged that these were indeed remnants of organic forms, and when it was realized that fossil strata revealed many chronologically distinct levels of extinct life, it became necessary to posit not one but several acts of divine violence (Catastrophism), Noah's flood being the last, each followed by a restocking of the planet. It became increasingly clear, however, that the higher (later) strata contained remnants of creatures of greater complexity than those of the lower (earlier) strata. In an attempt to defend the biblical position, the doctrine of Progressionism maintained that such an increase in complexity was the result of a series of staggered acts of creation leading to forms of increasing complexity (Miller 1992: 15–16), not to what Darwin would later call 'descent with modification through natural selection' (1996: 371).

The developing science of geology further contributed to the credibility of evolutionary interpretations when it was realized that the earth was not stable but undergoes constant physical change as a result of climatic and volcanic action. Formulated in the work of James Hutton and, later, Charles Lyell, whose *Principles of Geology* strongly influenced Darwin, the doctrine of Uniformitarianism overturned the idea of one or more discrete catastrophes (Miller 1992: 28–9). The notion of an ever-changing physical environment thus lent support to the idea of biological forms altering in order to adapt to that environment.

Various 'facts in favour of evolution before Darwin' (Miller 1992: 30–38) led Lamarck to develop the first important and influential dynamic view of the living world in the early nineteenth century. Drawing on the notion of the 'Great Chain of Being', Lamarck saw nature as 'a graded series of natural types, arranged in order', all constantly engaged in a struggle for complexity (Miller 1992: 41). The motion up this ladder, Lamarck argued, was driven both by an organism's immanent tendency to development and by the moulding force of the environment. This latter influence, he asserted, would lead to physical changes in the organism which would be inherited by its descendants (: 41–2). This doctrine, the inheritance of acquired characteristics, is Lamarck's chief intellectual legacy and had a profound influence upon the thinking of both Darwin and his opponents.

1.2.2. *Evolution by Natural Selection and the Neo-Darwinian Synthesis*

> If I were to give an award for the single best idea anyone has ever had, I'd give it to Darwin, ahead of Newton and Einstein and everyone else. In a single stroke, the idea of evolution by natural selection unifies the realm of life, meaning, and purpose with the realm of space and time, cause and effect, mechanism and physical law. But it is not just a wonderful scientific idea. It is a dangerous idea.
>
> (Dennett 1995: 21)

Initially an advocate of Paley's Argument from Design, Darwin had formulated the ideas underpinning his *Origin of Species* as early as 1838, in the period after his return to England following his voyage on the *Beagle* (1831–36). The view of nature which he developed during the *Beagle* years, the essence of the theory of evolution by natural selection, was as follows (for an overview, see Beer's *Introduction* in Darwin 1996):

1. The earth, as Lyell maintained, is in constant change. As a result, organisms must adapt to their new environment or a fatal disequilibrium would arise.
2. Despite the fact that living things breed true to type, Nature provides a steady supply of 'random unsolicited novelties' (Miller 1992: 104).
3. As Thomas Malthus argued in his *Essay on the Principle of Population* of 1798, the disparity between supply of and demand for resources in nature – food, space, mates – exacted a terrible price on those least suited to the prevailing conditions. Fierce competition for resources by large numbers of organisms inevitably leads to winners and losers.
4. Those individuals in possession of favourable novelties will tend to have the advantage over those in possession of less favourable novelties and, therefore, will tend to survive to propagate their advantages to the next generation. This concept is often called, in a phrase suggested to Darwin by Herbert Spencer, 'the survival of the fittest' (Dawkins 1983a: 179).
5. The successive accumulation of favoured novelties over time gives rise to considerable morphological change. Darwin conceived this using the metaphor of a branching tree, whereby a species gives rise to offshoots, creating a network of twigs all sharing a common ancestor represented by the trunk (Darwin 1996: 96).

Such was Darwin's concern over the implicit critique of Christian theology in his theory that he withheld publication of the work he had provisionally titled *Natural Selection* in the 1850s for almost twenty years. He may well have delayed longer were it not for the stimulus of receiving a letter in 1858 from Alfred Russell Wallace which suggested Wallace had independently arrived at the same theory. Appearing in 1859, the first edition of the *Origin* at last offered a convincing mechanism to explain the by then widely accepted fact of evolution. It should be noted, however, that the principle Darwin called natural selection was suggested by other writers before him, including Empedocles (Zirkle 1941).

Summarizing the mechanisms underlying the fundamentally algorithmic nature of the theory of evolution by natural selection, Dennett argues that

> evolution occurs whenever the following conditions exist: (1) variation: there is a continuing abundance of different elements [;] (2) heredity or replication: the elements have the capacity to create copies or replicas of themselves [;] (3) differential 'fitness': the number of copies of an element that are created in a given time varies, depending on interactions between the features of that element and features of the environment in which it persists.
>
> (1995: 343)

It is churlish, but undoubtedly true, to suggest that the *Origin of Species* would be an even greater work had it been written with knowledge of Gregor Mendel's studies in heredity, which were first published in 1866. The principal weakness of Darwin's theory was that it was formulated without knowledge of the mechanisms by which the characteristics of living things – let alone 'random unsolicited novelties' – were propagated. This allowed critics to suggest that whatever factor gave rise to favourable variations would be steadily dissipated over time through division and dispersal, such that a vibrant, multicoloured nature would eventually become a bland, muddy grey. Unable to rebut this charge, Darwin retreated to a distinctly Lamarckian position, suggesting in the sixth and final edition of the *Origin*, of 1872, that natural selection is complemented in large part by the inheritance of characteristics acquired, in response to the environment, during the course of an organism's lifetime (Beer, in Darwin 1996: xxiii).[2]

One of the few scientists to question the resurgent Lamarckian orthodoxy was August Weismann, who proposed, in 1883, a distinction between a mortal 'soma line' (the cells of the body) and an immortal 'germ plasm' (the hereditary material) (Miller 1992: 144). By the turn of the twentieth century, in conjunction with the rediscovery of Mendel's work, Weismann and others had shown that the nucleus of the cell contained, arranged on chromosomes, the information of heredity and that the unit of this information – the 'element' of which Dennett speaks and later termed the gene – was particulate in nature. That is, it retained its identity over the generations rather than becoming mixed and diluted, as critics of Darwin had

---

[2] This difference is fundamental. From a Lamarckian viewpoint, the giraffe's neck is long because successive generations of giraffes have stretched their necks in attempting to reach the juicy leaves on higher branches and the cervical extensions achieved in individual animals have been passed on to their offspring. From a (modern) Darwinian viewpoint, those giraffes which happened, as a consequence of random genetic variation, to be born with necks longer than those of their peers would be better able to reach the higher branches, would be better nourished and, as a result, would tend to have higher reproductive success, thereby transmitting the gene which caused this advantage to their descendants.

earlier claimed. From this flowed the so-called 'Central Dogma' of modern genetics, the principle that the genetic code controls the synthesis of proteins which, in interaction with the environment, give rise to the morphology of the organism. Contrary to the Lamarckian position, the dogma maintains that this process does not work in reverse (: 146–9).

By the 1930s, after thirty years of dispute between Mendelians, who believed evolution to consist of a series of dramatic mutations, and Darwinians, who advocated a process of gradualistic variation, the New (or Neo-Darwinian) Synthesis, which related Darwin's observations on changes in the morphology and behaviour of organisms to changes in their genetic constitution, was consolidated with the work of R.A. Fisher and J.B.S. Haldane (Miller 1992: 158–60). The final major element in the puzzle, the molecular structure of the genetic material itself, was identified in 1953 with the discovery of DNA by James Watson and Francis Crick. They determined that permutations of four nucleotides (adenine, cytosine, guanine and thymine) encoded the genetic information within the DNA molecule.

1.2.3. *The Selfish Gene*

> We are survival machines – robot vehicles blindly programmed to preserve the selfish molecules known as genes.... The selfish gene theory is Darwin's theory, expressed in a way that Darwin did not choose but whose aptness, I should like to think, he would instantly have recognized and delighted in. It is in fact a logical outgrowth of orthodox neo-Darwinism, but expressed as a novel image. Rather than focus on the individual organism, it takes a gene's-eye view of nature. It is a different way of seeing, not a different theory.
>
> (Dawkins 1989: v, viii)

One of Dawkins's many achievements, initially expounded in *The Selfish Gene* (1989), has been to recast an old argument in evolutionary biology in the most radical and striking terms and in doing so to breathe fresh life into the new synthesis. Biologists have long debated the question of the hierarchic level at which natural selection operates, an issue known as the 'units of selection' controversy (Lewontin 1970). In the following, the implication is that selection acts upon the species as a unit. This so-called species-selection hypothesis maintains that a species

> is to all intents and purposes a super-individual, exemplifying two complementary tendencies. On the one hand it displays *invariance*; i.e. by virtue of its hereditary mechanism it tends to preserve and perpetuate a certain standard form. But on the other hand, it displays an unavoidable tendency to vary or depart from this form, through the random intervention of mutation and genetic recombination.
>
> (Miller 1992: 169; his emphasis)

In opposition to species selection (the differential survival of species, selected for survival or extinction *en bloc*), to group selection (the differential survival of specific groups within a species, one group being favoured at the expense of another within the larger collective), and to individual selection (the differential survival of individual organisms, the species being simply a useful term for discussing a collection of morphologically similar but functionally independent agents), Dawkins insists that

> the best way too look at evolution is in terms of selection occurring at the lowest level of all.... the fundamental unit of selection, *and therefore of self-interest*, is not the species, nor the group, nor even, strictly, the individual. It is the gene, the unit of heredity.
>
> (1989: 11; my emphasis)

Taking this standpoint means that all aspects of the form, function and behaviour of living organisms can be understood from the perspective of 'the fundamental unit of selection', a working definition of which Dawkins offers as

> any portion of chromosomal material that potentially lasts for enough generations to serve as a unit of natural selection.... a genetic unit that is small enough to last for a large number of generations and to be distributed around in the form of many copies.... a unit which, to a high degree, *approaches* the ideal of indivisible particulateness.
>
> (1989: 28, 32, 33; his emphasis)

Although first suggested by Weismann in the late nineteenth century and articulated by G.C. Williams in the 1960s, gene-selectionism represents the neo-Darwinian synthesis taken to its logical conclusion. In this view, evolutionary change is regarded as the consequence of mutations in individual genes which, if they confer competitive advantages upon the individuals in which they reside, tend to increase their likelihood of being transmitted to the next generation. Within the gene pool of a species, such genes tend gradually to increase their representation, leading to change in the genetic profile of the species.

More fundamentally, a central thesis of a gene-centred view of biology is that only those genes which in some way tend to promote their replication will survive. 'This', Dawkins observes, 'is not a theory; it is not even an observed fact: it is a tautology' (1989: 86). In practice, this means that acts of selfishness at the level of the individual are the norm in ethology, this being a recursive function of the selfishness – to use Dawkins's anthropomorphic metaphor – of the individual gene, which either acts in its own self-interest or perishes.

Key to the argument of this book, Dawkins also contends that the gene is but one member of a class of entities he calls replicators (see the quotation from

Dennett in 1.1 above). These are information-encoding structures capable of giving rise to copies of themselves which may sometimes diverge slightly from the original form. These properties lead Dawkins

> to claim almost limitless power for slightly inaccurate self-replicating entities, once they arise anywhere in the universe. This is because they tend to become the basis for Darwinian selection which, given enough generations, cumulatively builds systems of great complexity.
>
> (1989: 322)

As the study of replicators in culture, memetics is itself ultimately predicated upon the properties of such 'slightly inaccurate self-replicating entities' including, I argue, those in the sphere of music.

Genotypes and (Extended) Phenotypes

For all their 'limitless power', genes require certain levers in order to exert their control over the world and, thereby, influence their fate. One of the most important of these levers is the 'phenotype', the form an organism assumes as a result of the interaction between its 'genotype' – its total genetic complement, acquired from its parent(s) – and the environment in which it develops and lives. Developing this, one of the most important relationships in evolutionary biology, Dawkins's notion of the 'extended phenotype', enlarges the definition of the phenotype to incorporate

> All effects of a gene upon the world. As always, 'effect' of a gene is understood as meaning in comparison with its alleles.[3] The conventional phenotype is the special case in which the effects are regarded as being confined to the individual body in which the gene sits. In practice it is convenient to limit 'extended phenotype' to cases where the effects influence the survival chances of the gene, positively or negatively.
>
> (1983a: 286)

As examples of extended phenotypes, Dawkins cites the bird's nest, the beaver's dam and the effects upon organisms engendered by parasites, all of which are

---

[3] 'Each gene is able to occupy only a particular region of chromosome, its locus. At any given locus there may exist, in the population, alternative forms of the gene. These alternatives are called alleles of one another.… there is a sense in which alleles are competitors of each other, because over evolutionary time successful alleles achieve numerical superiority over others at the same locus, in all the chromosomes of the population' (Dawkins 1983a: 283).

phenomena evolved to 'influence the survival chances of the gene'. I return to this subject and its application to memetics in Chapter 2.

1.3. Mediating between Nature and Culture: Interdisciplinary Analogy and Universal Darwinism

> The origin of life and the origin of human thought constitute two particularly significant turning points in the history of our distinctive planet. The prebiotic world was radically transformed by living, evolving cellular organisms; likewise, the world of prelinguistic animals was profoundly modified by the advent of human-style cognition and cultural evolution. Many have been prompted to compare these two evolutionary systems; both depend on a new form of information-accretion not found in the pre-existing worlds.
>
> (Sereno 1991: 467)

From at least the mid-eighteenth century it has been a common theme among commentators in a variety of disciplines – from both of C.P. Snow's 'two cultures' (1964) – that there exists a correlation between the natural and cultural worlds. Along a varied continuum, what might be termed the 'weak' manifestation of this tradition holds that culture manifests broad analogical or metaphorical affinities with nature; the 'strong' manifestation maintains that evolution in nature is paralleled in a structural sense by cultural change. It is certainly the case that, taking our definition of evolution as '[t]he origination of species of animals and plants, as conceived by those who attribute it to a process of development from earlier forms, and not to a process of "special creation"', and analogically substituting cultural forms for living forms, culture does appear evolutionary, in a 'Darwin-neutral sense' (Dennett 1995: 345), for the prevailing ethos of post-Renaissance Western societies is one of improving, developing and refining the general categories and types particular cultural products exemplify.

Nature-culture analogies often attempt to link the integrated functions and life history of the (human) organism with the perceived unity of a work of art and the historical development of a genre respectively (Solie 1980, Dahlhaus 1983: 44–5). Music has, arguably, been a particular focus of such organicist-evolutionary speculation, nature-culture analogies having been defining aspects of thinking in music historiography and music theory and analysis over the last two centuries and more (see Clarke and Rehding 2001).

This tradition reaches its apogee with Schenker, whose notion of structural-hierarchic transformation is the locus for both organicist and evolutionary speculation. Nevertheless, as Solie points out, there is a 'certain confusion of modality between the temporal and spatial' in Schenker, whereby he fails to distinguish between the idea of a diachronic growth process, manifested in the temporal unfolding of a piece – its 'perceptual [esthesic/evolutionary] progress' –

and the idea of synchronic growth structures, whereby the foreground is seen as the logical outgrowth of the background – its 'conceptual [poietic/organic] progress' (1980: 153). Moreover, Schenker's perspective is complicated by his invocation of the distinction between the ontogeny (individual synchronic/diachronic development) of the artwork over the phylogeny (diachronic species development) of its parent genre or formal archetype, and his belief that 'ontogeny recapitulates phylogeny in art and culture as well as in genetics' (: 153).

While it is easy to posit such relationships between nature and culture, it is more difficult to describe their properties and define their terms. There are two main problems in this respect. First, the relationship often appears to operate only at the weak level of analogy, the dimension of culture being a merely figurative equivalent to the natural world. Thus, whereas nature is conceived as the all-powerful arbiter of organic processes on earth, culture is often seen as something of a poor relation, often having to draw its conceptual vocabulary, and therefore its intellectual legitimacy, from biology.

Secondly, there is not one but several ways to relate nature and culture analogically. Sereno identifies four historically distinct and discipline-specific models, arguing that

> Most serious work on this topic has grown out of three focal comparisons: *species/language*, *genes/culture*, and *organism/concept*.... In historical and comparative linguistics, species with similar individuals capable of interbreeding are compared to language communities of mutually comprehensible speakers. In sociobiology and the study of animal behavior, genes coding for physical and behavioral traits are compared to fragments of culture capable of transmission and expression. And in evolutionary epistemology in the history and philosophy of science, interacting organisms in an environment are compared to competing scientific concepts and theories in an 'intellectual ecology'. In the years after the discovery of the structure of DNA in the 1950s and its relation to protein structure in the early 1960s, there was a burst of excitement about a fourth kind of comparison – the *cell/person* analogy
>
> (1991: 467; his emphases)

The model upon which the present study – and memetics as a whole – rests is 'gene/culture', the comparison of the gene with a fragment of culture, the meme. The reason that this is so will emerge after a consideration of the first problem. Put more formally, this problem maintains that the attempt to relate the two spheres is weakened epistemologically by the apparent subservience of the 'target' system (culture) to the 'source' system (nature), to use Sereno's terminology, even if the mapping satisfies his injunction that 'part-whole relationships be kept parallel across several levels of organization' (1991: 469, 470).

A solution is to invoke the notion of 'universal Darwinism', developed by Dawkins and Henry Plotkin and based on the former's assertion that 'we must begin by throwing out the gene as the sole basis of our ideas on evolution....

Darwinism is too big a theory to be confined to the narrow context of the gene' (1989: 191). Plotkin notes, however, that Dawkins's formulation of universal Darwinism (1983b)

> has been the more restricted one that wherever in the universe life has evolved, it has done so by the processes of Darwinian evolution. The version of universal Darwinism adopted here is that in addition to biological evolution as it is normally understood, Darwinian evolution is also operating to produce the transformations in time that we see in certain other spheres, such as immune system function and even the way science itself [as a component of culture generally] operates. This is not a new position. It began with Darwin himself and with his friend T.H. Huxley. It has been developed by a number of eminent scholars in the last 140 years.... in at least some respects, our brains are Darwin machines[4] too, and the way in which we gain knowledge is another form of universal Darwinism.
>
> (1995: xvii)

Universal Darwinism is therefore the notion that the processes evolutionary biology describes in DNA-based organisms on earth are merely a subset of a potential infinity of systems wherein complexity is engendered by the differential survival of selfish replicators (Dawkins 1983b). These systems – both inter- and intra-organismic (Plotkin 1995: 256) – are united by the operation of the evolutionary algorithm Dennett outlines in the passage (1995: 343) cited in 1.2.2 above. From a universal-Darwinian perspective, cultural evolution is not (weakly) analogical to biological evolution – as an inferior, dependent partner – but is (strongly) parallel to it as an equal and equivalent member of a set of replicator systems operating on earth in a variety of media (such as DNA molecules, alphabetical characters, musical sounds and electromagnetic signals), themselves subsumed by the cosmic ambit of universal Darwinism.

On this basis Dennett contends that

> Meme evolution is not just analogous to biological or genetic evolution, not just a process that can be metaphorically described in these evolutionary idioms, but a phenomenon that obeys the laws of natural selection exactly. The theory of evolution by natural selection is neutral regarding the differences between memes and genes; these are just different kinds of replicators evolving in different media at different rates.
>
> (1993: 202)

---

4 '[T]hat happy phrase of the American neurobiologist William Calvin' (: xvii). See Edelman 1987 and Calvin 1996 for accounts of the brain as a Darwin machine. I briefly consider the relevance of Calvin's theories to memetics in Chapter 3.

Distin makes the same point in terms of the type-token distinction. She maintains that

> A meme is not, strictly speaking, an analogue of a gene: rather, since both are replicators, a meme is a different *token* of the same *type* of entity as a gene. (…. A *token* is any 'particular specimen of any general class. All these specimens may be described as the several tokens of that single *type*.'). Similarly, cultural evolution is a different example [that is, token] of the same type of process as neo-Darwinism, rather than a simple analogue of it. This means that the two processes have the same description at a sufficiently functional, abstract level.
>
> (2005: 12; her emphases)

An important corollary of this line of argument is that genes and memes, as with all replicators, are fundamentally means of encoding information and that this information is essentially substrate-independent. It is therefore possible to represent the information content of a given replicator in various ways. In the case of a gene, we could represent its information content by means of a symbolic system other than the biochemical sequence of nucleotides (adenine, cytosine, guanine and thymine) which naturally encode it. One method, generally used in printed sources on genetics, is to use the initial letters of the constituent nucleotides (A, C, G and T), but other representational systems are possible – the HTML code of the Human Genome Project website is another way of representing the information content of a gene.[5] In both cases, the information is amenable to two-way conversion, from a nucleotide to another representation system and then (via genetic engineering) back again to a nucleotide sequence.

One could even use musical notation to represent the information content of a gene, for adenine, cytosine and guanine may be represented using the pitch of their initial letters, A, C and G; thymine might be assigned an arbitrary pitch value, perhaps E, creating a 'scale' consisting of rising thirds. Moreover, any replication of 'musical-genetic' melodic sequences based on these four pitches and encoding the nucleotide sequence of a gene would create a meme expressing the information content of that gene. Example 1.2 below, for instance, represents the initial part of the information content of the calmodulin-binding transcription activator 1 gene (CAMTA1), found on human chromosome one.[6]

5 At <http://www.ornl.gov/sci/techresources/Human_Genome/home.shtml>.

6 Apropos this example, and in a reversal of the traditional 'balance of power' between genes and memes, Lynch reports – uneasily – that 'some have said that since "the meme" is just propagating information without regard to medium, that even genes are just a special case of memes' (1998b: Section 11).

Example 1.2: Meme Encoding the Information Content of the Calmodulin-Binding Transcription Activator 1 (CAMTA1) Gene

Conversely, it is possible to represent the information content of a meme in a variety of ways. While memetics is predicated on the view that memes exist fundamentally as patterns of neuronal interconnection, they may also be encoded in other substrates. One of the most interesting and significant of these is as electromagnetic signals in computers and on the internet, an issue I return to in Chapter 7.

To summarize these points, the precepts of universal Darwinism and Dawkins's notion of the smallest unit of selection reject as superficial all correspondences between nature and culture except that operating between genes and memes. This correspondence is not a (weak) analogy but a (strong) parallelism based on the transmission of information in different substrates.

1.4. Memetics: An Overview and A Review of the Literature

> Actively contagious ideas are now called *memes* … by students of the newly emerging science of *memetics*. Though the analogy between cultural and biological contagion was recognized at least by the 1950s, the evolutionary biologist Richard Dawkins expressed it at full strength in the last chapter of his 1976 book, *The Selfish Gene*. This short chapter, in which Dawkins coins the word *meme*, launched a slowly smoldering first twenty years of memetics. Those decades also saw comparable contributions by Douglas Hofstadter and Daniel Dennett, among others.
>
> (Lynch 1996: 2–3; his emphases)

For Dawkins, a meme – Lumsden and Wilson use the term 'culturegen' (1981: x) – is

> a unit of cultural transmission, or a unit of *imitation*. 'Mimeme' comes from a suitable Greek root,[7] but I want a monosyllable that sounds a bit like 'gene'. I hope

---

[7] Namely μνημ (mnem). Μνημοσυνη (Mnemosyne) was the Greek goddess of memory – and one of the first goddesses of music.

> my classicist friends will forgive me if I abbreviate mimeme to *meme*.[8] If it is any consolation, it could alternatively be thought of as being related to 'memory', or to the French word *même*. It should be pronounced to rhyme with 'cream'. Examples of memes are tunes, ideas, catch-phrases, clothes fashions, ways of making pots or of building arches. Just as genes propagate themselves in the gene pool by leaping from body to body via sperms or eggs, so memes propagate themselves in the meme pool[9] by leaping from brain to brain via a process which, in the broad sense, can be called imitation.
>
> (1989: 192; his emphases)

Dawkins formulated this definition over thirty years ago, in the first edition of *The Selfish Gene*, pulling together various strands of nature-culture analogizing from the previous two centuries and more and recasting them in the crucible of his powerful selfish gene hypothesis – the notion that, ultimately, the driving force of evolution is the single gene, whose phenotypic effects (that is, those on the organism's morphology and behaviour) influence the reproductive prospects of that gene in ways which justify Dawkins's metaphor of apparent selfish intentionality.

While the idea of cultural equivalents to biological replicators cannot wholly be ascribed to Dawkins – many other commentators made this connection before *The Selfish Gene*, most notably Cloak, who spoke of 'corpuscles of culture' (1975: 168) – he must be given credit for the characteristic elegance of its formulation, for the coining of a singularly memorable and apposite term for the cultural replicator and, perhaps most importantly, for yoking the meme concept together with the selfish gene idea under the aegis of universal Darwinism.

Nevertheless, one should acknowledge the tradition of evolutionary epistemology (Campbell 1960, 1974) as a parent of memetics. Campbell's theory is based on the assertion that 'all processes leading to expansions of knowledge involve a blind-variation-and-selective-retention process' (1960: 397). He identifies that '[t]hree conditions are necessary: a mechanism for introducing variation, a consistent selection process, and a mechanism for preserving and

8 Semon's *The Mneme* (1921), a text not listed in the bibliography of Dawkins 1989, is an interesting anticipation of the term 'meme'. Semon notes that 'instead of speaking of a factor of *memory*, a factor of *habit*, or a factor of *heredity*, and attempting to identify one with another, I have preferred to consider these as manifestations of a common principle, which I shall call the *mnemic* principle'. He suggests that 'the immediate effect of stimulation on the irritable substance [that is, an organism] is only one half of the problem with which we are concerned …. The other and distinctive half of the mnemic problem … is the effect which remains in the stimulated substance *after* the excitement produced by the stimulation has apparently ceased. The capacity for such after-effect of stimulation constitutes what I have called the *Mneme*. Its result, namely, the enduring though primarily latent modification in the irritable substance produced by a stimulus, I have called an *Engram*' (: 11–12; his emphases). See also Laurent 1999.

9 That is, the totality of memes in the brains of the members of a given cultural group.

reproducing the selected variations' (: 381). This exactly parallels Dennett's summary of biological evolution given in 1.2.2 above. Despite their being subsumed under different analogical schemes in Sereno's system (organism/concept and genes/culture respectively), it is perhaps not too impertinent to the distinguished tradition of evolutionary epistemology to regard it as a subset of memetics. That is, the concepts blindly varied and selectively retained are verbal-conceptual memes, and their assemblage into larger systems (scientific theories and other complex intellectual frameworks) results in the formation of high-level cultural 'memeplexes'.

After its inception in the final chapter of *The Selfish Gene*, Dawkins returned to memetics in the early 1980s in *The Extended Phenotype* (1983a) – some would claim with a toning-down of his earlier enthusiasm for the ideas expressed in 1976. Nevertheless, after a decade and more of relative obscurity, the meme meme – that is, the idea of memetics, functioning itself as a replicator; what might also be termed the memetics metamemeplex (Brodie 1996: 97) – had gained considerable prominence in the early 1990s and began to prompt serious thought from such commentators as Dennett (1995) and Blackmore (1999) as to its validity and applicability to a wide variety of situations and problems. To help foster this development, the online *Journal of Memetics* was launched in 1997.[10]

By the end of the 1990s, two distinct traditions were developing within memetics (perhaps even amounting to a polarization), a populist, journalistic branch and a rigorous, scientific branch. In the work of Brodie (1996), to take arguably the most extreme practitioner of the former tradition (discounting the wilder shores of memetic speculation found in some corners of the internet), the emphasis is clearly on the epidemiological aspects of memetics and the alleged (but possibly real) threat of human enslavement by memes – all expressed in language somewhere between that of the personal development seminar and that of the fevered television evangelist. In Lynch's work (1998b), by contrast, memetics is coolly and rigorously systematized, its 'units, events and dynamics' being rendered in algebraic notation in order to facilitate the mathematical modelling of meme flows and prevalence – rather in the manner of the (not-explicitly-memetic) work of Cavalli-Sforza and Feldman (1981).

Dennett asks '[c]ould there be a science of memetics?' (1995: 352). As is clear from the degree of scepticism evident in several quarters, touched upon in Chapter 7, it is by no means an established scientific discipline at present. More fundamentally, in Blackmore's view,

10 At <http://www.jom-emit.org/>.

> It seems that there is no ready-made science of memetics waiting to be taken over. If we need a science of memetics, as I am convinced we do, then we shall have to build one up from scratch. The main tools available are the basic principles of evolutionary theory, the founding ideas of Dawkins, Dennett and other early memeticists, and … relevant ideas from … cultural anthropology …. Of course, we can also draw on more than a century of research in psychology and several decades of cognitive science and neuroscience.
>
> (1999: 36)

If Blackmore is to be taken as representative of the mood of current thought in this area, memetics clearly has a grasp of its intellectual antecedents, an understanding of the problems it seeks to address, and a sense of what related disciplines it may draw on for its continued development. While this reliance on established disciplines may at first appear somewhat parasitic, advocates of memetics hope it will eventually become a unifying force, linking neighbouring disciplines under the umbrella of common concerns, methodologies and ways of viewing the world – it is, after all, difficult to imagine a more all-encompassing principle than universal Darwinism. What is clear is that proponents of memetics intend it to serve as a metatheory of cultural evolution (and as such intend it to be able to support and sustain numerous diverse subtheories), just as memetics, and biological evolution, are themselves subject to the metatheory of universal Darwinism.

This brief review has necessarily ignored many interesting sources on memetics; and constraints of space mean that this book as a whole has had to be very selective in its citations from the memetics literature, my References including only a relatively small subset of the available sources. For a comprehensive listing, the reader is referred to the bibliography of the *Journal of Memetics*.

I return to the question of the relationship between nature and culture in Chapter 7. Whereas here, I have attempted to sketch the different ways in which the two spheres and their interaction has been conceptualized over recent decades, in Chapter 7, by contrast, I aim to examine how natural and cultural replicators themselves – genes and memes – co-operate with and challenge each other in their real-world struggle for existence.

1.5. Methodological and Conceptual Issues in Theorizing A Memetics of Music

In theorizing a memetics of music there are a number of methodological issues which need to be addressed in order for the investigation to proceed on a secure (epistemo)logical foundation. One of these stems from the tension between *a priori* (deductive, axiomatic, top-down) and *a posteriori* (inductive, empirical, bottom-up) arguments in memetics. Given that memetics has assimilated a broad and deep theoretical base from its sister discipline evolutionary biology, it is inclined – on the grounds of the axiomatically rigorous and empirically endorsed authority of the latter – to make strong *a priori* claims about the nature of culture. Nevertheless, its application to real-world musical contexts necessarily involves the tempering of axioms by the results of empirical investigations.

What then might constitute evidence in support of the axioms of memetics? One immediate problem is that it is in the nature of memetics that it aims to identify chronologically and geographically disparate patterns and configurations (memes) related by homological similarity and then posits a relationship of connection by imitation (replication) between them. It is, however, often difficult and sometimes impossible to prove that two particles are related by imitation, as against similarity resulting from 'convergent evolution' (Dennett 1995: 357). This is particularly the case in the absence of what Nattiez would term 'poietic documents' (1990: 141) – such as proven interactions between composers and documented cases of borrowing and influence. In the absence of strong evidence, it may be the case that a minimum threshold of proof (cast in terms of a certain degree of homological similarity and a certain strength of poietic connection) may have to be established in order to regulate the investigation and description of memetic relationships.

A more fundamental problem in developing a science of memetics, the 'problem of induction' besets all *a posteriori* theory building and all attempts empirically to verify *a priori* hypotheses. As Papineau observes,

> [inductive] arguments are not logically valid. The truth of the particular premisses does not guarantee the truth of the universal conclusion. That all bodies observed so far have fallen with constant acceleration does not guarantee that all future ones will do so too.
>
> (1995: 809)

Applied to memetics, this problem implies that however much data we amass in support of the hypotheses of memetics, and however many items of positive evidence we uncover, such premisses cannot logically support the 'universal conclusion' – in this case, that human culture is best understood in terms of the replication of discrete entities in a neo-Darwinian process of variation, transmission and differential selection.

Given that memetics aspires to the status of a scientific discipline, one solution to the problem of induction might be to subject its hypotheses not to the notion of (positive) proof by the amassing of highly suggestive evidence but to Popper's test of falsification (O'Hear 1995). This stipulates that it should logically be possible for contradictory evidence to be found, even if it has not yet been located. A theory which does not satisfy this test is, in Popper's terms, unscientific, but not necessarily illogical or useless. Note also that there is an important distinction to be drawn between falsifying 'specific memetic hypotheses' – such as those concerning the transmission of particular elements of culture – and falsifying the 'premises or the logic and mathematics based on those premises' of '[t]he overall theory' (Lynch 1998b: Section 18).

It could be argued, however, that even the theory of evolution by natural selection is a hypothesis intrinsically incapable of falsification, given the enormous geographical and chronological frames within which it is believed to operate. Despite this, the overwhelming majority of biologists hold the theory to be true on account of the body of (positive) evidence, not least among which is the fossil record, amassed in its favour. An anti-falsificationist view would maintain that, given this weight of evidence, evolution by natural selection is highly unlikely to be false. Dobzhansky (1973) adopts this line of argument, accumulating evidence in favour of evolution which he holds, by virtue of its extent and pervasiveness, to be incontrovertible.

In this spirit, a 'probabilistic' alternative to Popper's denial of 'our entitlement to believe in the truth of scientific theories, rather than their falsity' (Papineau 1995: 809), may be found in the form of Bayesian confirmation theory. This theory aims to 'identify the epistemic support evidence confers on a hypothesis with probability, usually understood in terms of dispositions to take risks whose outcome would depend on the correctness of the hypothesis of interest' (Bogen 1995: 79). Of course, believing in memetics is in no sense a risk akin to believing in the safety of a new medicine or the airworthiness of a new type of airliner. Nevertheless, we can adopt the Bayesian paradigm, without its rather convoluted mathematical underpinning, in the sense that we can aim to amass a body of evidence which would suggest that, if memetics were a mortal risk, it would probably be a risk worth taking.

The following two points summarize the epistemological foundations of this study. My bias throughout is, of course, in favour of memetics – I should not want to write a negative, debunking book – but I will not be insensitive to controversies, some of which will be fleshed out, although not necessarily resolved, in Chapter 7. First, memetics may draw upon the reflected *a priori* coherence and *a posteriori* support of Darwinian (biological) evolution by natural selection because universal Darwinism affords an epistemic link between biological evolution and memetics. Secondly, memetics may be judged probably true if sufficient evidence is amassed in its support. While I cannot guarantee to have satisfied this particular test here, I shall certainly aim to do so, and it is hoped that others may contribute to this goal in future research.

1.6. Summary

Darwin's natural selection algorithm offers a robust explanation for the mechanism of evolutionary change in the natural world, Dawkins's Selfish Gene theory positing that it operates primarily at a molecular level. In the work of Plotkin, analogues to natural selection have been shown to operate in several dimensions of the biological world, and there are many who hold that it is the best candidate to explain the evolution of complexity in all realms, from the molecular to the universal. One important consequence of universal Darwinism is that culture may be understood as operating on selectionist principles. While evolutionary thought has provided several metaphorical and narrative tropes for music historiography and music theory and analysis, memetics offers a neo-Darwinian theory of cultural transmission, selection and evolution. With it comes the opportunity to set thinking about music in a genuinely evolutionary context and thus to see how far 'Darwin's dangerous idea' can take our understanding of the art.

Chapter 2

Memory, Replication and Style: Memes in Music I

2.1. Introduction

In this chapter I outline some of the central precepts of memetics and begin to develop some definitions of what might constitute a meme in music. After examining some views on the neurobiological basis of memetics, drawing mainly on the work of Juan Delius, I begin the definition of the musical meme with a consideration of the genotype/phenotype distinction in biology and its application to memetics. I conclude by considering the relationship between memetics and Meyer's conception of style in music and look at some ways in which the parameters of music might sustain memetic replication.

2.2. Memory, Memes and Mnemons

Memory is one of the most remarkable capacities of the human brain and since it underpins all of our musical competences it is of central concern to memetics, as is made explicit in the quotation from Dawkins on p. 16 above. While memory, as with so much of the brain's function, is imperfectly understood, and while a detailed treatment of memory and its neurobiology is well beyond the scope of this book, some comments on memory – here and in Chapter 3 – are necessary to highlight one of the most fundamental and audacious concepts in memetics: that memes exist physically in the brain in the form of patterns of nerve-cell interconnection. For general overviews of memory, see Deutsch *et al.* 2001 and Dunsby 2001.

2.2.1. *Memory and Mnemobiology*

We might usefully classify memory into various categories one of which is according to the criterion of volatility. (Another criterion of memory categorization, information type, is considered in Chapter 3.) It should be remembered, however, that memory classifications are primarily psychological categories and may not necessarily map neatly onto distinct and/or localized neurobiological structures and processes in the brain.

As with the use of the term in computing, volatility refers to the stability of information stored in memory over time. The most volatile type is working (or sensory) memory, 'a short period of time during which relationships between successive events can be perceived directly, without cognitive reference to earlier periods'. This 'psychological present … is normally estimated to lie in the range of two to seven seconds' (Deutsch *et al.* 2001: 538). Short-term memory is responsible for storing relatively small amounts of information over a relatively short period of time, generally measured in terms of seconds, minutes and hours. Long-term memory, which encompasses larger quantities of information stored over days and years, is imprinted by highly salient experiences (a particularly striking or memorable event, for example), by specific education and training (learning), or by repeated exposure, including exposure during development (enculturation).

All three volatility types of memory are important for the storage and propagation of memes. Working memory allows patterns to be apprehended and processed as discrete units in real-time listening experiences. Short-term memory allows a listener to comprehend a whole symphonic movement and trace its unfolding thematic and tonal structure, mediating the diachronic with the synchronic by retrospectively reinterpreting past events in the light of present experiences. Long-term memory allows the listener to discern intertextual (memetic) connections between a work currently being heard and one stored as a result of past hearings. Despite the seeming primacy of long-term memory, all that is required for memetic transmission to occur is for a brain-stored copy of a meme to be converted into an external form, where it may attain great stability and durability, even long after this form has given rise to a new brain-stored copy. This contingency only rules out working memory as directly implicated in memetic transmission.

One of the cornerstones of memetics is that the meme exists fundamentally as a mental representation, as 'self-replicating brain structures, actual patterns of neuronal wiring-up that reconstitute themselves in one brain after another' (Dawkins 1989: 323). Moreover, Dawkins strengthens this assertion by noting that

> … my colleague N.K. Humphrey neatly summed up an early draft of this chapter: '… memes should be regarded as living structures, not just metaphorically but technically. When you plant a fertile meme in my mind you literally parasitize my brain, turning it into a vehicle for the meme's propagation in just the way that a virus may parasitize the genetic mechanism of a host cell. And this isn't just a way of talking – the meme for, say, "belief in life after death" is actually realized physically, millions of times over, as a structure in the nervous systems of individual men the world over'.
>
> (: 192)

For all Dawkins's confidence, it would be a mistake to claim that neuroscience had verified his assertion. Yet despite the need for more research on this aspect of brain function, his proposition seems intuitively sensible and will be accepted as a working hypothesis for the purposes of this study. The 'reconstitution' he speaks of is a function of memory, which, seen in these terms, consists of the encoding of information by patterns of neuronal interconnection. It may be the case that the less volatile the memory type, the more stable the neuronal interconnections formed, with long-term memory being characterized by more or less permanent changes in brain structure.

Developing the concept of 'mnemobiology' – the study of the physical characteristics of the meme as a brain entity – Delius estimates that the human brain contains somewhere in the region of 10^{15} 'variable synapses', interconnections between neurons which are established or modified when a unit of information is assimilated (1989: 43–4). He maintains that

> Such plastic synapses have to be thought of as the critical components of neural networks functioning as associative arrays. It has been shown mathematically and confirmed empirically that neural networks incorporating large numbers of modifiable junctions are able to store vast quantities of information in a very organized manner. An important property of associative network storage is that the information is content- and not address-retrievable (as in computers), and furthermore that it is stored in a highly distributed but still partially overlapping way …. Special versions of these networks show interesting additional properties, such as being capable of self organization, stimulus pattern categorization, pattern completion or complex stimulus-response conversions ….
>
> (1991: 82)

Therefore, if Dawkins and Delius are correct, the meme exists as a physical structure in the brains of its hosts; and if this is true, it follows that

> Any cultural trait taken over by a given individual from another individual must accordingly be thought of as the transfer of a particular pattern of activated/inactivated synapses from the associative networks of one brain to another. Different traits must be thought of as being coded by topologically different synaptic patterns, that is, a given cultural trait borne by an individual is encoded informationally as a particular configuration of modified synapses in his or her brain …. Naturally the synaptic constellation that a trait has in one brain will not be geometrically arranged in exactly the same way as the pattern that the same trait has in another brain: the brains of different individuals are likely to be too different for that. Functionally however, the two patterns could still be equivalent when effectively identical traits were represented in memory. In any case, following Dawkins … synaptic patterns that code cultural traits will be called memes, by analogy with the molecular patterns that code biological traits and which are called genes.
>
> (Delius 1991: 82–3)

The process of reconstitution which transforms the information content of a meme from a mental representation to an external form and back to a mental representation must occur through the agency of another symbolic system, for patterns of neuronal interconnection clearly cannot be directly transmitted between brains. In the verbal-conceptual realm the intermediate symbolic systems are spoken and written language; with musical memes they are sound waves and musico-graphic notation.

Despite the foregoing, one should acknowledge a central problem encountered in drawing analogies between constellations of neurons (the fundamental components of memes) and sequences of nucleotides (the fundamental components of genes). This difficulty is identified by Dennett when he observes that

> what is preserved and transmitted in cultural evolution is *information* – in a media-neutral, language-neutral sense. Thus the meme is primarily a *semantic* classification, not a *syntactic* classification that might be directly observable in 'brain language' or natural language. In the case of genes, we are blessed by a gratifyingly strong alignment of semantic and syntactic identity: there *is* a single genetic language, in which meaning [that is, what phenotypic feature(s) the gene codes 'for'] is (roughly) preserved across all species.
>
> (1995: 353–4; his emphases)

Music, however, has the propensity of having no fixed (verbal-conceptual) semantic structure, but a relatively stable syntactic structure – whether or not the constituent parts of that syntactic structure are consistently mapped onto topologically specific patterns of neuronal interconnection, which, as Delius suggests above, is perhaps unlikely. Thus, unlike primarily referential symbolic systems such as language and representational painting, music has the attribute of consisting of particles which have no necessary external verbal-conceptual referent. Musical particles combine in ways independent of verbal-grammatical content or functional logic – they obey the laws of what Schoenberg terms 'musical logic' (1995) – although the principle of memetic co-adaptation discussed in Chapter 3 permits specific musical configurations to become associated with verbally expressible concepts. In this sense, music – especially as represented by its most 'analytical' form, the score – is a medium lending itself particularly well to memetic analysis. The issue of the neural encoding of memes – in particular, Calvin's views on the topography and mechanics of the neural architecture – will be considered further in Chapter 3.

2.2.2. *Memes and Mnemons*

Lynch has developed Delius's ideas on the neurobiology of memes in order to formalize the entities studied by memetics. He notes that

> Many psychological phenomena other than ideas can be observed to self-replicate. These include certain habits, attitudes, class identities, cognitive associations, education, emotional dispositions, addictions, and even neurotic and psychotic symptoms. All these traits may be broadly classified as human memory content. This category is more general than the word 'idea' or even 'memory' usually connote. It includes everything in the fairly broad meaning of 'memory', [defined as] 'the store of things learned and retained from an organism's activity or experience as evidenced by modification of structure or behavior or by recall and recognition'. Thus, the principle [*sic*] abstractions manipulated with memetics theory are memory abstractions, or *mnemons*.
>
> (1998b: Section 4; his emphasis)

Here Lynch is defining Delius's 'particular pattern of activated/inactivated synapses from the associative networks of one brain' (1991: 82) – which interconnects, in 'analogue' fashion, with myriad other elements of the associative networks – as a discrete, 'digital' unit of memory content representing a single 'particle' of information. More formally, he suggests that

> Treating ~A [that is, the absence of memory abstraction A] as a mnemon along with A [the presence of mnemon A] may seem rather strange. People labelled '~A' may be called ~A-mnemon hosts or A-mnemon non-hosts. (A and ~A are called complements of each other.) But can a person's lack of the A-mnemon justifiably be called a mnemon itself? It sounds like saying that nothing is something. The meaning of the term 'mnemon' provides an answer to this question. Mnemons are merely memory abstractions. As such, a negatively defined mnemon – which only states what a person does not have – is just as much of a memory abstraction as is a positively defined mnemon.... the term 'memory is expanded in a way that somewhat resembles its usage in computer science: it now includes some (partly) 'empty memory' states ....
>
> (1998b: Section 6)

Centrally for memetics, '[w]hen copied from one brain to another, [a positively defined mnemon] becomes a meme' (Lynch 1998a). In theory, however, there may be no copying 'from one brain to another': a mnemon might not give rise to patterning in an intermediate symbolic system, and even if it does this might not lead to the reconstitution of the mnemon in another brain. In these situations no replication occurs and so the mnemon is not reified as a meme. This issue – and with it a distinction between what are termed 'strong' and 'weak' senses of memetic replication – is taken up again in Chapter 4.

2.3. Defining the Musical Meme I: The Geno/Memotype-Pheno/Phemotype Analogy

2.3.1. *Cultural Genotypes and (Extended) Phenotypes*

Formulating a workable and, more importantly, fruitful analogy to the biological genotype-phenotype distinction in the realm of cultural transmission and evolution is not without its problems. More fundamentally, however, one must ask: why attempt to formulate such an analogy between genes and memes in the first place? After all, while genes and memes are related by their shared status as replicators, it is not necessarily the case that genes have any special primacy (other than that arising from their obvious chronological priority on this planet), such that other replicator systems should slavishly adopt all their attributes. Indeed Blackmore goes so far as to say that '[t]he analogy between genes and memes has led many people astray .... There is an analogy there but only because both are replicators. Beyond that the analogy is weak' (1999: 66).

Nevertheless, one of the abiding concerns of universal Darwinism is to find underlying commonalities which connect the apparently diverse replicator systems operative on the earth and beyond. As a first step in this mediation, it seems the case that genes and memes are related by their sharing dual modes of existence. That is, they both clearly possess what might be regarded as a fundamental, hidden form (genotype, mental incarnation of the meme) and a resultant physical manifestation (phenotype, meme products). Given this apparent structural connection, it makes sense at least to try to adapt useful genetic concepts and terminology to see if it proves constructive for memetics.

Thus, after the broadly comparable formulations of Dawkins 1983a, Ball 1984 and Delius 1989, 1991, I regard what might be termed the 'memotype' as a constellation of interconnected neurons, analogous to the genotype; and what might be termed its 'phemotype' as the behaviours and resultant artefacts (the latter including the 'intermediate symbolic systems' discussed in 2.2.1 above) these neurons motivate and control, analogous to the phenotype. This binary formulation has the advantage of mirroring its biological analogue closely and being relatively simple and clear-cut. Moreover, it preserves the distinction Dawkins draws between replicators and 'vehicles', whereby the microscopic, invisible, units of replication are clearly distinguished from the large, visible, structures engendered by the replicators to facilitate their replication (1983a: Chapter 6).[1]

Nevertheless, despite the gravitation of some major figures around the analogy, no broad consensus on the details has yet emerged in the memetics literature, and the arguments pro and contra the various stances (which range from a rejection of the analogy to various fine tunings of it) are convoluted (for discussion, see Distin 2005, Chapters 8 and 9). For the purposes of this book, however, it seems to me that the formulation offered here – that musical memes exist fundamentally as neuronal interconnections but are manifested in the form of graphical and sonorous patterning – is clear and workable.

As with gene phenotypes, the phemotypic effects of memes may be reduced to the two spheres of somatic and extrasomatic effects. The first of these is relatively constrained and includes culturally-determined alterations to the form of a body holding the meme, such as tattooing and piercing. Of considerably greater importance are the extrasomatic effects, which include behaviours and the artefacts they produce. A musical meme, for instance, gives rise to the activities (behaviours) of composition and performance (playing and conducting); in terms of artefacts, the meme engenders configurations of sound waves and their symbolic representations in such media as paper, magnetic discs and compact discs.

As noted in 1.2.3 above, Dawkins's term extended phenotype enlarges the definition of the phenotype to incorporate '[a]ll effects of a gene upon the world' (1983a: 286). Yet whereas the phenotypic effects of the gene are both somatic and extrasomatic, the phemotypic effects of the meme are, as noted above, almost entirely extrasomatic. Moreover, we cannot usefully distinguish between a meme's phemotype and its extended phemotype. A meme may both influence the behaviour of, and artefacts produced by, the individual in whose brain it resides and also exert

[1] One potential criticism of this formulation, however, is the fact that the two replicator systems are not independent: the memotype of the meme (the neuronal constellation) is an element of the phenotype of the gene.

its behavioural and artefactual effects at considerable geographical and temporal remove.

For instance, memes which appeared initially in symphonies composed by Haydn in the isolation of Eszterháza in the 1770s continue to copy themselves into the brains of concert goers on the West coast of America in the twenty-first century; and paper copies of these memes continue to roll from the printing presses of the developed world. It follows from this and earlier observations that, whereas the gene is propagated non-phenotypically (ultimately genes, not bodies and other gene products, reproduce themselves), the meme, of necessity, must be propagated phemotypically, via intermediate symbolic systems. This contingency, as we shall see, has important implications for the evolution of musical style.

Summarizing the discussions in 1.2.3, 2.2.2 and 2.3.1, and adapting the concepts of the memotype and phemotype to the mnemon, Table 2.1 below gives an overview of the forms of genes and memes.

Table 2.1: Overview of Gene and Meme Forms (after Ball 1984: 156, Figure 2)

Gene	**Genotype**	**Phenotype**		
A unit of biological replication. Usefully regarded as manifesting itself as:	A constellation of nucleotides encoding a discrete, particulate unit of protein-generating information which is replicated (via its phenotype) in more than one body.	The somatic and extrasomatic products of a genotype, by virtue of which genes are reconstituted in other bodies.		
		Somatic	**Extrasomatic**	
			Behaviour	**Artefacts**
		feathers	nest building	nests
Meme	**Memotype**	**Phemotype**		
A unit of cultural replication. Usefully regarded as a composite of:	A constellation of neurons encoding a discrete, particulate unit of cultural information which is replicated (via its phemotype) in more than one brain.	The somatic and extrasomatic products of a meme, by virtue of which memes are reconstituted in other brains.		
		Somatic	**Extrasomatic**	
			Behaviour	**Artefacts**
		culturally-determined modifications to the body	playing, singing, conducting	scores, configurations of sound waves, recordings
Mnemon	**Mnemotype**	**Phmnemotype**		
An item of brain-stored memory. Usefully regarded as a composite of:	A constellation of neurons encoding a discrete, particulate unit of information which is not (yet) replicated in another brain.	The somatic and extrasomatic products of a mnemon, by virtue of which reconstitution of the mnemon in another brain (creating a meme) may occur.		
		Somatic	**Extrasomatic**	
			Behaviour	**Artefacts**
		As phemotype.		

Whereas the precise structure and function of the brain and the ways in which it supports human musicality still continue to elude neuroscience, the phemotypic manifestations of musical memes are all around us. So while there is, to me, great wonder in the notion of self-replicating clusters of neurons carrying musical information across expanses of time and space, our inability to identify the precise configurations and topography of the neurons which code 'for' certain musical patterns compels us to adopt the more pragmatic position of taking the musical meme to be represented by, even broadly equivalent to, its phemotypic manifestations – most accessibly in the printed score. While this recourse is primarily pragmatic, the discussion of the neural encoding of memeplexes in Chapter 3 suggests that it may nevertheless afford insights into the memotypic aspects of musical memes.

2.3.2. *The Ontology of Musical Memes and Musical Works*

Memetic transformation from memotype to phemotype and vice versa raises the question of the conceptual identity of the musical meme and, by extension, of the cultural products, the musical works, which consist of collections of memes. The single meme *versus* work-as-meme complex distinction is important, although music-philosophical writing is largely insensitive to it, being both focused on musical works and unfamiliar with the notion of the individual selfish replicator. Of course, the notion of the work is itself problematic (Goehr 1992), being the product a number of historically- and culturally-specific verbal-conceptual memeplexes; and even when commentators consider those musics which do not invoke a work concept, the single meme is not part of their perspective. In this study, I conceive the work in a more neutral, analytical sense, as a collection of independent memes which, nevertheless, band together to form a larger musical unit for the purposes of their mutual self-advancement.

In Nattiez's broadly work-centric perspective, 'music's irreducible dimension is *sound*. The musical work *manifests itself*, in its *material* reality, in the form of sound waves' (1990: 69; his emphases). Nevertheless, he acknowledges the complications which ensue when the work's 'mode of *being*' is considered, noting Ingarden's assertion that

> the work is a purely intentional object, immutable and permanent, whose heteronomous *existence* is no more than a reflection of its *being*: the existence of the work finds its source in the 'creative act' of the performer, and its foundation in the score …. The score constitutes the work's 'schema', which guarantees its identity over the course of history, even though numerous elements not fixed by the score 'play an essential role for the aesthetic Gestalt of the work' …, and even though the 'schema' allows an enormous number of possibilities for the work's realization.
>
> (: 69–70; Nattiez's emphases)

In Siohan's view, however, the notation 'is a graphic element, is neither music, nor its reflection, but a solely mnemonic device. There is no music except in the state of sonorous manifestation' (in Nattiez 1990: 71).

By contrast, memetics maintains that the meme is the central unit of reference, not the work, which merely represents the tendency of memes to form temporary, expedient alliances in the service of their individual, selfish replication. In contrast to the phemotypically-orientated score-sound dualism underpinning traditional work-centric music-philosophical discourse, the musical meme's ontological states are both neuronal configurations and their various manifestations, giving rise to a memotypic-phemotypic, brain-score/sound dualism. Furthermore, to paraphrase Dawkins, a musical meme is 'not just one single physical bit of [cultural information, however encoded].... it is *all replicas* of a particular bit of [cultural information], distributed throughout the world' (1989: 88; his emphasis). The meme therefore not only transcends the particular alliances it selfishly forms but also any of its particular instantiations.

As noted, despite being 'the thing that renders the work peformable and recognizable as an entity, and enables the work to pass through the centuries' (Nattiez 1990: 71), the score and its resultant sound image could be regarded as mere artefacts of memetic alliances. In contrast to Nattiez's assertion that 'music's irreducible dimension is *sound*', memetics suggests that music's 'irreducible dimension' is that of memotypic memes, and that sound waves are just one of their (extended) phemotypic artefacts, albeit overwhelmingly the one of greatest cultural importance.

These distinctions – memotype-phemotype, meme-work – raise two important issues at the heart of developing a memetics of music. The first, namely which phemotypic form one should take as one's medium of investigation (sound or score), has already been addressed: as noted in 2.3.1 above, one can be guided by pragmatic considerations and take the score as generally the most efficient means by which the nature of musical memes might be discerned. The second, more fundamental issue concerns the level one should focus upon (meme or work). Here there is no hard-and-fast rule; there are various strategies possible depending upon one's purpose and whether the aim of an investigation is broadly theoretical (centred on the properties of memes in general) or broadly analytical (centred on particular works). I deal with this issue in Chapter 6.

2.4. Defining the Musical Meme II: Replicator Attributes – Longevity, Fecundity and Copying-Fidelity

The survival of individual memes is determined by three attributes shared with all replicators: longevity, fecundity and copying-fidelity (Dawkins 1989: 18, 194). I now examine the relevance to musical memes of all three in turn, returning to the third in more detail in Chapter 3.

2.4.1. *Longevity*

Dawkins suggests that '[t]he longevity of any one copy of a meme is probably relatively unimportant, as it is for any one copy of a gene' (1989: 194) for, as argued in 2.3.2 above, a meme has a wider existence as an equivalence class, being '*all replicas* of a particular bit of [cultural information], distributed throughout the world'. For the class as a whole to survive, each individual copy must have a certain durability in order to persist long enough to engender its replication by imitation.

The key to memetic longevity lies in the stability of the meme's phemotypic form. Some such forms, such as behaviour patterns and sound waves, are inherently transient, vanishing almost immediately they are produced; whereas others, such as physical artefacts, are more durable, and can survive for millennia (see Table 2.1 above). Because of this, memes may well attain greater longevity in a stable phemotypic form, such as written or printed symbols, than in the fragile individual human brain itself.

For the longevity of musical memes, the greatest advance was the development of notation, '[a] visual analogue of musical sound, either as a record of sound heard or imagined, or as a set of visual instructions for performers' (Bent *et al.* 2001: 73). Moreover, because notation, and then printing, made it possible for performers and composers to see as well as to hear the music of their predecessors and contemporaries, they fostered an analytical and contemplative perspective whereby music could be studied free from the real-time cognitive and memory constraints of live performance. Thus, notation and printing not only increased the phemotypic longevity of musical memes but also greatly expedited their transmission.

2.4.2. *Fecundity*

Fecundity – the power of the meme to spread itself within and between cultural communities – 'is much more important than longevity of particular copies' (Dawkins 1989: 194). Although a meme in the mind of a composer or listener is subject to the vicissitudes of human frailty, it will survive if it can continue to make copies of itself, even if the individual phemotypic products of these copies are not especially long-lived. In this sense, its survival is ultimately contingent upon its fecundity, not upon the longevity of its phemotypic manifestations.

Fecundity is essentially a function of a meme's 'perceptual-cognitive salience'. While this issue will be covered in more detail in Chapter 4, the latter concept essentially refers to the degree to which a meme is perceived as standing out from its context. The higher the perceptual-cognitive salience of a meme, the more prominent it is to the members of a cultural community and, provided the meme is easily memorable, the more rapid its spread through the meme pool.

As implied above, not only did music notation and printing increase the longevity of memes, they also had a considerable impact on memetic fecundity, the latter in particular vastly increasing the number of phemotypic copies in circulation and therefore increasing the opportunities for further memetic replication on the basis of these copies. The explosive growth of information technology in the last few decades has further increased that fertility, allowing memes to be encoded in a new phemotypic form – digitally, as electromagnetic impulses – and rapidly transmitted across the internet.

2.4.3. *Copying-Fidelity*

A replicator cannot be long-lived if it is fragmented into smaller units or distorted upon replication – although fragmentation may itself engender a new potential replicator. Copying-fidelity is one of the defining characteristics of the gene, which, to recall his definition from 1.2.3 above, Dawkins considers to be

> any portion of chromosomal material that potentially lasts for enough generations to serve as a unit of natural selection.... a genetic unit that is small enough to last for a large number of generations and to be distributed around in the form of many copies.... a unit which, to a high degree, *approaches* the ideal of indivisible particulateness.
>
> (1989: 28, 32, 33; his emphasis)

As an undifferentiated segment of a chromosome, the longer a gene the greater the likelihood that it will be divided, and its information content destroyed, during the random cutting and splicing of the chromosome, known as 'crossing-over', which occurs during reproductive cell division (meiosis).

Similarly, a meme cannot be long-lived if it is fragmented into smaller units or its content distorted upon replication. The more concise a meme the greater the likelihood that it will survive the travails of replication intact. Ultimately, the meme shares with the gene a fundamental attribute of all replicators – that it is 'a unit of convenience, a length of [information] with just sufficient copying-fidelity to serve as a viable unit of natural selection' (Dawkins 1989: 195).

2.5. Memetics and Musical Style

Having outlined some of the abstract foundation principles of memetics, I now consider how they apply concretely to music. A useful bridge between memetics and more traditional music-historiographic and music-analytic concerns is the issue of style. In particular, Meyer's approach to conceptualizing style leads us very smoothly into the territory of memetics and will set the context for the more detailed considerations of Chapter 3.

2.5.1. *Analogue* versus *Digital: Two Models of Style in Music*

There are perhaps two principal models of style in music, what might be termed the analogue-parametric, represented most clearly by the work of LaRue and the digital-hierarchic, represented by the work of Meyer. While both are illuminating, it is the latter which accords most smoothly with memetics and I shall only briefly review the former in order to make clear what distinguishes it from the latter.

LaRue's view of style represents an example of what Bent and Pople term category analysis (2001: 560). As such, it is orientated to the parameters that are almost always present in music, such as rhythm and harmony. In his system these parameters are graded on a scale which, while in principle analogue, needs some means of making the measurements manageable. For this reason, LaRue invokes Aristotle's 'rule of three', an attempt to assign (that is, digitize) values on a sliding scale into one of three categories, high, medium and low. As a consequence of this parametric focus, LaRue's system necessarily plays down consideration of discrete sequential units in music, such as motives and phrases.

In contrast to LaRue's analogue approach, Meyer's perspective is firmly digital. He maintains that '[s]tyle is a replication of patterning, whether in human behavior or in the artifacts produced by human behavior, that results from a series of choices made within some set of constraints' (1989: 3). Thus, to paraphrase one of his later observations, a single (unreplicated) pattern cannot define a style (: 13, note 25).

Meyer identifies several hierarchical levels upon which the constraints governing pattern replication operate. His first group of levels consists of: laws, which are 'transcultural constraints … the principles governing the perception and cognition of musical patterns' (: 13); rules, which are 'intracultural, not universal' and which 'constitute the highest, most encompassing level of stylistic constraints' (: 17); and strategies, which are 'compositional choices made within the possibilities established by the rules of the style' (: 20). Below these three levels, Meyer notes that rules and strategies may themselves prevail at three further levels, each level hierarchically including the level(s) below it. These strata are: dialect, 'substyles that are differentiated because a number of composers … employ (choose) the same or similar rules and strategies' (: 23); idiom, constraints 'a composer repeatedly selects from the larger repertory of the dialect' (: 24); and intraopus style, 'concerned with what is replicated within a single work' (: 24).

Implicit in Meyer's framework is the notion that style analysis is not only hierarchical but also statistical in nature (Meyer 1992). In other words, a replication of patterning may only be identified if a sufficiently representative sample of material is considered. The size of the sample depends upon which broad class of data is observed or, to use a term of Nattiez's, upon which 'level of stylistic relevance' the analysis is situated (1990: 135–6), a concept analogous to Meyer's hierarchical perspective of laws, rules and strategies. To stress the inclusive nature of levels of stylistic relevance, Figure 2.1 below takes the pyramidal illustration of this principle from Nattiez (: 136, Fig. 6.2) and reworks it in order to represent the cultural/style-hierarchic configuration of the meme pool (see also Jan 1995: 6–7).

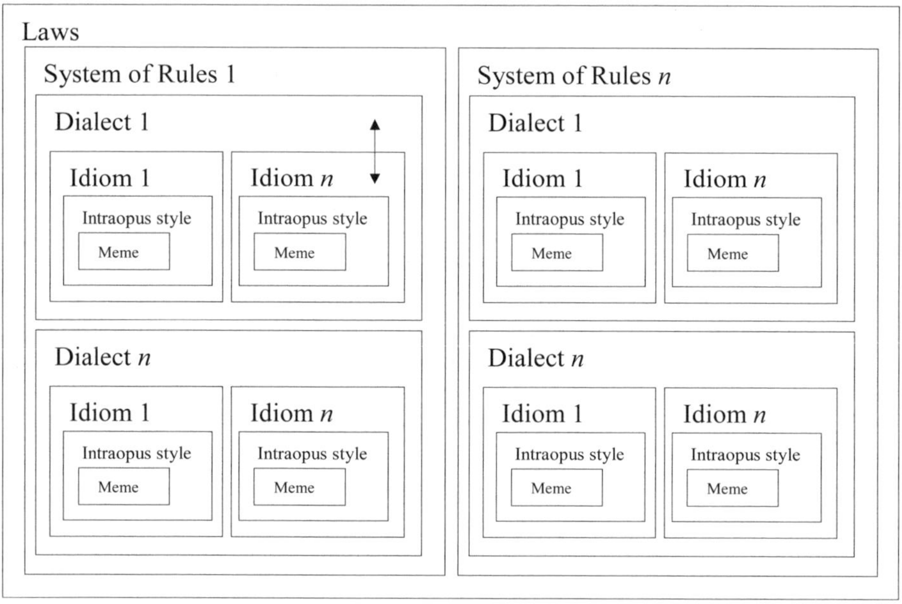

Figure 2.1: Cultural/Style-Hierarchic Realms and the Meme Pool

The boundaries of a musical meme pool are ultimately circumscribed by Meyer's concept of laws, within which several systems of rules (that is, distinct organizational systems) prevail, disposed both synchronically (geographically) and diachronically (chronologically). Concomitantly, each system of rules is generated by several dialects, again both synchronically and diachronically organized. In turn, a substantial number of idioms give rise to each dialect. Dialects, idioms and intraopus styles are defined by the particular community of memes assimilated by imitation from the including pool that is the level above them (rules, dialects and idioms respectively). Conversely, rules, dialects and idioms can only be generated by the totality of memes in the level(s) below them. Other aspects of Figure 2.1 will be discussed in Chapter 3.

In the Meyer-Nattiez formulation, the representative sample size diminishes as we move towards the centre of each nest of boxes, such that whereas the analysis of the 'universals of music' (Nattiez 1990: 62–8) takes as its theoretical sample every phenomenon subsumed under the aegis of 'music' – the boundaries of which are sometimes problematic to define – the analysis of the style of a work consists only of the identification of pattern replication within that work. Nevertheless, logic dictates that pattern replication may consist merely of an identity class of two, at any level of stylistic relevance.

2.5.2. *Style, Intertextuality and Memetics*

Meyer's conception of style as 'a replication of patterning' implies that what is replicated may arise both from a composer's own work and from the works of others. The latter situation, the borrowing of musical material from other composers, sometimes also treated under the concept of influence, is an aspect of the wider concept of intertextuality – the issue of 'quotation, borrowings, compositional modelling.... [and] the use of conventions' (Korsyn 1991: 6).[2] It covers all instances of composers reusing pre-existing musical ideas or compositional procedures in the act of producing new works. In Burkholder's view, however,

> If we are to understand the variety of borrowing methods, their history over time, and the relation of individual composers and repertoires to the problem as a whole, we must .... regard the study of musical borrowings *as a field*.... Most attempts to consider the problem in a broad context share a tendency to construe it too narrowly, focusing on 'quotation' within music of the last three centuries and excluding forms of borrowing that are so close to the heart of our tradition that they are seldom considered problematic, from cantus firmus to variations.... The most general term [for this field], and the one I prefer, is 'the uses of existing music'.[3]
>
> (1994: 861; his emphasis)

Cope, whose concerns include the field of computer recognition and recreation of style, uses the term 'referential analysis' for this field (2003: 11). Whereas Burkholder identifies no fewer than fourteen categories of 'the uses of existing music' in the music of Ives (: 854), Cope proposes a more generic five-part scheme designed to help operationalize a software utility (*Sorcerer*) he has developed for detecting allusions in a variety of musics. He explains that

---

[2] While none, to my knowledge, invokes the memetic paradigm, a number of studies of intertextuality are listed in note 5 of Korsyn 1991. For a memetic critique of his 'new poetics of musical influence', see Jan 2001.

[3] Burkholder's Appendix 1 lists a series of questions designed to generate a 'typology of the uses of existing music in new compositions or improvisations' (1994: 867–9). Giger 1994 describes a project to compile a bibliography of sources on musical borrowing. An online and regularly updated version of this bibliography is available at <http://www.music.indiana.edu/borrowing/>.

> My taxonomy for referential analysis includes Quotations (as in citations, excerpts, or renditions); Paraphrases (as in variations, caricatures, or transcriptions); Likenesses (as in approximations, translations, or similarities); Frameworks (as in outlines, vestiges, or redactions); and Commonalities (as in conventions, genera, or simplicities).... Clearly, potential for listener recognition proceeds from strong to weak through these categories and the potential for stylistic integration proceeds inversely.
>
> (2003: 11)

This referential-analytic continuum – 'the boundaries of these categories are imprecise and may, at times, overlap' (: 11) – and its properties are summarized in Figure 2.2 below; it is also incorporated, for reasons which will be outlined in due course, into Figure 3.2 below.

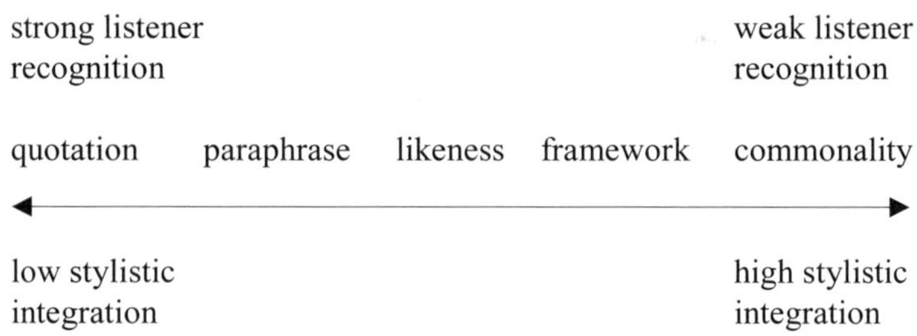

Figure 2.2: Cope's Continuum for Referential Analysis

It is important to stress that whereas events situated at the left-hand end of the continuum are striking and provocative, the caviar of this field so to speak, those at the right-hand end form the overwhelming bulk of borrowings, its daily bread. This region of the continuum encompasses all the patterns composers pass down the generations and which form the unremarkable bulk of a given style. Seen in these terms, composers do not invent such figures as the perfect cadence afresh: rather, they assimilate (inherit) them from the works of their predecessors and contemporaries.

In this study, I shall mainly focus on the central and right-hand end of Cope's continuum, for while quotations and paraphrases are exciting for any researcher working in this field to discover, from a statistical point of view they are relatively uncommon. Moreover, from the perspective which underpins this study, all borrowing – from the most audacious and arresting quotation (such as Berg's citation of the opening of *Tristan* in the *Lyric Suite*, shown in Example 4.14 below) to the most trivial and commonplace particle (such as the ascending triad c^1–e^1–g^1) – falls under the aegis of pattern replication, and the field most appropriate for its consideration is therefore not 'the uses of existing music' but memetics itself.

For memetics, since human culture is composed of myriad replicating particles each metaphorically pursuing its own selfish interests, the existence of intertextual connections between works is simply an inevitability; and compositions automatically attain the status of 'relational events rather than as closed and static entities' (Korsyn 1991: 15). Moreover, as will be discussed in Chapter 4, memetics argues that we should take the 'meme's eye view', not that of the composer: we should ask what attributes of a given pattern cause it to be replicated, not why a particular composer chose to borrow the pattern from a work of his or her musical culture.

2.5.3. *'Style-Identifying Signatures' as Memes in the Parameter of Pitch*

The replication of patterning which defines musical style occurs in several parameters and, within some of these, at various structural-hierarchic levels. To delineate the stylistic (memetic) profile of an idiom or dialect taking account of this two-dimensional framework (parameter-level) is a substantial undertaking, yet there is an area of pattern replication which is amenable to a preliminary investigation and which offers a relatively unproblematic way of moving from the abstract to the concrete aspects of musical memetics. This is the phenomenon of pitch particle recurrence, whereby relatively localized and discrete units are propagated on both an intra- and, most importantly, an inter-work level. It is perhaps especially transparent in eighteenth- and early-nineteenth-century music but demonstrable in all periods of western musical history and in many non-western musical traditions.

These patterns are perhaps the most obvious manifestations of memes in music, having 'just sufficient copying-fidelity to serve as a viable unit of natural selection' (Dawkins 1989: 195). They generally exist as self-contained, foreground-orientated segments consisting of a pitch sequence disposed either solely in melody or as part of a two-voice (melody-plus-bass) pattern and often associated with distinctive rhythmic shapes. Cope uses the term 'signature' to refer to a subset of such patterns, defining them as

> a set of contiguous intervals (i.e., exempt from key differences) found in more than one work by the same composer. Signatures typically contain two to nine notes melodically and more if combined with harmonies. They are generally divorced from rhythm, though rhythmic ratios often remain intact. Signatures are work-independent. They do not sound as if they come from a certain work of a composer but rather from the style of a composer (or a group of composers).
>
> (1991a: 46)

Location is clearly a factor in their disposition but, contrary to Cope's assertion (1991b: 25), 'style-identifying signatures' are by no means confined to cadences and may be deployed at various positions within the periodic structure. Moreover, they are not always confined to 'the same composer', but may be found, as Cope acknowledges, replicated intact in the work of several composers. Such wider propagation is, of course, fundamental for memetics.

Example 2.1 i and ii below show a pitch pattern/signature – a meme – from the dialect of the late-eighteenth century. The underlying voice-leading configuration is shown in part iii of the example. (Chapter 3 begins with an explanation of the symbols used in this and subsequent examples.)

Example 2.1: Meme in the Parameter of Pitch

i) Mozart: Serenade in C minor K. 388 (384a) (*c.* 1782/3), I, bb. 66–8

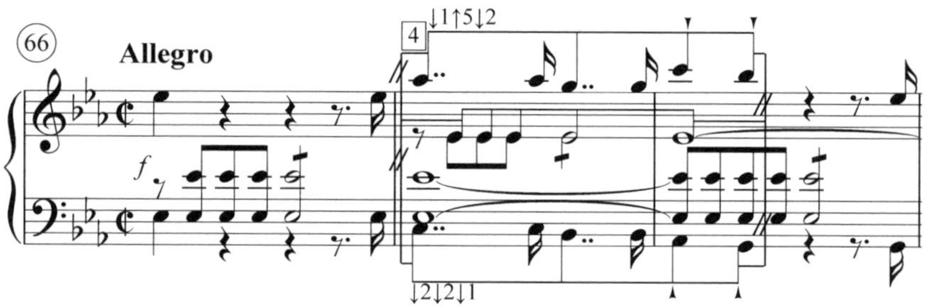

ii) Beethoven: Quartet in E♭ major op. 127 (1825), IV, bb. 219–22

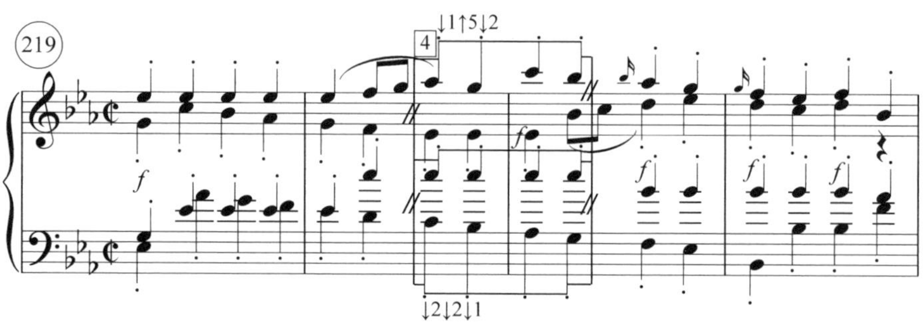

iii) Voice-Leading Schema

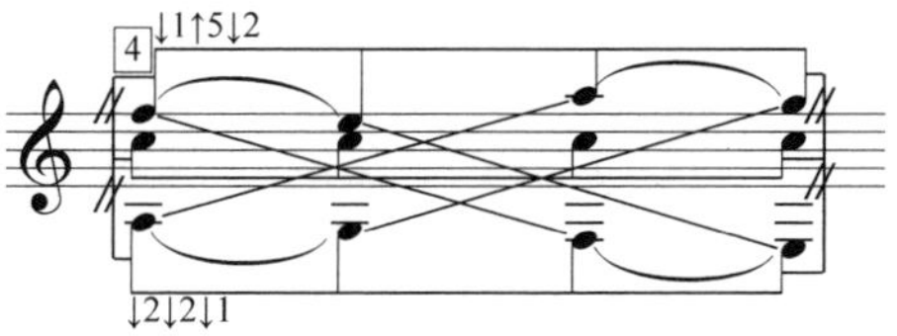

The meme consists of a three-part texture, the outer parts moving in parallel tenths and sixths around an inner pedal, expressing the harmonic progression $IV^6{}_3$–$I^6{}_4$–IV–$I^6{}_3$ and articulating a double interlocking voice exchange. Although occurring in different rhythmic, textural and registral garbs, each passage is essentially based upon the same pitch structure, therefore justifying its description as a meme replicated in the two contexts.

2.5.4. *Syntacticism and the Other Musical Parameters*

In addition to pitch, other musical parameters, such as rhythm, texture, timbre and even dynamics, might also support configurations which lend themselves to replication. As a general principle, however, the capacity for a parameter to sustain replication seems contingent upon the degree to which it possesses the attribute of 'syntacticism'. As Meyer notes,

> In order for syntax to exist ..., successive stimuli must be related to one another in such a way that specific criteria for mobility and closure are established. Such criteria can be established only if the elements of the parameter can be segmented into discrete, nonuniform relationships so that the similarities and differences between them are definable, constant, and proportional.
>
> (1989: 14)

However such stimuli are related to each other – whether they generate what George Mandler terms 'coordinate', 'subordinate', or 'proordinate/serial' structures (in Gjerdingen 1988: 12–14) – they must exist in syntactic relationships to each other within the boundaries of a particle, such that some degree of what might broadly be termed 'information' is encoded by virtue of the configuration of the component elements. On this reasoning, the greater the number of components within a particle, and the more complex and networked the syntactic relationships between those components, the higher the information content, in an abstract sense, of the particle.

In the Western tradition, syntacticism is most developed in the realm of pitch, and this is perhaps why this domain has been so extensively theorized over the last two millennia. In rhythm it is present to a lesser degree, hence the arguably less elaborate hierarchical organization of rhythm compared with pitch (and the relative under-theorization of rhythm compared with pitch). Nevertheless, rhythm possess sufficient syntacticism for Meyer to regard it, together with pitch, as a primary parameter (1992: 476).

In texture, timbre and dynamics – what Meyer terms the secondary parameters (: 476) – syntacticism exists only at a rudimentary level, relationships between events in these parameters being rather loose and often difficult to perceive. Another way to conceive this distinction might be to say that pitch and rhythm have a clarity which is digital in character (at least in conception and notation, if not in performance), whereas texture, timbre and dynamics have a more nebulous, analogue quality. The relevance of syntacticism and the related notion of information to a memetic perspective on music is explored more fully in Chapter 3.

Memes in the Parameter of Rhythm

In some contexts, rhythmic memes exist independently of the pitch configurations with which they are (temporarily) associated. Example 2.2 i below illustrates configurations in pitch (labelled meme *x*) and rhythm (meme *y*) which, as shown in ii and iii, have independent existence owing to their replication in association with (respectively) different rhythmic and pitch patterns in these other contexts, the latter patterns themselves potentially existing as memes. (It is assumed that a given meme in two different keys is essentially the same meme, in that it retains its defining internal intervallic structure.)

Example 2.2: Memes in the Parameters of Pitch and Rhythm

i) Memes *x* (Pitch Sequence ↑2↓3↑1) and *y* (Rhythmic Pattern ♩. ♬ | ♪3: 0.5: 0.5: 1): Mozart, *Die Zauberflöte* K. 620 (1791), no. 13, 'Alles fühlt der Liebe Freuden', bb. 1–2

ii) Meme *x*: Brahms, *Akademische Festouverture*, op. 80 (1880), bb. 88–90

iii) Meme *y*: Beethoven, Symphony no. 9 in D minor op. 125 (1824), I, bb. 74–6

In some musics, notably west African drumming, rhythm is the primary musical parameter, existing without associated pitch structures in complex durational and accentual hierarchies. In the first two 'bars' of Example 2.3 i and ii below, the rhythms are related by their replication of a core rhythmic texture in the bell II, castanet, rattle, tambourine I and small drum parts (marked with an asterisk in the example). This acts as a foil for the more rhythmically complex playing of the bell I, tambourine II and big drum parts.

Example 2.3: Memes in the Parameter of Rhythm. Two Fragments of African Northern Ewe Music (after Agawu 1995: 102)

i) Fragment of *Gàbàdà* music

ii) Fragment of *Égbaníbà* music

This replication engenders a rhythmic meme consisting of several strata, from the 'background' (crotchet) rhythm of the bell II, castanet and rattle, through the 'middleground' (quaver) rhythm of the tambourine I, to the 'foreground' (semiquaver) rhythm of the small drum.

Memes in the Parameters of Texture, Timbre and Dynamics

> [A] tutti was not necessarily overpowering; in most 18th-century music, it served principally to establish a clear perspective between solo and ensemble, either by contrasted material or by fuller scoring of a chamber music texture. Such sharp demarcations are typical in classic symphonies. [The opening of Boccherini's Symphony in B♭ major op. 22 no. 1 of 1775] illustrates a minimum standard tutti for classic music; the three-part chamber music texture, layered in parallel thirds and *Trommel-bass*, is reinforced by oboe, horn, and viola doublings.... [The opening of Cherubini's Overture to *Médée* of 1797] illustrates a typical grand tutti of around 1800. Winds and middle strings are deployed in full chords for sonority and rhythmic reinforcement of the treble-bass polarity. The Storm and Stress style here exemplifies an orchestral idiom cultivated by Gluck, which became prevalent at this time.
>
> (Ratner 1980: 151–2)

That Ratner can identify two distinct textural types here – the 'minimum standard tutti' and the 'grand tutti' – indicates that there are configurations of instrumentation and orchestration which recur (are replicated) in many contexts and which might potentially be regarded as memetic. Naturally these configurations arise in part from the constraints of instrumental range and capability and players' aptitude (and, equally importantly, from the social and economic factors impinging upon instrumental ensembles); but such 'environmental' constraints do not necessarily militate against our regarding such recurrent patterns as memes, albeit somewhat diffuse ones, in the parameters of texture and timbre.

In Example 2.4 ii below, the minimum standard tutti is accommodated by Mozart to the more restricted palette of the piano trio; the Boccherini passage cited by Ratner as an instance of this textural type is shown in Example 2.4 i. While the three-part texture is replicated, the timbre is clearly quite different; yet there is a distinct evocation of the orchestral antecedents of this texture and, therefore, a memory of 'oboe, horn, and viola doublings'.

Example 2.4: Meme in the Parameter of Texture

i) Boccherini: Symphony in B♭ major op. 22 no. 1 (1775), I, bb. 1–3

ii) Mozart: Piano Trio in B♭ major K. 502 (1786), I, bb. 1–4

Replicated dynamic patterns are common in some musics, yet they are often associated with pitch and rhythmic replication, simply 'tagging-on' to the replicated syntactic parameters. In some cases, however, dynamic memes became an integral element of the style of a period and may be found in numerous instances independent of replicated pitch and rhythmic patterns. One such example is the 'motto' opening of classical-period symphonies and sonatas where, irrespective of the nature of the pitch and rhythmic material, a *piano-forte* dynamic antithesis is stereotypical.

It could be argued, however, that there is a substantive difference between the concrete nature of a replicated pitch or rhythmic pattern – with which this study is principally concerned – and the rather fuzzy, abstract quality of a replicated texture, timbre or dynamic sequence. The question boils down to the issue of syntacticism, and the degree to which 'the elements of the parameter can be segmented into discrete, nonuniform relationships so that the similarities and differences between them are definable, constant, and proportional'. Because texture, timbre and dynamics cannot satisfy this condition to the degree that pitch and rhythm can, they cannot sustain a comparable 'ecology' of memetic replication.

Nevertheless, the notion of replication in the secondary parameters might be rehabilitated to some degree by regarding it as giving rise to 'musico-operational' memes. That is, it may sometimes be the case that what is replicated between two or more works is not explicit musical patterning, such as a chord progression, a melodic shape or a rhythmic ratio, but a particular procedure, a generic, material-independent way of manipulating musical material which is as much operational as it is purely musical. The most obvious examples of such operations are perhaps the contrapuntal/serial procedures of augmentation, diminution, inversion and retrogression; but there are numerous others, some common to a wide range of musics, others limited to a particular repertoire or musico-historical period. A replicated operation may therefore be common to a set of musical patterns, none of which is necessarily related in its primary-parametric configurations to any other patterns in the set by a process of imitation.

In view of this, we might say that Mozart replicates the abstract idea, the procedure, of loud-soft dynamic contrast in such contexts as the opening of the Symphony in D major K. 297 (300a) ('Paris') (1778), a scheme he probably assimilated most directly from J.C. Bach (in such works as the Sonata in D major op. 5 no. 2 (1766), I, bb. 1–4). That Mozart presumably acquired this technique by imitation makes it memetic, but in a more abstract sense than those several cases where Mozart assimilated a pitch or rhythmic meme by imitation of his contemporaries.

A daunting vista emerges from these considerations: the several parameters of music have the capacity to support particulate configurations at various levels of structure, which may be replicated by imitation within a cultural group. This is perhaps nothing more than an unfamiliar way of acknowledging the great richness and complexity of music and the reliance of composers, directly and indirectly, on their predecessors. Nevertheless, the full significance of this perspective will become evident later, when the notion of memetic replication is employed to consider the related issues of synchronic organization (Chapter 3) and diachronic change (Chapter 4) in music.

2.6. Summary

Defining the musical meme, while not unproblematic, is facilitated by drawing upon the central principles of replicator theory, most importantly the notions of longevity, fecundity and copying-fidelity. The last of these suggests that small packets of musical information – which balance the need for having sufficient information content to ensure perceptual-cognitive salience with the need to avoid corruption during replication as a consequence of excessive length and complexity – are the most likely candidates for musical memes. Such particles, principally taking the form of discrete configurations of pitch and rhythm, are persistent, surviving across the expanses of musical history by virtue of their being replicated in the works – and ultimately the brains – of successive generations of composers.

They are easily accommodated within a Meyerian conception of musical style, which also offers a useful framework for conceptualizing the hierarchic organization of culture.

Chapter 3

Replicating Sonorities, Replicating Hierarchies: Memes in Music II

3.1. Introduction

I build upon the groundwork of Chapter 2 here to consider the more technical aspects of the musical meme. After introducing an analytical symbology for musical memes, the central issues underpinning their definition are examined, beginning with the related concepts of meme particulateness, coindexation and segmentation. This leads to an investigation of memetic co-adaptation and the formation of memeplexes, complex agglomerations of memes at different structural-hierarchic levels. I conclude with attempts to draw analogies between cultural (memetic) and biological (genetic) hierarchies.

3.2. An Analytical Symbology for Musical Memes

To facilitate the analytical study of musical memes it is useful to devise a symbology which is capable of showing a meme's initial and terminal nodes, its medial components and its structural-hierarchic location. To this end, the following symbology – intended to be suitable for, or adaptable to, memes in all musical parameters and designed to be applied as an analytical overlay to musical notation – is proposed and will be employed in this study:

1. The components of a meme are identified with a stem arranged in the opposite direction to the 'rhythm' stem of the note if the disposition of the other parts permits or, if not, with a stem extending the rhythm stem.
2. These elements are linked by a beam which, while largely horizontal, may in parts be drawn diagonally according to the direction of the added stems.

3. The hierarchic location of the meme is indicated by a boxed numeral placed to the left of the beam. The number '4' is used to indicate a meme at the foreground level, '3' for a meme at the shallow middleground level, '2' for a meme at an intermediate middleground level and '1' for a meme at a deep middleground level (Schenker's 'erster Schicht'). The three *Ursatz* memes are, therefore, situated at level '0'.
4. The direction of motion of the meme and its intervallic content, expressed in semitones, is indicated as a vector (for example, '↑4↑4', '↑4↓9') placed at the left-hand edge of the beam.
5. Where a meme comprises upper and lower component strata (for example, as separate voices), or more than two strata, the initial and terminal stems of each stratum are connected by left and right braces ('[ ]') connected to the mid-point of the stem. Braces broken with two '//' symbols (or more, depending on the number of strata) indicate that the components are judged to have independent memetic existence – they are also replicated separately – and that the complex is therefore a memeplex.
6. Hierarchical relationships between members of a memeplex are indicated by a tree structure of 'nested' beams within an overarching beam. Circled pitches within such a complex indicate those of structural importance at the higher hierarchic level.
7. Other analytical information – in particular, Roman numerals and figured bass symbols for harmonic memes; and implication-realization analysis symbols to indicate the perceptual-cognitive basis for memetic segmentation – may be added to the overlay.

This symbology is illustrated in Figure 3.1 below, which shows the system abstractly, followed by an illustration of its use in two concrete musical contexts.[1]

[1] While the compilation of a catalogue of musical memes is an undertaking well beyond the scope of this study, it will require a system of categorization. This might consist, for instance, of two pairs of bracketed numbers, each pair of numbers within the brackets being separated by a dash – for example, (3–24)(3–23) – in the manner of Forte's pitch-class set labelling system (1973). The first number of the first pair (analogous to Forte's procedure) indicates the number of elements in the meme and the second the ordinal position of the meme in a listing of all memes with this number of elements. The second pair indicates, using the same format as the first, its nearest evolutionary antecedent, where this relationship can be verified or estimated with an acceptable degree of probability.

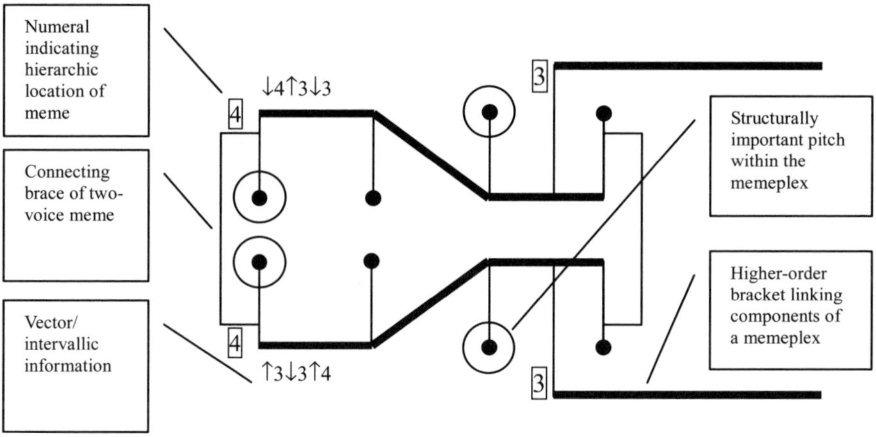

Figure 3.1: An Analytical Symbology for Musical Memes: Abstract Symbols

Example 3.1: An Analytical Symbology for Musical Memes: Two Examples

i) J.C. Bach: Sonata in E♭ major op. 5 no. 4 (T. 338/1) (1766), I, bb. 77–8

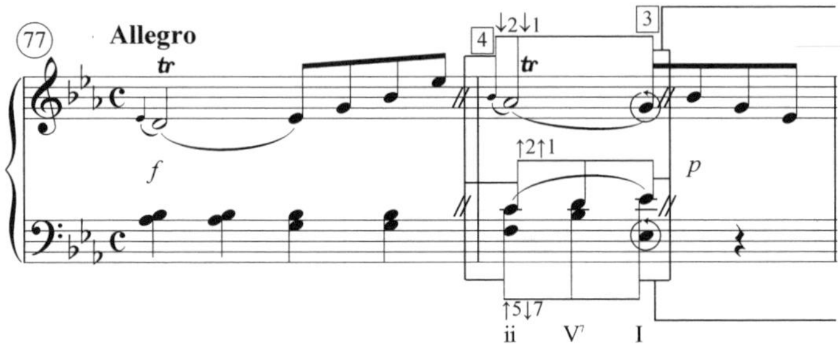

ii) Haydn: Symphony no. 94 in G major Hob. I: 94 ('Surprise') (1791), IV, bb. 1–4

Here, three melodic memes – the patterns $\hat{5}$–$\hat{4}$–$\hat{3}$, $\hat{6}$–$\hat{7}$–$\hat{1}$ and $\hat{2}$–$\hat{5}$–$\hat{1}$ – generate the harmonic meme ii–V^7–I. These melodic memes are linked by braces to demarcate the structure which results from their conglomeration, but the '//' symbol indicates that each has independent existence; thus the composite structure is a memeplex, not just a single unit-meme. The memeplex is situated at the foreground level, signified by the '4', but it also generates a component of a higher-level memeplex (not shown in the example), indicated by the '3'.

3.3. Defining the Musical Meme III: The Issues of Particulateness, Segmentation and Coindexation

I return to the definition of the musical meme, fleshing out some of the points made in 2.5 above. To do so, I shall invoke the notions of particulateness, coindexation and segmentation. I treat them separately here for expositional clarity and convenience; in reality, they are closely interdependent.

3.3.1. *Particulateness*

Particulateness refers to the tendency of musical memes – certainly those in the parameters of pitch and rhythm – to exist as discrete and closed units, an extension of the digital (as opposed to analogue) quality referred to in 2.5.4 above. As with the gene, however, there is no hard-and-fast definition of what constitutes a meme. Indeed, the biologist Seymour Benzer proposed refining the somewhat imprecise concept of the gene by focusing it into the categories of 'muton' ('the minimum unit of mutational change'), 'recon' ('the minimum unit of recombination') and 'cistron' ('the unit responsible for synthesizing one polypeptide chain') (Dawkins 1983a: 81).

Dawkins's definition of the gene ('any portion of chromosomal material …') given in 1.2.3 above is perhaps the most utilitarian. As a condensation of this definition, he speaks, adding to Benzer's categories, of the 'optimon', 'the unit of natural selection' (1983a: 81). The definition is founded on his observation, made apropos the notion of copying-fidelity, that the smaller the gene the greater the statistical probability that it will survive the process of crossing-over intact. He does not, however, apply the same logic to the meme. Using musical memes as his examples (as in his canonic definition of the meme in 1.4 above), he notes that

> So far I have talked of memes as though it was obvious what a single unit-meme consisted of. But of course it is far from obvious. I have said a tune is one meme, but what about a symphony: how many memes is that? Is each movement one meme, each recognizable phrase of melody, each bar, each chord, or what?
>
> (1989: 195)

The biological analogy, indeed replicator theory itself, suggests that memes tend towards the latter end of the continuum Dawkins outlines – towards existence as short and clearly demarcated rather than long and diffuse units. The reason for this is directly analogous to that given for the gene: the more concise a meme the greater the likelihood that it will survive the travails of replication by imitation intact. This is probably a function of memory: the more complex a piece of information, the greater the likelihood that it will be altered upon reconstitution, creating a tendency to privilege discrete, simple units. The following example illustrates the application of this principle to musical memes.

Example 3.2: Smallest Indivisible Units

i) Hummel: Concerto for Trumpet and Orchestra in E major (1803), I, bb. 54–7

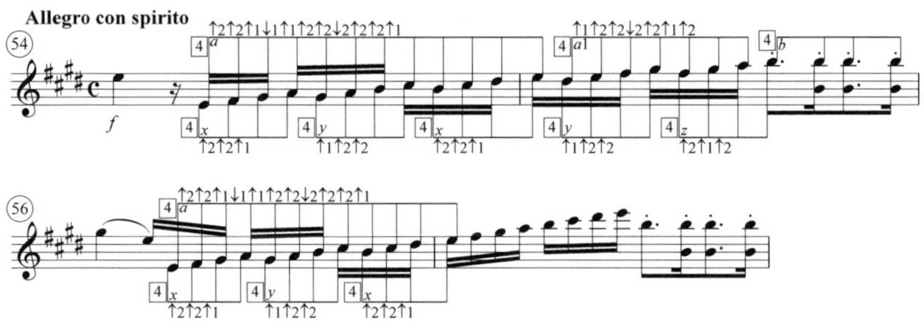

ii) Beethoven: Symphony no. 5 in C minor op. 67 (1808), IV, bb. 1–12

In Hummel's phrase, unit *a* (upper bracket) is subjected to extension at a^1 then combined with a contrasting unit, *b*. The complex a–a^1–b may theoretically exist as a meme in that it may be propagated intact in other contexts. In the extract from Beethoven, unit *a* demonstrates an existence independent of a^1 and *b* (even though its third statement, at bb. 10f., is extended to form a complex *a*–*y*), illustrating the tendency for smaller units to achieve the more stable memetic existence. However, as the subdivisions of *a* and a^1 in the extracts indicate (lower brackets), the smallest indivisible unit in these passages is the filled-in ascending fourth, in its three interval-sequence variants *x*, *y* and *z*.

Dennett, however, is reluctant to admit very small particles as memetic. His definition of the meme, also invoking a musical example,[2] asserts that

> *D–F♯–A* isn't a unit and the theme from the slow movement of Beethoven's Seventh Symphony is: the units are the smallest elements that replicate themselves with reliability and fecundity. We can compare them, in this regard, to genes and their components: *C–G–A*, a single codon of DNA, is 'too small' to be a gene. It is one of the codes for the amino acid arginine, and it copies itself prodigiously wherever it appears in genomes, but its effects are not 'individual' enough to count as a gene. A three-nucleotide phrase does not count as a gene for the same reason that you can't copyright a three-note musical phrase: it is not enough to make a melody.
>
> (1995: 344; his emphases)

Aside from his confusion of memes and melodies in the final sentence of this passage, his somewhat oversimplistic alignment of notes and nucleotides, and his reliance on copyright law to decide questions of musical perception, Dennett seems to suggest that while three notes cannot be memetic, four can, for he claims that

> The first four notes of Beethoven's Fifth Symphony are clearly a meme, replicating all by themselves, detached from the rest of the symphony, but keeping intact a certain identity of effect (a phe[m]otypic effect), and hence thriving in contexts in which Beethoven and his works are unknown.
>
> (: 344)

Nevertheless, many listeners familiar with American popular song would recognize the following, Johnny Burke's and Erroll Garner's 'Misty', from its distinctive opening vocal gesture ('Look at me …'), a collection of just three pitches, $b\flat^1$–g^1–d^1, in a distinctive rhythm, ♫ | 𝅗𝅥. – and they may even be able to do so without its characteristic harmonic support. If the memory of a melody can be accessed (cued) by hearing its opening notes, even in the absence of a harmonic and/or timbral context, this implies that these notes themselves have the potential for independent memetic existence.

---

2 Commentators often employ musical examples because, apropos the quotation from Dennett in 2.2.1 above, musical memes may be discussed in purely syntactic-informational terms – as configurations manifested in the form of symbols on a printed score – without the need to appeal to a complicating semantic-informational dimension, as would be the case with memes in referential symbolic systems such as poetry or painting.

Example 3.3: Burke and Garner, 'Misty' (1954), bb. 4–7

Moreover, Dennett's argument blurs the parameters of pitch and rhythm. Even the shortest and most self-contained musical meme is seldom an indivisible particle, by which I mean divisible not vertically (by length, segmentationally), or horizontally (by pitch strata, voices), but parametrically. Almost invariably it is itself a complex of memes – a memeplex – in different musical parameters, principally pitch (and therefore register) and rhythm, but also in the realms of dynamics and texture; Example 2.2 above is an example of this phenomenon of parametric co-adaptation, consisting of configurations in pitch and rhythm which, as shown in parts ii and iii of the example, have independent existence in other contexts. One consequence of this is that a three- or four-component pitch sequence may have relatively low salience in one rhythmic context – it may not be distinctive enough to engender imitation – yet the same sequence may acquire greater prominence by virtue of its co-adaptation with a more striking rhythmic pattern in another context, and so be subject to the replication which renders it, and the partnership, memetic.

Having established the parametric interaction of musical memes, Dennett's example, the motive from the opening of Beethoven's Fifth Symphony, could be read as not just four 'notes' but as two pitches, g^1 and $e\flat^1$, articulated by four rhythmic attacks, 𝄾♪♪♪ | 𝅗𝅥 |. One might even say that the most distinctive aspect of the figure is not the pitch content but the rhythmic profile which, at bb. 182ff., becomes reduced to a three attack rhythm, ♫ | ♩., a memetic unit of wide currency at this time and indeed throughout musical history.

A further complicating factor in the definition of musical memes is the fact that, in most musics, several pitch strata interact, giving rise to harmony and counterpoint. A fragment of music from the common-practice period may consist of a melody line, a bass and one or more inner parts, each of which may have its own linear-memetic identity, but which may also generate a harmonic memeplex. Contrary to Dennett's assertion, Example 3.4 below shows a three-vertical-component cadential meme, the harmonic structure generated by three melodic memes.

Example 3.4: A Three-Vertical-Component Cadential Meme

i) Corelli: Trio Sonata in D major op. 1 no. 12 (1681), III, bb. 11–12

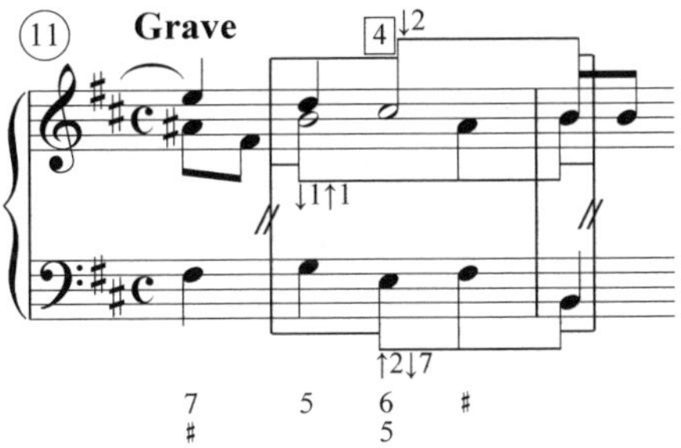

ii) Bach: *Matthäus-Passion* BWV 244 (*c.* 1727–42), no. 25, Chorale 'Was mein Gott will, das g'scheh' allzeit', bb. 3–5

One could even assert the memetic status of the two-vertical-component perfect cadential patterns shown in Example 3.5 below, for the end-segments, the harmonic progression V–I, are to all intents and purposes identical, despite being preceded by different penultimate configurations.

Example 3.5: A Two-Vertical-Component Cadential Meme

i) Mozart: Sonata in D major K. 284 (205b) (1775), I, bb. 126–7

ii) Beethoven: Piano Trio in D major op. 70 no. 1 ('Ghost') (1808), I, bb. 268–70

Dennett's assertion of the memetic status of the theme from the slow movement of Beethoven's Seventh Symphony – all forty-five notes of it (bb. 27–42) – is problematic in that he does not distinguish between listeners and composers *qua* listeners. Although 'there is a limit to the complexity of musical phrases that can be memorized' (Gatherer 1997: 81), this particular theme is probably not too elaborate to be held intact in the memory of many musically literate listeners – today and in 1812. If so retained, it would qualify in its entirety as a meme. Of course, it also survives, rather more durably, in the form of countless phemotypic representations – in printed scores and CD recordings. In the work of the composers who were Beethoven's contemporaries and successors, however, this theme, although also stored in their brains as a single unit-meme, was not replicated as such in their compositions, for what might be called the 'anti-plagiarism' verbal-conceptual meme (prolific in western European culture certainly from the beginning of the nineteenth century) would have inhibited this type of copying, making it, in Dawkins's words, far too long to be 'a viable unit of natural selection' (1989: 195). Memorizing and then replicating whole chunks of the music of their predecessors and contemporaries is obviously not what composers did at this time and in this place; they tended, as I have suggested, to replicate the small component units of the musical continuum – either remembered from musico-aural experience or viewed as musico-graphical symbols on paper – thereby navigating the straits between the siren voices of memorability and the rocks of plagiarism.

On this reasoning, as Example 3.6 below illustrates, Beethoven's theme might be regarded not as a single unit-meme, but as a collection of memes. The example shows copies of just two of the memes – bracketed and labelled *x* and *y* in the example – which make up this melody.

Example 3.6: Memes in Beethoven's Seventh Symphony

i) Meme *x*: Mozart, Piano Concerto in C major K. 467 (1785), I, bb. 413–17

ii) Memes *x* and *y*: Beethoven, Symphony no. 7 in A major op. 92 (1812), II, bb. 27–34

iii) Meme *y*: Schubert, Piano Quintet in A major D. 667 ('Trout') (1819), I, bb. 1–6

To review the foregoing, any discrete musical segment which a composer assimilates from his or her cultural environment may be regarded as memetic. Such a segment will tend to be the union of a short melodic fragment, a simple chord progression and a concise rhythmic pattern. Thus, to demarcate musical memes one needs 'to break the stream of music into component units (or "unities" – i.e. units that either could not be further subdivided or did not need to be because their sub-units never occur independently)' (Bent and Pople 2001: 566). While offered as a summary of the working methods of distributional analysis, this principle both holds for the definition of the meme and neatly parallels that Dawkins gives for the gene.

Nevertheless, we have still not determined the minimum number of components a pattern must have in order to function as a meme. Dennett concedes, after Dawkins, that 'there is no "principled" lower limit on the length of a sequence that might come to be considered a gene or a meme' (1995: 344), despite previously asserting four as this nominal value in his discussion of Beethoven's Fifth Symphony. Observing that 'Beethoven is the favourite example for illustrating this problem' (1999: 53), Blackmore also sidesteps the issue of meme size, essentially taking Dennett's 'smallest elements that replicate themselves with reliability and fecundity' (Dennett 1995: 344) – or, to take Pocklington's and Best's inverse formulation, 'the largest units of socially transmitted information that reliably and repeatedly withstand transmission' (1997: 81) – as the most secure criterion (Blackmore 1999: 54).

To help resolve the matter, we might invoke issue of syntacticism. As noted in 2.5.4 above, this implies the storage and transmission of what might be termed information.[3] The more pitch or rhythmic elements a meme contains, the greater the potential for information-bearing relationships to exist between the meme's elements. In a three-element meme, for instance, element one can relate to elements two and three, element two can relate to elements one and three, and element three can relate to elements one and two. Such relationships may be intervallic in the case of pitch and proportional in the case of rhythm. They may also, in a more abstract sense, be 'positional' ('nodal' or 'sequential'), in that an element which occupies position one in a sequence may relate in positional terms to an element which occupies position five, even if these elements are of the same pitch or have the same duration.

With three elements, there are six possible intra-meme relationships in each parameter. With a four-element meme, the number increases to twelve and with five elements, to twenty. Modelled by the formula $r = n \times (n-1)$, where r is the number of intra-meme relationships and n is the number of meme elements, this principle means that a pitch meme such as that shown in Example 1.1 i above, has, in its upper voice, $9 \times (9-1) = 72$ possible pitch relationships. Factoring in rhythmic and positional parameters gives a total 'relational network' of $72 \times 3 = 216$ 'connections'.[4]

I hypothesize that if a particle consists of so few elements that its information content is low or even zero, it may possess insufficient perceptual-cognitive salience to attract the attention of a listener, to be encoded in memory, or to be transmissible to other listeners. Conversely, if it contains enough elements to afford it a high information content, it will possess high salience but there will be an increased probability that its information content may be degraded on replication owing to miscopying. Even where the mutation of a replicator does not result in informational degradation, there is by definition some reconfiguration, such that even though the number of memetic 'bytes' of information is preserved, their disposition is altered.

Given this, three components is probably the lower threshold for a parametric element sequence, such as melodic pitches or durations in a rhythmic relationship. Because harmonic patterns involve vertical as well as horizontal relationships, two components, as in Example 3.5 above, is probably their lower threshold. With r values of zero and one respectively, one- and two-element melodic or rhythmic patterns probably have too low an information content to function as memes whereas, as noted above, a three-component pattern has $r = 6$, a clear differential from the two-component value.[5]

---

3 I employ the term in a different sense to its use in information theory, as implemented for music in such studies as Knopoff and Hutchinson 1981.

4 Discussing pitch relationships in terms of interval-class content, Straus arrives at values not modelled by $r = n \times (n-1)$ but of similar order (2000: 10, Figure 1–7).

5 As discussed below, Lerdahl's and Jackendoff's 'Grouping Preference Rule 1' expresses this notion as '[s]trongly avoid groups containing a single event. (Alternative form: Avoid analyses with very small groups – the smaller, the less preferable.)' (1983: 43).

By way of a summary of the points discussed in this section, Figure 3.2 below hypothesizes the relationship between various meme attributes and the number of component elements.

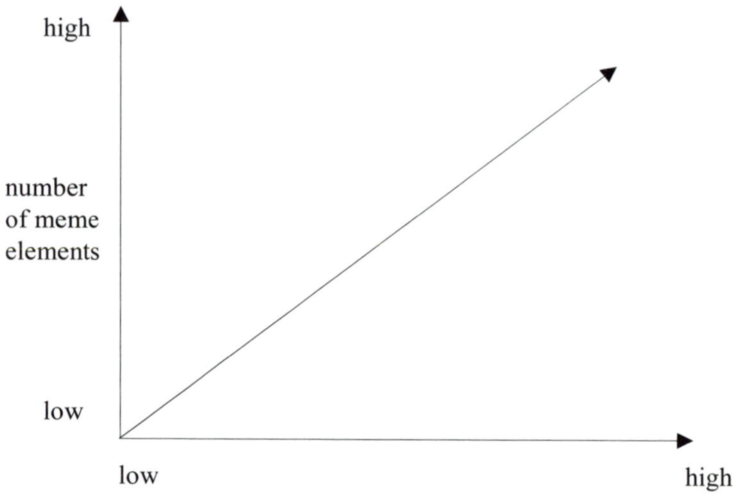

copying-*in*fidelity
perceptual-cognitive salience
memorability
individuality (style structure) *vs.* generality (style form/shape)
information content (given by *r* value)
perception of quotation/borrowing/plagiarism
[Cope:
listener recognition
commonality framework likeness paraphrase quotation
stylistic *non*-integration]

Figure 3.2: Attributes of Memes Plotted Against Number of Component Elements

On the *x* axis, it is hypothesized that there is a high degree of correlation between copying-*in*fidelity; perceptual-cognitive salience; how memorable a meme is; whether the meme is perceived as stylistically individual or general (Narmour's concepts of style structure and style form – style shape in his later writings – respectively); its information content (as represented by its *r* value); and to what degree a competent listener will perceive the meme as having been 'lifted' from a specific antecedent context. Lastly, the stages of Cope's continuum for referential analysis (shown in Figure 2.2 above) are adapted, by simple reversal of the sequence, to the figure.

While this chart is in no sense scientific – for one thing, it combines quantitative (y axis) with qualitative (x axis) values – it does, I hope, encapsulate a central tenet of replicator theory, namely that the more elements a particle contains, the more distinctive and 'singular' it is yet, by the same token, the more likely it is to be subject to miscopying and fragmentation.

3.3.2. *Segmentation*

Segmentation is the process whereby the memetic structure of music – the organization of the sound stream into a series of discrete replicated particles – is perceived by the listener as a result of the effect of various articulations between particles. As a key aspect of perception and cognition, we automatically subject music to segmentational operations, dividing the stream of sound information into discrete units in order to facilitate efficient processing. Whether this occurs synchronically (in analytical contexts) or diachronically (during real-time listening experiences), it may be characterized as the drawing, literally or metaphorically, of vertical and horizontal lines over the sound stream of music in order to mark points of articulation and closure.

Segmentation is an issue often discussed in the music-analytical and music-psychological literature in terms of the concept of grouping structure, 'which describes how the mind articulates a chronological stream of musical events by associating events into groups that seem to belong together in some way' (Pople 2004a: 133). Such association is often engendered by the separation of a unit from its surrounding material by means of strong initial and terminal articulations. From a memetic perspective, it appears that unless a unit of musical information is demarcated in this way, it will have insufficient particulate identity to function as a unit of imitation.

There are clearly several ways in which a musical continuum may be partitioned into its constituent units, but for memetics it is important that segmentation operations possess psychological validity and are not merely abstract analytical operations. In this section I shall consider what I see as the two fundamental ways in which segmentation is brought about: first, and perhaps most importantly, bottom-up segmentation resulting from processes described by Gestalt psychology and derived music-theoretical perspectives; and secondly, segmentation engendered by top-down (schematic, experiential) knowledge.

Bottom-Up: Gestalt Segmentation

At an innate level, our comprehension of patterning is controlled by processes formalized by the Gestalt school of psychology. In summarizing its central precepts, Deutsch observes that

> we group elements into configurations on the basis of various simple rules …. One is proximity: closer elements are grouped together in preference to those that are spaced further apart.… Another is similarity …. A third, good continuation, states that elements that follow each other in a given direction are perceptually linked together …. A fourth, common fate, states that elements that change in the same way are perceptually linked together. As a fifth principle, we tend to form groupings so as to perceive configurations that are familiar to us.
>
> (1999: 300)

In a reinvigoration of this area of research, Gestalt thinking informs several avenues of music-theoretical and music-psychological research developed during recent decades. Lerdahl's and Jackendoff's Generative Theory of Tonal Music (1983; hereafter 'GTTM') relies on Gestalt precepts for the formulation of its five grouping 'well-formedness rules' and seven grouping 'preference rules'. In Lerdahl's and Jackendoff's formulation,

> Grouping well-formedness rules (GWFRs) establish the formal structure of grouping patterns and their relationship to the string of pitch-events that form a piece …. Grouping preference rules (GPRs) establish which of the formally possible structures that can be assigned to a piece correspond to the listener's actual intuitions ….
>
> (1983: 36–7)

Thus the GWFRs define what is formally possible; and the GPRs predict, on the basis of Gestalt grouping principles (see 1983: 40–42), what structure(s) our innate perceptual-cognitive systems are most likely to detect. I cite the twelve grouping rules from GTTM in full below. All are strongly predictive of the groupings into which replicated patterns in music fall. In the discussion which follows, they will be invoked where relevant and situations where memetics suggests contrary interpretations will be identified.

> **GWFR 1** Any contiguous sequence of pitch-events, drum beats, or the like can constitute a group, and only contiguous sequences can constitute a group.
> **GWFR 2** A piece constitutes a group.
> **GWFR 3** A group may contain smaller groups.
> **GWFR 4** If a group G_1 contains part of a group G_2, it must contain all of G_2.
> **GWFR 5** If a group G_1 contains a smaller group G_2, then G_1 must be exhaustively partitioned into smaller groups.
> **GPR 1** Strongly avoid groups containing a single event. (Alternative form: Avoid analyses with very small groups – the smaller, the less preferable.)
> **GPR 2 (Proximity)** Consider a sequence of four notes $n_1n_2n_3n_4$. All else being equal, the transition n_2–n_3 may be heard as a group boundary if
> a. (Slur/Rest) the interval of time from the end of n_2 to the beginning of n_3 is greater than that from the end of n_1 to the beginning of n_2 and that from the end of n_3 to the beginning of n_4, or if

b. (Attack-Point) the interval of time between the attack points of n_2 and n_3 is greater than that between the attack points of n_1 and n_2 and that between the attack points of n_3 and n_4.
GPR 3 (Change) Consider a sequence of four notes $n_1n_2n_3n_4$. All else being equal, the transition n_2–n_3 may be heard as a group boundary if
a. (Register) the transition n_2–n_3 involves a greater intervallic distance than both n_1–n_2 and n_3–n_4, or if
b. (Dynamics) the transition n_2–n_3 involves a change in dynamics and n_1–n_2 and n_3–n_4 do not, or if
c. (Articulation) the transition n_2–n_3 involves a change in articulation and n_1–n_2 and n_3–n_4 do not, or if
d. (Length) n_2 and n_3 are of different lengths and both pairs n_1, n_2 and n_3, n_4 do not differ in length.
GPR 4 (Intensification) Where the effects picked out by GPRs 2 and 3 are relatively more pronounced, a larger-level group boundary may be placed.
GPR 5 (Symmetry) Prefer grouping analyses that most closely approach the ideal subdivision of groups into two parts of equal length.
GPR 6 (Parallelism) Where two or more segments of the music can be construed as parallel, they preferably form parallel parts of groups.
GPR 7 (Time-Span and Prolongational Stability) Prefer a grouping structure that results in more stable time-span and/or prolongational reductions.

(1983: 37–52)

Temperley's model (2001) of grouping structure in music, a development of the preference-rule methodology of Lerdahl and Jackendoff, also draws on Gestalt theory. Unlike Lerdahl and Jackendoff, however, Temperley subjects his theory to empirical testing via computer models, on the grounds that 'if a model does *not* perform a process successfully, then one knows that the process is *not* performed cognitively in that way' (: 6; his emphases). His formulation of 'melodic phrase structure' (that is, grouping) is summarized in three preference rules, the first of which encapsulates the Gestalt rule of proximity and, therefore, Lerdahl's and Jackendoff's GPR 2.

PSPR [phrase structure preference rule] **1 (Gap Rule).** Prefer to locate phrase boundaries at (a) large inter-onset intervals [that is, the interval between note onsets] and (b) large offset-to-onset intervals [the interval from the end of one note to the beginning of the next].
PSPR 2 (Phrase Length Rule). Prefer phrases to have roughly 8 notes.
PSPR 3 (Metrical Parallelism Rule). Prefer to begin successive groups at parallel points in the metrical structure.

(: 68–71)

Note that PSPR 2 is broadly in accordance with the observations made in 3.3.1 above concerning copying-fidelity and the tendency of memes to exist as shorter rather than longer configurations – although a 'phrase'[6] is not necessarily the same as a meme – and also that Lerdahl's and Jackendoff's GPR 1 is in accordance with the observations on the information content of memes in 3.3.1.

Perhaps the most comprehensive application of Gestalt principles to music analysis, however, is Narmour's implication-realization (henceforth 'i-r') model (1977, 1984, 1989, 1990, 1992, 1999), which builds on Gestalt-inspired foundations established by Meyer (1956, 1973, 1989). Categorizing Gestalt grouping principles into innate (bottom-up, genetically transmitted) and acquired (top-down, memetically transmitted) phenomena, Narmour notes that

> the separate registral and intervallic aspects of small intervals ... are said to be implicatively governed from the bottom up by the Gestalt laws of similarity, proximity, and common direction (sometimes called common fate).... As perceptual-theoretical constants, what is important to notice about the invocation of such Gestalt laws is (1) that they have been shown to be highly resistant to learning and thus may be innate ...; (2) unlike the notoriously interpretive, holistically supersummative, top-down Gestalt laws of 'good' continuation, 'good' figure, and 'best' organization ..., the Gestalt laws of similarity, proximity, and common direction are measurable, formalizable, and thus open to empirical testing ...; and (3) they are applied here from the *bottom-up* as nonclosural (implicative) *hypotheses*.
>
> (1989: 46–7; his emphases)

Corroborated by such empirical studies as Schellenberg 1996, 1997 and Thompson and Stainton 1996, the i-r model offers a means of assessing the bottom-up, note-to-note implicative flux of a passage and identifying its points of procession and closure at various hierarchical levels. Narmour proposes a number of basic i-r structures which he identifies using a distinctive terminology and symbology. His central premise is that, in melodic motion, an interval of a perfect fourth (5 semitones) or smaller moving in a given registral direction implies a continuation of similar intervallic magnitude in the same registral direction (process, symbolized by 'P'); while an interval of a perfect fifth (7 semitones) or larger moving in a given registral direction implies a continuation of smaller intervallic magnitude in the opposite registral direction (reversal, 'R'). To summarize the varying implicative properties of intervals, Narmour gives the following scale.

[6] Nattiez notes the 'fuzzy and ill-defined terminology' in received definitions of such conventional surface-analytic concepts as 'cell', 'motif' and 'phrase' (1990: 159).

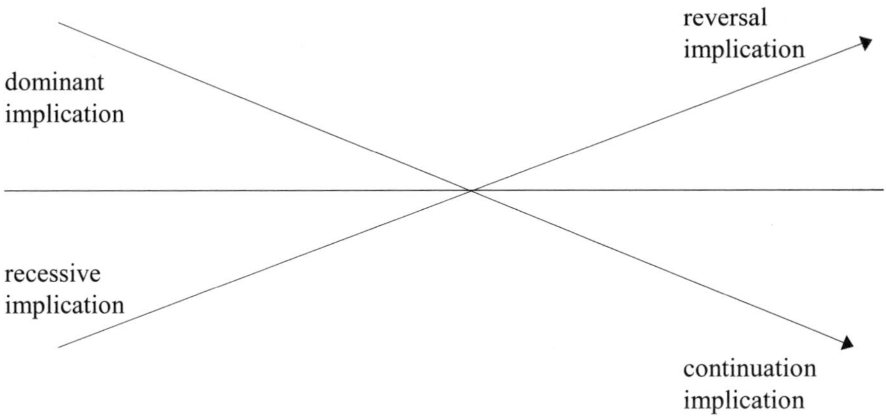

semitones:

0	1	2	3	4	5	6	7	8	9	10	11

interval description:

u	m2	M2	m3	M3	P4	A4/ D5	P5	m6	M6	m7	M7

sameness.........similarity differentiation.........

(a + a) (a + a^1) (a + b)

continuation implied (threshold) reversal implied

weak implication ←- - - - - - - - - - - - - -→ strong implication

Figure 3.3: Scale of Intervallic-Implicative Functions, after Narmour 1989: 51; 1990: 80, Fig. 5.1

A minimum of three melodic pitches is required to instantiate i-r functions (•*x*•*y*•), the motion between pitches one and two (interval *x*) engendering the implication and the motion between pitches two and three (interval *y*) either furnishing or denying the realization. Creating overlaps and interconnections between i-r units, the motion between pitches two and three may of course itself engender a further implication, a melody consisting of a string of nodes across which the i-r dynamic jumps.

The primary functions P, D and R give rise to a number of secondary functions. Symbols without brackets indicate prospective realizations and symbols within brackets indicate retrospective realizations. A retrospective structure is a pattern which despite (for instance) implying registral continuation (C–↑D, implying –↑E)

– process, P, not reversal, R – changes registral direction (C–↑D–↓B), giving '(R)', 'retrospective reversal' (Narmour 1990: 90–91). A fuller account is given in Chapter 4, where the various functions are considered in terms of the notions of perceptual-cognitive salience and memetic selection.

Most significant for the issue of memetic segmentation is the fact that, retrospective structures notwithstanding, these implicative 'potentials' may not be fulfilled, being terminated – as early as the second pitch in the •*x*•*y*• scheme outline above – by three factors which serve to define the initial and terminal boundaries of a grouping. Summarizing these, Narmour asserts that

> incisive points of melodic closure creating pitch groupings take place when in the parameter of duration a short note moves to a long note …; we may mark such durationally cumulative places analytically with the symbol (d) over the closed melodic note, the 'd' standing for durational interference in the continuation of the melodic line [cf. Lerdahl's and Jackendoff's GPR 3, d] …. Points of melodic closure also occur when in the parameter of harmony a sufficiently dissonant note goes to a sufficiently consonant one; this we mark with the symbol (h) over the closed melodic note, the 'h' standing for harmonic interruption in the melodic line …. Lastly, the parameter of meter may also impose closure upon a melodic pattern. I mark this with the symbol (b) which signifies metric [beat] differentiation that is sufficiently emphatic by itself to segment a melodic line ….
>
> (1989: 45–6)

Closure may also be achieved by the realization of an implication, yet this is often reinforced by a 'd', 'h' or 'b' event in order to attenuate the implicative potential generated by interval *y* in •*x*•*y*•.

Thus, the dynamic forces generated by P, D and R structures (and their associated secondary functions) serve to impel music forwards and create drive and momentum; whereas d, h and b events serve to attenuate this momentum and engender stability and repose. It is the victory of the latter forces over the former which brings about the segmentation of the sound-stream necessary for memetic propagation.[7]

The following example illustrates the relationship between i-r/closural principles and memetic replication. The opening of Example 3.7 i, from the Act I finale of Mozart's *Die Zauberflöte*, is replicated at the opening of Schubert's song 'Heidenröslein', Example 3.7 ii. In particular, Schubert imitates the segment marked *x*, allowing us to regard it as a meme. This component exists as a discrete particle because first, it occurs at the beginning of this section of Mozart's finale (after a whole silent bar with pause) and at the start of Schubert's song and so it is

---

[7] The concept of a grouping defined by an implication which is realized and/or terminated by end-closure is to some extent reminiscent of Riemann's notion of the *Motiv*, 'a single unit of energy (*Lebenskraft*) passing through phases of growth, peak and decay' (Bent and Pople 2001: 541–2).

demarcated at its opening by silence; and secondly, according to Narmour's segmentation principles, the minim/crotchet a[2] in the second bar of each melody is a point of closure engendered by durational interference. Given that the two segments are functionally identical (Schubert's halved rhythmic notation aside), it follows that they share a common i-r/closural structure, consisting of three melodic-implicative units and a terminal durational interference, D, IP, P, (d).

Example 3.7: Memetic Segmentation and Coindexation

i) Mozart: *Die Zauberflöte* K. 620 (1791), no. 8, 'Zum Ziele führt dich diese Bahn', bb. 327–30

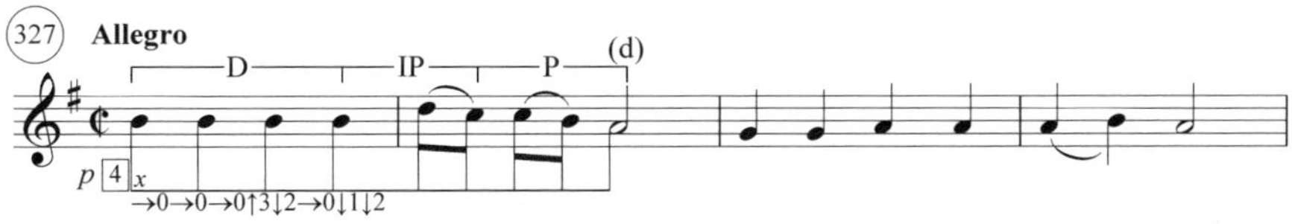

ii) Schubert: 'Heidenröslein' D. 257 (1815), bb. 1–4

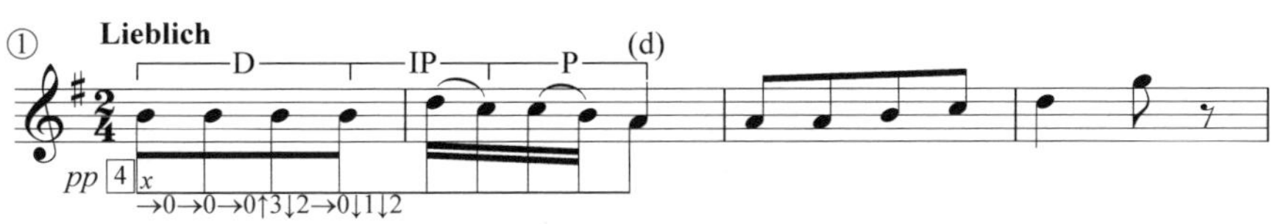

This example leads us, briefly, to a much bigger point concerning the interface, and tensions, between genetic and memetic replication. Given that genes define the perceptual and cognitive environment (Meyer's level of laws) within which memes are propagated – after all, they control the building of the brain – memes appear, to a large extent, to be operating on terms dictated by genes. Therefore to say that a meme will prosper if it takes advantage of the environment provided by genes is insufficient; a meme is in large part defined by the template of that environment. Nevertheless, despite this axiomatic sociobiological view – that '[t]he genes hold culture on a leash. The leash is very long, but inevitably [cultural] values will be constrained in accordance with their effects on the human gene pool', in Wilson's famous formulation (1978: 167) – other commentators see more complex interactions at work. This issue of gene-culture (meme) coevolution will be discussed further in Chapter 7.

Top-Down: Schematic and Conceptual Segmentation

While one can understand Narmour's suspicion of 'the notoriously interpretive, holistically supersummative, top-down Gestalt laws of "good" continuation, "good" figure, and "best" organization' (1989: 47), there are certain situations where top-down processing may counteract a bottom-up segmentation implied by Gestalt principles. Such an override might reunify a span of music which would normally be perceived as articulated on such criteria as 'similarity, proximity, and common direction' (: 47) and would therefore contradict GTTM's GWFR 1. By way of illustration, the integrity of a $\hat{5}$–$\hat{1}$ schema (a shallow-middleground-level archetype) abstracted from meme *x*, Example 3.8 i below, might be strong enough to override the segmentation initially imposed by the minim rest in a mutant form x^1, Example 3.8 ii.

Example 3.8: Schematic Segmentation

i) Meme *x*, $\hat{5}$–$\hat{4}$–$\hat{3}$–$\hat{2}$–$\hat{1}$

ii) Mutant form x^1, $\hat{5}$–$\hat{4}$–$\hat{3}$–$\hat{2}$…$\hat{1}$

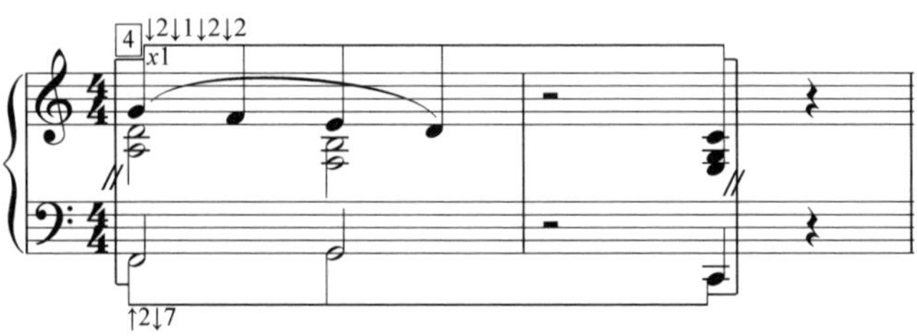

In conjunction with schematic segmentation, it is sometimes the case, as illustrated in Example 3.9 below, that our verbal-conceptual (intellectual, theoretical) understanding of a passage may cause us to impose or reject a segmentation in contradiction to a perception motivated by bottom-up factors.

Example 3.9: Conceptual Segmentation: Chopin, Nocturne in G minor op. 37 no. 1 (1838), bb. 41–4

While our segmentation of this phrase is to some extent facilitated by its 2 + 2 bar periodicity (GTTM's GPR 5), our verbal-conceptual knowledge of the closural importance of a perfect cadence in this style motivates us to impose a grouping boundary at *x*, despite the undifferentiated crotchet movement and invariant, chorale-like texture of the passage. Nevertheless, the schematic memory abstracted from numerous other memes terminating with a perfect cadence is presumably also operative in such situations. Thus, having distinguished in theory between segmentation engendered by schematic and by verbal-conceptual knowledge, it is difficult in practice to determine the respective strengths of these top-down factors with respect to segmentation decisions made in any given (analytical or real-time-listening) situation.

3.3.3. *Coindexation*

As discussed in 2.2.2 above, an information-encoding neuronal constellation existing in only one brain (a mnemon) and its somatic and extrasomatic products (its phmnemotype) have a provisional status. 'When copied from one brain to another, [a positively defined mnemon] becomes a meme' (Lynch 1998a). For the neuronal constellation to be regarded as a meme, one must therefore:

- Verify its derivation from an antecedent mnemotypic form, as evidenced by conformance between the antecedent's phmnemotypic products and its own phemotypic products. (I speculate on the ultimate origin of musical memes in Chapter 7.) This cross-linking back in time might be termed the 'retrospective memeticization' of the constellation.

and/or

- Verify its generation of a consequent memotypic form, as evidenced by conformance between its own phmnemotypic products and the consequent's phemotypic products. This cross-linking forward in time might be termed the 'prospective memeticization' of the constellation.

I term such an antecedent or consequent copy a 'coindex', borrowing this idea from Temperley, who speaks of '*coindexing* – "labelling as the same"' (2001: 326; his emphasis). Engendering an intertextual connection between works, two or more coindexes might be regarded as existing as hyperlinks to each other in conceptual space. In an abstract sense, a meme and its coindex(es) can exist at various levels of the stylistic hierarchy discussed in 2.5.1 above, although they exist in concrete form fundamentally at the level of idiom (memotype) and intraopus style (phemotype).

In its cognition of coindexation, the brain is postulating what Ockelford terms a 'zygonic' relationship between two or more groups. In defining this principle, he notes that

> The interperspective relationships through which perceived derivation (or generation) is presumed to be cognized are termed 'zygonic' ['[f]rom the Greek term for "yoke", implying a union of two similar things (2004: 71)] .... It is hypothesized that, at the level of frames ['vertical' slices through musical time, consisting of a number of 'horizontal' parametric-perceptual 'slots' (pitch, rhythm, dynamics, etc.) each filled with an appropriate value (2004: 32–3)], zygonic relationships (or 'zygons') reasonably model a link thought to be constructed in cognition between any pairs of perspective values of the same type, where one is deemed to derive from the other.
>
> (2004: 37–8)

While zygonic relationships exist, at their most basic level, between narrow time slices, from note to note, they also obtain, at a higher hierarchic level, between groups of notes, between particles which may potentially be memetically related. The brain perceives a connection between two groups in which it is sensed that one

> is wholly or partly implied by another or, more persuasively, derives from it.... greater degrees of similarity and salience are more likely to result in a sense of direct derivation, corresponding to strong elements in music-structural cognition ....
>
> (: 58)

The primary orientation of Ockelford's zygonic theory is towards the idiomatic (intra-work) level: he is mainly concerned with how the listener relates the component units of a piece to each other in order to model its large-scale unity and coherence and to trace its 'structural narrative' (: 70). But there seems no reason against extending the theory to encompass the higher levels of Figure 2.1 above and, therefore, memetic connections between particles.

Having endorsed the importance of the Gestalt principles of proximity, similarity, good continuation and common fate for establishing grouping boundaries in music, Ockelford suggests that

> three zones are distinguishable on the continuum of [inter-group] derivational[/relational] possibilities, defined as follows: (a) one group is perceived to derive as a whole from another; (b) an aspect of one group is perceived to derive from another; (c) there is no perceived derivation between groups. Analysing relationships of type 'a' as zygonic invariants suggests that similarity between groups is ultimately dependent on one or more of three processes: the modification of material …, its omission or addition ….
>
> (: 53)

Of these zones, the first is clearly most pertinent to memetics – provided of course the derivation is a consequence of neuronal constellation transmission. '[T]he modification of material …, its omission or addition' are mutational operations as a result of which one particle is transformed into another. I defer their consideration until Chapter 4.

The hyperlinking of coindexes to each other is potentially one of the most problematic aspects of memetics, bringing into play complex issues of morphological conformity and chronological relationship between patterns. One of the most significant of these is the difficulty of locating a convincing coindex for a mnemon/phmnemotype, often because of the sheer magnitude of that which one has to investigate. In this situation, one might instead have to invoke a probabilistic perspective, positing the statistical probability that a coindex of a given mnemon exists somewhere in the dialect at a particular geographical or chronological locus.

Another complication results from the fact that, if a coindex of a meme *M* is located, one has to determine whether the coindex is the direct (causal) antecedent or consequent of *M* or whether the resemblance is adventitious. Dennett argues that

> This is the same epistemological problem, in the science of culture, that taxonomists confront when they try to sort out homology [resemblance between two organisms or between features of two organisms owing to direct evolutionary descent or descent from a common ancestor] from analogy [resemblance due to fortuitous *convergent evolution* toward features of common morphology and/or function], ancestral from derived characters, in cladistic [species' family-tree] analysis ….
>
> (1995: 357)

It may be impossible to resolve this question, for the complexity of human cultural communities and the convoluted modes of interaction between their members make verification of causality highly problematic, even when relationships and interactions between individuals can be reconstructed. A workable definition of the meme probably ought not, in consequence, to contain a stipulation that a direct causal connection be verified between two equivalent particles, simply that a given particle has a morphologically unambiguous coindex.

A further difficulty arises in the case of two mnemons, *Mn-x* and *Mn-y*, which are similar but not identical in configuration, for in such situations one must determine whether they merit the status of coindexes, and hence memes. Given a verified relationship of replication between *Mn-x* and *Mn-y*, if *Mn-x* and *Mn-y* are considered sufficiently similar to warrant identity as coindexes, then they may be regarded as instantiations of meme *M*. If, however, *Mn-x* and *Mn-y* are considered sufficiently different to preclude identity as coindexes, then their individual memetic status, as *M-x* and *M-y*, would logically depend upon the existence of a coindex for each.

Figure 3.4 i below represents this issue and leads to another complication. To regard *Mn-y* as a mutant form of *Mn-x* (or *vice versa*) implies direct evolution, by definition a linear-causal process, whereas in reality the relationship might be one between independently generated variants of a single antecedent (a common ancestor), *Mn-w*, Figure 3.4 ii. Cone also identifies this issue, noting that '[*Mn-*]x and [*Mn-*]y may both be derived from some common source (a previous [*Mn*]w such that [*Mn-*]w→[*Mn-*]x and [*Mn-*]w→[*Mn-*]y), in which case [*Mn-*]y is not necessarily also derived from [*Mn-*]x' (1987: 240). Alternatively, the relationship may be one of similarity (analogy not homology) between two independently generated mnemons, each deriving from its own antecedent, *Mn-v* and *Mn-w*, Figure 3.4 iii.

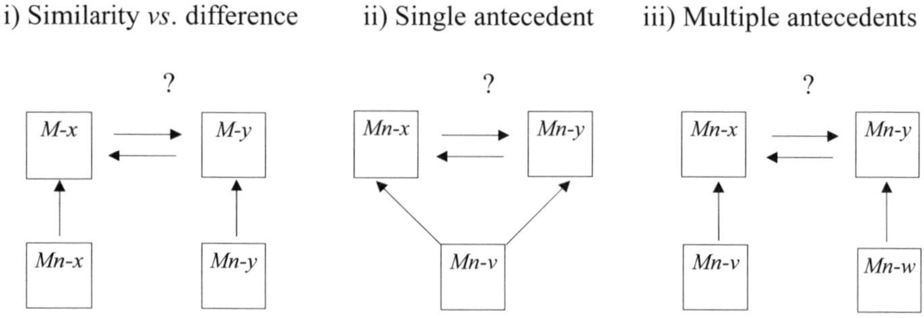

Figure 3.4: Potential Ambiguities in Relationships Between Mnemons

Discrete, Overlapping and Nested Coindexation

It is possible to identify three categories of coindexation. A given span of music may be parsed not only into discrete (proximate, adjacent or abutting) memes but also into overlapping and nested memes, each segmentation of the pitch or rhythm matrix being defined and verified by reference to a coindex in another context. Figure 3.5 below represents these situations, where the 'sound stream' is chronologically anterior to the coindexes.

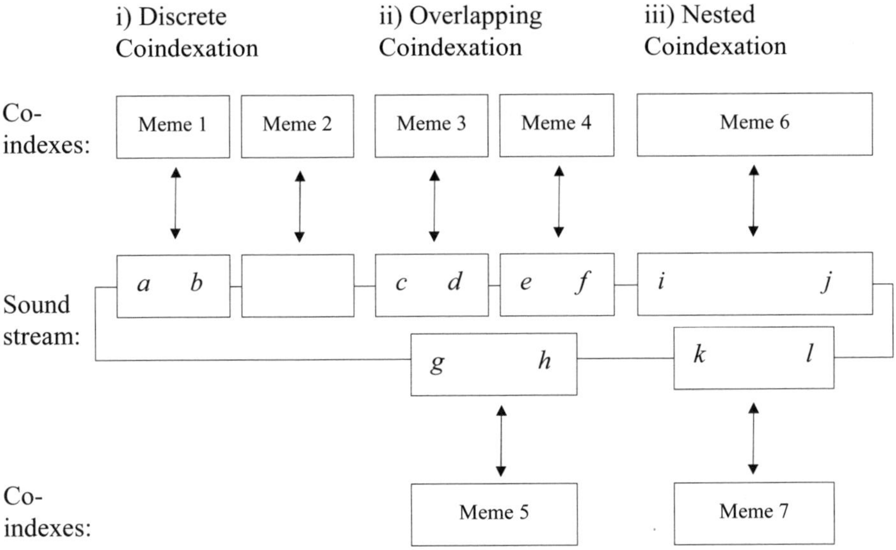

Figure 3.5: Discrete, Overlapping and Nested Coindexation

In all three types of coindexation, the initial and terminal nodes of each meme must, of course, have some means of articulating the sound stream of the source composition so as to mark the configuration out for consciousness and thus make it distinct from the surrounding sound information.

With overlapping coindexation, however, the articulation between points *d* (the terminal node of Meme 3) and *e* (the initial node of Meme 4) in Figure 3.5 ii should not be so strong as to militate against the alternative perception of Meme 5, which straddles these points, as a unitary configuration. Conversely, the initial and terminal nodes of Meme 5 (points *g* and *h* respectively) must not be so strong as to militate (by bisection, *c…g*/*g…d*; *e…h*/*h…f*) against the alternative perception of Memes 3 and 4 as unitary configurations.[8] Note that overlapping coindexation contradicts the stipulations of GTTM's GWFR 4 and GWFR 5, in that the GWFRs in general, and these two in particular, 'define a strict, nonoverlapping, recursive hierarchy' (Lerdahl and Jackendoff 1983: 37).

Nested coindexation is subject to the same logic: in Figure 3.5 iii, articulations *k* and *l* need to be strong enough potentially to mark Meme 7 out as a discrete unit, but must not be so strong as to militate (by trisection, *i…k*/*k…l*/*l…j*) against the alternative perception of Meme 6 as a unitary configuration. Example 3.10 below

8 Overlapping coindexation may also consist of a meme sharing its initial and/or terminal pitch with the terminal and/or initial pitch of memes directly preceding and/or following it, situations which perhaps warrant a fourth category of elided coindexation.

illustrates these situations (see Jan 2001 for more on the relationship between the two Mozart pieces in this example).

Example 3.10: Discrete, Overlapping and Nested Coindexation

i) Anonymous: Pasagalio (Italian MS, *c.* 1750–75)[9]

ii) Gluck: *Iphigénie en Tauride* (1779), no. 26, 'Chaste fille de Latone', bb. 1–4

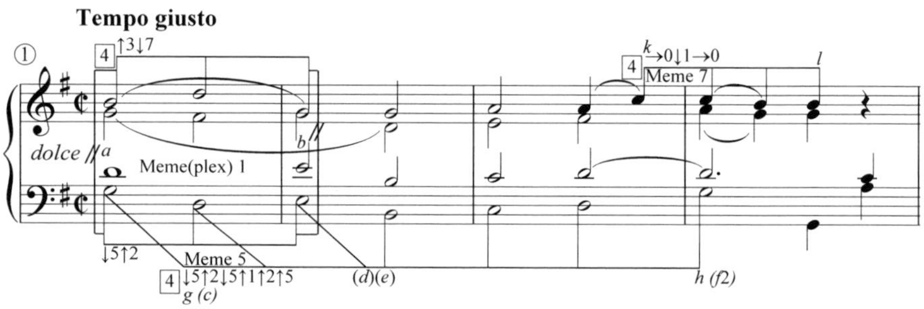

iii) Mozart: *Idomeneo, re di Creta* K. 366 (1781), no. 25, bb. 1–4

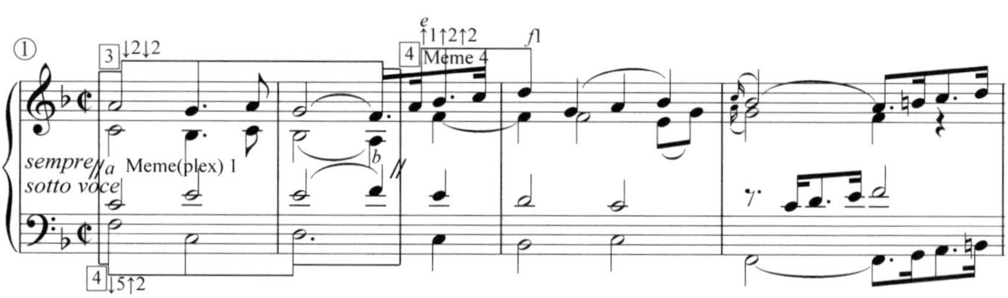

9 The $\hat{1}$–$\hat{5}$–$\hat{6}$–$\hat{3}$–$\hat{4}$–$\hat{5}$–$\hat{1}$ bass line of this example, associated with the chaconne tradition, has a long provenance. One of its earliest appearances was in the final *ballo* ('O che nuovo miracolo') of Emilio de' Cavalieri's music to the *intermedi* for *La Pellegrina* of 1589. Monteverdi also used the figure in his madrigal 'Zefiro torna' (pub. 1632). I am grateful to John Bryan for this information.

iv) Wranitzky: *Oberon, König der Elfen* (1789), no. 4, 'Hör, o Gottheit, meine Klagen', bb. 1–4

v) Mozart: *Die Zauberflöte* K. 620 (1791), no. 9, bb. 1–4

Discrete coindexation of Meme(plex) 1 (*a…b*) in Example 3.10 ii recurs in v and, in a slightly different form ($\hat{3}$–$\hat{2}$–$\hat{1}$/I–V–vi as against $\hat{3}$–$\hat{5}$–$\hat{1}$/I–V–vi), in iii, all three clearly demarcated from the following material by means of metric differentiation. Overlapping coindexation is seen in Example 3.10 i, ii and v, where Meme 5 (*g…h*) in i and ii overlaps the articulation (*d*/*e*) between Memes 3 (*c…d*) and 4 (*e…*f^{2}) in v. Nevertheless, this case is more complex than Figure 3.5 implies for three reasons. First, and contrary to the situation represented in the figure, $g = c$ and $f = h$. Secondly, a rest occurs in v after the third pitch of the passacaglia bass, separating Memes 3 and 4 but also bisecting Meme 5. Thirdly, the second half of the passacaglia bass in v (if this is indeed the source) is mutated. Nested coindexation is shown in Example 3.10 ii, iv and v, where Meme 6 (*i…j*) in iv and v encompasses Meme 7 (*k…l*) in ii and iv. Paralleling the situation with i, ii and v, however, $j = l$ in Example 3.10 iv. Such overlaps suggest that in a given phemotypic context certain pitches may represent the overdetermined products of several simultaneously (co-)operative memes.

Coindexation-Engendered Segmentation

As the above demonstrates, the subdivision of music into the 'unities' Bent and Pople speak of (3.3.1 above) may take place by reference to other copies of that unit, identifying that portion of the pitch and/or rhythmic continuum which is replicated. With such coindex-engendered segmentation, a component segment of a passage stands out in relief from its surrounding context, and initial and terminal nodes are thereby defined, by virtue of its concordance with a previously encountered passage stored in long-term memory. The normal requirement that a group of musical information be clearly demarcated from its surrounding material in order to serve as a unit of memory and imitation implies that the passage standing out as a coindex of a previously memorized pattern should itself be segmentationally demarcated from its context.

Nevertheless, a comparison with language suggests that this may not invariably be the case. When read on the page, the pangram 'the quick brown fox jumps over the lazy dog' is easily segmented into its nine words by virtue of the strong Gestalt cues provided by the gaps between the words, the brain taking white space as a powerful visual grouping cue. When heard in spoken form, however, the brain employs different parsing algorithms to group the unbroken stream of sound into units of meaning. According to Liberman and Studdert-Kennedy, '[t]he segmentation of speech sounds is a process that imposes boundaries based on the grammatical structure of the language, not on the physical structure of the acoustic wave' (in Dennett 1993: 51).

In music, a comparable situation obtains. When considering a musical score, it is easy to segment the music into particulate units by virtue of such Gestalt aspects as long notes, rests, pauses and other factors, as formalized in the GTTM grouping rules and Narmour's d, h and b closural functions. Yet while such articulatory functions are clearly evident in performance – GTTM and Narmour's theory would have little explanatory force if they merely commented on typographical aspects of the printed score – it is also the case that 'the acoustic wave' may be segmented even in the absence of such strong Gestalt clues as to the initial and terminal nodes of a musical group. This occurs as a result of top-down processes analogous to the imposition of 'boundaries based on the grammatical structure of the language'. As such it constitutes a type of schematic segmentation (3.3.2 above).

If we heard a sentence such as '*celeris fulva* fox *saluit super ignovum canem*', and knew no Latin, it would be the replication of patterning – the recognition that we have heard the acoustic profile of the non-Latin word 'fox' before and can map it against a pre-memorized morpho-grammatical category – that allows us to perceive it as a distinct acoustic group within an otherwise unarticulated sound stream. We would not, of course, make this distinction if, in the same situation, we had heard '*celeris fulva vulpes* …'. In musical contexts, such an overlap between a pre-memorized pattern (which would probably have strong Gestalt-engendered articulations at its initial and terminal nodes) and a 'fox' allows us to draw a relationship of coindexation between the two, even when the fox blends into the long grass of its surrounding acoustic context.[10]

[10] A comparable situation obtains in Ancient Greek epigraphy, where no spaces articulate the stream of letters carved into the stone and where words are demarcated by their mapping against coindexes in other contexts.

Thus, as argued earlier, coindexation cannot be considered in isolation from particulateness and segmentation. These aspects of the meme are interdependent, for particulateness (the existence of a sequence of musical elements as a discrete, self-contained group) arises from segmentation (the tendency of the sound stream to divide/be divided into discrete groups of musical elements). Moreover, coindexation, in mapping one discrete group against another (in tracing meme reification by replication), imposes articulation and segmentation on the contexts in which the replication occurs and thereby engenders a particulate, quasi-digital order within streams of musical data inhering ultimately at the level of the psychological representation.

3.3.4. *What is Not a Musical Meme?*

Having considered, in 2.3, 2.4 and 3.3 above, the attributes of memes in music, having asked 'what is a musical meme?', it is pertinent at this point to ask the converse question: 'what is *not* a musical meme?' In other words, are some elements of particular pieces, however important they may be to the music's structural and expressive processes, not derived by imitation from antecedent music and therefore not part of the nexus of replication which hyperlinks memes within a musical culture?

The answer to this question is contingent upon a number of factors: the degree to which the element's parameters possess the attribute of syntacticism (2.5.4 above); the number of strata constituting the element; the degree of articulation separating the element from adjacent patterning; the information content of the element (3.3.1 above); and its structural-hierarchic location (an issue considered below). While constraints of space prevent a full treatment of the interaction of these issues, there seems one obvious situation in which non-memetic material might exist. This is where a passage contains two proximate memes enveloping an articulated and unharmonized monad or dyad. The latter, by virtue of its low element/information-content, may have insufficient perceptual-cognitive salience to function as a meme and thus is not likely to have been memetically (homologically) derived. Any apparent 'coindexes' in other contexts would therefore have arisen (analogically) through spontaneous generation, and not by replication.

With the exception of such patterns, it seems likely that the overwhelming majority of musical material within a culture is memetic; there is, to answer my question, very little which is not a musical meme, just as very few elements of verbal-conceptual thought are not memes. This is because all humans are born with a brain which, in the Lockian view, is a *tabula rasa*. Consequently, composers must assimilate the vast bulk of their musical pattern repertoire (as opposed to their genetically-acquired musical competences) memetically from the society within which they are enculturated. Other than monads and dyads, any 'new' patterns they bring into being are therefore almost always mutations of pre-assimilated memes and not *de novo* formulations.

3.4. Memetic Co-Adaptation and Memeplexes

> The integrated multicellular organism is a phenomenon which has emerged as a result of natural selection on primitively independent selfish replicators. It has paid replicators to behave gregariously. The phenotypic power by which they ensure their survival is in principle extended and unbounded. In practice the organism has arisen as a partially bounded local concentration, a shared knot of replicator power.
>
> (Dawkins 1983a: 264)

Up to now I have tended to treat musical memes as unitary entities and have not explored in detail the possibility of their further subdivision. Motivated by the neo-Darwinian tendency to privilege the smallest independent unit of replication, I have also focused largely on the single meme. These two perspectives were necessary for the sake of theoretical exposition, but they are oversimplifications for two reasons.

First, as argued in 3.3.1 above, single unit-memes are themselves normally multiparametric collections, consisting of often independently replicated particles in each of the meme's constituent parameters. Secondly, in both its memotypic and phemotypic incarnations and at both parametric and multiparametric levels, a given meme has to reach an accommodation with other memes as part of the price of being replicated, simply because cultural products are richly multimemetic, not unimemetic. Just as a living organism is 'a colony of genes' (Dawkins 1989: 46), so a piece of music is (the phemotypic product of) a colony of memes. These intraopus associations are essentially temporary alliances, strategic marriages of convenience forged by memes for their long-term survival. The individual memes may well find themselves in different alliances in the next 'generation'.

In discussing these issues, Dawkins makes an important point about replicator collaboration when he argues that

> Memes, like genes, are selected against the background of other memes in the meme pool. The result is that gangs of mutually compatible memes – coadapted meme complexes or memeplexes – are found cohabiting in individual brains. This is not because selection has chosen them as a group, but because each separate member of the group tends to be favoured when its environment happens to be dominated by the others.
>
> (in Blackmore 1999: xiv)

The uniparametric memes constituting a multiparametric meme must therefore be compatible, or at least not strongly incompatible, with each other. Moreover, the memes constituting a musical work must be subject to similar constraints, for the lower the level of the stylistic hierarchy a meme is situated, the greater the need for memetic compatibility. While a dialect (many brains) may have the capacity to sustain strongly divergent memes, this seems less so at the idiomatic and intra-work (single-brain) levels. Moreover, beyond a general co-operation between memes, there are more specific situations where a meme, although retaining the 'indivisible particulateness' discussed in 2.4.3 above, combines well with other memes such that it is propagated not singly, but as part of a complex.

'Delius .... reiterates the importance of coadapted meme-complexes, in which memes are selected for their mutual compatibility' (Dawkins 1989: 323; see also Delius 1989: 54–5). In preference to the somewhat unwieldy 'coadapted meme-complex', I shall use the term 'memeplex', coined by Speel (1999: 241; see also Blackmore 1999: 19) and employed by Dawkins in his more recent writings. In this chapter I use it in two specific senses of memetic co-adaptation: in the local sense of the meme as a multiparametric complex, and the more extended sense of the span or passage of music as a multimemetic complex. In Chapter 5, I extend the second sense to encompass a global conception of the movement or work as a superordinate-level multimemetic complex of memes and memeplexes.

3.4.1. *Multiparametric Complexes: The Components of Memes*

A meme is divisible not only segmentationally from adjacent patterns but parametrically, principally into pitch and rhythmic configurations, the parameters most capable of engendering syntacticism. In this sense, a meme can be regarded as a multiparametric 'molecule' composed of uniparametric 'atoms'. This concept is represented in Figure 3.6 below.

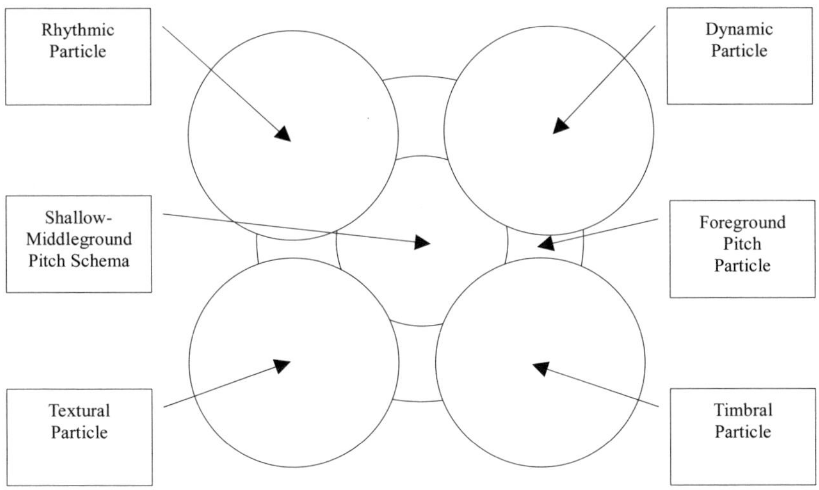

Figure 3.6: The Meme as a Multiparametric Complex

A useful framework for conceptualizing the relationship between uniparametric and multiparametric phenomena is provided by Narmour's distinction between style forms/shapes and style structures. He conceives style forms as

> those parametric entities which achieve enough closure so we can understand their functional coherence without reference to the specific intraopus contexts from which they come – all those seemingly time-*independent* patterns, large and small, from parameter to parameter, which recur with statistically significant frequency.
>
> (1977: 173; his emphasis)

When studying such patterns,

> the style analyst will attempt to restore the syntactic function of style forms by arranging them in various specific contexts according to their statistically most common functional occurrences. The contexts which result from such arrangement can be called *style structures* in the sense that they are directly tied to and contribute to the structure of real pieces, not just to constructed classes of things, as are style forms. Unlike the description of style forms, the identification of style structures involves ascribing time-*dependent* function to patterns … in intraopus relationships.
>
> (: 174; his emphases)

Despite their different structural-hierarchic locations, patterns in both categories – exemplified by the independently replicated uniparametric pitch and rhythm shapes in Example 2.2 above and the multiparametric complexes in Example 3.7 above – are memetic, on account (as argued in 3.3.4 above) of their replicated status.

At a higher structural level, sequences of style structures

> create a network of relationships I will call the *idiostructure*.... The idiostructure ... is defined chiefly by nonclosure. That is, within a piece idiostructure will often be exemplified by those things that keep the motive, phrase, or section ongoing and processive, and style structure will be exemplified by those things that create articulation and disjunction between events.
>
> (: 164, 181; his emphasis)

Because the idiostructure may encompass replicated sequences of style structures, its configuration may be accounted for by the properties of the multimemetic complexes discussed next.

3.4.2. *Multimemetic Complexes: Pitch Memeplexes and Replication Hierarchies*

Multimemetic complexes are replicated sequences of segmentationally discrete pitch memes. Logically, any memeplex may only consist of units which are also replicated independently of their preferred partners and which as a complex form a class of at least two. If a replicated conglomeration of discrete units exists only in this form, one must regard this larger, encompassing, unit as the meme, in which case no memeplex exists.

A complication arises, however, from the issue of the structural-hierarchic location of the replicated patterns. The notion that memes may exist at levels other than the foreground has been touched upon several times earlier, but its detailed treatment has had to be deferred until now. Whereas the voice-leading schema of Example 2.1 iii above is evident on the lightest reduction, Example 3.11 below, which shows a familiar linear-harmonic sequence replicated in two very different contexts, suggests that musical memes can exist at deeper structural levels.

Example 3.11: Middleground-Level Meme

i) Handel: 'Arrival of the Queen of Sheba' from *Solomon* HWV 67 (1748), bb. 7–10

ii) Mozart: *Die Zauberflöte* K. 620 (1791), no. 5, 'Hm Hm Hm', bb. 214–17

iii) Voice-Leading Schema

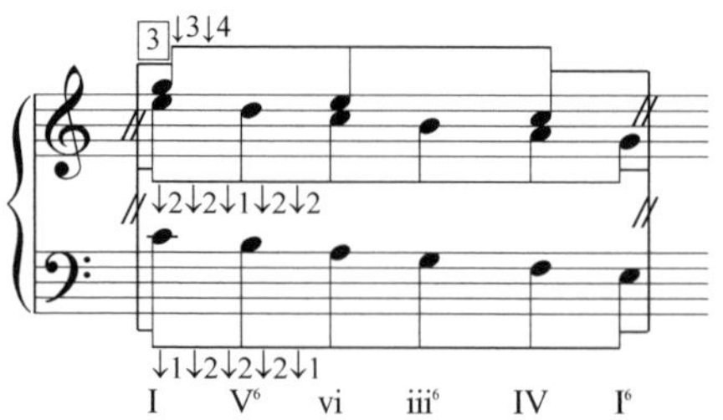

As shown by the schema in Example 3.11 iii, the harmonic structure I–($V^6{}_3$)–vi–($iii^6{}_3$)–IV–($I^6{}_3$) and associated voice-leading pattern is common to both phrases.

The generative surface figuration of Example 3.11 i is not replicated in ii, but the figuration of each is itself almost certainly memetic.

If such a middleground meme were to result from the replication of the same foreground figuration, we may or may not be dealing with a memeplex, depending on the nature (number, segmentation) of the generative elements. Conversely, when a memeplex is replicated, the same middleground-level structure will almost inevitably be generated in each copy, and this 'piggyback' replication renders the middleground structure itself memetic. This point is made, albeit obliquely, by Agawu when he argues that

> T[opic]'s may be organized hierarchically, so that a sequence such as T1–T2–T3, which in the first instance describes a simple succession of T's, may, in this particular disposition, yield a secondary topic (T4) or topics (T5, T6, T7), where T4, T5, T6, and T7 arise solely from the conjunction of T1, T2, and T3. T's are therefore subject to replication as (at least) second-order semiotic systems.
>
> (1991: 129)

The concept of the memeplex nevertheless holds that Agawu's observations apply not just to topics, but to all types of musical patterning. (His views on the 'conjunction' of topics – that several different patterns may be abstracted from the same sound-stream – echo my observations on discrete, overlapping and nested coindexation made in 3.3.3 above.)

These issues of memetic conglomeration and structural hierarchy are further illustrated by Example 3.12 below.

Example 3.12: Pitch Memeplexes and Replication Hierarchies

i) Mozart: Flute Quartet in A major K. 298 (?1778/1786), II, Minuet, bb. 0–8

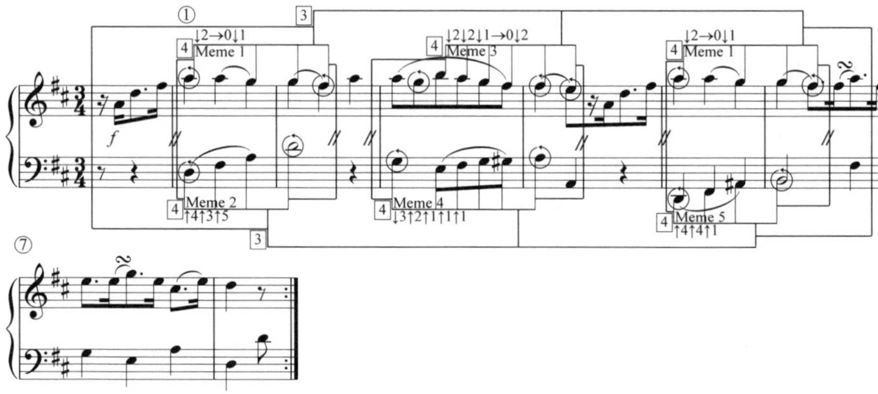

ii) Voice-Leading Reduction of i

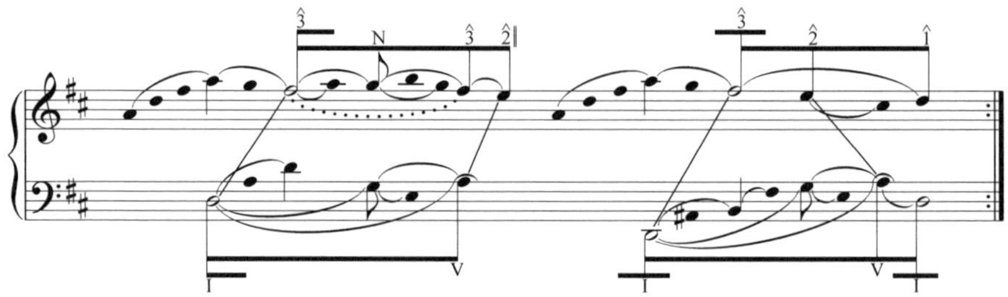

iii) Mozart: Adagio in C major for Glass Harmonica K. 356 (617a) (1791), bb. 1–8

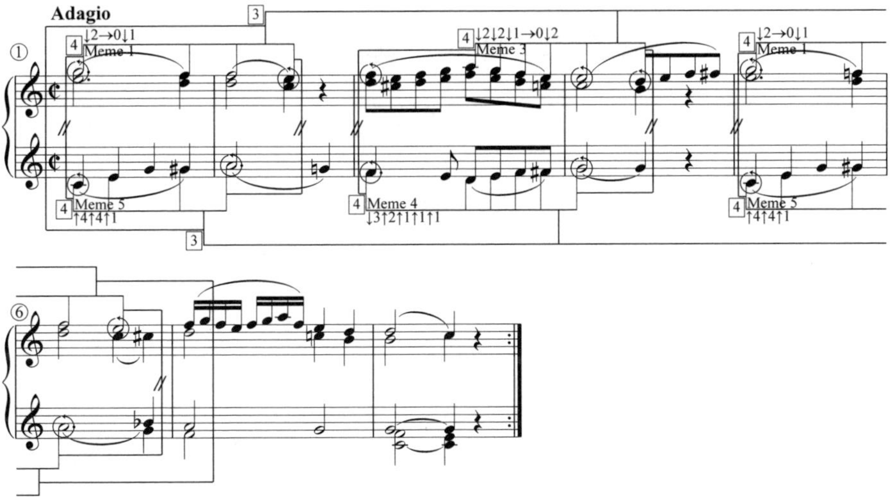

iv) Voice-Leading Reduction of iii

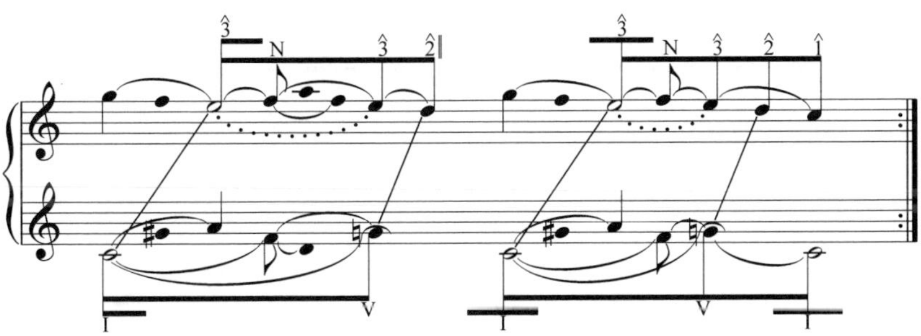

v) Mozart: Flute Quartet in A major K. 298, II, Trio, bb. 0–8

vi) Voice-Leading Reduction of v

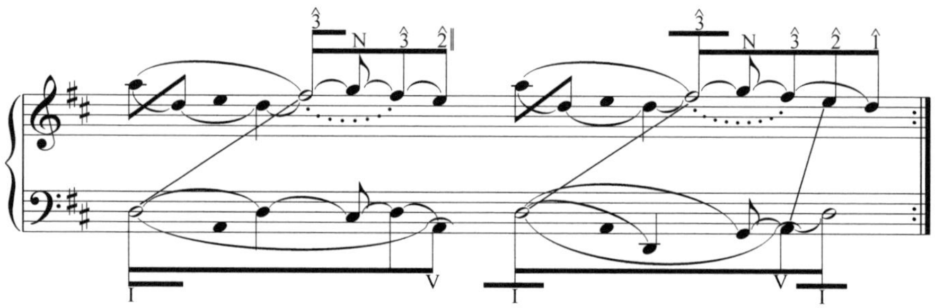

vii) Coindexes of Memes 1–5:

a) Meme 1: Beethoven, Symphony no. 9 in D minor op. 125 (1824), III, bb. 91–3

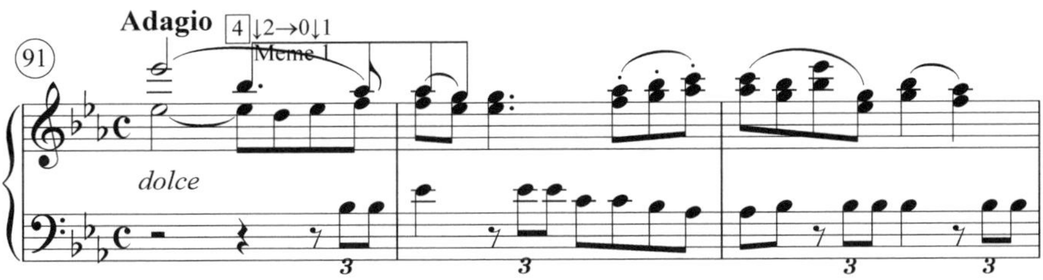

b) Meme 2: Mozart, Symphony in C major K. 338 (1780), I, bb. 1–4

c) Meme 3: Haydn, *Die Schöpfung* Hob. XXI: 2 (1798), no. 32, 'Holde Gattin!', bb. 14–16

d) Meme 4: Beethoven, Symphony no. 8 in F major op. 93 (1812), I, bb. 5–8

e) Meme (1 +) 5: Mozart, Piano Quartet in G minor K. 478 (1785), II, bb. 1–4

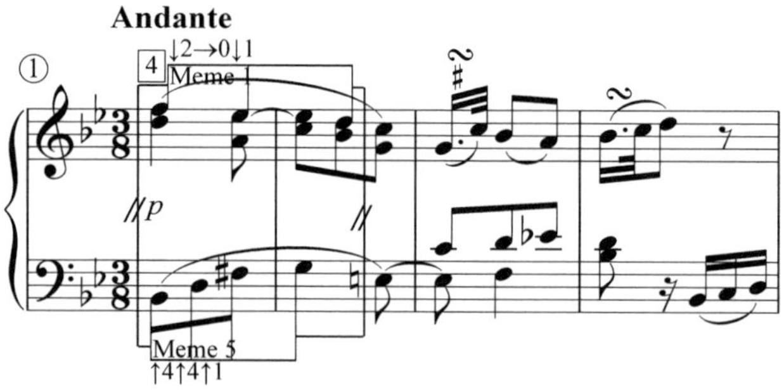

Several segments from the flute quartet passage are copied almost exactly in the Adagio; these are labelled Memes 1–5 in Example 3.12 i and iii. Indeed, the segmentation of each passage is carried out, as discussed in 3.3.3 above, on the basis of that which is copied in the other. While memetics suggest that these segments are discrete, independent memes, an alternative reading of the passages would regard them as components of a single unit-meme, even though its length, and the presence of connecting material not replicated in both examples, somewhat militates against this interpretation.

To discount the single unit-meme reading properly, it is necessary to ascertain that segments 1–5 are independent memes. Although one might simply assume – on probabilistic grounds – the existence of copies of these patterns elsewhere in the dialect, it is prudent to attempt definitively to locate them. Example 3.12 vii a–e shows a coindex for segments 1–5 from other works from the dialect of Viennese Classicism. Having ascertained that segments 1–5 are indeed independent memes, their sequential replication in Example 3.12 i and iii allows us to speak of the replication of a memeplex in these phrases.

Turning to the reductions at Example 3.12 ii and iv, it is evident that, as in Example 3.11 above, the foreground-level events of the passages in i and iii generate a shallow-middleground-level structure – the interrupted linear progression $\hat{5}$/I–$\hat{4}$–$\hat{3}$–$\hat{2}$/V|| $\hat{5}$/I–$\hat{4}$–$\hat{3}$–$\hat{2}$/V–$\hat{1}$/I – which, aside from a few minor details of voice alignment and disposition of scale degrees, is essentially common to both passages. Because this structure is replicated, it is a meme.[11] It is situated at the shallow-middleground level, but is not necessarily confined to this level; one might easily find examples of replicated patterns expressing this scale-degree succession situated closer to or at the foreground level.

While the foreground-level configurations of Example 3.12 i and iii are real – as discrete, localized entities they are readily accessible to perception – the structure of Example 3.12 ii and iv (and that of Example 3.11) is in a sense virtual – it is an artefact, a product of the operation upon the real pitch configurations of verbal-conceptual memes articulating notions of rhythmic reduction and hierarchical structuring. At this level and in this context it has no autonomous musical existence beyond the patterns which express it. Nevertheless, provided that two or more people share the verbal-conceptual memes necessary for generating such virtual structures, they are easily accessible and may therefore be regarded as invariant, replicated relationships resulting from the replication of, in this case, a sequence of (themselves individually replicated) patterns. The implications of this are considerable. Far from surviving only at the surface, a hierarchy of overlapping and interrelated memes exists, stretching from the immediate foreground to the deepest background and encompassing replicated middleground patterns and, ultimately, the various *Ursätzen* which, as one means of representing the replicated sequences into which foreground memes tend to fall, schematize memes at the most fundamental level of musical organization.

Owing to the more 'distributed' nature of deeper-level musical structures, a meme will have a greater horizontal extent the farther away from the foreground it is situated, a background or middleground structure being of greater temporal span than the same configuration situated at the foreground. However, a foreground-orientated meme based upon an $\hat{8}$–$\hat{1}$ linear progression is, in terms of the number of its components, larger than a $\hat{5}$–$\hat{1}$ *Ursatz* and it may therefore be less stable during replication, even though it will occupy a fraction of the time required for the expression of the *Ursatz*. (This perspective might account for the historical durability of the *Ursatz* species $\hat{5}$–$\hat{1}$ and $\hat{3}$–$\hat{1}$ and the comparative rarity of the species $\hat{8}$–$\hat{1}$.) Further to the arguments in 3.3.1 above, one might assert that the greater stability is attained by memes with the smaller number of components, at whatever hierarchic level they are situated. At the foreground they may only occupy a few beats, at the middleground they cover large spans of music and at the background they traverse a whole movement.

Example 3.12 v shows the theme of the first half of the Trio of K. 298 III. Despite the fact that its foreground patterning is quite different from that of Example 3.12 i and iii, its middleground organization, vi, is essentially the same as

[11] As discussed in Chapter 4, it may (only) be a meme in the 'weak' sense of memetic replication for, to simplify this concept, it may be confined to Mozart's idiom. Nevertheless, one might conceivably find copies in the wider dialect, the 'strong' sense of replication.

that of the passages in which the memeplex is replicated, ii and iv. Clearly a middleground-level meme may be expressed by a variety of foreground configurations; in the present case, that in ii, iv and vi is expressed both by a memeplex located at the foreground, i and iii, and by a sequence of foreground events, v, which – to my knowledge – is not a memeplex.

To review the position so far, Example 3.12 suggests two replication-hierarchic scenarios. First, a shallow-middleground-level meme may be generated/replicated in two or more contexts by unique foreground-level conglomerations. Not replicated as such, these conglomerations exist in the form of only one instantiation; but they will almost certainly consist of independent memes. In this first scenario, the only memetic elements are the independent foreground-level patterns and the resultant shallow-middleground-level structure. Secondly, a shallow-middleground-level meme may be generated/replicated by a foreground-level conglomeration which is replicated in two or more contexts; if this consists of independent memes it is, by definition, a memeplex. In this second scenario, the independent foreground-level patterns, the foreground-level conglomeration and the resultant shallow-middleground-level structure are all memetic.

Developing the second scenario further, it is logical to suggest that, in addition to foreground-located memeplexes, such complexes may also be situated at the middleground level. Independently memetic middleground-level events in one piece would be replicated in sequence in another, both complexes generating a common background-level pattern. This is analogous to the situation presented in Example 3.12 i–iv, but located at one level of structure deeper (assuming, for simplicity's sake, three principal structural levels). Figure 3.7 below represents these relationships.

i) *Urlinie* $\hat{5}$–$\hat{1}$

$\hat{5}$ $\hat{4}$ $\hat{3}$ $\hat{2}$ $\hat{1}$

ii) Middleground Structures: Constituent Scale Degrees

a	*b*	*c*	*d*	*e*
$\underline{\hat{5}}$–$\hat{4}$–$\hat{3}$–$\hat{2}$–$\hat{1}$	$\underline{\hat{4}}$–$\hat{3}$–$\hat{2}$	$\underline{\hat{3}}$–$\sharp\hat{4}$–$\hat{5}$	$\hat{5}$–$\natural\hat{4}$–$\hat{3}$–$\underline{\hat{2}}$	$\hat{5}$–$\hat{4}$–$\hat{3}$–$\hat{2}$–$\underline{\hat{1}}$

iii) Foreground Memes M^1–M^{20}

M^1–M^5	M^6–M^8	M^9–M^{11}	M^{12}–M^{15}	M^{16}–M^{20}

Figure 3.7: Memeplexes at Various Structural Levels

At level iii of this hypothetical example, twenty foreground memes, M^1–M^{20}, each express (are principally orientated around) a single scale degree. These memes are shown as associating to form five groups. The first group of memes, M^1, M^2, M^3, M^4 and M^5, for instance, might express the scale degrees $\hat{5}$, $\hat{4}$, $\hat{3}$, $\hat{2}$ and $\hat{1}$ respectively, giving rise to a middleground linear progression $\hat{5}$–$\hat{1}$, shown in Figure 3.7 ii *a*. Each of these middleground structures might, in turn, express a component (underlined in Figure 3.7 ii) of the $\hat{5}$–$\hat{4}$–$\hat{3}$–$\hat{2}$–$\hat{1}$ *Urlinie* shown in Figure 3.7 i. Similarly, the fifth middleground structure, ii *e*, another $\hat{5}$–$\hat{1}$ linear progression and itself generated by the group of memes M^{16}–M^{20}, might express the final pitch, the $\hat{1}$, of the *Urlinie*.

Each middleground structure in Figure 3.7 ii is a meme: for instance, countless examples may be found in tonal music of $\hat{5}$–$\hat{4}$–$\hat{3}$–$\hat{2}$–$\hat{1}$ middleground linear progressions, such as that expressed in bb. 18–22 of the first movement of Mozart's Sonata in C major K. 545 (1788) (illustrated in Schenker 1979 as Fig. 88 4 c). If, by analogy with the foreground memes in Example 3.12 i, these five middleground structures *a*–*e* were replicated in sequence in another work at the same level, as is analogically the case in Example 3.12 iii, they would constitute a middleground memeplex. As with the foreground memeplex in Example 3.12 i and iii, such a middleground memeplex will generate a meme at a still deeper structural level: in the same way that the foreground memeplex of Example 3.12 i and iii gives rise to the middleground meme of Example 3.12 ii and iv, the middleground memeplex of Figure 3.7 ii and its coindex in another work will engender the background meme of Figure 3.7 i and its coindex in that other work.[12]

[12] As argued in Chapter 5, memetics supports a bottom-up generative-conglomerational view of musical structure in contrast to the orthodox Schenkerian top-down generative-transformational perspective.

To summarize these central but rather convoluted issues, we might posit two related hypotheses. First, as the 'second scenario' discussed above asserts, if a complex of independent foreground-level memes is replicated in another context, then while existing as a memeplex at the foreground level, it also generates/replicates a middleground-level meme. Secondly, applying the same principle recursively to higher levels, if a complex of independent middleground-level memes is replicated in another context, then while existing as memeplex at the middleground level, it also generates/replicates a background-level meme. Logically, the 'first scenario' also applies recursively: just as the middleground structure of Example 3.12 ii, iv and vi is not dependent upon a specific set of foreground memes for its expression – evident from the divergence between the passages in Example 3.12 i and iii on the one hand and v on the other – so the background structure in Figure 3.7 i is not contingent upon a specific set of middleground memes for its expression.

Having now considered pitch memeplexes in some detail, it seems that memes also exist below the foreground in the parameter of rhythm: the *Gàbàdà* and *Égbaníbà* rhythms shown in Example 2.3 above consist of three structural levels (rhythmic background, middleground and foreground) at each of which is situated a rhythmic meme. A hierarchical view of rhythmic organization was developed by Yeston by the application of Schenkerian principles to duration. He argues that rhythmic stratification – the process whereby 'slower moving rhythmic configurations … combine to produce a rhythmic foreground' – is determined by five criteria: disposition of attack points, timbre, dynamics, density and pattern recurrence (1976: 54). In predominantly pitch-based music, however, another criterion must be added, namely the recurrence of pitch shapes. Moreover,

> The notion that pitch configurations may generate rhythmic structures has been shown to be at least as old as the eighteenth-century analyses of compound lines made by Heinichen. In its most general form, this principle rests on the recognition that a rhythmic sub-pattern may be derived from a gross, attack-point rhythm by either of two criteria: (1) the recurrence of a pitch, or (2) the occurrence of a pitch event that corresponds to a prior pitch event of the same level of significance.
>
> (1976: 55)

As an example of this process, one might read three hierarchic levels, i, ii and iii in Example 3.13 below, in the opening theme of Beethoven's Piano Concerto no. 4.

Example 3.13: Pitch-Generated Rhythmic Stratification

i) Pitch-Generated Rhythmic Meme; ii) Pitch-Generated Rhythmic Meme; iii) Pitch-Generated Rhythmic Meme; iv) Beethoven: Piano Concerto no. 4 in G major op. 58 (1805), I, bb. 1–5; v) Voice-Leading Reduction of iv; vi) Alternative Voice-Leading Reduction of iv; vii) Duple Diminution of i; viii) Duple Diminution of ii; ix) Duple Diminution of iii.

Example 3.13 iv may be read as prolonging a $\hat{3}$/I–$\hat{2}$||/V interruption (b^2–a^2) with the $\hat{3}$ prolonged by a neighbour note $\hat{4}$/V (c^2). Based on the musical surface, rhythmic level iii results from those attacks which introduce a change of pitch, ignoring ‘the recurrence of a pitch’. Derived from the first reduction (v), ii takes into account ‘the occurrence of a pitch event that corresponds to a prior pitch event of the same level of significance’, the points of rhythmic articulation arising from the introduction of the neighbour note c^2 in b. 3, its subsequent resolution to b^1 in b. 5 and the further motion to a^1. Taking the alternative reduction (vi), i downgrades the $\hat{3}$/I in b. 5 to the status of a passing harmony, placing greater emphasis upon the span $\hat{4}$–$\hat{2}$/V in bb. 3–5 and giving rise to a rhythmic structure slightly different from that of ii.

Example 3.13 vii, viii and ix are duple diminutions of i, ii and iii respectively, allowing us more easily to conceive the three rhythmic structures as potential shallow-middleground-level rhythmic memes of increasing remove (iii, ii, i). Naturally a coindex for each would need to be located; and each coindex will almost certainly be generated by foreground pitch configurations different from those generating the patterns in vii, viii and ix. To a greater degree than foreground-level rhythmic memes, those at the middleground are contingent upon (replication in) the parameter of pitch. By analogy with higher-order pitch memes, such rhythmic memes are virtual entities, existing beyond the realm of immediate perception and amenable to cognition largely through the mediation of verbal-conceptual memes.

3.4.3. *Psychological Representation and Neurobiological Encoding of Memes and Memeplexes: Schemata, Connectionism and the 'Cerebral Code'*

Psychological Representation

A key principle of cognitive psychology is that 'the brain abstracts recurrent commonalities from the environment and encodes them in the form of schematic representations as a basis for future categorization and comprehension' (Bharucha 1987: 2). Schemata are perceptual-cognitive frameworks determining, and being determined by, the nature and disposition of a number of lower-level elements, termed 'features' by Gjerdingen.[13] Thus, '[s]chemata can be defined as meaningful sets of features, and features can be defined as meaningful elements in sets of schemata' (Gjerdingen 1988: 6). Put another way, features are discrete entities whose interrelationships are controlled by, and at the same time give rise to, schemata. From the point of view of the composer schemata are primarily synthetic, generative tools, guiding the creative process; from the point of view of the listener they are analytical aids, directing the processes of perception and cognition. The relevance of schemata from the point of view of the meme will be explored in Chapter 4.

The principle of replication is intrinsic to schemata: they are replicated relationships and are, by virtue of this, necessarily memetic. As with all memes, schemata exist fundamentally as neuronal constellations in the brain and so, having

[13] Meyer regards them as 'patterns that, because they are congruent both with human perceptual/cognitive capacities and with prevalent stylistic (musical and extramusical) constraints, are memorable, tend to remain stable over time, and are therefore replicated with particular frequency' (1989: 51). He also uses the term 'archetype' to refer to structural classes which are the consequence of innate physiological and psychological attributes as opposed to those – schemata – which are generated by learning. In practice, however, Gjerdingen believes '[t]he two categories commingle' (1988: 46). Leman 1995 is a comprehensive treatment of this subject.

covered some of these issues in 2.2.1 above, a return to this question is warranted in order briefly to examine the issue of structural-hierarchic location in musical memetics in terms of the psychology and neurobiology of memory organization. However, to reiterate the caveat made in that earlier section, a detailed treatment of the subject is well beyond the scope of this book.

If we regard the schema as a middleground structure and its constituent features as foreground patterning, it will be evident in the light of 3.4.2 above that a diversity of features may assemble to generate a particular schema. A passage such as bb. 9–12 of the Trio from Mozart's Symphony in A major K. 114 (1771) is an instantiation of what Gjerdingen terms the prototypical $\hat{1}$–$\hat{7}$...$\hat{4}$–$\hat{3}$ 'changing-note archetype' (1988: 53, 65, Example 4-11, 94).[14] Aside from the obligatory $\hat{1}$–$\hat{7}$...$\hat{4}$–$\hat{3}$ melodic motion, metric and periodic articulation into parallel initial and terminal events and the underlying I–V...V–I harmony are invariant in all but a handful of cases. More variable is the bass motion which, although predominantly articulating scale degrees $\hat{1}$–$\hat{2}$...$\hat{7}$–$\hat{1}$ in examples with high typicality, can also diverge within the parameters specified in the prototype (: 103). (The concepts of typicality and prototypicality are discussed further in Chapter 4.) Despite the complexity of these relationships, Gjerdingen emphasizes that the essence of this structure lies in its

> coordinated sets of movements. For example, across the first metric boundary there is movement from the melodic scale degree 1 to degree 7, movement in the bass from 1 to 2 (or occasionally 3 → 2 or 1 → 5), and harmonic movement to the dominant, usually but not always from the tonic. *It is such a coordinated set of movements and not the presence or absence of any single feature that characterizes each schema event.*
>
> (1988: 64, his emphasis)

In outlining the schema-features dualism, Gjerdingen notes that, according to the criterion of information type, we demonstrate two kinds of memory structure, termed semantic and episodic by Tulving. These correspond to the classifications categorical and schematic, respectively, proposed by Mandler (Gjerdingen 1988: 59). While these represent primarily psychological models, it seems reasonable to suggest that, while not as separate as the following necessarily simplified discussion implies, they may nevertheless be based on structurally or functionally distinct neurobiological substrates.

Semantic/categorical memory takes the form of an associative network of information-encoding memory nodes and their interconnections. The memory

14 Some of the passages Gjerdingen analyzes as instantiations of the $\hat{1}$–$\hat{7}$...$\hat{4}$–$\hat{3}$ schema can be interpreted as conforming to other schematic types. His Example 5-14a, for instance, from Mozart's Sonata in C major K. 309 (284b) (1777), can be read as a $\hat{1}$–$\hat{7}$...$\sharp\hat{2}$–$\hat{3}$ type if the criterion of strict symmetry is employed to determine the pitches 'rhyming' with those instantiating the $\hat{1}$–$\hat{7}$ dyad (1988: 78).

patterns for foreground features such as memes *a–e* in Example 3.12 i and iii would seem to be subject to this synchronic type of organization. In contrast, episodic/schematic memory structures the diachronic recall of discrete events anchored in linear time. The memory patterns for a middleground schema such as that shown in Example 3.12 ii and iv, with its clear sequence of component events, would appear to be subject to this type of organization. Figure 3.8 below represents these two models of memory organization.

i) Semantic/Categorical Nodes ii) Episodic/Schematic Sequence

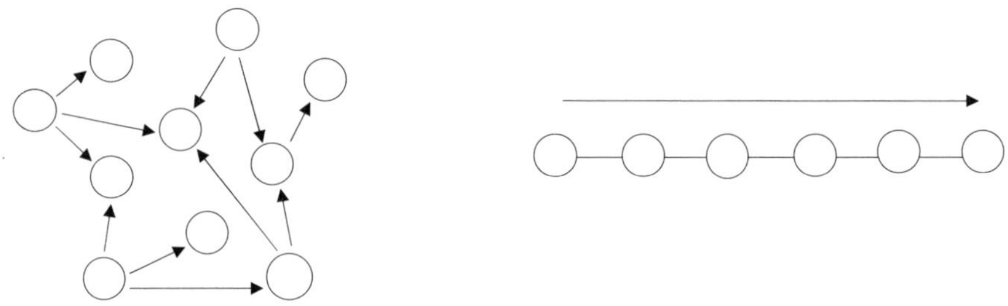

Figure 3.8: Semantic/Categorical and Episodic/Schematic Memory (after Gjerdingen 1988: 60–62, Figures 4-1–4-3)

Having outlined their differences, Gjerdingen asserts that

> These two types of memory organization commingle if we allow the term *feature* for event schemata to coincide with the term *concept* for semantic[/categorical] networks.... in music, *dominant seventh chord*, for example, can be both a concept linked to the memory nodes *instability*, *dissonance*, and so on, and a feature in the [episodic/]schemat[ic] *perfect authentic cadence* and *1–7...4–3 changing-note*.
>
> (1988: 61; his emphases)

In the light of the discussion in 3.4.2 above, it could be argued that (memotypic) foreground-orientated memes (features) are coded by the individual nodes in a semantic/categorical associative network; and that (memotypic) middleground-orientated memes (schemata) are the consequence of the organization of these nodes into sequential configurations fixed in and mediated by episodic/schematic memory. These middleground schema memes may then themselves act, via functional transformation, as features coded by the nodes of a higher-order semantic/categorical associative network. The highest level semantic/categorical nodes (after several levels of recursive schema-to-feature transformation) may be fixed sequentially into a superordinate episodic/schematic configuration, the highest level schema, of which the *Ursatz* is one viable representation. In this sense, the hierarchic, embedded, nature of memory organization gives rise to the hierarchic, embedded, nature of the musical phemotype.

Neurobiological Encoding

Might such hierarchic psychological representations of memes and memeplexes be paralleled in the neurobiology of the brain? A view increasingly supported by studies of brain structure is that interconnections between nerve cells form neural networks, the varying connections, and connection strengths, of which can account for pattern recognition and schema abstraction. As noted in 2.2.1 above, Delius believes that '[s]uch plastic synapses have to be thought of as the critical components of neural networks functioning as associative arrays' (1991: 82; see also his Figure 6.1; and Gjerdingen 1988: 60–61, Figures 4-1 and 4-2). These connectionist architectures may be simulated in computer models (see Todd and Loy 1991, Griffith and Todd 1999). For Bharucha, such models

> have a number of properties that recommend them as models of music cognition.... they can account for how we learn musical patterns .... their assumptions are either known or plausible principles of neuroscience.... they shed light on the observation ... that aspects of pitch and harmony involve the mental completion (or Gestalt perception) of patterns.... they are capable of recognizing varying shades of similarity and are therefore well suited to modeling similarity-based accounts ... of tonality or modality.... [and] they can discover regularities in musical styles that may elude formal music-theoretic analysis .... [Moreover,] a neural net can learn temporal composite patterns so that they function as schemas and as sequential memories.
>
> (1999: 413, 424)

Other studies, including ones by Gjerdingen (1989, 1990), accord with these claims. His research using an adaptive-resonance-theory (ART) system suggests that 'self-organizing neuronlike networks are ... able to sort ... dozens of diverse musical features into stable, meaningful schemata' (1990: 339). In this study, Mozart's six earliest compositions (KK. 1a–d, 2 and 3) were used to entrain the network, which abstracted a number of simple voice-leading schemata from them, such as cadences and arpeggiations. Gjerdingen's Fig. 12 (: 365) suggests that the notion of hierarchic embedding discussed above (whereby schemata can themselves function recursively as features in higher-level schemata) may easily arise in multileveled networks.

A computer simulation of a connectionist system is implemented by, among other things, program code, memory addresses and CPU switches. Such networks are physically implemented in the brain, according to Calvin, by neuronal 'mosaics of the mind'. These are hexagonal areas of neocortex (the outer 2mm-thick layer of the cerebral hemispheres) 0.5mm across, consisting of numerous minicolumns – 'a cylindrical group of about 100 neurons extending through all the [six] layers of neocortex and about 0.030 mm in diameter' (1996: 205). Calvin insists that

> *mosaics of the mind* is not just a literary metaphor. It is a description of mechanism at what appears to be an appropriate level of explanation for many mental phenomena – that of hexagonal mosaics of electrical activity, competing for territory in the association cortex of the brain.... The pattern within each hexagon of this mosaic may be the representation of an item of our vocabulary: objects and actions such as the cat that sat on the mat, tunes such as Beethoven's dit-dit-dit-dah, images such as the profile of your grandmother, a high-order concept such as a Turing Machine – even something for which you have no word, such as the face of someone whose name you haven't learned. If I am right, the spatiotemporal firing pattern within that hexagon is your cerebral code for a word or mental image.
>
> (1996: 2; his emphasis)

As 'the representation of an item of our vocabulary', each mosaic might be regarded as the memotypic form of a meme, including 'tunes such as Beethoven's dit-dit-dit-dah'. Moreover, as is clear from the extract, Calvin envisages an element of competition between these mosaics. According to his hexagonal cloning theory (: 99–101), the hexagons can implement what he regards as the 'six essentials' (: 21) of the Darwinian algorithm; these augment, but do not contradict, Dennett's tripartite formulation cited in 1.2.2 above. Copying, variation and selection of hexagons makes the brain a Darwin machine and can account for meme evolution at the memotypic level.

3.4.4. *Replicated Symbolism: Memeplexes and Meaning*

> [T]he linguistic sign unites not a thing and a name, but a concept and a sound-image. The latter is not the material sound – a purely physical thing – but the psychological imprint of the sound, the impression that it makes on our senses: the sound-image is sensory, and if I happen to call it 'material', it is only in that sense, and by way of opposing it to the other term of the association, the *concept*, which is generally more abstract.
>
> (Saussure, in Nattiez 1990: 3)

The musico-operational memes considered in 2.5.4 above are a subset of a much broader grouping, verbal-conceptual memes. As noted earlier, these are the ideas, notions and concepts which underpin our lives, our social interactions and ultimately our consciousness; Dennett asserts boldly that '[h]uman consciousness is *itself* a huge complex of memes (or more exactly, meme-effects in brains)' (1993: 210, his emphasis). To take Hamlet's celebrated phrase 'To be, or not to be, that is the question' (III, i, 56) as an example of a verbal-conceptual meme, the whole unit is a meme, as are the individual words, existing independently of the larger phrase. The individual words are themselves signifiers of meaning, 'question' being not just a replicated sequence of letters but also a marker of a concept which registers at the deepest level of our consciousness.[15] From the argument of 3.3.1 above, it seems that, like nucleotides in genetics and single notes in music, the individual phonemes in language probably do not qualify as memetic. Only their assemblage into larger units gives them the necessary information content to function as memes, their status as part of a relativistic network of interpretants, in Peirce's sense (Nattiez 1990: 6), affording them conceptual content.

The idea of the memeplex enables us to understand how replicated patterning acquires symbolic/referential signification, and to illustrate this I begin with the topics of late-eighteenth-century music (Ratner 1980, Allanbrook 1983, Agawu 1991). Of the two principal schools of semiology identified by Keiler (1978) – the taxonomic empiricists (represented by Nattiez) and the semanticists (represented by Saussure) – it is the views of the latter which are invoked by Agawu to explain the semiological functioning of topics (1991: 11f.). For the semanticist tradition, configurations such as patterns of notes acquire verbal-conceptual meaning by means of the process Meyer term connotation, whereby 'associations [are] made between some aspect of the musical organization and extramusical experience' (1956: 258). To have cultural force, such associations must be memetically replicated.

Nevertheless, many topics are most easily conceived in terms of textural and timbral configurations and it is not always straightforward to define them in terms of the replicated pitch and rhythmic patterns which most often constitute memes. Agawu, however, attempts to identify the structural patterns underlying topics, mediating between what Jakobson terms introversive (structural) and extroversive (referential) modes of semiological functioning (1991: 23). More importantly, and perhaps with greater specificity than Ratner, he attempts to define the more foreground-orientated pitch and rhythmic shapes characteristic of particular topics. Adopting the terminology of Saussure, Agawu observes that

[15] Constraints of space prevent my discussing the complex question of whether verbal-conceptual memes are the working currency of the brain (which implies that without language we can have no conceptual thought), or whether they are the result of the conversion into natural-language memes of some more fundamental meme incarnation, a 'machine code' or 'brain language', as is implied to some degree in the passage from Saussure at the head of this section. Dennett argues against the latter view (1993: 234).

> A topic, T, may be defined as a musical sign. Each T embodies the union of a signifier and a verbally mediated signified. Signifiers are purely musical dimensions such as texture, timbre, rhythm, melody, and harmony *in a particular disposition* …. The signified or concept is represented by an arbitrary label drawn from U[niverse of] T[opic]. Signifieds normally point to dimensions of historical or sociocultural specificity, including the elements of a contemporary compositional code.
>
> (1991: 128–9; his emphasis)

Thus, the scale degree succession $\hat{8}$–♯$\hat{7}$–♮$\hat{7}$–♯$\hat{6}$–♮$\hat{6}$–$\hat{5}$ (existing as part of a musical memeplex which may also contain rhythmic, textural, timbral and dynamic memes) forms the defining element of the 'purely musical dimension' of the 'lament' topic memeplex which was widely propagated in the seventeenth and eighteenth centuries (Rosand 2001, Williams 1998). As a topic, this musical signifier also had a non-musical signified, a verbal-conceptual memeplex comprising 'socioculturally specific' concepts of lamentation and death, which existed in such phemotypic forms as Nahum Tate's text for Dido's lament from Purcell's *Dido and Aeneas* (*c.* 1689). The musical memeplex and the verbal-conceptual memeplex, in forming a 'union of a signifier and a verbally mediated signified', engendered an even larger musico-conceptual memeplex which was propagated intact in seventeenth- and eighteenth-century culture. Thus, a memeplex may encompass not only 'pure' complexes of memes, propagated in only one cultural medium, but also hybrid complexes, formed from memes in different symbolic systems.

Despite its congruence with observed musical phenomena, Gjerdingen's synthesis of the two forms of memory organization in the passage (1988: 61) cited in 3.4.3 above tends to blur the semiotic distinction between signifiers and signifieds. One means of clarification would be to regard the spoken (verbal-phonetic) and written (verbal-graphical) patterning 'chromatic tetrachord' – to adapt Gjerdingen's example to the case of the lament topic – as the phemotypic products of memotypic memes which, as a class, act as signifiers at what might be termed level-one semiosis, illustrated in Table 3.1 i below. To this category one should add the written (musico-graphical) patterning of the chromatic tetrachord. Together, and in co-adaptation with an array of other memes, these various representations structure our verbal-conceptual cognition of this pattern, forming a network of interpretants. Given that we are dealing with a musico-conceptual memeplex, Table 3.1 i also illustrates the conceptual elements, showing two language signifier memes, verbal-phonetic (Saussure's 'sound-image') and verbal-graphical, in addition to the three musical signifier memes. (Table 3.1 nevertheless oversimplifies matters by ignoring the motor-control memes which govern the muscular actions engendering writing, speaking and the production of musical sounds.)

While to some extent independent, the three musical signifier memes shown in Table 3.1 i also exist in semiotic co-adaptation with the memotypic sonority meme, our mental image of the sound – the sound internalized ('heard') in the brain – which operates as their signified and whose phemotypic product, via the intercession of musical instruments, is the physical sonority through which the chromatic tetrachord figure impinges upon us most directly. Similarly, the two conceptual signifier memes exist in semiotic co-adaptation with the memotypic verbal-conceptual interpretant memeplex which defines the concepts (in this case) of death and grief.

At a higher level of referring, level-two semiosis, the association between the musical meme (the tetrachord, as signifier) and the verbal-conceptual meme (concepts of death and grief, the signified) forms a (topical) musico-conceptual memeplex, Table 3.1 ii below.

Table 3.1: The Memetic-Semiotic Nexus of the 'Lament' Musico-Conceptual Memeplex

i) Level-One Semiosis

	Memotype		**Phemotype**	
	Musical	**Verbal-Conceptual**	**Musical**	**Verbal-Conceptual**
Signifiers	Verbal-Phonetic Meme → 'Chromatic Tetrachord'	Verbal-Phonetic Memes → 'Death, Grief…'	→ Verbal-Phonetic Pattern 'Chromatic Tetrachord'	→ Verbal-Phonetic Patterns 'Death, Grief…'
	Verbal-Graphical Meme → 'Chromatic Tetrachord'	Verbal-Graphical Memes → 'Death, Grief…'	→ Verbal-Graphical Pattern 'Chromatic Tetrachord'	→ Verbal-Graphical Patterns 'Death, Grief…'
	Musico-Graphical Meme → 		→ Musico-Graphical Pattern 	
Signified	Sonority Meme →		→ Physical Sonority	
		Verbal-Conceptual Interpretant Memeplex → 'Death, Grief…'		→ (Verbal-Conceptual Interpretant Memeplex 'Death, Grief…')

ii) Level-Two Semiosis

	Memotype		**Phemotype**	
	Musical	**Verbal-Conceptual**	**Musical**	**Verbal-Conceptual**
Signifiers	Sonority Meme →		→ Physical Sonority	
Signified		Verbal-Conceptual Meme → 'Death, Grief…'		→ Verbal-Conceptual Meme 'Death, Grief…'

In verbal-conceptual signification systems, the memotypic signifier – the verbal-phonetic and/or verbal-graphical memes antecedent to the language-specific spoken and/or written word – and the memotypic signified – the interpretant-mediated idea or 'concept' (Saussure) with which they are stably united – give rise to a unitary phemotypic manifestation, in that at the phemotypic level the concept is inseparable from its verbal-phonetic or verbal-graphical manifestation (hence the brackets in the bottom right-hand corner of Table 3.1 i). In music, by contrast, a separation is maintained, in that the memotypic signifier – the memes antecedent to a verbal-phonetic, verbal-graphical or musico-graphical representation – and the memotypic signified – the memes antecedent to a physical sonority – give rise to separate manifestations which preserve the level-one signifier-signified dualism at the level of the phemotype.

It is not only eighteenth-century topics, with their relatively stable referential associations, which may partake of the signifier-signified dualism, but all musical memes. Any replicated configuration of musical elements may become associated with (refer to) a replicated configuration of verbal-conceptual elements to form a musico-conceptual memeplex, if only at the idiomatic level. As represented by the double-headed arrows in Figure 2.1 above, there may be transmission of memes from the dialect into the idiom of the composer and vice versa. The topic memeplex may not survive intact when crossing from dialect to idiom: new verbal-conceptual memes (signifieds) may be attached by the composer to the signifying musical meme. Conversely, musical memes situated at the level of idiom may, in passing out into the dialect, lose any verbal-conceptual memes with which they were originally co-adapted in the brain of the composer and exist without co-adapted verbal-conceptual memes, or in co-adaptation with different verbal-conceptual memes, in the brains of other composers.

From the perspective of taxonomic empiricism, relatively few memeplexes, most prominently the topics, are grounded upon an elision between the poietic and the esthesic in the sense that 'strategies of perception will correspond to strategies of production because the producer has internalized laws of perception' (Nattiez 1990: 212). Perhaps the majority of musico-conceptual memeplexes exist only on the poietic side, as idiomatic associations between musical memeplexes and verbal-conceptual memeplexes forged in the brain of the composer and not accessible at the esthesic level, at which are situated other composers who replicate the musical memeplex but, in so doing, inadvertently disconnect it from the co-adapted verbal-conceptual memeplex.

3.5. The Hierarchies of Nature and Culture: An Analogy

Developing a memetics of music presupposes a meditation between the biological and cultural realms, not because memes are necessarily dependent or contingent upon genes – although this happens largely to be the case at present – but because, as replicators, genes and memes might reasonably be expected to demonstrate certain common properties which transcend their different substrates. One aspect they do seem to have in common is their tendency towards multileveled hierarchical organization – from single genes and memes to large-scale biological and cultural structures and systems. This is an issue partly covered in 3.4.1 and 3.4.2 above – and, as noted, will be revisited in Chapter 5 – but it is now expanded upon to cover levels beyond the individual musical work and to encompass mappings from one replicator system to the other.

In hypothesizing correspondences between natural and cultural levels, it is fruitful to attempt to relate aspects of the genetic hierarchy to the stylistic hierarchy propounded by Meyer (2.5.1 above). In doing this, one might distinguish between two types of replicator hierarchy, the genetic/memetic-structural and the genetic/memetic-cultural; together, these form a continuum from the lowest to the highest points in the hierarchy. The former type describes the structural relationships which obtain between replicators at the level of the individual (the single vehicle: the organism and the unitary musical work) and all lower hierarchic levels. The latter type describes the 'cultural' relationships which obtain between replicators at the level of the group (the collection of vehicles: the group of organisms and various associations of musical works) and all higher hierarchic levels. Adapting the format of Figure 2.1 above, Figure 3.9 below summarises and extends this interpretation of these correspondences.

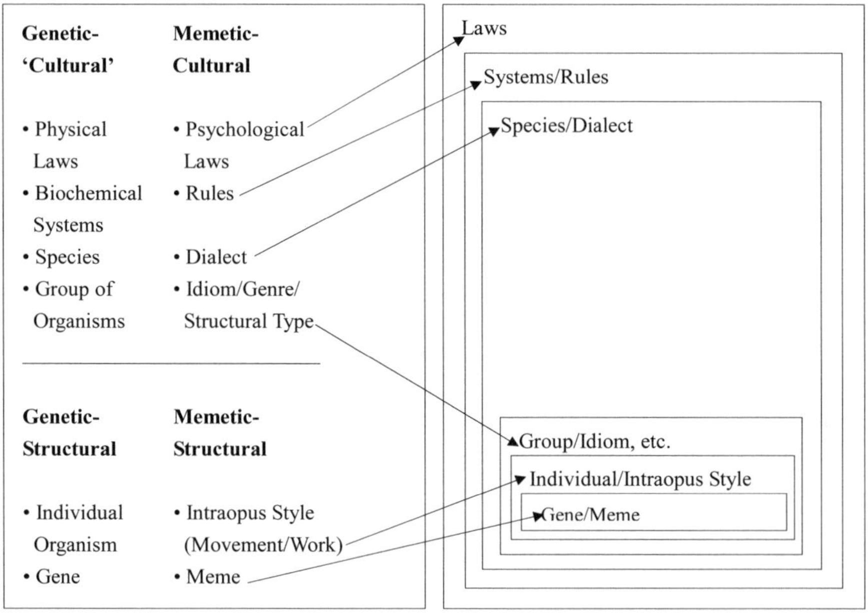

Figure 3.9: Correspondences and Inclusion Relationships in Natural and Cultural Hierarchies

Of the genetic/memetic-cultural correspondences, the physical laws which enable several possible biochemical systems on Earth (of which carbon-based biochemistry is predominant) are analogous to the psychological laws which support several systems of rules, such as modality and tonality. Whereas a species is defined by the similar geno/phenotypic profile of a collection of chronologically and geographically circumscribed organisms, a dialect may be regarded as the similar memo/phemotypic profile of a group of similarly constrained composers. Groups (subtypes) within a species map onto the idioms of individual composers, and also onto genres and formal/structural types, for these possess sufficient genetic/memetic individuality to differentiate themselves from the species/dialect as a whole, yet are not definable without reference to the larger group within which they are subsumed and from which they draw. Moving to the genetic/memetic-structural correspondences, as a bounded, discrete collection of genes and their phenotypic effects, the individual organism corresponds to the self-contained cultural product (movement or work), the phemotypic effects of a functional complex of memes. At the level of the individual replicator, and as is the central thesis of this study, the meme is analogous to the gene.

If accepted, these mappings are significant for two principal reasons. First, they suggest that replicators in different substrates will behave in analogous ways in respect of hierarchic organization. Secondly, and warranted by the authority of universal Darwinism, they offer the opportunity systematically to apply the large body of established theoretical knowledge on the nature of genetic hierarchies, both intra- and inter-level, to those of memetics.

3.6. Summary

The concepts of particulateness, coindexation and segmentation – corollaries of the notions of longevity, fecundity and copying fidelity – are at the core of the definition of memes in music. Stemming from the precepts of Gestalt psychology, particularly their operationalization in Narmour's implication-realization model, they offer a useful framework for understanding how memes configure themselves in order to facilitate their passage through the human perceptual-cognitive filter and into the relative security of memory. Despite their tendency to relative concision, memes in music retain their digital identity even as they form rich multiparametric and multimemetic networks at several structural-hierarchic levels. Considering the full range of these hierarchies – on a continuum which moves from the level of uniparametric patterns, through multiparametric and multimemetic complexes, right up to the complex interactions which constitute musical dialects – the presence of certain suggestive affinities with organic hierarchies allows us to identify structural parallels between genetic and memetic replicator systems.

Chapter 4

Evolutionary Dynamics: The Selfish Musical Meme

4.1. Introduction

Whereas Chapter 3 focused mainly on the static aspects of the musical meme and the issues surrounding its definition and intra-work organization, this chapter addresses its dynamic aspects – principally the inter-work (inter-brain) transmission of memes, the attributes that make them differentially transmissible and the consequences of cumulative meme mutation. After a consideration of the epidemiological aspects of memetics, I examine the mechanisms of memetic transmission, mutation, selection and evolution, using perspectives drawn from semiology and from the implication-realization tradition of analysis. At the heart of this discussion is what Blackmore terms the 'meme's eye view', a way of thinking which regards cultural phenomena from the selfish perspective of the meme.

4.2. *Ein Echter Ohrwurm*: Memetics as Cultural Epidemiology

> Colleague at Bochum University: 'Sie haben mir einen Floh ins Ohr gesetzt' ['you have put a flea in my ear']. Discjockey on German radio: 'Der Song ist ein echter Ohrwurm' ['the song is a real "ear-worm"']. Report in an English newspaper: 'The idea was obviously infectious'. Passenger on an international flight: 'What a contagious, nonsensical habit!'. American performance artist: 'Language is a virus'.
>
> (Delius 1989: 26)

Regarding human beings as 'strange creatures' – on the grounds that, despite evolving by natural selection like other animals, we do so many extraordinary and diverse things that other animals do not – Blackmore begins her study of memetics with a discussion of 'what makes us different?' (1999: 1, 3). She concludes that the distinguishing feature is 'our ability to imitate' (: 3) – that we so naturally and automatically copy the actions, behaviours and ideas of other members of our species. If the propensity to imitate is the defining characteristic of *Homo sapiens*, then transmission by imitation/copying is the defining characteristic of the meme, for as argued, a mnemon only becomes a meme when it is copied in at least two brains, being transmitted between these individuals via a process of imitation. It follows from this that the most successful memes, defined as those most widely copied, will be those with the greatest propensity to imitation. As noted, this attribute, fecundity, is a function of – is partly synonymous with – the meme's perceptual-cognitive salience, the property of 'standing out', in psychological terms, from the mass of surrounding memetic information, and thus of being relatively more distinctive, striking and memorable.

When a meme is transmitted widely within a meme pool – such as when a fashion trend or a craze spreads within a socio-cultural group – it is functioning in a similar way to an infective agent, such as a bacterium or virus (Dawkins 1993). Some members of the group are infected and some are uninfected according to whether or not they have been exposed to individuals who encode the meme in memory and who, by engendering the meme's phemotypic products in various media, act as vectors in the meme's transmission. This attribute of the successful meme – its tendency to behave, as Delius reports, as an *Ohrwurm* – means that both the (real) transmission of memes 'horizontally' within a socio-cultural community and their (virtual) transmission 'vertically' within a memetic-cultural hierarchy (Figure 3.9 above) may be understood not only in terms of the sophisticated models developed in population genetics and cultural transmission theory (for the latter, see Cavalli-Sforza and Feldman 1981, Lynch 1998b and Witten 1991), but also in terms of those formulated in epidemiology to map the spread of gene-based infections.[1]

To take the real/horizontal aspect first, Lynch conceives memetics as to some extent the study of 'thought contagion' (1996). He argues that

> Different modes of thought contagion usually occur together. Thus, a single idea has a *propagative profile* consisting of any advantages it has in each mode. Memetic theory analyzes these propagative profiles in a manner resembling that used in epidemiology. An epidemiologist might conclude, for instance, that sneezing out virus particles accounts for much of the common cold's propagation; the virus's way of causing sneeze-triggering nasal irritation is what makes the cold so common. Similarly, a memeticist might determine that the [country-suffers-from-a-]weapons-shortage belief spreads largely by proselytism; the idea's way of producing proselytism – motivating fear [–] is what makes the belief so common. Memetics is, in part, an *epidemiology* of ideas.
>
> (1996: 9; his emphases)

If a meme is an infective agent, then the individual in whose brain it resides is its host. This opposition requires the meme to be regarded as functionally distinct

---

1 My use of the terms horizontal and vertical here differs from their standard usage in cultural transmission theory. See Shennan 2002: 48–51.

from the organism it inhabits, despite (as noted in 2.3.1 above) being instantiated by constellations of neurons, a component of the gene phenotype.

More subtly, Delius draws an analogy between, on the one hand, organisms which live in symbiotic relationship with each other – in which the invading organism may function as mutualist (beneficial; the host's genes gain from the association), commensal (neutral; the host's genes neither gain nor lose appreciably) or parasite (harmful; the host's genes are disadvantaged) – and, on the other hand, humans and the memes with which we are, in an equivalent sense, symbiotic – in which the infecting replicators may similarly function as mutualist, commensal or parasite in relation to the human host's genes (1989: 48–65; see also Ball 1984: 147, Figure 1). The relationship between the genetic and the memetic spheres is discussed further in Chapter 7.

The virtual/vertical aspect is a function of the real/horizontal. When a mnemon arises at the level of intraopus style, it is, by definition, unreplicated. It may be a mutation of an existing meme, or a nascent entity. If the composer uses it in another work, it spreads outwards and 'upwards' to the level of his or her idiom. If it is imitated by another composer, the mnemon not only becomes a meme but it infects the intraopus style of that composer's work. It may be further replicated by the second composer in other works, moving outwards and upwards to the level of his or her idiom. At the same time, it moves upwards to, and begins to colonize, the dialect. If enough composers adopt the meme, and it attains a certain critical mass within the dialect, it may even contaminate the level of rules. This aspect is epidemiological because moving from the lower to the higher hierarchic levels in Figure 3.9 implies the transmission of a pattern outwards from a centralized memotypic locus (the brain of an individual composer) to a distributed one (the brains of many members of a musico-cultural community), and from a localized phemotypic representation (in the score of a single work) to a generalized one (in the scores of works by several composers).

4.3. Memetic Transmission and Mutation

Dennett's 'maximally abstract' definition of evolution by natural selection (1995: 343) given in 1.2.2 above identifies variation, heredity/replication and differential fitness as necessary conditions for the operation of the Darwinian algorithm. As a replicator, the meme satisfies these and will therefore 'tend to become the basis for Darwinian selection' (Dawkins 1989: 322), the engine which drives memetic-cultural evolution. Memetic transmission (heredity/replication) results from our distinguishing human tendency to imitation and the propensity of memes to assume the most appropriate forms to take advantage of this.[2] Given the finite attentional and memory capacities of the human brain, some memes will be inaccurately transmitted, giving rise to mutant (variant) forms. Some of these mutants will be more effective replicators than their progenitors, resulting in selection in favour of the mutants (differential fitness). The result of this differential transmission of mutant memes will be cultural evolution. While mutation can be regarded as a form of meme evolution, it is the larger-scale, systemic consequences of mutation which are normally regarded as evolutionary.

In biological transmission, variation tends to occur before heredity/replication, for the crossing-over which forms a component process of meiosis shuffles the genetic material creating new configurations, and sometimes new genes, prior to transmission. In memetics, by contrast, the variation often occurs as a consequence of the process of transmission, miscopying or mutation being intrinsic to memetic transmission. This contingency means that it is appropriate to treat memetic transmission and mutation together, as closely related processes.

Cavalli-Sforza and Feldman argue that

> the centrality of the concept of transmission to evolutionary thinking is patently obvious. In biological material, however complex, there exists an almost perfect mechanism of genetic transmission. Evolution is the result of mutational exceptions to perfect transmission and the differential success of the products of this imperfect transmission.
>
> (1981: 341)

In cultural material, the 'mutational exceptions to perfect transmission' are more extensive than in biological material. Such deficits in copying-fidelity, while intrinsic to all replicators, are a particular characteristic of the meme. Indeed, this 'Chinese Whispers' effect may at times even outweigh 'perfect transmission', generating a plethora of mutant forms which stoke the engine of Darwinian selection and result in the meme 'achieving evolutionary change at a rate that leaves the old gene panting far behind' (Dawkins 1989: 192).

Figure 4.1 below represents the mechanism of memetic transmission and mutation. Because cultural products are transmitted from a producer to a receiver via an intermediate (phemotypic) form, an effective means of representing the process is Molino's notion of the semiological tripartition, as applied to musical semiology by Nattiez. The figure traces the movement of a meme through five hosts as it passes between the poietic, neutral and esthesic poles and across the somatic (memotypic)–extrasomatic (phemotypic) boundary which bisects it.

---

[2] In memetics, transmission implies the replication of information. In the present discussion this will be regarded as a given, but it should be noted that there are objections to the notion of replication in cultural transmission and evolution. Because I regard these as non-fatal (refutable by memetics), they will be treated briefly in Chapter 7, not here.

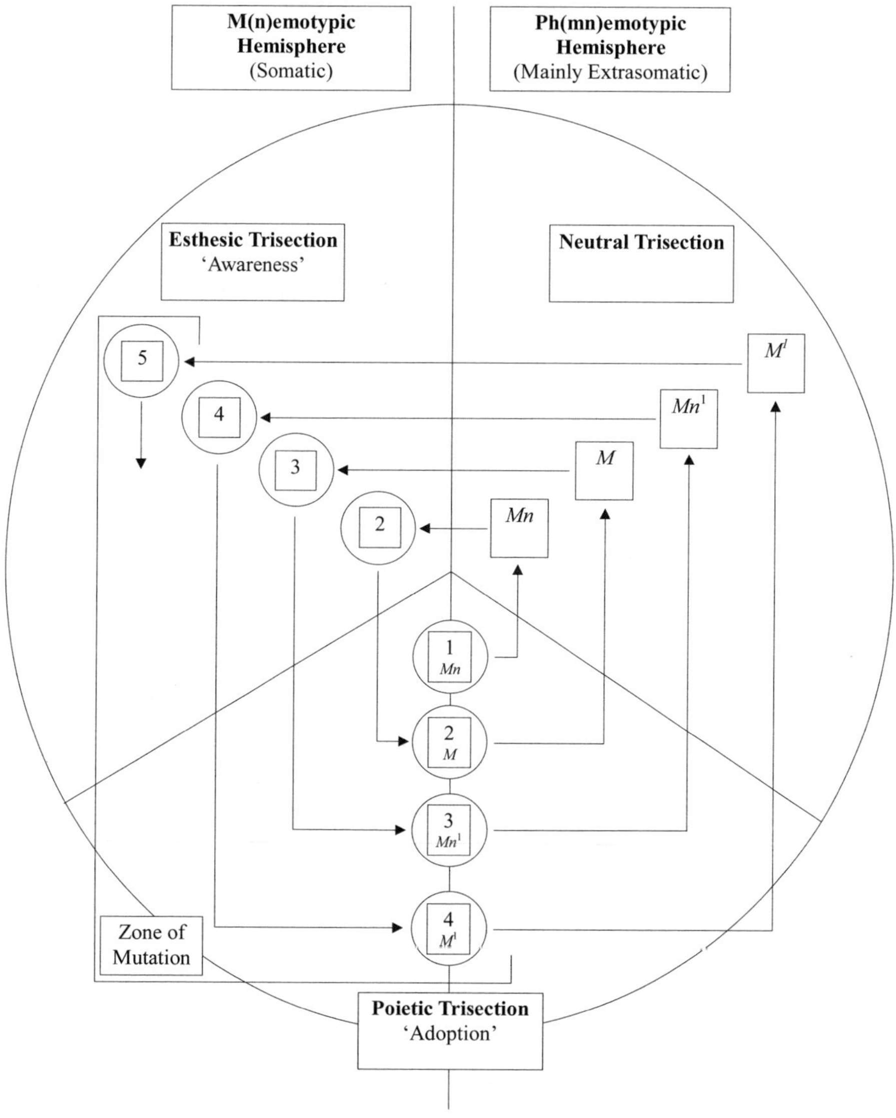

Figure 4.1: Memetic Transmission and Mutation and the Semiological Tripartition

One can regard a mnemon *Mn*, located in the brain of the first (originating) host (1), as situated at the poietic level. The process of conversion into the phmnemotypic form, a musico-graphical or aural incarnation, first moves the mnemon across the somatic-extrasomatic boundary within the poietic level, whereupon the phmnemotype exists in the context of compositional sketches and drafts; and then from the poietic to the neutral level, where it constitutes part of a completed, notated and performed composition.

The second host (2) encounters the mnemon from the standpoint of the esthesic pole, by exposure to its phmnemotypic products. The movement from the esthesic back to the poietic pole within the second host corresponds to the two principal stages of memetic transmission identified by Cavalli-Sforza and Feldman: awareness (knowing a musical idea; memotypic storage) followed by adoption (employing it in real compositional contexts; memotypic storage plus conversion to phemotypic form) (1981: 62–5). Irrespective of whether there is adoption – a composer may be aware of a meme, but not go on to adopt it – awareness (internalized imitation) is the necessary condition for the conversion of a mnemon into a meme.

After adoption, meme *M* – as the unit of cultural information has now become – resides in the brains of both the first and second hosts and may continue to be transmitted largely unaltered to numerous other hosts. Given that a meme is rarely imitated with complete accuracy over any length of time, some changes are almost inevitable during this process. As Figure 4.1 shows, a third host (3) might encounter *M* and subject it to alteration at some stage in the course of its progress through the esthesic-m(n)emotypic, poietic-m(n)emotypic, poietic-ph(mn)emotypic and neutral-ph(mn)emotypic sectors. This 'zone of mutation', the area within which a transmutation can occur, is indicated by a bracket in the figure.

At this stage, the mutant form Mn^1 is mnemonic but not memetic for, like *Mn* earlier, it exists at its moment of genesis (the point of its fixation by a new array of neuronal interconnections) as a theoretically unique unreplicated entity. Forms similar to Mn^1 may exist within the dialect (or may be presumed, in a probabilistic sense, to exist), but these have not been derived causally by means of imitation of Mn^1, or *vice-versa* (homology); by coincidence, they share the same configuration (analogy). If such a particle is imitated by a fourth host (4), it becomes the mutant meme M^1. M^1 may then be subject to further imitation, and possible mutation, by a fifth host (5), and subsequent hosts *ad infinitum*. M^1 may overwrite *M* in the brain of the third host or coexist with it; the mutant may even be encountered by the first two hosts and assimilated, again either overwriting *M* or coexisting with it.

The changes imposed on *M* which result in M^1 might be intentional, accidental or obligatory. While partly overlapping with the first, the third latter category encompasses changes determined by the new context into which the meme must be inserted, for because memes almost always form part of larger complexes, they must reach potentially mutation-inducing accommodations with their temporary partners.

4.3.1. *'Strong' and 'Weak' Memetic Replication*

This model of memetic transmission may be developed further by identifying what may be termed strong and weak senses of memetic replication. These depend in part on the potentially complex interactions between awareness and adoption and between the m(n)emotypic and ph(mn)emotypic forms of the meme. These two senses may be defined as follows. Assuming for the sake of argument in both cases either its *de novo* genesis or its mutation from an extant meme:

- The strong sense of memetic replication ascribes memetic status to a mnemon on the grounds that its phmnemotypic form in one or more works of the originating composer leads to the creation of a memotypic form in the brain of one or more members of that composer's cultural community; and this awareness is then followed (and verified) by adoption. Without such adoption (production of phemotypic forms by one or more subsequent hosts; what might be termed dialect-expression) it is not possible to ascertain the awareness which actually constitutes the memeticization of the mnemon.
- The weak sense of memetic replication ascribes memetic status to a mnemon on the grounds that i) although its phmnemotypic form occurs in one or more works of the originating composer; and that ii) although this form may have led to awareness of the mnemon in that composer's cultural community there are no phemotypic products marking adoption (and therefore awareness), it might still be possible to admit the memeticization of the mnemon on the grounds of a presumed awareness by members of the cultural community owing to their exposure to the phmnemotypic form.

The definition of the weak sense of memetic replication is intended to take into account the truism that it is easier to prove a positive (inherent in the definition of the strong sense) than a negative: it is not possible definitively to assert that a mnemon was not adopted by a member of a cultural community, let alone whether there was no awareness of it in brains long turned to dust. One might easily extend the weak sense to encompass awareness in later cultures, including our own. In this situation, and as a consequence of exposure to what may have been a 'dormant' phmnemotypic form, a long-perished mnemon may be revivified and memeticized and then weak or strong replication may be initiated in contemporary culture.

Strong replication is perhaps most pertinent (certainly in the context of common-practice European musics) to the work of major figures who exerted a clear influence on their musical cultures and whose memes were widely copied in the brains, and manifested in the works, of their contemporaries and immediate successors. Weak replication is arguably most relevant to the music of less significant figures who imitated the music of their major counterparts but whose own innovations, such as they were, were not adopted in their own cultural milieu.

4.3.2. *Mutational Operations*

The music-analytic literature is rich in discussion of the issue of musical similarity and difference and the operations on musical material needed to transform passages exhibiting one relationship into passages exhibiting the other. Ockelford reviews a number of similarity-difference classification taxonomies by such commentators as Serafine (whose scheme is arranged '"relative repetition" … "ornamentation" … and "substantive transformation"'), Réti (who moves through 'imitation … varying … [and] transformation … [to] indirect affinity') and LaRue (who identifies '"recurrence", "development" … "response" … and "contrast"'), noting their rather imprecise and therefore arbitrary divisions (2004: 52, 53; see also Schoenberg 1970: 8–15).

At the heart of all such taxonomies there are three basic operations upon musical material which engender mutation; put in more specifically memetic terms, we could say there are three fundamental ways in which musical memes may be subject to miscopying. What makes for complication are the degrees to which these types of miscopying occur and the various outcomes of their combination. The three basic operations are identified by Ockelford in discussing zygonic relationships between groups (3.3 above). To recall part of an earlier cited passage, he notes that

> Analysing relationships of type 'a' [where 'one group is perceived to derive as a whole from another'] as zygonic invariants suggests that similarity between groups is ultimately dependent on one or more of three processes: the modification of material …, its omission or addition ….
>
> (2004: 53)

Ockelford argues that these three operations – modification, subtraction (omission) and addition – are comparable to several other 'string-matching' processes, including the measurement of pianists' errors in performance, as studied by Repp (: 53). They are also directly analogous to the Damerau-Levenshtein 'edit-distance' metric (Orpen and Huron 1992), in which the number of additions, deletions (subtractions) and substitutions (modifications) required to move from an antecedent to a consequent text/character string are measured. This metric is discussed more fully in Chapter 6.

The mutational operations may be formally defined as follows:

- *Modification*. A pitch or rhythmic element of a meme is changed, the stability of the surrounding elements clarifying its identity as a variant of the antecedent component ($a–b–c \rightarrow a–b^1–c$).
- *Subtraction*. A pitch or rhythmic element of a meme is removed and the surrounding elements, which formerly were discontiguous, are juxtaposed ($a–b–c–d \rightarrow a–c–d$).

- *Addition*. An extra pitch or rhythmic element is interposed between two formerly adjacent elements of the meme, rendering them discontiguous (*a–b–c* → *a–b–d–c*).
- *Substitution*. A composite (two-step) operation consisting of a subtraction followed by an addition (*a–b–c* → *a–c*; *a–c* → *a–d–c* ≡ *a–b–c* → *a–d–c*), the outcome of which is analogous to modification.

These operations are illustrated in Example 4.1 below. For the sake of argument it is assumed that the passages shown in i a, ii a, iii a and iv a are memes (if only in the weak sense), and that the patterns in i b, ii b, iii b and iv b, respectively, are their direct or indirect derivatives which themselves went on to be memeticized (again, if only in the weak sense).

Example 4.1: Unitary and Composite Mutational Operations

i) Modification

a) Haydn: Sonata in E minor Hob. XVI: 47 (before 1766), I, bb. 12–18

b) Mozart: *Don Giovanni* K. 527 (1787), no. 21b, 'In quali eccessi' (1788), bb. 23–30

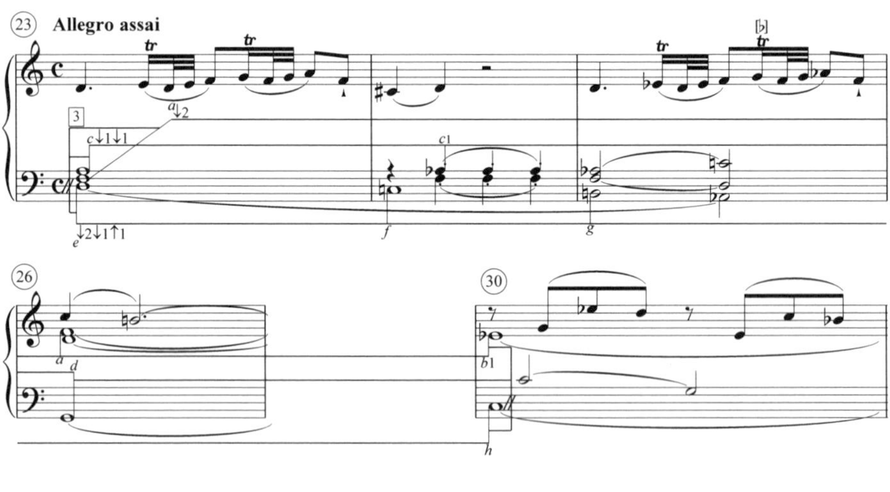

ii) Subtraction

a) Mozart: Sonata in A minor K. 310 (300d) (1778), I, bb. 15–16

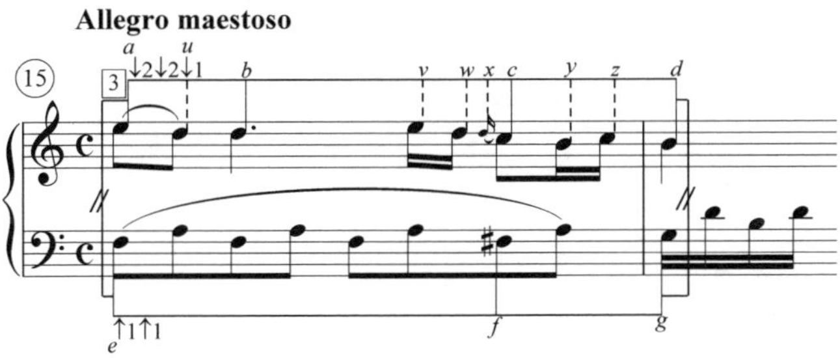

b) Haydn: Quartet in D major op. 64 no. 5 ('Lark') (1790), I, bb. 25–7

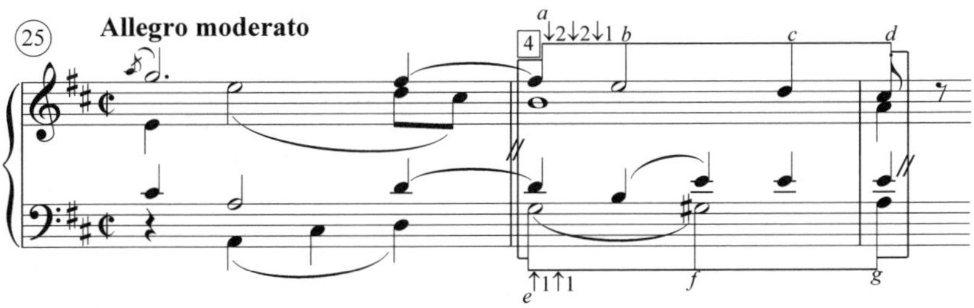

iii) Addition

a) Beethoven: Sonata in E♭ major op. 81a (‘*Les Adieux*’) (1809), I, bb. 1–2

b) Mahler: Symphony no. 9 (1909), IV, bb. 1–3

iv) Composite Operations

a) Mozart: *Die Zauberflöte* K. 620 (1791), no. 17, 'Ach, ich fühl's', bb. 1–4

b) Verdi: *La Traviata* (1853), no. 6, 'Ah, fors'è lui che l'anima', bb. 26–32

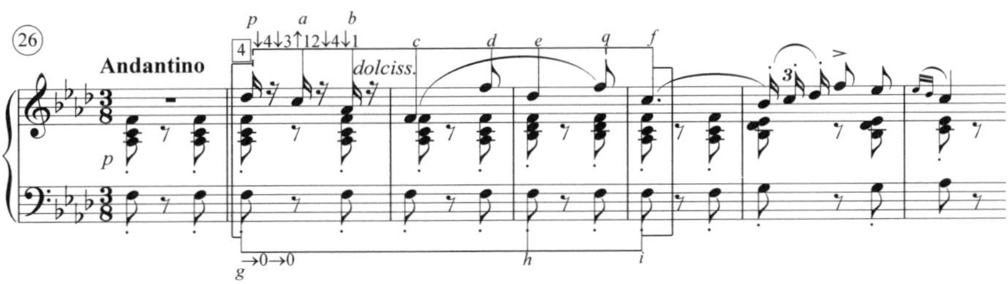

In Example 4.1 i a, the fifth of the local supertonic chord in b. 14 is modified in bb. 17–18 by chromatic change of one note, element *c*, as part of an elaborated restatement. A similar sequence, in a different tonal context and at a deeper structural level, is shown in i b.

In Example 4.1 ii a, Mozart's meme, variants of which are commonly used to articulate the V/V/V (or, as here, V/V/III) before the imperfect cadence on V/V at the end of a sonata form expositional transition (Rosen 1988: 235), is reduced to its basic components – the $\hat{2}$–$\hat{1}$–$\hat{7}$ motion over $\hat{4}$–$\sharp\hat{4}$–$\hat{5}$; elements *a–g* – in the Haydn passage ii b by the removal of the diminutions *u–z*. An interpretation of the passages as examples of subtraction might, however, be weakened if it were shown that patterns such as ii b had an earliest antecedent which predated the earliest antecedent of ii a. If this scenario were demonstrated to be generally true – that the basic tendency in all replicator mutations is towards increasing not decreasing complexity (subject to the constraints of a copying-infidelity and memorability threshold situated somewhere on the *x–y* axis of Figure 3.2 above) – then subtraction would be undermined as a valid memetic-mutational category.

In Example 4.1 iii, Beethoven's 'Lebewohl' descending figure is modified by the simple addition (repetition) of the f^1, creating an appoggiatura, element *z*, in Mahler's version. In a sense, the passage shown in i b might also be regarded as an example of addition, for while it consists of the same replicated elements as the second statement in i a (bb. 17–18), its deeper structural location means that it is prolonged by the interpolation of components which are not also replicated in i a.

These examples of modification, subtraction and addition represent simple and clear-cut cases of processes which, while regularly occurring in isolation, are also often combined. The Mozart and Verdi passages in Example 4.1 iv show such composite operations. As a shallow-middleground-level meme, most of the Verdi copy can be seen as subtracting foreground diminutions from the Mozart, in particular the elements *t–z*, yet it also adds the diminutions *p* and *q* to the basic framework, making the relationship more than one of simple subtraction.

Another type of composite mutation, which might be called memetic hybridization, is represented in Figure 4.2 below. This is the memetic analogue to genetic crossing-over during meiosis, where 'bits of each paternal chromosome physically detach themselves and change places with exactly corresponding bits of maternal chromosome' (Dawkins 1989: 27). The 'bits', in question may be whole genes, which therefore remain intact during crossing-over, or parts of genes, which are consequently fragmented and recombined. In Figure 4.2, which uses various changing-note schemata to illustrate this process in memetics, feature memes comprising the first halves (initial events) of two schemata in effect 'detach themselves' from the feature memes of the second halves (terminal events) and then one or both of each corresponding pair changes places and reattaches to its associated event, giving rise, at the middleground (schematic) level, to a hybrid form.

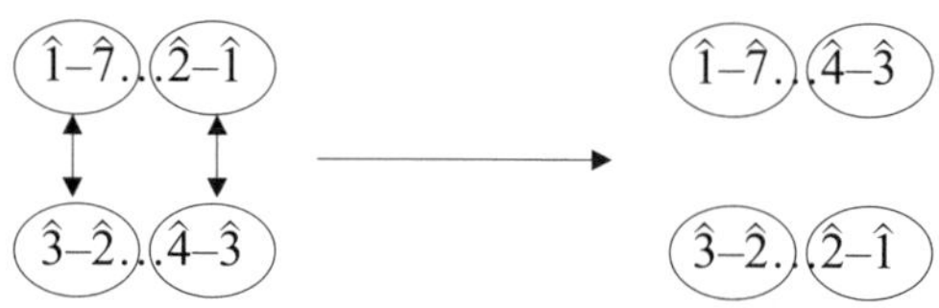

Figure 4.2: Memetic Hybridization via Schematic 'Crossing-Over'

The notion of copying fidelity implies that the more extended and elaborate a meme, the greater the likelihood that fragmentation, and thus potential crossing-over, will occur. Those middleground memes resulting from binary associations of foreground patterning, such as the changing-note schemata, would seem especially susceptible to such hybridization.

Pitches in Example 4.1 above are not only marked with the *a–b–c* symbols from the bullet points preceding it but also with letters from the end of the alphabet: stable meme components are marked with an alphabetic sequence starting at *a*, whereas those elements subject to mutation (specifically to addition and subtraction) are marked with an alphabetic sequence ending at *z* and also with dotted lines. Apart from such cases as element *a* in Example 4.1 i, the former tend to be situated at the shallow-middleground level whereas the latter are foreground-orientated. Structural-hierarchic location is therefore important in any consideration of mutational operations, for while modification acts upon meme components at a variety of levels – such as the chromatic change in Example 4.1 i b – addition and subtraction tend to act upon the diminutions which separate the components of memes orientated at deeper levels – such as the appoggiatura f^1 in Example 4.1 iii b. In the latter case, it might be argued that the meme itself is not mutated; only if the entire sequence of events represented by elements *a*, *b*, *c* and *z* were replicated unchanged in two or more contexts (in addition to the two or more contexts in which elements *a*, *b* and *c* were replicated) would it be possible to speak of a new, mutant meme being replicated. Consequently, one might say that:

- To speak of mutational operations upon a meme, as opposed to those upon a mnemon, the antecedent particle must be replicated in two or more contexts before the mutational operation is applied to it; and the consequent (mutated) particle will remain a mnemon until it is itself replicated.
- If a meme exists at the extreme foreground level, any mutation will, by definition, affect meme elements, for every pitch between the meme's initial and terminal nodes is replicated, even if some elements of the meme are situated at deeper structural levels, as a shallow-middleground-level framework.
- If a meme exists at a deeper structural level (the shallow-middleground or above), then mutation may affect meme elements only (components whose replication is necessary for the definition of the meme), or the patterning in the interstices of meme elements only (components not necessary for the definition of the meme), or some combination of both.
- While interstitial patterning may itself form part of generative foreground-level memes, if monadic or dyadic it may alternatively constitute a further class of non-memetic material to add to that outlined in 3.3.4 above.

The stringency of the first of these points may mean that, in many cases, what is most often altered are the non-memetic foreground-level diminutions separating and prolonging elements of a shallow-middleground-level meme which, in consequence, remains relatively stable over time.

Finally, whereas genes are propagated as such (genes reproduce, not bodies), memes are propagated phemotypically (via the behaviours and artefacts they engender). It follows that whereas genetic mutation is purely a result of mechanisms operative at the level of the genotype and is not influenced by phenotypic factors, memetic mutation may occur as a result of the process of transformation between a meme's memotypic and phemotypic states. However, when a meme is transformed from one form to another in the brain of a single individual, such mutation is non-phemotypic; conversely, the necessarily phemotypic propagation of memes does not invariably give rise to mutation.

The evolutionary pressure exerted by the phemotypic propagation of memes means that whereas Weismannism (1.2.2 above) holds unconditionally true for genetic evolution – changes in the form of the body do not feed back into changes in the genetic structure – a neo-Darwinian view of memetic evolution is compelled to make a small, Lamarckian concession (1.2.1 above). It must acknowledge that '[t]he equivalent of Weismannism is less rigid for memes than for genes: there may be "Lamarckian" causal arrows leading from phe[m]otype to replicator, as well as the other way around' (Dawkins 1983a: 112).

4.3.3. *Implication-Realization and Memetic Mutation*

As discussed in 3.3.2 above, Narmour's i-r model is a useful tool in understanding the segmentation of the musical continuum into discrete units which, as a consequence of their resultant particulateness, have the potential to serve as units of musico-memetic transmission. Here, I consider how the i-r model can also facilitate our understanding of memetic mutation and selection. There are two main aspects to this issue: the role of implications and their realizations in acting as a driving force for memetic mutation; and the role of implications and their realizations or denials in determining the perceptual-cognitive salience (and therefore the selection prospects) of individual memes. I examine the first of these here and the second in 4.4 below.

In a revealing passage discussing the relationship of the i-r model to the process of stylistic development, Narmour notes that

> Style – intra- and extraopus norms – [is] both the source of specific implications and the framework by which they are evaluated. Strength of implication would be directly related to the number of times such and such a realization had followed such and such an implication.[3] From without, a listener would recognize an implicative pattern and judge its strength by remembering various statistical recurrences of syntactic relationships in the style. From within, the realization of an implication already anticipated by the listener on the basis of prior knowledge and learning would contribute to the systematic aspect of the style. Further repetitions of these implied realizations would serve to reaffirm the systematic (synchronic) aspect, whereas a novel realization or a novel denial would weaken the system and emphasize the diachronic aspect of style – as a historical process undergoing change. A new style would be established once a novel realization or a novel denial recurred.
>
> (1977: 127)

In this sense,

---

[3] Here, Narmour is referring to implications motivated by top-down (learned, schematic) factors. In later work (1990, 1992), he prioritizes bottom-up (innate, Gestalt-driven) implications.

> musical works do seem to have implicative ancestors. The high-level descending chromatic linear bass lines that generate such striking changes of harmony in the works of Beethoven …, Brahms …, and Tchaikovsky …, for instance, find their progenitors in the more localized, diatonic chaconne and passacaglia basses of the Baroque. What I wish to argue here, however, is not just that familial relationships exist among certain structures in the history of music – which is well-known – but rather that structural changes in style result partly from realizations of latent implications.
>
> (: 130)

He gives an example (1977: 129, Example 44) showing a schematic representation of style change driven by the realization of implications. A hypothetical style, consisting of just two melodies outlining the fifth c^1–g^1 in $\frac{3}{4}$ 𝅗𝅥 ♩ rhythm, is shown to have certain melodic and rhythmic implications. On their realization, these broaden the style's melodic range to encompass the upper neighbour note a^1, giving rise to the new pitch structure g^1–a^1–g^1; and they create new rhythmic (𝅗𝅥 ♩ | ♩ 𝅗𝅥) and, consequentially, metrical ($\frac{4}{4}$) structures.

By realizing such implications a composer may create a new mnemon; if such 'a novel realization … recurred' – if it were replicated – then a new meme would be created. Musical memes therefore carry within them, as a result of their internal implicative tendencies, an inherent mutational drive, a propensity to generate variant forms which realize the 'latent implications' of their antecedents.

4.4. Memetic Selection

Selection and differential fitness represent two sides of the same coin: selection is a process whereby some replicators are differentially (preferentially) copied in the relentless competition for representation in the next 'generation'; whereas differential fitness is an attribute which measures a replicator's reproductive success in the face of various selection pressures. Costall notes the importance of the 'selection analogy' to theories of culture change, recalling that in the late-nineteenth century the anthropologist Alfred Haddon studied

> the 'life-histories of designs'.... he argued that the determination of the provenance of a decorative form should, as in biology, be informed by careful classification of its structure complemented by an analysis of its geographical distribution .... Furthermore, in order to clarify the processes of transformation, the anthropologist should again follow the biologist's lead and conduct 'breeding' experiments where changes in cultural forms are recorded as they occur across different 'generations' .... Haddon cites the experiments conducted by Pitt-Rivers and Balfour in which they asked one person to copy a design and then pass it on to another person who, in turn, copied it, and so on. Haddon's basic point, however, concerned the analogy of selection, the idea that the fate of a design is to be 'subject to vicissitudes very similar to those which beset the existence of any organism' ....
>
> (1991: 324–5)

Passing over Costall's subtle discussion of the role of intentionality in both biological and cultural selection, one should note his relegation of memetic selection to the status of a 'mere analogy' with that in biology (: 331). To reiterate the argument outlined in 1.3 above, universal Darwinism holds that the operation of selection in culture is not (weakly) analogous to its operation in biology but is instead a (strong) parallelism based upon commonalities in the properties of replicators in a variety of substrates.

4.4.1. *Cultural Selection and the Units of Selection Controversy*

Regulating the replication of memes within cultural systems, cultural selection is Cavalli-Sforza's and Feldman's parallel to the natural selection which mediates the replication of genes within living systems. They define it as

> the rate or probability that a given innovation, skill, type, trait, or specific cultural activity or object – all of which we shall call, for brevity, *traits* – will be accepted in a given time unit by an individual representative of the population.
>
> (1981: 15; their emphasis)

Differential replication leads to change in the relative frequency of memes – traits, in Cavalli-Sforza's and Feldman's terminology – and their mutants in the meme pool over time, for a variant of an existing meme may persist and increase its numerical and statistical representation or it may become extinct, according to whether it is more or less susceptible to imitation as a result of the changes it has undergone. This notion of propensity to imitation (fecundity) is directly analogous to the biological concept of reproductive fitness; it is an index of a replicator's capacity for motivating its duplication which Cavalli-Sforza and Feldman term cultural fitness (1981: 17). In biological replication, a gene's fitness is contingent upon the phenotypes it plays a role in engendering in collaboration with its allies. A corresponding situation obtains in cultural replication, for a meme is not selected directly but by virtue of its phemotypic consequences and those of its allies in particular cultural products.

An account of cultural selection would be incomplete without consideration of the relevance of the units of selection controversy to memetics (1.2.3 above). In terms of the hierarchy represented in Figure 3.9 above, does cultural selection function at the level of the individual movement or work, at the level of idiom, genre or structural type, or even higher, at the level of dialect and rules? In the light of Haddon's 'basic point', it might initially seem appealing to suggest that changes in the configuration of works constituting and defining a musical dialect – his 'designs' – are subject to selection, the dialect moving towards the configuration of those works which are selected. But does selection actually operate at the level of the work, equivalent to the level of the individual organism in biological terms?

The logic of universal Darwinism dictates that because the core orientation of evolutionary replicator theory is toward the lowest level of replicator-structural/cultural hierarchies; and because the gene-selection hypothesis asserts that 'the fundamental unit of selection, and therefore of self-interest' (Dawkins 1989: 11) in living organisms is the near-indivisibly-particulate segment of chromosome, then the meme should be regarded as the unit of cultural selection. On this reasoning, evolutionary change in biology and culture is the consequence of mutations in individual genes or memes which sometimes confer competitive/perceptual-cognitive advantages upon the individuals or works in which they reside such that, after selection, these replicators are more likely to be represented in the next generation. Within the replicator pool of a species or dialect, these variants tend automatically to increase their representation, leading eventually to bottom-up-driven structural change in the genetic or memetic profile of the species or dialect.

4.4.2. *Implication-Realization and Memetic Selection*

The i-r model (3.3.2 above) contends that, beyond their purely structural (processive, closural) function, the delay or denial of a realization is one source of the affective power of music. To recall, a minimum of three events are needed to allow for an implication (between events one and two) and an associated realization or frustration (between events two and three). The pattern may of course go on to incorporate further events, or be terminated by a 'd', 'h' or 'b' interruption. Put simply, implications that are quickly realized are experienced as affectively weak, whereas delayed or even suppressed realizations are perceived as affectively charged. Such affect is generally non-connotative: the denial is registered in a physiological and subconscious manner rather than in verbal-conceptual terms, so we feel the emotion viscerally rather than process it cerebrally (Meyer 1956: 31, 256ff.). Sometimes, however, denials are so slight as barely to disturb our affective equanimity. Either way, in Narmour's opinion,

> what we are talking about here is surprise not in the sense of astonishment or being startled but rather in the sense of tiny cognitive 'jolts' to the neuronal electrical system governing our subconscious cognitive expectations. So minute are these 'renunciations' that natural-language terms like *surprise* and *denial* (as well as traditional symbols like exclamation marks) seem too strong.
>
> (1990: 138; his emphases)

Of course, many independent variables are at play in such considerations, but, as he observes,

> The important empirical point is that similarity, proximity, and common direction [the innate, bottom-up Gestalt laws, upon which the implication-realization model is based] can be measured and defined in a rigorous sense, whereas notions of 'good' and 'best' [associated with the top-down Gestalt laws, which the implication-realization model rejects as variable and culturally determined] cannot.
>
> (: 63)

In theory at least, this distinction allows the possibility of measuring the 'tiny cognitive "jolts"' objectively, and therefore of comparing intra-meme implications systematically.

The i-r dynamic may be a factor in memetic selection because when a meme mutates a form may arise which has what might be termed a greater i-r 'potential' (hereafter 'i-r*p*') than its antecedent.[4] By this, and further to the opening remarks in this section, I mean that if a weak intra-meme implication is realized immediately, or if the realization is delayed only briefly, then the meme might be said to have a low i-r*p* and, concomitantly, low perceptual-cognitive salience. By contrast, if a strong intra-meme realization is delayed significantly, or is not forthcoming – perhaps as a result of closure of the meme by means of an interruption – then the meme might be said to have a high i-r*p* and, concomitantly, a high perceptual-cognitive salience.

A more significant factor in calculating i-r*p* than this aspect of proximity of realization, however, is the internal intervallic structure of implications and realizations. To formalize the i-r*p* of a given meme, one must account for the fact that i) as an interval approaches the limen of the augmented fourth (6), its 'continuation implication' declines and its 'reversal implication' increases (Narmour 1990: 80, Fig. 5.1); and that ii) realizations of similarity

---

[4] I use the word 'potential' here in analogy to its sense in physics, as an i-r 'charge' or pressure arising between two pitches which is either 'discharged' (realized) or intensified (frustrated) at the third pitch.

> decrease or increase the degree of ongoing implication with reference to the initial (modeling) interval. Moreover, this is measurable: an ascending C–D–F constitutes a stronger implicative process [P] than an ascending C–D–E (by a half step), whereas C–D–E♭ is slightly weaker (again by a half step).
>
> (: 88)

Narmour attempts to categorize the i-r patterns according to 'the aesthetic effect inherent in the various structures' (: 343). While not adhering strictly to his categorizations, my numerical weightings reflect his differentiation between patterns engendering 'no surprise', 'some surprise' and 'great surprise' (: 343).

Table 4.1 below, which takes into account the intervallic-implicative distinctions shown in Figure 3.3 above, assigns i-r*p* values to the fifteen i-r functions identified by Narmour. While the absolute sizes of the i-r*p* values is perhaps not crucial, the differentials between them need to reflect the variable salience of the different i-r structures; and it is naturally important that the values are used consistently in any comparative exercise. To this end, I employ five basic strategies, summarized below, to calculate i-r*p*. These attempt to mediate between and quantify the aspects of initial (x) and terminal (y) interval size and, therefore, the degrees of realization or denial of x's intervallic implications within and between each group of function-exemplars:[5]

- *For P, (R) and (IR)*, the integer value of the i-r*p* derives from the initial interval (x) and the decimal value derives from the intervallic difference (y–x); therefore i-r*p* = $x.(y–x)$.
- *For IP, (IP), R, IR and (VR)*, the integer value of the i-r*p* derives from the initial interval and the decimal value derives from the terminal interval; therefore i-r*p* = $x.y$.
- *For (P), VP, (VP) and VR*, the i-r*p* value is an integer derived by summing the component intervals; therefore i-r*p* = $x + y$.
- *For D*, the i-r*p* is assigned a fixed value of 0.5.
- *For ID and (ID)*, the i-r*p* is an integer deriving from the first interval; therefore i-r*p* = x.

5 This approach is supported in principle by Professor Narmour (personal communication, 2 December 2004).

Table 4.1: Implication-Realization Functions and I-R*P* Values

Key
The first column shows the names of and symbols for the various i-r functions and indicates the strategy employed for calculating the i-r*p* value (see above). The second column defines each function formally (after Narmour 1989 and 1990 *passim*). In the third column, the wedge symbol ('▶') indicates the beginning of a group of configurations with the same *x* value. Under 'Intervallic Profile (•*x*•*y*•)', arrows and integers separated by dots ('•', representing pitches) indicate the size (in semitones) and direction (up, down, lateral) of melodic motion within an i-r pattern. Positive or negative integer values under 'Intervallic Difference (*y*–*x*)' indicate intervallic differentiation within an i-r pattern. The final (decimal or integer) number on each line is the i-r*p* value itself.

Function and Symbol/ I-R*P* Calculation Strategy	**Definition**	**Group**	**Intervallic Profile (•*x*• *y*•)**	**Intervallic Difference (*y*–*x*)**	**i-r*p* Value**
Prospective (registral-intervallic) Process ┌—P—┐ i-r*p* = *x*.(*y*-*x*)	After small interval (≤ P4 (5 semitones)): • implication of intervallic similarity realized (**I** = **A+A**; defined as 2 adjacent intervals differing by *y*–*x* = –m3…+m3 (–3…+3 semitones)); • implication of registral continuation of ascent or descent in same direction realized (**V** = **A+A**).	▶	•↑/↓1•↑/↓1•	0	**1.0**
			•↑/↓1•↑/↓2•	+1	**1.1**
			•↑/↓1•↑/↓3•	+2	**1.2**
			•↑/↓1•↑/↓4•	+3	**1.3**
		▶	•↑/↓2•↑/↓1•	–1	**2.1**
			•↑/↓2•↑/↓2•	0	**2.0**
			•↑/↓2•↑/↓3•	+1	**2.1**
			•↑/↓2•↑/↓4•	+2	**2.2**
			•↑/↓2•↑/↓5•	+3	**2.3**
		▶ etc.			
Retrospective (registral-intervallic) Process ┌—(P)—┐ i-r*p* = *x* + *y*	After large interval (≥ P5 (7 semitones)): • implication of intervallic differentiation denied (**I** = **A+A**; defined as 2 adjacent intervals differing by *y*–*x* = –m3…+m3); • implication of registral reversal denied (**V** = **A+A**).	▶	•↑/↓7•↑/↓10•	+3	**17**
			•↑/↓7•↑/↓9•	+2	**16**
			•↑/↓7•↑/↓8•	+1	**15**
			•↑/↓7•↑/↓7•	0	**14**
			•↑/↓7•↑/↓6•	–1	**13**
			•↑/↓7•↑/↓5•	–2	**12**
			•↑/↓7•↑/↓4•	–3	**11**
		▶	•↑/↓8•↑/↓11•	+3	**19**
			•↑/↓8•↑/↓10•	+2	**18**
			•↑/↓8•↑/↓9•	+1	**17**
			•↑/↓8•↑/↓8•	0	**16**
			•↑/↓8•↑/↓7•	–1	**15** etc.
		▶ etc.			
Prospective Intervallic Process ┌—IP—┐ i-r*p* = *x*.*y*	Partial denial of **P**. After small interval (≤ P4): • implication of intervallic similarity realized (**I** = **A+A**; defined as 2 adjacent intervals differing by *y*–*x* = –M2…+M2 (–2…+2 semitones)); • implication of registral continuation denied (**V** = **A+B**).	▶	•↑/↓1•↓/↑2•	+1	**1.2**
			•↑/↓1•↓/↑3•	+2	**1.3**
		▶	•↑/↓2•↓/↑1•	–1	**2.1**
			•↑/↓2•↓/↑3•	+1	**2.3**
			•↑/↓2•↓/↑4•	+2	**2.4**
		▶ etc.			

Table 4.1 Continued

Function and Symbol/ I-R*P* Calculation Strategy	Definition	Group	Intervallic Profile (•*x*• *y*•)	Intervallic Difference (*y*–*x*)	i-r*p* Value
Retrospective Intervallic Process ┌─(IP)─┐ i-r*p* = *x.y*	After large interval (≥ P5): • implication of intervallic differentiation <u>denied</u> (**I** = **A+A**; defined as 2 adjacent intervals differing by *y*–*x* = –M2…+M2); • implication of registral reversal <u>realized</u> (**V** = **A+B**).	▶	•↑/↓7•↓/↑5•	–2	**7.5**
			•↑/↓7•↓/↑6•	–1	**7.6**
			•↑/↓7•↓/↑8•	+1	**7.8**
			•↑/↓7•↓/↑9•	+2	**7.9**
		▶	•↑/↓8•↓/↑6•	–2	**8.6**
			•↑/↓8•↓/↑7•	–1	**8.7**
			•↑/↓8•↓/↑9•	+1	**8.9**
			•↑/↓8•↓/↑10•	+2	**9.0**
		▶ etc.			
Prospective Registral (Vector) Process ┌─VP─┐ i-r*p* = *x* + *y*	Partial denial of **P**. After small interval (≤ P4): • implication of intervallic similarity <u>denied</u> (**I** = **A+B**; defined as 2 adjacent intervals differing by *y*–*x* ≥ +M3 (4 semitones)); • implication of registral continuation <u>realized</u> (**V** = **A+A**); Intervallic and symmetrical opposite of **IR**.	▶	•↑/↓1•↑/↓5•	+4	**6.0**
			•↑/↓1•↑/↓6•	+5	**7.0**
			•↑/↓1•↑/↓7•	+6	**8.0** etc.
		▶	•↑/↓2•↑/↓6•	+4	**8.0**
			•↑/↓2•↑/↓7•	+5	**9.0** etc.
		▶ etc.			
Retrospective Registral (Vector) Process ┌─(VP)─┐ i-r*p* = *x* + *y*	After large interval (≥ P5): • implication of intervallic differentiation <u>realized</u> (**I** = **A+B**; defined as 2 adjacent intervals differing by *y*–*x* ≥ +M3); • implication of registral reversal <u>denied</u> (**V** = **A+A**);	▶	•↑/↓7•↑/↓11•	+4	**18**
			•↑/↓7•↑/↓12•	+5	**19**
			•↑/↓7•↑/↓13•	+6	**20** etc.
		▶	•↑/↓8•↑/↓12•	+4	**20**
			•↑/↓8•↑/↓13•	+5	**21** etc.
		▶ etc.			
Duplication ┌─D─┐ i-r*p* = 0.5	Iteration of a pitch (x–x–x), creating 'lateral' registral motion (**V** = **A+A**) and unison intervallic structure (**I** = **A+A**).		•→0•→0•	0	**0.5**
Prospective Intervallic Duplication ┌─ID─┐ i-r*p* = *x*	Partial denial of **P**. After small interval (≤ P4): • implication of intervallic similarity <u>realized</u> (**I** = **A+A**); • implication of registral continuation <u>denied</u> (**V** = **A+B**). 'Zigzagging' intervals (up–down; down–up) are identical.		•↑/↓1•↓/↑1•	0	**1.0**
			•↑/↓2•↓/↑2•	0	**2.0**
		▶ etc.			

Table 4.1 Continued

Function and Symbol/ I-R*P* Calculation Strategy	Definition	Group	Intervallic Profile (•*x*• *y*•)	Intervallic Difference (*y*–*x*)	i-r*p* Value
Retrospective Intervallic Duplication ┌─(ID)─┐ i-r*p* = *x*	Partial denial of **R**. After large interval (≥ P5): • implication of intervallic differentiation denied (**I** = **A+A**); and • implication of registral reversal realized (**V** = **A+B**). 'Zigzagging' intervals are identical.		•↑/↓7•↓/↑7•	0	**7.0**
			•↑/↓8•↓/↑8•	0	**8.0**
		▶ etc.			
Prospective (intervallic-registral) Reversal ┌─R─┐ i-r*p* = *x.y*	Intervallic and registral opposite of **P** and **D**. After large interval (≥P5): • implication of intervallic differentiation realized (**I** = **A+B**; defined as 2 adjacent intervals differing by *y*–*x* ≤ –m3); • implication of registral reversal realized (**V** = **A+B**).	▶	•↑/↓7•↓/↑4•	–3	**7.4**
			•↑/↓7•↓/↑3•	–4	**7.3**
			•↑/↓7•↓/↑2•	–5	**7.2**
			•↑/↓7•↓/↑1•	–6	**7.1**
		▶	•↑/↓8•↓/↑5•	–3	**8.5**
			•↑/↓8•↓/↑4•	–4	**8.4** etc.
		▶ etc.			
Retrospective (intervallic-registral) Reversal ┌─(R)─┐ i-r*p* = *x*.(*y*–*x*)	After small interval (≤P4): • implication of intervallic similarity denied (**I** = **A+B**; defined as 2 adjacent intervals differing by *y*–*x* ≤ –m3); • implication of registral continuation denied (**V** = **A+B**).	▶	•↑/↓4•↓/↑1•	–3	**4.3**
		▶	•↑/↓5•↓/↑2•	–3	**5.3**
			•↑/↓5•↓/↑1•	–4	**5.4**
Prospective Intervallic Reversal ┌─IR─┐ i-r*p* = *x.y*	Partial denial of **R**. After large interval (≥P5): • implication of intervallic differentiation realized (**I** = **A+B**; defined as 2 adjacent intervals differing by *y*–*x* ≤ –M3); • implication of registral reversal denied (**V** = **A+A**).	▶	•↑/↓7•↑/↓3•	–4	**7.3**
			•↑/↓7•↑/↓2•	–5	**7.2**
			•↑/↓7•↑/↓1•	–6	**7.1**
		▶	•↑/↓8•↑/↓4•	–4	**8.4**
			•↑/↓8•↑/↓3•	–5	**8.3**
			•↑/↓8•↑/↓2•	–6	**8.2**
			•↑/↓8•↑/↓1•	–7	**8.1**
		▶ etc.			

Table 4.1 Concluded

Function and Symbol/ I-R*P* Calculation Strategy	**Definition**	**Group**	**Intervallic Profile (•*x*• *y*•)**	**Intervallic Difference (*y*–*x*)**	**i-r*p* Value**
Retrospective Intervallic Reversal ┌─(IR)─┐ i-r*p* = *x*.(*y*–*x*)	After small interval (≤ P4): • implication of intervallic similarity <u>denied</u> (**I** = **A**+**B**; defined as 2 adjacent intervals differing by *y*–*x* ≤ –M3); • implication of registral continuation <u>realized</u> (**V** = **A**+**A**).	▶	•↑/↓5•↑/↓1•	–4	**5.4**
Prospective Registral (Vector) Reversal ┌─VR─┐ i-r*p* = *x* + *y*	Partial denial of **R**. After large interval (≥P5): • implication of intervallic differentiation <u>denied</u> (**I** = **A**+**B**; defined as 2 adjacent intervals differing by *y*–*x* ≥ +m3); • implication of registral reversal <u>realized</u> (**V** = **A**+**B**). Registral and symmetrical opposite of **VP**.	▶	•↑/↓7•↓/↑10•	+3	**17**
			•↑/↓7•↓/↑11•	+4	**18**
			•↑/↓7•↓/↑12•	+5	**19** etc.
		▶	•↑/↓8•↓/↑11•	+3	**19**
			•↑/↓8•↓/↑12•	+4	**20** etc.
		▶ etc.			
Retrospective Registral (Vector) Reversal ┌─(VR)─┐ i-r*p* = *x*.*y*	After small interval (≤ P4): • implication of intervallic similarity <u>denied</u> (**I** = **A**+**B**; defined as 2 adjacent intervals differing by *y*–*x* ≥ +m3); • implication of registral continuation <u>denied</u> (**V** = **A**+**B**).	▶	•↑/↓1•↓/↑4•	+3	**1.4**
			•↑/↓1•↓/↑5•	+4	**1.5**
			•↑/↓1•↓/↑6•	+5	**1.6** etc.
		▶	•↑/↓2•↓/↑5•	+3	**2.5**
			•↑/↓2•↓/↑6•	+4	**2.6** etc.
		▶ etc.			

By summing the i-r*p* weightings for each of the component i-r structures of a meme, one arrives at a numerical quantification of the meme's perceptual-cognitive salience. One may use this value to compare the meme with others, including its evolutionary antecedents and consequents. The application of i-r*p* will be illustrated in the next section, but before this it is necessary to outline three important caveats to the concept of i-r*p*.

First, it seems likely that rising i-r*p* values do not map indefinitely onto rising estimations of perceptual-cognitive salience and rising memorability. There must come a threshold when the perceptual-cognitive load imposed on the listener by a meme with a high i-r*p* militates against that meme's comprehension and/or storage – the meme is too complex to process and/or to memorize. At the very least, memes with a high i-r*p* seem more likely to have a lower copying-fidelity than those with a lower i-r*p* value. We might represent this relationship diagramatically as in Figure 4.3 below. It is hypothesized that perceptual-cognitive salience will continue to rise slightly in tandem with rising i-r*p* even as memorability begins to fall, for we may find certain patterns striking even if we cannot memorize them successfully. Thus, given that a high i-r*p* often (but not invariably) correlates with a high number of meme elements, the regular $x = y$ relationship between number of meme elements and rising perceptual-cognitive salience and memorability posited in Figure 3.2 above is over simplistic.

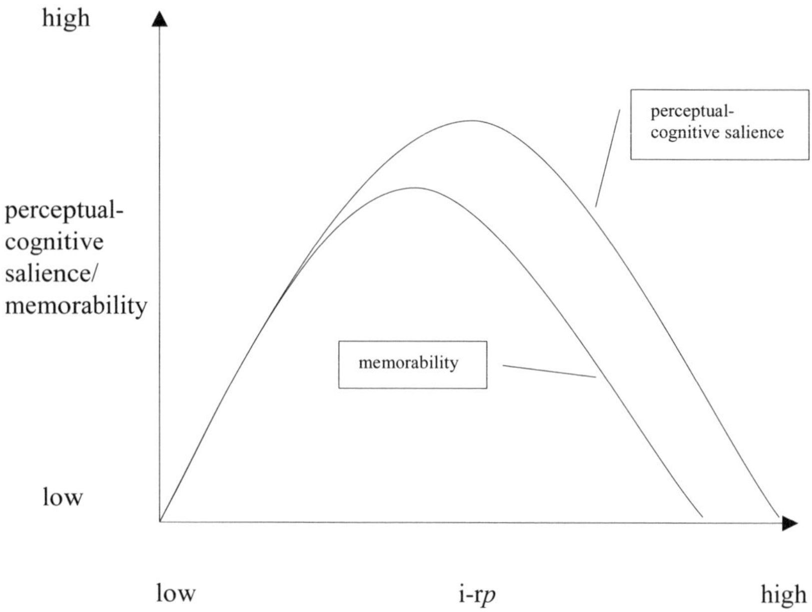

Figure 4.3: Hypothesized Relationship Between I-R*P*, Perceptual-Cognitive Salience and Memorability

As a second caveat, Narmour is careful to point out that such bottom-up implications as are quantified in my system by i-r*p* values have to be reconciled with top-down, culturally-acquired schemata (style structures), and with the prevailing tonal context.[6] He cautions that

---

[6] As an example of the influence of tonal context, the magical horn $b\flat^1$ (replacing the normative $\hat{6}$ with $\flat\hat{6}$) in b. 59^3 (from b. 30^3) of 'September' from Strauss's *Vier Letzte Lieder* (1948) seems to impart to its parent ii–ii$^{6}{}_{5(\flat)3}$ meme a perceptual-cognitive salience greater than that explicable in terms of the difference in i-r*p* between the diatonic and the chromatic forms. This salience may also be augmented by the 'echo-effect' of verbal-conceptual memes co-adapted (as evidenced by their alliance at b. 30) with the musical meme.

> a representative style-structural complex with denial as one of its learned properties can inhibit the implication of the melodic style-shape simplex that in part invokes it.... if one wants to evaluate the degree of implication inherent in any initial interval, one has to show empirically which conformant extraopus style structures are relevant to the context of the melodic interval at hand.... though style shapes literally constitute style structures, paradoxically, noncongruent implications between the shapes and structures of style frequently exist.
>
> (1990: 138–9, 142)

As a third and broader caveat, while the notion of i-r*p* offers a means of formalizing a class of bottom-up meme attributes and thereby predicting which patterns may be generally most salient, it does not account for the myriad other factors which affect how we perceive patterns in music. Not only must we take into account the various extraopus schemata particular to a given style (the second caveat), we must also consider the various intraopus (idiostructural) processes which highlight or downplay the salience of patterns in their diachronic context. Most dauntingly of all, we must show awareness of – although, by definition, we cannot realistically hope fully to account for – the various personal and emotional factors each individual person brings to the experience of musical listening, which may intensify or attenuate perceptions of salience arising from bottom-up processes.

Despite these various obstacles, it seems prudent to begin to answer the question 'what makes a meme memorable?' with a consideration of those elements of musical perception and cognition that are innate and objective, and which may therefore be modelled and quantified to some degree, and then, when this ground is secure, to move on to those factors which are acquired and subjective. In this sense, the conclusions one might draw from an index such as the i-r*p* are necessary but not sufficient for a comprehensive assessment of the perceptual-cognitive salience of a meme.

Bearing these three caveats in mind, and *ceteris paribus*, it is nevertheless logical to assert that if the i-r*p* of a mutant meme is greater than that of its antecedent – the mutant perhaps intensifying and delaying (or even denying) the realization of what was a weak and quickly satisfied implication in the antecedent form – then this will increase, in direct proportion, its perceptual-cognitive salience. This will thereby increase its propensity to imitation by the members of a cultural community. In this way, its differential/cultural fitness (and therefore its statistical prevalence in the meme pool), compared with that of its antecedent, will increase in direct proportion to the increase in its i-r*p*. Thus, the i-r*p* offers an index not only of perceptual-cognitive salience but also of Darwinian fitness and, concomitantly, of likely distributional frequency within the meme pool.

4.5. The Selfish Meme and the Meme's Eye View

> An i-culture builds and operates m-culture features whose *ultimate function* is to provide for the maintenance and propagation of the i-culture in a certain environment.... the ultimate function of both an i-culture *and* an m-culture is the maintenance and propagation of the i-culture.... the survival value of a cultural instruction is the same as its function; it is its value for the survival/replication of itself or its replicas(s) ....
>
> (Cloak 1975: 170, 172; his emphases)

From Dawkins's perspective of the gene as 'the fundamental unit of selection' arises his celebrated appellation 'selfish'. Central to the striking image embodied in his phrase 'the selfish gene' is the notion of the gene appearing to act egotistically in furtherance of its own interests. To paraphrase him, an entity, such as a baboon or a gene, is said to be selfish if it has the effect (not the purpose) of promoting its own welfare at the expense of that of another entity (1983a: 284). The most significant competitors of the gene in this sense are its alleles, its close equivalents or 'alternative forms', which act as rivals for the slots (loci) on a chromosome (: 283). Devoid of consciousness, the gene cannot be selfish, selfless or in possession of any other attribute of higher organisms, yet the anthropomorphic metaphor of conscious intentionality effectively articulates the truism that those genes which tend to act – engender phenotypic effects – in such a way as to increase the chances of their survival via that of their encompassing organism will self-evidently prevail and be replicated, to the disadvantage of those less phenotypically consequential genes. Powerful as the selfish gene metaphor is, it is founded upon a (tauto)logical and mechanistic process entirely without conscious agency or intentionality, yet it is in the nature of such processes that they often appear to be strongly goal-directed and intentional.

Applying this logic to culture, a meme, to reiterate Dawkins's maxim, can be said to be selfish if it has the effect (again, not the purpose) of promoting its own welfare – its survival by replication – at the expense of that of another meme. To reword my earlier assertion, we may say that, devoid of consciousness, the meme cannot be selfish, selfless or in possession of any other attribute of higher organisms, yet the anthropomorphic metaphor of conscious intentionality effectively articulates the truism that those memes which tend to act – engender phemotypic effects – in such a way as to increase the chances of their survival via that of their encompassing cultural object will self-evidently prevail and be replicated, to the disadvantage of those less phemotypically consequential memes. As noted in 1.2.3 above, '[t]his is not a theory; it is not even an observed fact: it is a tautology' (1989: 86). It is in this sense that we may comprehend the reflexive 'themselves' in Dawkins's statement that 'memes propagate themselves in the meme pool by leaping from brain to brain via a process which, in the broad sense, can be called imitation' (1989: 192); and it is in the same sense that all references in this book to the apparent conscious intentionality of memes should be understood.

Developing this argument, a meme's most significant competitors would appear to be its alleles, but is this concept pertinent to memetics? In genetics, most of the body cells of higher animals are diploid, meaning that they have paired chromosomes and possess two copies of each gene coding for a particular phenotypic effect, one on each corresponding chromosome. An allele is one of several analogous but alternative forms of a gene occupying a particular locus. In cases where both copies are identical (where it is the same allele), the organism is said to be homozygous; where the copies differ, it is said to be heterozygous. In the latter case, one allele may be dominant and the other recessive, in which situation only the former allele's effects will be expressed. The definition of an allele therefore includes the aspects of phenotypic effect (the allele codes for blue eyes or for red petals) and structural location (the allele occupies a locus *l* of a given chromosome).

In parallel with genetic alleles, it would appear that there are situations in which it may be possible to speak of memetic alleles. Two or more memes may be said to exist in allelic rivalry to each other if:

1. They are configurationally, functionally or structurally analogous or homologous. This implies that …
2. The memes are (equally) able to occupy a locus *l* in a 'structural meme', a concept discussed in Chapter 5.

The first condition requires that allelic memes have a similar shallow-middleground structural framework and foreground prolongations; as with the phenotypic effects of genetic alleles, the rival memotypic neuronal constellations code for similar phemotypic musical patterns. Generally, such structural/configurational relationships will most likely obtain between mutational antecedents and consequents, and therefore the relationship is, strictly, one of homology, not analogy. In this sense, memetic mutation and allelic rivalry are directly related.

Studies of text propagation on the internet offer a vivid illustration of meme selfishness. To investigate replication and evolution in this medium, Pocklington and Best developed

> an analytic technique to detect units of selection within a corpus of texts. These units or cultural replicators will be sets of words which repeatedly co-occur.... the repeated co-occurrence of words across texts indicates replication of the concepts signified by those word combinations. These replicating word combinations are taken to be units of selection as they fulfil the criteria of repeatable, reliable replication.
>
> (1997: 82)

A unit of selection – or 'term-subspace' in their terminology (: 84) – 'is composed of a number of terms [words] that when found together in a document represent the occurrence of a particular "cognitive motif" (: 85). As a meme, the 'cognitive motif' is the memotype and the term-subspace its phemotypic manifestation. The corpus in question was a set of postings to the USENET News (NetNews) internet discussion forum. The particular focus was a thread of 101 posts from September 1995 concerning 'a heated discussion about the behavior of … a prolific and controversial poster', whose name Pocklington and Best changed to 'James Smith' (: 84). They chose to track the distribution of a meme manifested phemotypically by the term-subspace 'james, smith, nazi', whose appearance was symptomatic of a move within the thread to heightened aggression and name-calling.

Their analysis of the data concluded that

> The significant trait [meme]/replicative success covariance is visually apparent [in their Figure 3]. As the density of posts in time went up, the average degree to which the posts expressed our particular trait also increased. In other words, when posts made greater use of the replicator, 'james, smith, nazi', the number of posts per unit time to that thread increased.
>
> (: 85)

This suggests that there is a clear correlation – a 'trait/replicative success covariance' – between the degree to which a meme is replicated and its intrinsic and/or associated attributes, including the degree to which it pushes our '[psychological] buttons' (Brodie 1996: 88). The meme 'James Smith is a Nazi' spread rapidly through the discussion group by virtue of its highly emotional connotations of tyranny and horror. One might hypothesize that a more sober allelic form 'James Smith is impolite' – perhaps manifested by the term-subspace 'james, smith, impolite' – would have considerably lower reproductive success. To re-paraphrase Dawkins's maxim, and thus to invoke his 'tautology', the meme 'James Smith is a Nazi' is selfish because it has the effect (not the purpose) of promoting its own welfare at the expense of that of alleles such as 'James Smith is impolite'.

A direct corollary of the selfish meme principle is Blackmore's notion of the 'meme's eye view'. While acknowledging that memes 'cannot see anything and they cannot predict anything', she explains that

> the point of this perspective is the same as the 'gene's eye view' in biology. Memes are replicators and tend to increase in number whenever they have the chance. So the meme's eye view is the view that looks at the world in terms of opportunities for replication – what will help a meme to make more copies of itself and what will prevent it?
>
> (1999: 37; see also Blackmore 2000)

Taking the meme's eye view is the basic methodological orientation of memetics and is the logical consequence of the notion of the meme as the fundamental unit of cultural selection – just as the gene's eye view accords with the notion of the gene as the fundamental unit of biological selection. Therefore, whenever a cultural system is being analyzed memetically, one should always ask how the replication of each of its component memes will be affected by changes in the conditions acting upon the system and how individual memes fare against their alleles.

Asking 'what will help a [musical] meme to make more copies of itself?' might lead to the identification of such factors as the mutation towards a more chromatic form (for example, the mixture-generating transformation of the harmonic progression I–IV–I^6_4–V–I, leading to the variant I–$IV^{\flat 3}$–I^6_4–V–I), or the mutation towards more syncopated rhythms (for example, the deformation of the pattern c^1–d^1–e^1–f^1 in the rhythm $\frac{4}{4}$ ♩♩♩♩ to the rhythm ♪♩♩♩𝄾). Of course, this leads to the ontological problem that the greater the degree of mutation, the greater the likelihood of engendering not the same meme altered but a new, quite different meme, one which might then compete allelically with its antecedent.

This meme-centric perspective, and more particularly the abstract notion of selfishness, may be quantified, at least in the dimension of pitch, using the i-r*p* metric. This is illustrated by Example 4.2 below, which shows three hypothetical memes synthesized, according to the two criteria listed above, as allelic rivals. Example 4.2 ii is, in terms of its i-r*p* value, slightly more perceptually-cognitively salient than its allele i, and it will therefore (*ceteris paribus*) stand a greater chance of imitation. If, however, Example 4.2 i gives rise to a mutant of the form shown in iii, the i-r*p* value of this mutant will exceed that of i and ii: the new terminal reversal carries a higher i-r*p* value (8.1) than the terminal process of the antecedent (2.1). This mutant form may therefore (again, *ceteris paribus*), acquire a replicative edge over its allelic rivals – both its antecedent, i, and the allele in ii.

Example 4.2: Selfishness as a Function of Variation in the Perceptual-Cognitive Salience of Memes

i) Hypothetical Meme 1

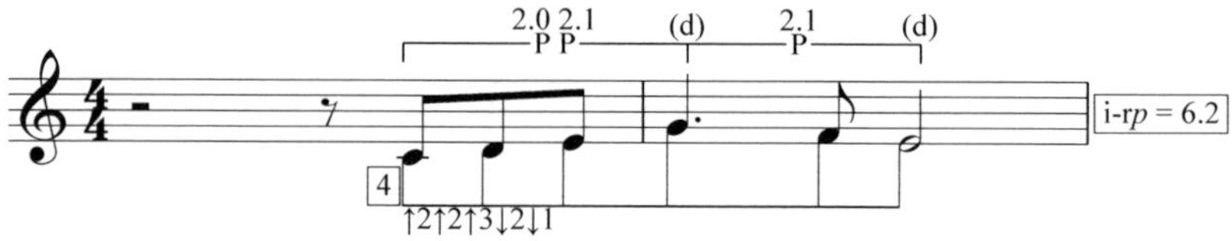

ii) Hypothetical Meme 2

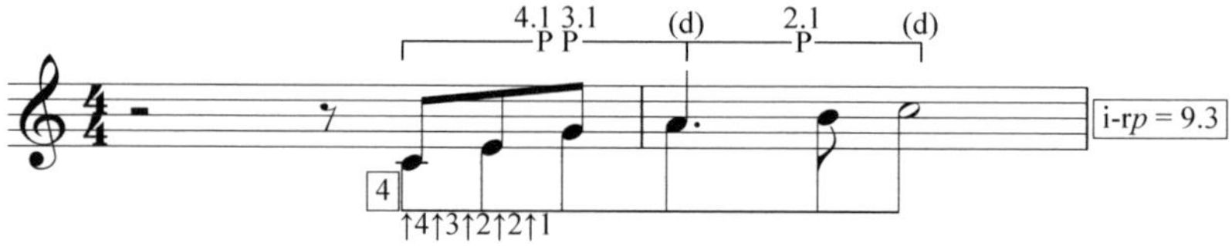

iii) Mutant form of Hypothetical Meme 1

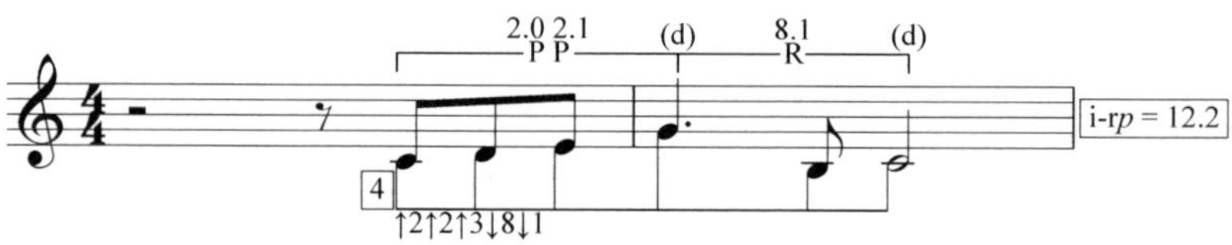

Following on from the point made at the end of 4.4.2, the i-r*p* therefore offers an index not only of perceptual-cognitive salience, differential/cultural fitness and distributional frequency but also – because all these phenomena are mutually interdependent – of meme selfishness itself.

4.6. Memetic-Cultural/Stylistic Evolution

In the musicological literature the manifest dynamism of musical styles is often described, in a pseudo-Darwinian sense, as a process of 'evolution'. In general, however, the term is rarely applied in anything other than a loosely (weakly) analogical sense. By contrast, memetics allows us to move beyond this to posit clear (strong) structural parallels between biological and cultural evolution and therefore to assert that style is evolutionary not only in the sense of manifesting continuous morphological variation (later styles are measurably different in several respects to earlier ones), but in a more fundamental, Darwinian sense predicated upon the attributes of the meme.

Deviations from exact copying-fidelity affecting the individual meme have been considered in terms of the concept of memetic mutation. To understand cultural/stylistic evolution one must move up a hierarchic level: in a cultural system such as a musical dialect there are a multitude of memes and memeplexes in a constant state of mutational change. It is the interactive and cumulative effect of these multiple meme-level changes which drives the continual change in the profile of a given meme pool and consequently the higher-level, systemic transformations of cultural evolution.

To examine some of the processes involved, and after a general consideration of evolutionary constraints, the sections which follow start from a low-level perspective which focuses on the fate of a single memeplex, move on to an intermediate-level perspective which examines issues surrounding a class of analogous memeplexes, and then conclude with a high-level perspective concerned with the most global repercussions of memetic evolution.

4.6.1. *Constraints on Evolution: Nature and/*versus *Nurture*

> [A]lthough *nature* – that is, the constraints of human cognition – establishes the conditions that make it possible for the cadential $^6{}_4$ progression [$I^6{}_4$–V–I] to imply and define a tonal center, the frequency with which the progression was replicated (chosen by composers) depended in large measure on cultural constraints – that is, on *nurture*.
>
> (Meyer 1992: 490; his emphases)

In considering memetic evolution it is necessary to understand which elements of a cultural-evolutionary system are invariant and which are mutable; that is, it is important to be clear about the distinction between nature and nurture in memetic evolution. One might say that processes operating on Meyer's level of laws determine the environment for memetic propagation, and then the outcomes of the selection processes which operate within the terms of these laws determine the complexion of the rules (included systems of organization) which arise. This position might be elaborated as follows:

1. For memetics, the level of laws encompasses two spheres, the physical-acoustic and the psychological:

- *The physical-acoustic*. There are certain fixed physical-acoustic constraints on sound spectra in our universe, such as the simpler mathematical ratios of some intervals (such as the octave, 1:2 and the perfect fifth, 2:3) compared with others (such as the major second, 8:9 and the minor second, 10:11).

- *The psychological*. Our perceptual-cognitive system has evolved by gene-based natural selection to process information, including acoustic information, as efficiently and parsimoniously as possible. This ultimately arose as a survival mechanism, but its consequences are recruited in musical processing. Whether this processing occurs through a 'modular' (domain-specific; Fodor 1983) or non-modular (domain-general) neurophysiological organization is perhaps incidental to this issue. More subtly, Lerdahl identifies other 'cognitive constraints on compositional systems', ranging from the necessity for music to be amenable to sequential discretization to the necessity for it to support a hierarchical 'pitch space' consisting of steps and skips (1992: 104, 114).

2. The environment of the meme consists of two components: i) the stable physical-acoustical and psychological environment outlined in point 1) above; and ii) the unstable (competitive) environment created by other memes. The former component acts effectively as a filter through which memes must metaphorically pass. Some memes are, in principle, highly unlikely to survive if they violate these physical-acoustic/psychological constraints too flagrantly.
3. As noted in 3.4.3 above, 'the brain abstracts recurrent commonalities from the environment and encodes them in the form of schematic representations as a basis for future categorization and comprehension' (Bharucha 1987: 2). These 'commonalities' are, of course, the configurations of the memes which have passed through the physical-psychological filter and which are made, therefore, in the filter's image.
4. As these memes mutate, the brain has to abstract new schemata based on the commonalities of the new memes.

The notion of constraint is a prominent theme in writings on schema theory by Meyer and Gjerdingen. In Meyer's formulation, constraints are 'learned and adopted as part of the historical/cultural circumstances of individuals or groups' (1989: 3). 'Learned' and 'adopted' clearly have somewhat different connotations and in general Meyer gravitates towards the second of these as a model for constraint formulation, somewhat downplaying the first. His term 'adopted' suggests that constraints are somehow separable from music, an external rulebook picked up or put down in an act of conscious choice by a composer.

The broad tenor of Meyer's claim is no doubt partly true, but his statement might be qualified by suggesting that whereas those constraints operating at the level of laws are immutable and inexorable, constituting the realm of nature, those operating at the levels of rules and dialects are the product of the characteristics of the memes propagated at these levels of the memetic-cultural hierarchy and are therefore transmissible and mutable, constituting the realm of nurture. Thus – in an interpretation which constitutes an argument against the conscious intentionality implicit in Meyer's view that '[d]ialects are substyles that are differentiated because a number of composers … employ (choose) the same or similar rules and strategies' (1989: 23) – whereas 'natural' constraints are externally imposed upon memes, 'nurtural' constraints are functions of the memes themselves and therefore have no existence independently of the intrinsic attributes of those memes. In short, learned – as opposed to adopted (chosen) – constraints are not phenomena separate from memes, selected (consciously) from a set of alternatives.

On this reasoning, if a small proportion of the memes in a given meme pool express melodic or harmonic progressions radically different to the remainder, then the constraints operative in that dialect would be determined by the statistical predominance of the majority; the constraints would, all other things being equal, be a simple consequence of predominance. Moreover, this predominance would tend to increase; as Cavalli-Sforza and Feldman express it, '[t]he basic assumption of the logistic model is that the probability of adoption is proportional to the fraction of individuals who have already adopted the innovation, and the residual fraction who have not yet adopted it' (1981: 35). The principal reason why certain phenomena – some harmonic progressions, for instance – are 'prohibited' by theory is because those memes expressing them are not widely propagated in the meme pool and therefore have insufficient cultural force to legitimize the progressions they instantiate. Such an explanation would seem to transcend more traditional interpretations predicated on such subjective notions as compositional utility and 'sounding good'.

The composer need never consciously formalize these constraints because they are not separate from the musical memes which constitute the raw materials of music. The degree to which such formalization by music theory feeds back into the practice of composers is difficult to determine. In general, it is perhaps the case that, aside from the elision of theory and practice in the work of such conservatives as Rameau and such progressives as Babbitt, '[n]obody has ever begun by manufacturing rules out of whole cloth. First came music itself; only later could the principles of its creation – its theory – be deduced' (Jeppesen 1992: ix).

Lastly, the degree of co-adaptation between memes also acts, indirectly, as a constraint on memetic evolution. Whether a mutant meme is imitated depends upon the equilibrium between the perceptual-cognitive advantage its novelty engenders and the degree to which it is compatible with established members of the meme pool (and, more immediately, with the memes which comprise its specific idiostructural context). Logically, the greater the extent to which a mutant is co-adapted with others in the meme pool, especially at the lower levels of stylistic relevance, the greater its chances of survival.

4.6.2. *A Low-Level Perspective: A Sketch for a Mutational-Evolutionary History of the* 'Tristan *Memeplex' from Palestrina to Wagner and Beyond*

To illustrate low-level mutational-evolutionary processes, the following series of extracts sketches a brief history of one of the most celebrated of musical entities, the '*Tristan* memeplex'.[7] (It will become clear during the course of this discussion why the term 'memeplex' is more appropriate than 'meme'.) While to a large extent speculative – a transmission-mutation nexus is posited the homological nature of which, by its very nature, is difficult to confirm – the patterns identified do constitute a convincing thread of transformation uniting seemingly disparate events in musico-stylistic history. To illustrate the concept of i-r*p* outlined in 4.4.2 above more fully, an i-r analysis is overlaid, and the i-r*p* is indicated, for each of these variants. Only those elements constituting the memeplex will be analyzed; i-r*p* values for other material not regularly replicated as part of the memeplex will not be incorporated. The significance of the memeplex's i-r*p* values for the mutational-evolutionary history of the *Tristan* memeplex is considered at the end of this section.

The antecedent of the memeplex may be traced at least as far back as the Renaissance. At this time, the modal system gave rise to a great variety of cadential types, the consequence of the particular intervallic configuration of each mode. One distinguishing characteristic of the Phrygian mode was the semitone between its first two pitches, E and F, reproduced in Example 4.3 below at a different transpositional level.

Example 4.3: Palestrina: 'Ave mundi spes, Maria' (*c.* 1584), bb. 50–51

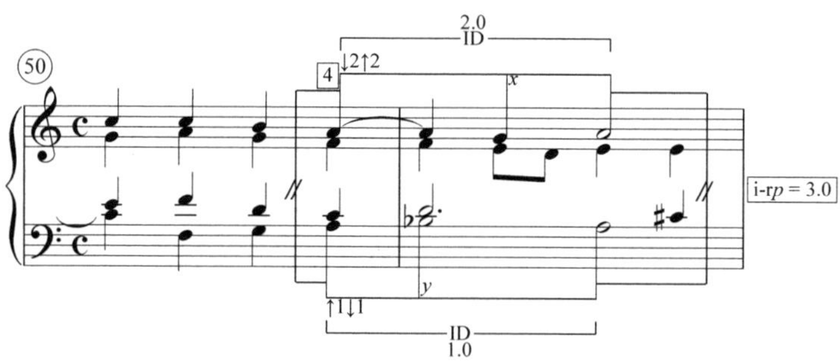

[7] Considering the vast amount of music from the period surveyed here – the sixteenth to the twentieth centuries – it is a very brief history, focusing on a mere eleven (hopefully representative) cases. Examples marked with an asterisk are identified by Cope as '[p]recedents to … Wagner's Prelude to *Tristan und Isolde*' (2003: 15, Figure 6).

By the mid-Baroque, this linear confluence had been assimilated into the newly-emerging tonal system as the scale degree progression iv$^6_3$–V, forming a pattern often replicated, as in Example 4.4 below, as the final gesture of open-ended movements or sections of works. Of course, in recognition of its evolutionary antecedents, theory calls this progression a 'Phrygian cadence'.

Example 4.4: Corelli: Concerto Grosso in G minor op. 6 no. 8 ('*La notte*') (*c.* ?1690), I, bb. 1–6

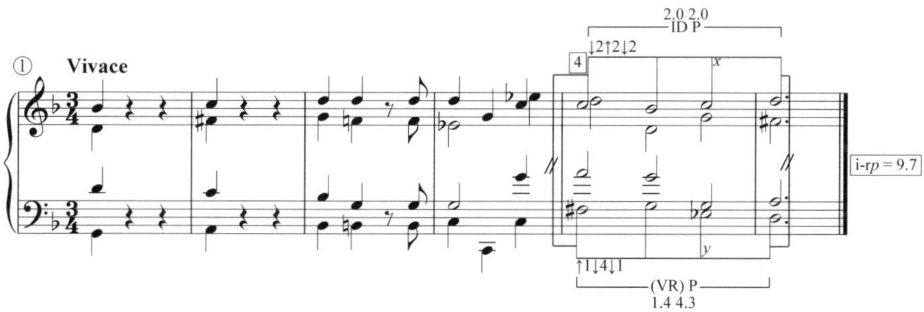

Other voices notwithstanding, it contains two contrapuntal-structural voices – an upper voice, which will hereafter also be referred to as line *x*; and a lower voice, which will also be referred to as line *y* – which move in contrary motion to reach the octave on the dominant. The notional upper voice in the schema in Example 4.5 below may not necessarily appear in this position in a real instantiation of the schema.

Example 4.5: Schematic Basis of the *Tristan* Memeplex

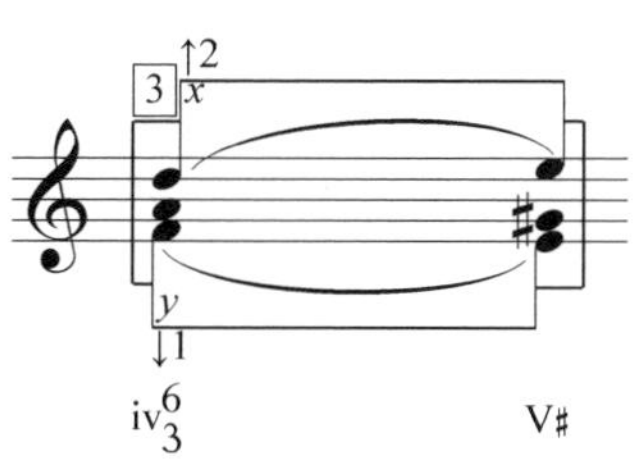

The three examples above illustrate that the identity of the object under investigation is not as straightforward as it might initially seem. We are (initially) concerned with the contrary-motion outer-voice pattern $\hat{4}$–$\hat{5}$/$\hat{6}$–$\hat{5}$ ($x + y$) and the iv$^6_3$–V harmonic structure which it generates, hereafter referred to as meme *z*; but the four melodic pitches of $x + y$ do not necessarily always constitute the entirety of the structure under investigation. Lines *x* and *y* are often subsumed by slightly longer melodic configurations which, by virtue of their initial and terminal articulations and replication in other contexts are the memes, not the more abstract *x* and *y*. (As noted in 3.3.1 above, two-unit particles such as *x* and *y* probably contain insufficient information to be a meme, unlike four-unit particles such as *z*.) This is the case in Example 4.3 above, where the upper-voice g^1–a^1 motion (*x*) is part of a longer a^1–g^1–a^1 structure and the lower voice b♭–a motion (*y*) is part of a longer a–b♭–a structure. Nevertheless, the $x + y$ motion forms the structural (shallow-middleground-level) foundation for such passages and serves as our central reference point in this account.

The distinction between lines $x + y$ on the one hand and meme *z* on the other is somewhat artificial: horizontal melodic strata ($x + y$) and vertical harmonic structures (*z*) are difficult to separate because they are mutually generative. The distinction here is intended to represent the fact that memes based on or subsuming lines *x* and *y* may exist independently of each other; but as a memeplex $x + y$ they overlap substantially with meme *z* (in this case, $x + y \equiv z$). Meme *z* is not, however, reducible to lines $x + y$; in an incarnation as a two-chord, four-part structure, as in Example 4.4, *z* will contain two other linear elements (in this case, $x + y \neq z$).

These various patterns in combination form a melodic-harmonic memeplex, the elements of which are the *z* chord-sequence meme generated by the $x + y$ outer-voice progression; a rising ♮$\hat{7}$–$\hat{1}$–♯$\hat{1}$–$\hat{2}$ melodic overlay, hereafter referred to as meme *p*, to be discussed later; and the opening melodic prefix of Wagner's version of the memeplex, hereafter referred to as meme *q*, also to be considered later. To assist orientation through the following examples, Figure 4.4 below is a Venn-diagram representation of the *Tristan* memeplex as manifested in Example 4.11 below.

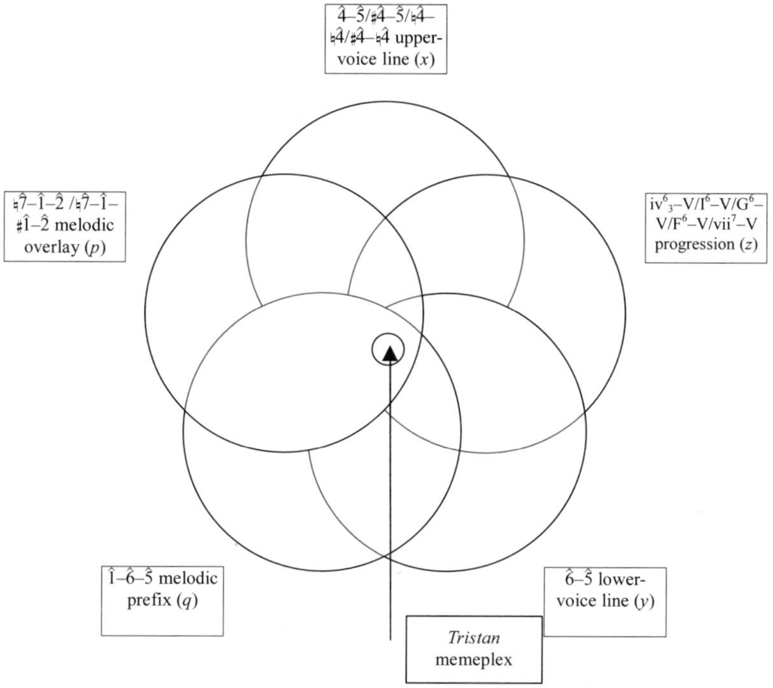

Figure 4.4: Components of The *Tristan* Memeplex

As a further complication, the classes represented by the sum of the circles of the figure are themselves subdivided; there are, for instance, several possible *x*-type memes, not just those based on 4̂–5̂. It is therefore more realistic to speak of classes of memes represented (and to a degree oversimplified) algebraically by the symbols *x*, *y*, *z*, etc.

By the mid-eighteenth century the first note of the upper voice was often chromaticized, this mutational variant giving the $x^1 + y$ progression ♯4̂–5̂/6̂–5̂. Theory interprets the harmonic root of the first chord of the resultant z^1 pair as ♯IV, terming the vertical an augmented sixth chord (A^6). Of course, further linear-harmonic infilling of this vertical – D♯/A/F in A minor, the 'Italian' sixth (I^6) – gives the 'German' form, D♯/C/A/F (G^6). Meme z^1, A^6–V, was often co-adapted in operatic contexts with verbal-conceptual memes concerning notions of hesitation and expectancy. In Example 4.6 below, it occurs at the point when Belmonte and Pedrillo vacillate before proceeding tentatively to question the fidelity of their partners.

Example 4.6: Mozart: *Die Entführung aus dem Serail* K. 384 (1782), no. 16, 'Ach Belmonte! Ach mein Leben!', bb. 139–42

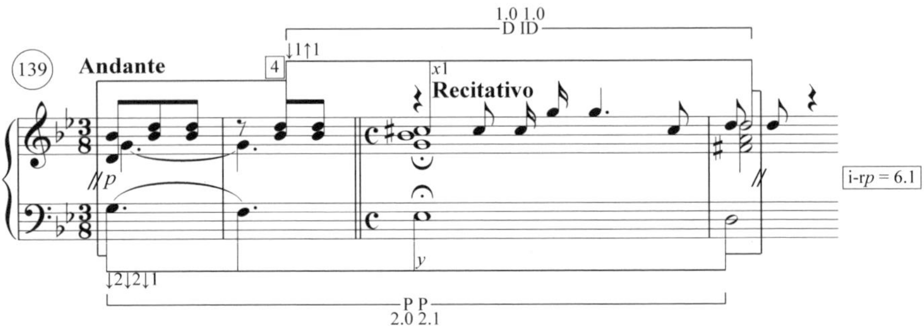

In Example 4.7 below x + y-based memes are absent (there is no A^6–V progression here), but the melodic line prefigures Wagner in its $\sharp\hat{7}$–$\hat{1}$–$\sharp\hat{1}$–$\hat{2}$ melodic progression, meme p. In the passage from *Tristan*, the $\sharp\hat{7}$ and $\sharp\hat{1}$ will become appoggiaturas to 'inner'-voice notes of the F^6 and V chords respectively. This example suggests that meme p existed as an independent particle before it became part of the *Tristan* memeplex.

Example 4.7: Beethoven: Sonata in C minor op. 13 ('*Pathétique*') (1798), I, bb. 7–8*

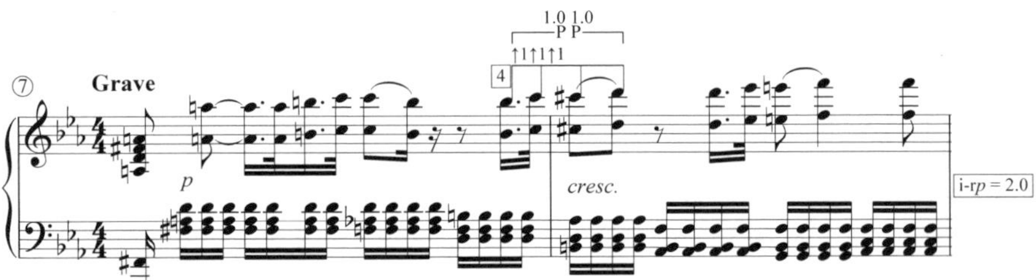

The assimilation of p-class memes into the $x + y + z$ memeplex appears to have been under way by the early-nineteenth century, as suggested by Example 4.8

below.[8] Here, the leading-note appoggiatura $g\sharp^1$ overshadows the harmonic note a^1 before the line moves to b^1. Yet the melodic line is $\sharp\hat{7}$–$\hat{1}$–$\hat{2}$, a simpler – evolutionarily prior? – allele of meme *p* and evidence that other *p*-class memes existed in co-adaptation with the $x + y + z$ memeplex. Schubert uses the 'French' variant of the A^6 chord here, D♯/B/A/F (F^6), this difference forcing theory to reinterpret the root of the chord, from D♯ (♯IV) to B (II). Characterized the interval of an augmented fourth above the bass, this form is possibly a later mutational variant than the Italian and German types. Although the change of root has no effect on the $x^1 + y$ motion underlying the memeplex, the astringency of the F^6 may confer upon it greater perceptual-cognitive salience than either the I^6 or the G^6.[9]

Example 4.8: Schubert: 'Kennst du das Land' D. 321 (1815), bb. 16–18

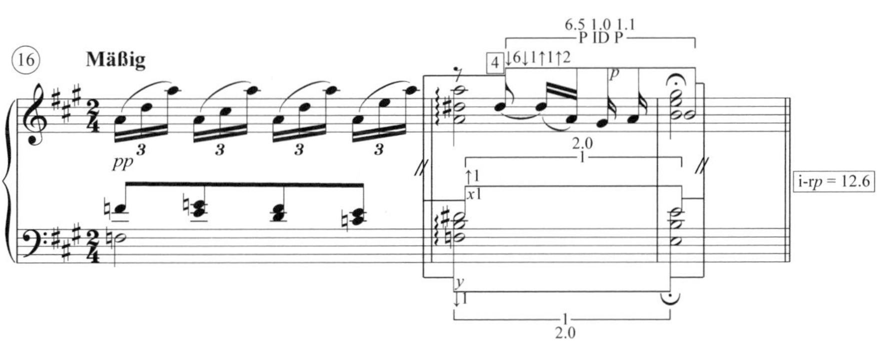

Example 4.9 below is the closest to Wagner's version of the memeplex encountered so far. It shows the association of all four elements of the memeplex identified previously, x^1, *y*, z^1 (as I^6–V) and *p* (in its fully chromatic, four-note form).

---

[8] In this example, and in Example 4.9 and Example 4.10, dyadic structures appear. Symbolized by a number indicating their interval size within the i-r bracket (Narmour 1990: 391ff.), these are not listed in Table 4.1 above. At the risk of oversimplifying a complex aspect of Narmour's theory, I regard dyads spanning fewer than 6 semitones as interrupted processes; thus, •1• (┌─ 1 ─┐) implies •1•1•. To calculate the i-*rp* of such dyads, I double the value of the realized process. The two-note duplications in Example 4.6 and Example 4.10 are similarly treated.

[9] In terms of the immediate nexus of imitation, these bars, and indeed much of the structure and detail of Schubert's version, derive directly from Beethoven's 1809 setting of Goethe's text, op. 75 no. 1. On the first pages of each song, for instance, the common features are: the shared tonic, A major; the ascending melodic line (e^1–$f\sharp^1$–$g\sharp^1$–a^1 in Beethoven, $c\sharp^2$–d^2–e^2–$f\sharp^2$ in Schubert); the modulation to ♮VI; and the cadence at 'Kennst du es Wohl?', Phrygian in Beethoven and, as shown in Example 4.8, French-6th-inflected in Schubert. I am grateful to Sarah Smeeton for pointing out these resemblances to me.

Example 4.9: Spohr: *Der Alchymist* woo57 (1830), no. 14, 'Abenhamet!', bb. 1–4*

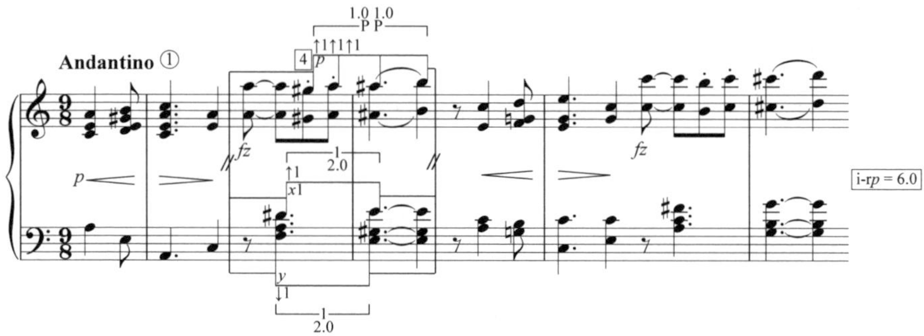

In Example 4.10 below, meme p is associated with the harmonic progression vii^7–V^7, the seventh of the second chord forming the terminal component of a new form of line x, x^2 ($\natural\hat{4}$–$\natural\hat{4}$).[10] This progression might be admitted to meme class z on the grounds that its bass line instantiates the motion of line y.

Example 4.10: Liszt: 'Ich möchte hingehn' N31 (?1844–56), bb. 124–5*

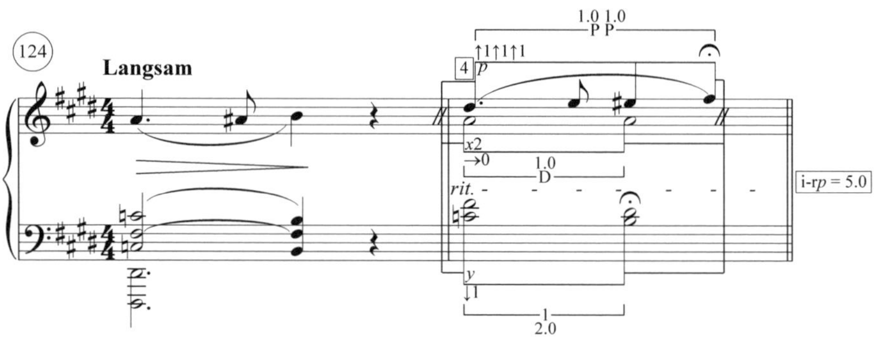

Example 4.11 below, Wagner's phrase itself, synthesizes p with another variant of x, x^3 ($\sharp\hat{4}$–$\natural\hat{4}$), y and z^1 (as F^6–V$^{\natural 7}$). The eschewing of the expected motion $\sharp\hat{4}$–$\hat{5}$ (x^1) in favour of $\sharp\hat{4}$–$\natural\hat{4}$ is perhaps influenced by the second pitch of x^2 ($\natural\hat{4}$–$\natural\hat{4}$) in Example 4.10, the mere semitone difference between the first pitches of x^2 and x^3 indicating the mutational proximity of these passages. In Wagner's version, mutation has affected the rhythmic placement of the voices such that the identity of

---

[10] Millington points out that the figure I term meme p is common in Liszt's song *Die Loreley* of 1841 (1992: 815).

the F[6] is obscured by a much heavier emphasis on the appoggiatura g♯[1] than occurs in Example 4.8 above.[11]

Example 4.11: Wagner: *Tristan und Isolde* WWV 90 (1859), *Einleitung*, bb. 0–3

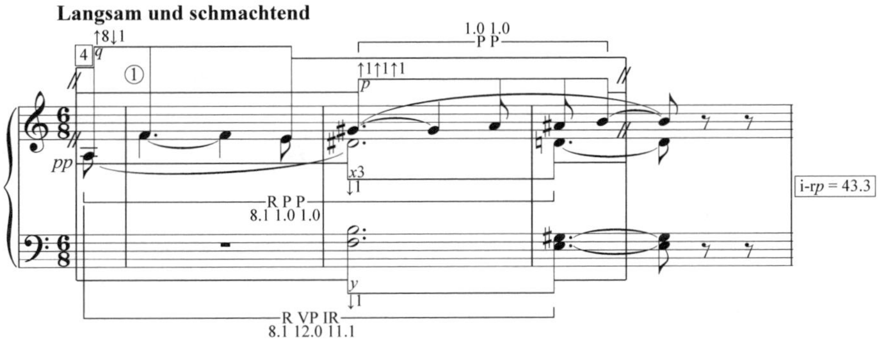

Of course, Wagner adds a distinctive opening prefix $\hat{1}$–$\hat{6}$–$\hat{5}$ to the memeplex, meme *q*, which – in a good example of memetic co-adaptation – connects smoothly to the d♯[2] of x^3. Meme *q* existed independently before its incorporation into the *Tristan* memeplex, as shown in Example 4.12 below.

Example 4.12: Berlioz: *Symphonie Fantastique* op. 14 (1830), I, bb. 3-6

After Wagner, the celebrity of *Tristan* meant that the replication of the memeplex was in part meditated by co-adapted verbal-conceptual memes, either related to the dramatic themes of the opera (especially the idea of longing) or, more abstractly, pro- or anti-Wagner aesthetic sentiments. The ironic, gently mocking tone of Example 4.13 below, with its cartoon-music-anticipating acciaccature, is clear.

---

[11] Resolving the resultant ambiguity – is the g♯ indeed an appoggiatura to a chord tone of a French sixth chord or itself a chord tone of a half-diminished seventh chord? – is the first 'analytical decision' necessary for defining the '*Tristan* Chord' (Nattiez 1990: 222). From a memetic-evolutionary perspective, and on the evidence of the examples considered, the g♯ is clearly an appoggiatura.

Example 4.13: Debussy: 'Golliwogg's Cake-Walk' from *Children's Corner* (1908), bb. 61–4

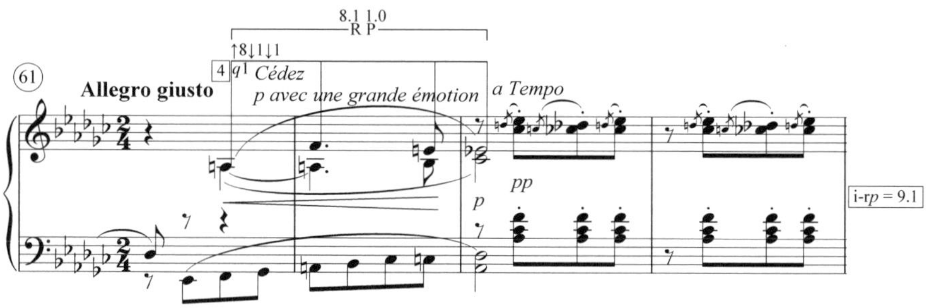

Nevertheless, what is replicated in this passage is not the complete memeplex as occurs in *Tristan*, but only meme *q*, together with the first note of line x^3, e♭[1] ($\hat{6}$ in G♭ major, equivalent to Wagner's ♯$\hat{4}$ in A minor); the complete $x^3 + y$ pattern, and therefore meme z^1, are absent, as is meme *p*.[12] Meme *q* was, of course, added late in the memeplex's history and is a separate entity to the phrygian-cadential structure ($x + y + z$) with which we have been principally concerned; but it serves as an effective cognitive marker of the whole complex.

In the final example in this series, Example 4.14 below, the row is contrived so as to permit Berg to quote the *Tristan* memeplex literally. No mutation has taken place here (aside from a change in the metrical placement of the memeplex), for the effect of the citation – and its place in the rich complex of musical and verbal-conceptual memes associated with the affair between Berg and Hanna Fuchs-Robettin – clearly requires that the memeplex be literally replicated and immediately perceptible.

12 Despite the attenuation, Wagner's sonority still manages to replicate itself, for the simultaneity on b. 62[3], c♭–a♮–f[2], sounds three notes of the F[6] chord f–b–d♯[1]–a[1].

Example 4.14: Berg: *Lyrische Suite* (1926), VI, bb. 26–7

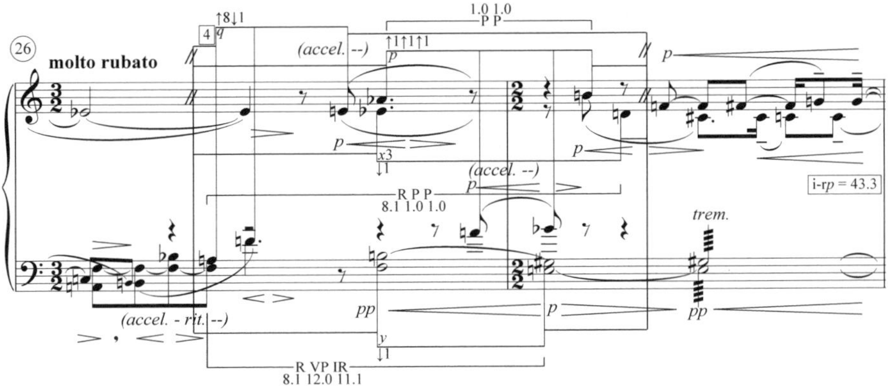

Turning now to the i-r*p* values, it is evident that the i-r*p* of the memeplex from Palestrina to Wagner broadly increases over time – in summary, the totals are: Palestrina, 3.0; Corelli, 9.7; Mozart, 6.1; Schubert, 12.6; Spohr, 6.0; Liszt, 5.0; Wagner, 43.3; Debussy, 9.1; and Berg, 43.3 – but that the values do not increase sequentially. Recall, however, that i-r*p* values are sometimes calculated from longer melodic segments which encompass lines *x* and *y*, and which thereby involve more complex i-r structures than the simpler (often dyadic) i-r structures in the 'exception' passages. Moreover, in the case of the Debussy phrase, all that remains of the memeplex is meme *q*; the other lines, incorporation of which would considerably increase the overall i-r*p* value (in this and indeed the other passages), are not included in the calculation. Despite these problems, which essentially stem from the fact that the memeplex is replicated in conjunction with diverse and complex ancillary material, it seems that with further refinement the i-r*p* might also serve as an index – in addition to serving as such for the attributes of perceptual-cognitive salience, Darwinian fitness, distributional frequency and selfishness, as discussed in 4.5 above – of the increasing evolutionary complexity of memes and memeplexes over time.

The most significant outcome of the i-r*p* analysis suggests that the conjunction of the $x^3 + y + z^1 + p$ structure with the *q* prefix in Wagner's phrase considerably increased the cognitive salience of the memeplex by virtue of the new ┌R VP IR┐ structure engendered between *q* and *y*; the ear, I suggest, is led from *p* both along into x^3 and down into *y*. As can be seen in the Debussy passage, despite considerably augmenting the i-r*p* of the memeplex as a whole, this alliance ultimately served the selfish interests of meme *q*.

This long and thin slice of musical history shows that a large musico-morphological distance – from a simple Renaissance cadence to a complex nineteenth-century harmonic sequence – is traversed not in a large leap, but by means of a series of small, incremental steps spread over some three hundred years. This subject, 'single-step' *versus* 'cumulative' selection, is taken up again in Chapter 5. While we may question d'Indy's particular interpretation of the scale degree upon which the '*Tristan* chord' is based (in Nattiez 1990: 224) – although my reading of the chord and its antecedents suggests scale degree location is a relatively insignificant consideration compared with voice-leading patterns – his reduction of it to iv^6 in the context of a Phrygian cadence offers a clear perspective back through evolutionary time to the Renaissance antecedents of Wagner's memeplex.

4.6.3. *An Intermediate-Level Perspective: Evolutionary Aspects of Changing-Note Schemata*

As argued in 3.4.3 above, the dichotomy between features and schemata is a means of understanding replicated patterns at various structural-hierarchic levels. Gjerdingen 1988 considers one such schema, the $\hat{1}$–$\hat{7}$…$\hat{4}$–$\hat{3}$ changing-note archetype, studying numerous incarnations spanning the years 1725–1900. By discussing the changes manifested by the schema over time, Gjerdingen is essentially charting a process of memetic evolution, a process which is initially operative at the feature (foreground) level but which, when changes to features become sufficiently momentous, results in change at the schema (shallow-middleground) level. To follow on from the rather focused study of the *Tristan* memeplex, and before the more global considerations of the following section, it is useful to examine Gjerdingen's model of schema change over time, which represents an intermediate-level memetic-evolutionary perspective.

A Memetic Perspective on Gjerdingen's First Hypothesis

Gjerdingen's model is grounded on two hypotheses, the first of which asserts that '[t]he variation across time in the number of instances of a musical schema approximates a normal, bell-curved statistical distribution' (1988: 100). He adds that '[t]he degree of pointedness in the population [bell] curve … varies directly with the number of constraints specified in the schema's definition' (: 101). This hypothesis, Gjerdingen notes,

> can predict that the constituent style forms in a composite style structure should all have broader historical distributions and less pointed population curves than the style structure itself, because the definition of the style structure stipulates additional constraints of context and interrelationship.
>
> (: 102)

To recall, style forms/shapes function as features in cognitive schemata and are encoded by semantic/categorical memory nodes; they approximate to foreground-orientated unit memes such as the opening I–V and closing V–I cadences, and the (sometimes sub-foreground/shallow-middleground) melodic dyads of the $\hat{1}$–$\hat{7}$…$\hat{4}$–$\hat{3}$ schema. While one would not normally expect such two-component patterns as the melodic dyads of changing-note schemata to be memetic, these are almost inseparable from their supporting harmonic progressions, the distinction between these parameters being merely a methodological convenience. Thus, the dyad-chord complex possesses the necessary informational richness for memetic replication. Style structures function as the schemata themselves, which organize features and are encoded by episodic/schematic memory sequences; they approximate to more extended memeplexes engendered by the co-replication, in fixed sequence, of a number of lower-order memes whose main structural nodes are situated at the shallow-middleground level or above. The synchronic and diachronic aspects of this relationship might be represented as follows.[13]

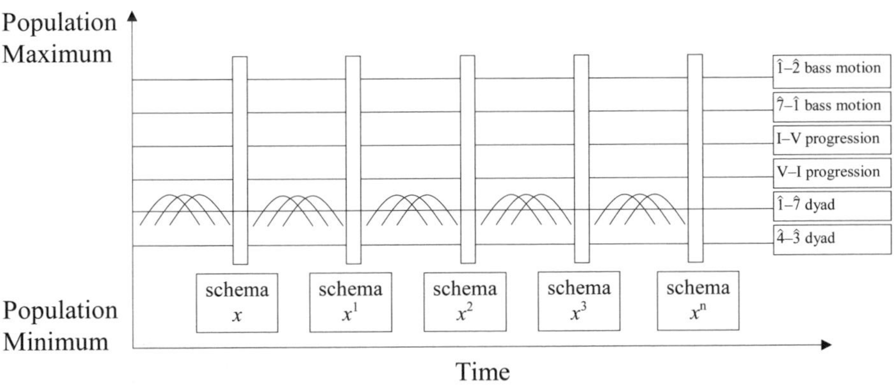

Figure 4.5: Population Distribution for Feature Memes and Schema Memeplexes (after Gjerdingen 1988: 99–105, Figures 6-1–6-9)

A given feature meme may itself be instantiated by many superficially different surface patterns, the sometimes sub-foreground/shallow middleground scale-degree motion of the initial $\hat{1}$–$\hat{7}$ melodic dyad, for instance, being revealed by minimal reduction of superficial diminutions. Thus there exist equivalence classes of allelic feature memes related by their expressing a 'common denominator' meme, such as a particular scale-degree sequence or chord progression.[14] Although neither of the passages in Example 4.15 below occurs in the context of the initial event of a $\hat{1}$–$\hat{7}$…$\hat{4}$–$\hat{3}$ changing-note schema, their configuration nevertheless

[13] Although, for clarity, the features listed on the right of Figure 4.5 are arranged one on top of another, no implication of relative predominance is intended by their particular vertical position on the population axis.

[14] Again for clarity, the population of these feature-classes is represented as stable over time in Figure 4.5, although in reality this may not have been so.

permits them to do so for their surface disparity lightly masks an underlying scale-degree affinity. In this sense, there is a parallelism between genes competing for loci on chromosomes and foreground-orientated feature memes competing for slots in shallow-middleground-level schemata.

Example 4.15: Two Instantiations of the $\hat{1}$–$\hat{7}$ Melodic Dyad

i) Haydn: Sonata in C minor Hob. XVI: 20 (1771), I, bb. 1–2

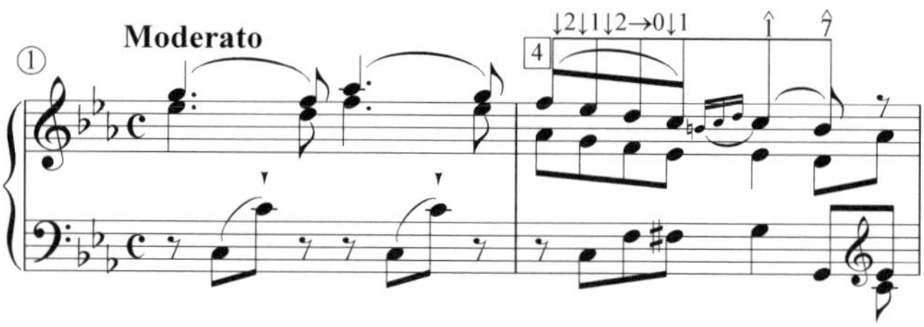

ii) Beethoven: Sonata in C♯ minor op. 27 no. 2 ('Moonlight') (1801), III, bb. 21–2

While the various feature classes in Figure 4.5 may remain relatively stable over time, the memes which instantiate them are subject to the same mutational pressures as any other meme and will therefore change relatively rapidly. The rise, peak and decline of such memes is represented in Figure 4.5 by the curves on the '$\hat{1}$–$\hat{7}$ dyad' line (the same principle applies, of course, to all feature memes), the (scale-degree/harmonic progression) attributes and population curve of the particular feature class being 'averaged out' (see below) from the generative set of feature memes.

Given that the horizontal axis of Figure 4.5 represents time, it is clear that the features and schemata towards the right-hand side are evolutionary descendants of those towards the left-hand side. Evolutionary change at the schema level is driven by change at the feature level – by internal changes to features and, concomitantly, by changes to feature interrelationship; like all patterns of memetic structural-hierarchic inclusion it is bottom-up, not top-down. It is therefore unlikely that new schemata will appear spontaneously, for this is counter to the gradualism intrinsic to the evolution of all replicators; such spontaneous generation would be akin to the saltationism underpinning some nineteenth- (and indeed twentieth-) century theories of biological evolution, now discredited.[15] Rather, new schemata must come into being through the evolution of extant forms, the innovations arising as a consequence of mutation in the component features of their precursors.

A Memetic Perspective on Gjerdingen's Second Hypothesis

The second hypothesis asserts that '[a] musical schema will exhibit a curve of typicality similar to its population curve' (1988: 103). Typicality, Gjerdingen contends, is evaluated by 'comparison of the instantiation at hand with a central tendency abstracted from previously encountered examples of the same schema. The most obvious … mechanism for this process of abstraction is an averaging of all the features of the set of known examples' (: 103). Moreover, he argues that 'the typicality of a musical structure will follow the structure's population curve'; and that '[t]he prototype of the structure will be found at the population peak, and increasingly atypical examples of the structure will be found farther and farther down either slope of the population curve' (: 104). He defines the prototype as 'a perfect example of a type … the most typical example of a category' (: 94).

Whether a given passage is held to be an instantiation of a particular schema depends upon its fulfilling certain criteria of typicality, or engendering a sufficient degree of 'confidence' in the perceiver that the pattern represents an instantiation of the schema (1988: 94–5). Of course those criteria of typicality can only be abstracted – averaged out from – a population sample already taken exclusively to represent instantiations of the schema, a population comprising 'the set of known examples', so there is inevitably a rather circular quality to the definition. Regarding typicality as a function of copying-fidelity may help alleviate this problem, in that the greater the copying-fidelity of a schema, the more homogeneous its population will become and the greater the probability that any given instantiation will closely resemble another.

Gjerdingen's discussion of the reception and propagation of schemata tends to blur the distinction between the esthesic and poietic poles. At the esthesic, the subject – the 'competent listener', in whose brain are copied many instantiations each of several schemata, and the composer-as-listener – utilize a predominantly top-down model of processing in which, after a number of cues have been registered, the appropriate schema is selected to organize this input and to predict what is still to come. Thus, when the first part of an unknown – but believed-to-be-schematically-based – passage is heard, its possible continuations are presumably rapidly rehearsed (simulated) in the listener's working memory. These might take the form of an array of alternative conclusions synthesized from the terminal

---

15 From the Latin *saltare*, to jump, saltationism contends that evolution can give rise to substantial changes in form over a relatively short space of time, creating radically new adaptations and features in the organism (Dawkins 1983b: 412–18). Such leaps, Richard Goldschmidt asserted, gave rise to 'hopeful monsters' (in Dennett 1995: 288).

events of specific schema instantiations resident in long-term memory, these being reconfigured to conform to the context of the initial event.

At the poietic pole, by contrast, the composer, despite having utilized a top-down model of perception and cognition when situated at the esthesic pole as listener, utilizes a predominantly bottom-up model of production in which features are assembled almost extempore, producing a schema 'unconsciously'. Composers have copied in their brains an array of feature memes which associate in a variety of ways and thereby repeatedly reinstantiate a set of schema memes. Drawing from and structuring a pool of essentially independent features (and apropos the set of I–V…V–I changing-note archetypes), the members of this 'complex network of associated schemata…. bear a family resemblance to each other based on their sharing of features, even though no single set of features defines each and every member of the family' (1988: 59).

Like much analysis, Gjerdingen's methodology seems conceived as a parallel to a model of perception and cognition assumed to be operative on the part of the esthesically-situated subject. As such, it specifies 'constraints of context and interrelationship' (1988: 102) to a much greater degree than is likely to have been the case for the eighteenth-century listener, part of whose listening experience was Gjerdingen's data. Although both situated at the esthesic pole, such a disparity between the analyst's perspective and that of the historical listener is almost inevitable in the work of the modern scholar writing with the benefit of comprehensive and authoritative modern editions and plentiful recordings at his or her disposal and needing relatively fixed categories within which to consider large quantities of information.

Caught up in the ebb and flow of information interchange, the eighteenth-century listener is denied such a conspectus and so tends not to form such clear and distinct categories. Therefore one consequence of Gjerdingen's charting the distribution of a specific configuration within a large sample size over a substantial period of time is the risk of implying that the arrangement of the set of features making up the $\hat{1}$–$\hat{7}$…$\hat{4}$–$\hat{3}$ schema was any more culturally salient and focused than the several other possible schematic arrangements of the same set of features replicated at the same time. This approach tends to impart to the $\hat{1}$–$\hat{7}$…$\hat{4}$–$\hat{3}$ schema to a degree of intellectual singularity and prominence unlikely to have been in accordance with the perceptions of a composer or listener of the period experiencing innumerable interacting features. Thus, one might come to the conclusion that 'the number of constraints specified in the schema's definition' (Gjerdingen 1988: 101) by the analyst is not necessarily comparable to the number of constraints placed by an individual experiencing this music *c.* 1775.

In fairness, Gjerdingen himself tacitly acknowledges the potential multiplicity of schematic types when he speaks of 'a fuzzy set – a category whose boundaries merge with the boundaries of other categories' (1988: 95). He is not alone in this respect, for '[i]n recent years, certain philosophers have been willing to countenance "cluster concepts", natural kinds defined by traits which covary only statistically. For them, the boundaries between natural kinds in character space are "fuzzy"' (Hull 1982: 283). For instance, Gjerdingen identifies a number of changing-note schemata based upon the I–V…V–I harmonic structure, whose conformant melodic dyads are $\hat{1}$–$\hat{2}$…$\hat{7}$–$\hat{1}$, $\hat{1}$–$\hat{7}$…$\hat{2}$–$\hat{1}$, $\hat{1}$–$\hat{7}$…$\hat{4}$–$\hat{3}$, $\hat{3}$–$\hat{2}$…$\hat{4}$–$\hat{3}$ and $\hat{3}$–$\hat{4}$…$\hat{2}$–$\hat{3}$ (1988: 56). As is shown in Figure 4.6 below, some dyads may appear in more than one of these schemata.

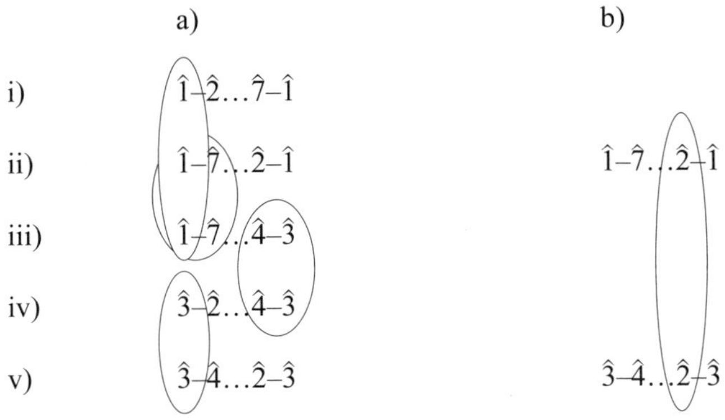

Figure 4.6: 'Fuzzy Sets' based on the I–V…V–I Harmonic Structure (after Gjerdingen 1988: 56, Example 4-1)

In Figure 4.6 a ii and iii, the initial melodic dyad acts as a cue for what might follow. It prompts the listener to be aware of a finite set of possible terminal melodic dyads (Gjerdingen notes the importance of bass-line cues in this respect; 1988: 71–5). Moreover, at a finer level of resolution, in all the examples the first component of the initial dyad may act as a cue for a finite set of second components. In Figure 4.6 b ii and v, the connection drawn between the first component of the terminal dyads indicates that, in addition to the schema forms $\hat{1}$–$\hat{7}$…$\hat{2}$–$\hat{1}$ and $\hat{3}$–$\hat{4}$…$\hat{2}$–$\hat{3}$, the forms $\hat{1}$–$\hat{7}$…$\hat{2}$–$\hat{3}$ and $\hat{3}$–$\hat{4}$…$\hat{2}$–$\hat{1}$ may also theoretically be cued, provided these types are replicated in the dialect.

Gjerdingen contends that 'the retention of older, established schemata will inhibit the recognition of early examples of a [new] schema' (1988: 104). Given that the initial events of established (widely propagated) schemata act as cues, prompting the listener to expect a conformant statement of the terminal event drawn from a finite set of possibilities, the composer-as-listener is subject to much the same play of implications, and may not be able to synthesize a top-down perspective to organize the new schema. The composer-as-composer, however, may not recognize early examples of a new structure, in the sense of being able to assign them to membership of an extant category, but this would not necessarily prevent the composer replicating the new configuration of (presumably) familiar features in subsequent compositional contexts by means of other, allelic, feature memes, once the structural characteristics of this higher-order meme have been abstracted. While established schemata may indeed inhibit the recognition of new schemata, it seems unlikely that they could impede the replication of the new form.

Finally, what of the meme's eye view in all of this? The caveat concerning 'fuzziness' notwithstanding, when the $\hat{4}$–$\hat{3}$/V–I meme became associated in schematic memeplexes with the $\hat{1}$–$\hat{7}$/I–V meme, their fates became interconnected. Indeed the fecundity of the $\hat{4}$–$\hat{3}$/V–I meme may even have been increased by participation in such schemata, for even though each was replicated independently, deployment of the $\hat{1}$–$\hat{7}$/I–V meme may have tended to cue the $\hat{4}$–$\hat{3}$/V–I meme in the mind of the composer in terminal conformance. In such situations, the terminal-event meme 'hitches a ride' on the back of the initial-event meme and, because this alliance leads to the existence of one more phemotypic copy of the terminal-event meme than would otherwise have been the case, there will be a statistical increase in the likelihood of the meme's further replication. In this sense, it is in the selfish interests of a meme to be able to form a component of a schema.

4.6.4. *A High-Level Perspective: System-Level Evolutionary Change*

Contrary to the view that the major-minor tonal system is ontologically privileged and Platonically stable owing to its primary structures being closely aligned with elements of the harmonic series (Schenker 1979: 10–11), the argument developed in this book suggests that, the inescapable physical-acoustic constraints of their environment notwithstanding (4.6.1 above), tonal systems are memetic phenomena operating at the levels of rules, strategies and dialects and are therefore subject to the operation of the evolutionary algorithm. Thus, for memetics, such higher-order aspects of musical organization as tonality – better 'tonalities', in Pople's sense (2004b), implying the multivalent, not the monolithic – are fluid and mutable.

In perhaps the most striking manifestation of universal Darwinism, Dennett suggests that even physical laws are fluid and evolutionary, and 'that the singularities known as black holes are in effect the birthplaces of offspring universes, in which the fundamental physical constants would differ slightly, in random ways, from the physical constants in the parent universe' (1995: 177). In a slightly different twist to this line of argument, physicists such as David Deutsch (1997) argue that our universe is but one of many encompassed by an all-encompassing multiverse. Within the 'parent' multiverse, the various 'child' universes may manifest different physical systems and laws of organization. If one such 'offspring universe' were to replicate more effectively than its 'siblings', then its systems of organization may overwhelm those of its siblings in a multiverse-level manifestation of the variation-heredity/replication-differential fitness algorithm. One would then be justified in speaking of evolution by means of multiversal Darwinism. The characteristics of such offspring universes are ultimately determined, in bottom-up fashion, by the properties of the smallest-level units of which they are composed, the individual subatomic particles and atoms.

Similarly, one might hypothesize that the characteristics of tonal systems are determined by the properties of their smallest functional units, namely individual memes, constrained by the properties of the physical-acoustic and psychological environment within which they are propagated, and by the perceptual-cognitive schemata which are abstracted from exposure to other memes. To extend the argument developed in connection with constraints in 4.6.1 above, the major-minor tonal system and its constituent dialects (represented by the 'system of rules' set in Figure 2.1 above) may therefore be regarded as the mean product of the attributes of the millions of memes extant at a selection of moments in musical history between *c.* 1700 and *c.* 1900. Narmour adopts this position, albeit expressed in different terminology, asserting that

> syntactic structures determine musical scales …, construct pitch hierarchies, and generate that elusive and changeable but permeating musical phenomenon we call tonality …. the notion of scale step *as a rigid system* is oversold by psychologists and overbought by music theorists.… scale steps in tonal systems are atomic schemata …, building-block variables at the bottom of the top-down stylistic hierarchy.… scale steps are nothing more than stored, abstract representations that depend on varying contextual cues.
>
> (1990: 143, 144; his emphasis)

As the memes that define the system change then the system itself is, of necessity, reconfigured – an offspring tonal universe arises from within the tonal multiverse. Yet any system can only tolerate a certain degree of internal change before it becomes not the same system altered but a quite different system, as happened to tonality towards the end of the nineteenth century. Moreover, within such a fluid continuum, drawing a dividing line to demarcate sectors is arbitrary: for instance, LaRue's concepts for categorizing the evolving stages of tonal organization – which he identifies as the stages of linear, migrant, bifocal, unified and expanded tonality, and then atonality (1970: 52–4) – however effectively they capture the essence of an evolving tonal system, can really only represent thin, static slices of this process of change, not the broad dynamic flow.

This perspective forces one to re-evaluate Meyer's notion of dialect. While differentiation between dialects may be made, he argues, on the basis of geography, nationality, artistic movements, social class or cultural function, 'most often dialects are distinguished historically' (1989: 23). One might therefore interpret the period *c.* 1700–*c.* 1900 as comprising three historical dialects, the Baroque, Classicism and Romanticism, operating within the constraints of a single set of rules, that of 'tonality'. Yet while no contemporary commentator claims a strict articulation between these periods – indeed the tendency is increasingly to emphasize lines of continuity – if one regards the evolution of musical style as the manifestation of a fluid meme pool reconfiguring itself through a succession of transient states, then the notion of discrete historically demarcated dialects cannot logically remain tenable. The meme pool of J.S. Bach's time evolved through a near infinity of such states until it became transmuted into that of Wagner's, and beyond.

Moreover, bearing in mind the caveats attendant upon LaRue's segmentation of the development of tonal organization, scepticism is needed concerning the rigidity of the distinction Meyer draws between (diachronic) changes from one dialect to another – which he terms 'trended changes', for example between 'Classicism' and 'Romanticism' *c.* 1800–*c.* 1820 – and changes from one system of rules to another – which he terms 'mutational changes', for example between tonality and serialism *c.* 1900–*c.* 1920 (1989: 102). Note, however, that Meyer is using the term 'mutational' in a different sense to that used here: memetics regards trended changes just as much the result of meme mutations as mutational changes. He conceives this distinction as one between differences of degree and kind respectively, yet argues that the two modes of style change are not necessarily related (: 103) and that '[i]t does not follow, however, that the trend *caused* the mutational change, only that the stylistic/cultural situation created by the trend made it possible for the mutation to endure – be replicated.... Nor is it supposed that if a stylistic consensus takes place, the new rules (mutations) will be a result of prior trends or strategies' (: 103, notes 79, 80; his emphasis).

While I am not suggesting the teleological inevitability of a given rule change arising from antecedent changes in the dialect(s) it encompasses, it must be the case – accepting my earlier contention that the nature of a system is a function of the properties of its smallest units – that the large-scale reconfiguration represented by a change in rules can only be defined in terms of the changes occurring upon lower hierarchic levels. A neo-Darwinian perspective would regard mutational changes as the inexorable outcome of cumulative trended changes, the latter acting not only as a necessary condition for the former but also as determinants of the configuration of the new higher-order system. In this respect, memetic-cultural evolution again parallels biological evolution, for 'all sane Darwinians are gradualists in the extreme sense that they do not believe in the *de novo* creation of very complex and therefore statistically improbable new adaptations like eyes. This is surely what Darwin understood by the aphorism "Nature does not make leaps"' (Dawkins 1983a: 287–8).

Furthermore, just as the notion of distinct, historically sequential dialects is undermined by a view of musical style as a succession of transient meme-pool states, so the idea of distinct, historically sequential systems of rules cannot logically be sustained. While the division of musical culture along the vertical/synchronic axis of rules, dialects and idioms is a powerful intellectual tool for structuring a complex field, and one which retains its clarity at any given point in musical time, when considered in association with the horizontal/diachronic axis representing temporal progression the distinctiveness of each of its first two categories is attenuated by the inexorable gradualism of memetic mutation and evolution.

Far from being an end-state to which cultural evolution has been purposely directed, tonality – leaving aside the question of which slice of musical history affords one the most representative view of it – is, essentially, an accident, albeit a glorious one. Just as life on earth might have been very different had this or that environmental or genetic event played itself out differently, so the tonal system of, for instance, Beethoven – and therefore that of his successors – might well have been very different had Haydn followed his father's craft, or had Mozart not been introduced to a selection of works of J.S. Bach by Gottfried von Swieten. Tonality, memetics contends, was merely the outcome of the confluence of millions of memes at a particular stage of their evolution, memes that were old by the time of Palestrina but which, like the gene, are potentially immortal. The alliances those memes found themselves in and which resulted in the formation of the tonal system have long since broken down. Nevertheless, their evolutionary descendants are still active and will probably remain so as long as humans – or intelligent machines, a subject I return to in Chapter 7 – make music.

4.7. Summary

Whereas the disposition of musical memes in intraopus contexts accounts for the synchronic memetic-structural and memetic-cultural hierarchies of works and styles at any given point in time, their mutability, transmissibility and differential perceptual-cognitive salience furnish the necessary and sufficient conditions to impel diachronic changes at higher levels of the memetic-cultural hierarchy. Gradually and non-teleologically, higher-order musical systems reconfigure themselves as rules and dialects transmute over time. For all their magnitude, these systemic changes are the consequence of the relentless, low-level competition for survival between selfish memes. Taking the meme's eye view in this process is facilitated by formalizing certain of its Gestalt-psychological attributes, such that a number of related properties which equate the notion of selfishness itself may be modelled.

Chapter 5

Cumulative Selection and The Evolution of Large-Scale Design in Music

5.1. Introduction

Having considered some of the attributes of the musical meme, and the processes underpinning its transmission, mutation and selection in Chapter 3 and Chapter 4, I turn now to the larger cultural products, musical works, of which memes form the component parts. As argued in 3.4 above, a unit meme is normally a multiparametric complex itself consisting of memes in the parameters of pitch, rhythm and perhaps other, secondary parameters; and a musical span (a phrase or section) is a multimemetic complex consisting of a number of interconnected pitch and rhythmic memes. By extension, a movement or work might be regarded as a superordinate-level multimemetic complex consisting of a multiplicity of memes and memeplexes in various parameters in selfish co-adaptation with each other. But how might such a complex come about? How is it 'designed' by the process of cultural selection over time?

To address these issues, I begin with an examination of the problem of design in nature and the controversies that engulfed evolutionary thinking when it was pressed by adherents of creationism to explain the origin of complex biological structures. Then the distinction between 'single-step' and 'cumulative' selection is outlined and applied to the evolution of what might be termed structural memes in music – the large-scale formal archetypes repeatedly instantiated by the tendency of memes to conglomerate in certain ways at particular points in their evolutionary history. Thereafter, Borges's notion of the 'Library of Babel' is adapted to model the relationship between musical structures in 'conceptual space'. The chapter concludes with a reconception of the notion of progress in culture in the light of ideas from memetics.

5.2. Arguments About Design

Arguments about the morphology and design of living things have shaped the course of debate in evolutionary theory from the eighteenth-century controversies between creationists and evolutionists to more recent developments in embryology. The parallels between genes and memes hypothesized by universal Darwinism and elaborated upon in previous chapters suggest that such arguments, some of which I outline here, bear a direct relevance to memetics.

5.2.1. *Paley's Watch and the Blind Watchmaker*

In *The Blind Watchmaker*, Dawkins maintains that

> The complexity of living organisms is matched by the elegant efficiency of their apparent design. If anyone doesn't agree that this amount of complex design cries out for an explanation, I give up. No, on second thoughts I don't give up, because one of my aims … is to convey something of the sheer wonder of biological complexity to those whose eyes have not been opened to it. But having built up the mystery, my other main aim is to remove it again by explaining the solution.
>
> (1991: xiii)

Dawkins's title refers to the metaphor used by William Paley in his *Natural Theology* to advocate the creationist Argument from Design (see 1.2.1 above). This holds that unlike an object such as a stone, which can easily be understood to have arisen through natural, physical means, a watch is so complicated as to have required the intercession of 'an artificer or artificers, who formed it for the purpose which we find it actually to answer; who comprehended its construction, and designed its use' (in Dawkins 1991: 4). From his watch, Paley moves to the even greater complexity of the human body, arguing that something so elaborate and well regulated could not possibly have originated except by the intercession of an intelligent, therefore divine, designer. For all its superficial appeal, however, this argument suffers from the fatal flaw of infinite regress: if a (presumably) complex, intelligent designer is needed to create the human form, who or what created the designer?

Dawkins's Darwinian counter-argument to the doctrine of special creation, and the solution to the infinite-regress problem, retains the terms of Paley's metaphor even as it subverts it. There is indeed a watchmaker responsible for creating the organized complexity of living things but the watchmaker is not a mysterious deity: it is process of evolution by natural selection of inherited genetic variation. Lacking teleological purpose, natural selection builds up complex forms in a manner which strongly suggests the action of a conscious creator, yet it 'has no purpose in mind. It has no mind and no mind's eye. It does not plan for the future. It has no vision, no foresight, no sight at all. If it can be said to play the role of watchmaker in nature, it is the *blind* watchmaker' (1991: 5; his emphasis). Unlike Paley's watchmaker, whom biblical doctrine assumes works over a relatively short time span (the six days of Genesis, Chapter 1), the blind watchmaker of natural selection acts over the millennia of geological time.

5.2.2. *Cultural Objects and Second-Order Organisms*

We find a parallel to this tension between creation and evolution in human culture, in which the extreme complexity evident in the products of artistic endeavour calls for an explanation. Conceiving cultural products as analogous to living organisms, Cavalli-Sforza and Feldman note that

> A particular cultural trait is chosen for study for the sake of convenience of observation and measurement, or because of its specific interest with respect to a more general context. Usually the trait is abstracted from a larger, more complex unit which can be truly defined as a *cultural object*. Modern technology offers many highly developed examples of cultural objects, which are almost as complex as a living organism: a jet, a car, or a washing machine, for example. These could be considered as 'organisms', because they are reproduced by some kind of assembly line, a procedure which puts together a number of pieces specifically molded or machined, so as to look as closely as possible like a prototype.... The artisan making a violin, or the engineers and factory workers making a car, are the living organisms or the *first-order organisms* that produce the pieces and assemble them. Without them, no *second-order organisms* like the violin and the car would be produced.
>
> (1981: 17; their emphases)

Works of art also constitute second-order organisms and are similarly conceived in terms of the notion of a complex of combined but separable traits (: 18). The latter are equivalent to the individual meme, the 'larger, more complex units' being such things as bagatelles, symphonies and music dramas. The second-order organism, be it a trouser press or a sonata, represents the phemotypic confluence of a large number of memes, the neurophysiological antecedent of which is an extended episodic/schematic memory string. Thus, a jet aircraft, as an ordered construction of metal, plastic, glass and numerous other materials, is not an assembly of memes *per se*, but a phemotypic artefact resulting from the interaction of the constituents of a memeplex.

In the critical language of romanticism, the term 'creation' was applied to artistic enterprise in a clear parallel to its religious sense, the artist being held to have brought a second-order organism into being by an act analogous to special creation. Even in the first decade of the nineteenth century, in a letter to Breitkopf and Härtel of 4 March 1809 apropos the Fifth and Sixth Symphonies, Beethoven is using such language, advising his publisher that

> Tomorrow you will receive a notice about some small corrections which I made during the performance of the symphonies – When I gave these works to you, I had not yet heard either of them performed – and one should not want to be so like a god as not to have to correct something here and there in one's created works[.]
>
> (In Anderson 1961: 217; letter 199)

Of course, for the composer, painter or poet the individual act of artistic production does indeed possess several of the attributes of special creation, in that a large and complex entity is fashioned over the course of a relatively short time span in a specific temporal and geographical locus. In this act, the artist acquires a God-like status in bringing something rich and complex into being. How might this tension between creation and evolution be conceived and resolved in memetics?

For artistic products, as opposed to technological artefacts, correspondence to a rigid prototype by means of the strictly controlled assembly of invariant components is true only in the loosest sense and is not a significant characteristic, certainly in the post-Renaissance European tradition. Clearly, a chronologically- or geographically-circumscribed series of sonata-form movements, for all their affinities, evidently lacks the large- and small-scale copying-fidelity intrinsic to a series of Boeing 747s. Nevertheless, there is usually sufficient conformance for us to speak of a structural archetype being instantiated when one compares such a series of movements. This is because in producing a work of art the artist will almost invariably draw upon specific structural models propagated within his or her culture. I regard such archetypes as memes operative at the level of global structure for they are replicated ways of organizing replicated patterns and are therefore higher-order replicated patterns. Providing a framework for organizing a movement's specific meme-sequence, structural memes are themselves the result of decades if not centuries of cultural evolution.

5.3. The Evolution of Structural Memes

I now turn to consider the nature of structural memes in music and the mechanisms driving their evolution in more detail. While it seems there is a connection between the evolution of structural memes and that of the genres within which they sit, the complex social, political, economic and mechanical factors which impinge on the development of genre render this particular subject beyond the scope of this study. Nevertheless, memetics contends that no cultural phenomenon, including the evolution of genre, can be understood without a neo-Darwinian model of meme variation, heredity/replication and differential fitness operating in multiple cultural realms.

5.3.1. *Structural Memes*

In developing his comparison between genes and memes, Dawkins reaches a point of apparent divergence. He suggests that

> Memes seem to have nothing equivalent to chromosomes, and nothing equivalent to alleles. I suppose there is a trivial sense in which many ideas can be said to have 'opposites'. But in general memes resemble the early replicating molecules, floating chaotically free in the primeval soup, rather than modern genes in their neatly paired, chromosomal regiments.
>
> (1989: 196–7)

While this may be true for many memes – for 'ideas, catch-phrases, clothes fashions, ways of making pots or of building arches' (: 192), and the like – it does not appear to be so for memes in the more formal domains of culture. In music, the tonal system has evolved structural archetypes for the organization of memes and these have comparably sophisticated analogues in many other modes of artistic discourse, such as the arrangement of verbal-conceptual memes to form poetic metres and verse types.

Of the two basic components of analysis defined by Bent and Pople – namely, 'the interpretation of structures in music, together with their resolution into relatively simpler constituent elements, and the investigation of the relevant functions of those elements' (2001: 526) – it is perhaps the second which has most exercised theorists. One of their major preoccupations of the past five centuries has been to construct archetypes for the sequential organization of musical material, and Bent and Pople review several models advanced to address this question. Chief among these are: the rhetorically-predicated schemata of Medieval and Renaissance theory, as in the work of Listenius and Burmeister; the periodic, cadence-sensitive models of eighteenth-century theorists such as Riepel, Kirnberger and Koch (from which, in the nineteenth century, the *Formenlehre* of Leichtentritt and Prout arose); Schenker's notion of hierarchic structural levels; Schoenberg's, Réti's and Keller's views of logical motivic proliferation (*Substanzgemeinschaft*); mathematical models derived from Cantorian set theory; generative/transformational grammars drawing principally on Chomskyan linguistics; and, fairly recently, the distributional syntaxes mapped by semiotics (2001: 530–70). It should be stressed, however, that in attempting to elucidate the organization of one cultural-syntactic system through the mediation of another, such models – even though they may to a limited extent feed back into and influence compositional practice – consist of verbal-conceptual memeplexes operating upon (interpreting) musical memes and memeplexes.

Although radically different, these theoretical viewpoints are related by their core assumption that the assemblage of musical units into larger wholes is not a purely random process, but is governed by the operation of certain (meme-derived) constraints, to use Meyer's term. Thus, if a classical sonata movement is comprised of n discrete particles, it is not necessarily the case that $n!$ (that is, n factorial: $n\times n\text{-}1\times n\text{-}2\times n\text{-}3$, etc.) more such movements may be created by the mechanical permutation of these units. Similarly, while the vast majority of classical sonata movements may be held to express the $\hat{3}$–$\hat{1}$, $\hat{5}$–$\hat{1}$ and $\hat{8}$–$\hat{1}$ Schenkerian archetypes, it seems likely that none is founded upon a $\hat{2}$–$\hat{1}$, $\hat{4}$–$\hat{1}$, $\hat{6}$–$\hat{1}$, or $\hat{7}$–$\hat{1}$ *Urlinie*. This finite number of ordering (co-adaptation) sequences is determined by the properties of a meme's initial and terminal nodes. It is akin to the finite number of ordering sequences of genes within chromosomes, which are the consequence of the ways in which a gene's initial and terminal nucleotides form bonds with neighbouring genes.

This tendency of memes to conglomerate in certain limited ways leads to the formation of a relatively small number of configurations – antecedent-consequent phrases, sonata forms, *Ursätzen* – which, because they are replicated, albeit indirectly, are themselves memetic. Naturally, different structural constraints are generated in different repertoires, but they arise by analogous (meme co-adaptational/conglomerational) means. Thus, if a chromosome is understood as essentially a string (a topological sequence) of genes, each of which is restricted by its biochemical properties to occupying a specific locus along the chromosome's length, a span of music may correspondingly be understood as a similarly circumscribed string (an episodic/schematic temporal sequence) of memes. It is a sonorous 'chromosomal regiment', whichever verbal-conceptual framework – Quintillian rhetoric, phrase assemblage, voice-leading strata, motivic elaboration, set-permutation, generative grammar, or distributional syntax – one employs to model the sequential disposition of the 'soldiers'.

On this reasoning it is clearly a mistake to regard the resultant archetypes as moulds, into which the ideas of composers may, in a crude sense, be poured. Rather, they exist because they are repeatedly reinstantiated – replicated – by memes at more immediate levels of musical structure. Despite their seemingly abstract quality, such fundamental patterns had clear reality for composers – even if, as Cook observes, they may have little tangible identity for listeners (1990: 57) – for, as Drabkin notes,

> we know that [Beethoven] studied the music of his predecessors Haydn and Mozart and modelled a number of sonata-type works of the 1790s and early 1800s on specific works by Mozart. If a piece by Mozart could suggest to Beethoven a set of procedures to be followed – with modifications – to produce another piece, then he probably did not regard the growth processes in a particular piece as the exclusive property of that piece.
>
> (1991: 15)

Thus Beethoven – and probably most composers working in traditions with strongly developed notions of genre and form – perceived a fairly clear distinction between a work's formal-structural archetype and its specific content, what Bonds terms a 'conformational approach' to form (in Smith 1996: 193). He realized that a given formal schema might receive many instantiations each of which was unique in its local details but all of which shared broadly analogous 'growth processes'. Given this replication by repeated instantiation, it is logical to assert that the structural archetypes of the music of the common-practice era – simple binary form, da capo aria form and other ternary designs, sonata form, the patterns of the multi-movement sonata cycle, etc. – are memes at the largest dimensions of musical organization; they are, to use Gjerdingen's terminology, high-level structural schemata which may be instantiated by the assemblage of a variety of lower-level features.

Structural memes need not be confined to the tonal-harmonic structures most often regarded as defining formal archetypes. On a more abstract level, were it not for clearly replicated regularities in dynamics, cadence structure and thematic character, Leeson and Levin would not have been able to abstract what Rosen terms a 'useful roadmap' of the opening ritornelli of Mozart's concerto first movements. Outlining this schema, Leeson and Levin note that

> The first theme (1), usually piano – or forte followed by piano – is extended to a perfect cadence in the tonic. It is followed by a more active forte passage (2), driving to a half-cadence (3) on the dominant.... A more lyric theme (4), piano,... is extended to a perfect cadence in the tonic and a forte passage (5).... This ... is often followed by a second concluding motive (6), piano and less assertive, which is itself succeeded by a brief flourish (7) on the tonic that rounds off the ritornello and immediately precedes the entry of the soloist ....[1]
>
> (in Rosen 1987: 83)

The same principles apply to verbal-conceptual patterning and the deeper-level structures to which this gives rise. For example, the text of the introductory sections of books and journal articles from a variety of disciplines often takes the form of 'common ground–disruption–resolution', this tripartite structure being further subdivided into consistently deployed subcomponents (Booth, Colomb and Williams 1995: 249). Given that such patterns are repeatedly articulated by a variety of 'surface' configurations, in texts of widely divergent form and content, we are perhaps justified in regarding the abstract pattern as a deep-level meme, a 'normative prolongational structure' (Lerdahl and Jackendoff 1983: 198) in the verbal-conceptual realm.

---

[1] In a typical instantiation, Mozart's Piano Concerto in C minor K. 491 (1786), I, has an opening ritornello organized as follows (bracketed numbers refer to Leeson's and Levin's 'roadmap'): (1) bb. 1–13; (2) bb. 13–34; (3) b. 34; (4) bb. 35–63; (5) bb. 63–73; (6) bb. 73–87; (7) bb. 88–99.

5.3.2. *The Mechanisms of Memetic-Structural Evolution*

To return to an issue raised in Dawkins's quotation at the start of the previous section, the extent to which we are justified in using the genetic term allele in connection with memetics has been partly treated in 4.5 above, where it was suggested (under point 1 on p. 137) that configurationally, functionally or structurally analogous or homologous memes might be said to exist in a state of allelic rivalry. It was also hypothesized there (point 2) that such memes might also be said to exist in a state of allelic rivalry if they are capable of occupying a given locus in a structural meme.

I have argued that structural memes are configurations replicated by means of their repeated reinstantiation by memes at more immediate structural levels, claiming that 'they are replicated ways of organizing replicated patterns and are therefore higher-order replicated patterns' (p. 168). Their generative lower-order memes are in a relationship of allelic competition with each other, in that a number of morphologically analogous memes may instantiate a given component of the structural meme. Moreover, each candidate for a given locus of the structural meme has a similar 'conglomerational grammar' to its alleles, such that an allele for locus *y* of a hypothetical three-component structural meme *x–y–z* forms similar structural relationships with alleles for components *x* and *z* as do other alleles for locus *y*. This phenomenon is illustrated in Figure 5.1 below.

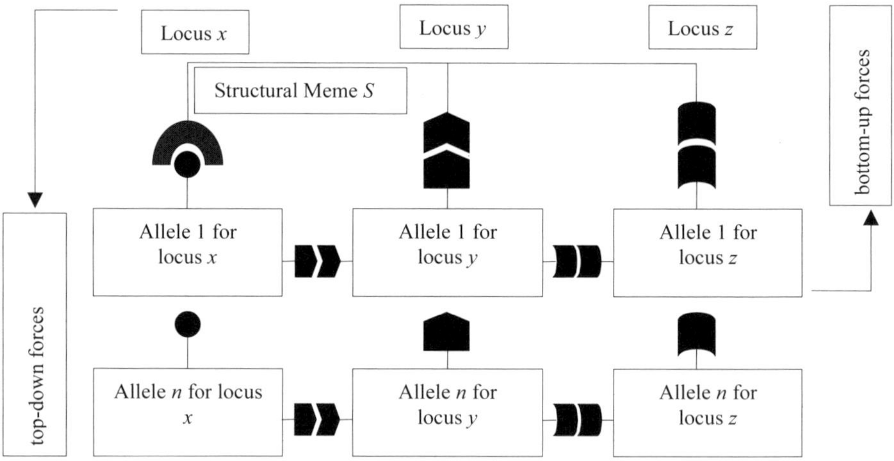

Figure 5.1: Allelic Rivalry and Conglomerational grammar

Having outlined its basic mechanism, the aetiology and evolution of a structural meme S^1 may be resolved into four stages:

1. The association of memes of specific nature and function (scale-degree emphasis, harmonic progression, rhythmic relationship, etc.) gives rise to a sequential configuration which generates a sequence of structural nodes, a structural mnemon MnS^1.
2. Because this sequential configuration has multiple modes of instantiation, its re-generation by memes of analogous (allelic) configuration, function or structure engenders a structural meme, S^1, a replicated structural relationship.
3. Lower-order-meme-driven mutation or reassortment of, or interpolation of other nodes into the interstices of, S^1's structural nodes on subsequent replication leads to the formation of a variant of S^1, a structural mnemon MnS^2.
4. Re-generation of MnS^2 by memes of allelic configuration, function or structure renders it memetic, creating a new structural meme, S^2.

Figure 5.2 below represents this sequence of events using the transmissional-tripartitional format of Figure 4.1 above.

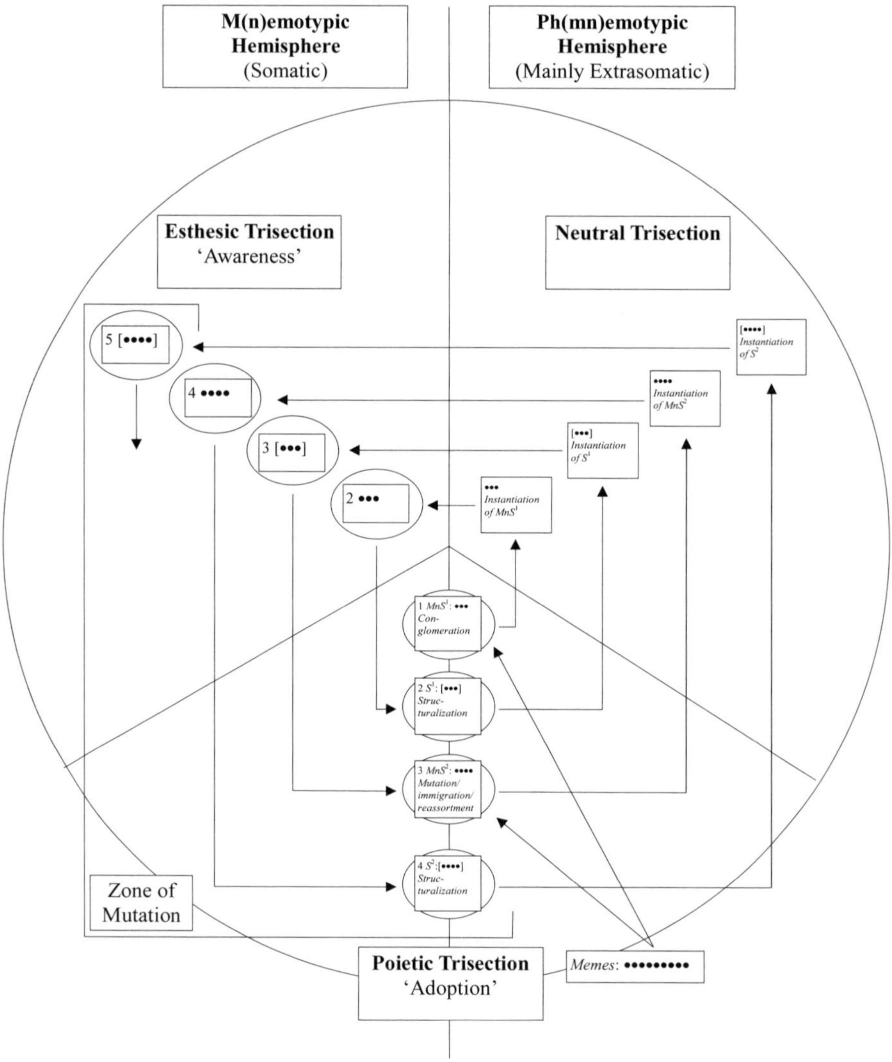

Figure 5.2: Memetic-Structural Transmission and Evolution and the Semiological Tripartition

In the first host (1), a collection of memes assembles to form a multimemetic complex MnS^1. This is embodied at the neutral-phmnemotypic level in the form of a notated or improvised composition. At its most abstract level, this conglomeration of memes gives rise to a series of structural nodes which represent the salient events of the movement's unfolding processes. A second host (2) imitates this sequence of nodes in the sense of replicating the 'growth processes', to use Drabkin's phrase, of the initial conglomeration, by means of foreground memes of analogous configuration, function or structure. In imitating the nodal sequence, the second host structuralizes it: the growth process becomes memetic, becoming in itself a unit of cultural replication, and a structural meme, S^1, is formed.

The parameters most likely to support such (re)conglomeration, certainly in music of the common-practice Western tradition, are global tonal/harmonic motion and associated upper- and lower-voice pitch structures, although 'co-parameters' such as rhythm and texture may also be significant. In the light of Leeson's and Levin's observations on Mozart's concerti ritornelli discussed in 5.3.1 above, one might even admit such configurations as those described by the phrase 'a loud *tutti* with trumpets and drums playing the rhythm ♩ ♪.♬ ♩ ♩' as capable of participating in such processes.

A third host (3) may then continue the process of structural imitation, either closely or with modifications. Such modifications, driven by changes at the level of the generative lower-order memes, may include the mutation of existing nodes of the structural meme, their internal reassortment and the interpolation of additional nodes into the structure – transformations underpinning the mutation of foreground-orientated memes (4.3.2 above) recursively writ large. Such a modified version of the original structural meme, MnS^2 may then be encountered by a fourth host (4) who, in imitating it, structuralizes it and renders it memetic. A second structural meme, S^2, is thereby formed.

Deliège and Mélen's theory of cue abstraction offers support for this model. While not without its critics (a refinement is offered in Ockelford 2004), their theory outlines a psychological mechanism for the mental representation and propagation of structural memes. They contend that

> A cue always contains rare but striking attributes that link it to that which it cues … in order that the latter may be recognised …. A cue is a kind of conspicuous point that becomes fixed in memory by virtue of its relevance and by repetition ….
>
> (1997: 390)

Such cues may play a central role in engendering structural memes for, invoking principles which I have treated under the rubrics of segmentation and coindexation, Deliège and Mélen argue that

> The musical surface is first segmented into sections of various lengths. The cue abstraction mechanism, on the one hand, the principle of sameness and the principle of difference, on the other hand, offer the basis for the processes operating at this level, allowing segmentation of the temporal flow … and the categorisation of musical structures …. In a later stage, the traces left by the reiterations of the cues lead to the formation of imprints in the long-term memory. The latter are forms of prototypes that integrate the main features of the style of the piece and enable an evaluation of the structures throughout listening.
>
> (: 389)

These 'imprints in the long-term memory' may be held to represent the nodes of the structural meme, and as such constitute a generalized image of the movement's structure as defined by its principal melodic, harmonic and tonal events and its points of articulation and closure. As such they also exert a degree of top-down pressure in partly determining the nature of the material which might, in later instantiations of that structural meme, occupy each topological locus.[2]

5.3.3. *Single-Step* versus *Cumulative Selection in the Evolution of Structural Memes*

Distinguishing between the circumscribed act of special creation which gives rise to the individual work of art and the long process by which the complex structural archetypes instantiated by that second-order organism arises (5.2.2 above) mirrors the first-order dichotomy between ontogeny and phylogeny. It also implies that the greater the complexity of such an archetype, the lower the statistical probability that it could come into being randomly. Indeed any complex configuration is much more likely to evolve by means of the 'stepwise' modification of a slightly less complex antecedent than by means of a 'leap' from a considerably simpler precursor. Thus, complexity can most easily evolve by building gradually on previous forms, a reliance on what Dennett terms 'cranes', not 'skyhooks' (1995: 73–5).

The phylogenetic evolution of complexity is illustrated by Dawkins using the Shavian notion of the monkey, given sufficient time, eventually reproducing the works of Shakespeare as a result of random tapping on a typewriter. Dawkins is somewhat less ambitious, being concerned only with the genesis of a single line from *Hamlet*, 'Methinks it is like a weasel' (III, ii, 388), spoken by Hamlet to Polonius in observing the resemblance of clouds to the shapes of animals. To attempt to create this line, which consists of twenty-three letters and five spaces, Dawkins programmed a computer to generate a random string of twenty-eight

---

[2] That the allelic competition between foreground memes to express the components of the structural meme of a movement tends repeatedly to be 'won' by a network of memes with a high degree of mutual compatibility is presumably a factor driving close memetic co-adaptation.

characters drawn from the twenty-six letters of the Latin alphabet and the space character. His experiment produced such bizarre, but entirely predictable, results as:

> WDLDMNLT DTJBKWIRZREZLMQCO P

and

> GEWRGZRPBCTPGQMCKHFDBGW ZCCF
>
> (1991: 47)

Indeed, Dawkins expresses the odds of the monkey typing METHINKS IT IS LIKE A WEASEL at its first attempt as $({}^{1}/_{27})^{28}$ – the odds of getting an individual character correct and in the correct locus in the sentence raised to the power of the number of characters in the sentence. Put another way, the monkey would need 27^{28} attempts – 'generations' – to be guaranteed to produce the sentence. On all reasonable estimates, it is clear that the hapless creature would never type the line, let alone the Bard's complete *oeuvre*.

This process is an example of what Dawkins terms 'single-step selection', a process in which each iteration selects afresh from the range of possibilities, taking no account of previously selected configurations (1991: 45). As a mechanism for evolutionary development, single-step selection is a very poor candidate indeed. If we have to wait an eternity for a single line to arise through the random assembly of a mere twenty-eight characters, how much longer must we wait for a first-order living organism to arise from the assembly of its myriad molecular constituents? On the same logic, how much longer must we wait for a second-order organism such as a play, a painting, or a symphony to come about from the association of its smallest units?

The alternative – and probably the only plausible – model of evolution is 'cumulative selection', whereby the configuration of members of one generation influence that of successive generations (1991: 45). Applying this model to the Shakespeare line, Dawkins modified his computer program in order to copy the first random string of characters generated many times with the potential for a small degree of random error in the progeny. The mutant form most resembling the target phrase was then selected as the basis for further copying and its own mutant offspring were similarly selected from. Using this second model it was possible to progress from

WDLDMNLT DTJBKWIRZREZLMQCO P

to

METHINKS IT IS LIKE A WEASEL

(1991: 47–8)

in the space of a mere forty-three generations, an eminently feasible process in comparison to the random stumblings of single-step selection. Although not goal-directed, cumulative selection is, in comparison to single-step selection, fundamentally non-random and allows developing structures to move in the direction of increasing refinement and complexity with respect to their antecedent forms.

Cumulative selection offers a parsimonious and convincing model for the evolution of structural memes in music. It is difficult to imagine this in terms of the established forms of Western music post 1700 for these have come to us by way of extended spans of structural evolution. To comprehend the process we must go back to *Urformen* and consider much less developed structural types. The earliest extant instrumental forms – as opposed to those dictated by the imperatives of a text – are those of Medieval and Renaissance dance music. Such pieces consist, in the main, of a few brief phrases assembled from a variety of memes. In this respect they are comparable to the line 'Methinks it is like a weasel' Dawkins synthesized by using his computer to generate an ordered sequence of 28 characters drawn from a universal set of 27.

It is clear what would happen if such a collection of memes were subject to the single-step selection mechanism Dawkins first employed in his experiment. On this model, every composer would start afresh, with a *tabula rasa*, assembling memes to make phrases without reference to the attempts of earlier composers. One can see how difficult it would be to move to such a 'target' configuration as that represented by sonata form. To estimate the odds involved, we would need to determine the number of events necessary to give rise to such a form.[3] If we decide, conservatively, that twenty specific characteristics are necessary to appear in a particular order for a given movement to belong to the class of sonata-form movements (to conform to what Carter terms the 'sonata principle' (1987: 89)), then, using Dawkins's equation, the statistical probability of a Josquin or a Palestrina spontaneously generating a sonata-form movement are $(^1/_{20})^{20}$, where for each of the twenty 'slots' there are classes each comprising thousands of alleles of

[3] These would certainly include the establishment of the tonic at the beginning; the modulation to, cadential reinforcement and harmonic elaboration of the dominant; and the reestablishment of the tonic, to give a very broad-brush view of the principal tonal events. In addition, one would also need to specify associated thematic, textural and gestural phenomena.

analogous configuration, function or structure suitable to occupy it. On these highly restricted parameters, the odds of spontaneously generating a sonata-form movement in the manner of special creation seem vanishingly small. It is clear that single step selection is statistically unlikely to give rise to an archetype as complex as sonata form in any reasonable time frame, certainly not over the course of the period *c.* 1500–*c.* 1750.

By contrast, the cumulative selection model can easily account for the aetiology and evolution of sonata form, and indeed any other complex structural archetype, provided we accept that '[e]ach successive change in the gradual evolutionary process was simple enough, *relative to its predecessor*, to have arisen by chance' (Dawkins 1991: 43; his emphasis). In these terms, it is clear that the complexity-distance – which one might conceive in terms of the Damerau-Levenshtein metric – between an entity such as a late-Renaissance proto-binary form and an early-nineteenth-century sonata form such as the first movement of Beethoven's '*Eroica*' Symphony is very large indeed.[4] Accordingly, the statistical probability of a composer 'leaping' this expanse in one bound, by means of single-step selection, is very low. Yet if the complexity-distance between any two such 'reference-point' structural memes is divided into a number of smaller 'steps', the span from any one of these intermediate structural memes to the one immediately after it decreases in direct proportion to the number of subdivisions. Concomitantly, the probability of composers being able to move, by means of cumulative selection, from one degree of structural complexity to the next increases in direct proportion to this value.

On this reasoning, it is intuitively clear that the probability of a work such as Beethoven's '*Eroica*' Symphony arising in any temporal or geographical locus other than the Vienna of 1803–04 is low; it could not have been composed by a member of the Notre Dame school, by Monteverdi, or perhaps even by Mozart. This is not, however, to adopt a determinist perspective: there is no sense in which Beethoven was destined or preordained to compose the '*Eroica*' in the form in which it now stands, just as Josquin was not destined to compose *Absalon fili mi* in 1497, and Stravinsky was not preordained to compose *Le sacre du printemps* just before the First World War. None of these works need ever have existed, although something like them probably would have been able to come into being. However, a symphony of the configuration represented by the '*Eroica*' would have been highly improbable outside (in both a chronological and a geographical sense) the lineage that led up to and away from it and of which it forms a part. This argument also implies that conditions theoretically existed for a plethora of potential '*Eroica*'-type works – each different but of equivalent scope and complexity, and using a similar memetic vocabulary – to have been written around the first five years of the nineteenth century in Vienna by a sufficiently (genetically,

---

4 An example of the former is Felice Anerio's 'Al suon' (from *Ghirlanda di Fioretti Musicali* of 1589), given in arrangements for harpsichord and lute in Davison and Apel 1949: 181 (no. 160 b).

memetically) gifted composer. Beethoven, as it happened, was the only composer in the right place at the right time able to bring any such structure into being.

This line of argument ties in closely with what is known of the embryological development of living creatures. Discussing the probabilistic differences between 'angel' wings (those sprouting directly out of the back) and those types of wings which evolved from arms, Dawkins notes that

> although any gene on any chromosome may mutate at any time, the consequences of mutation on *bodies* are severely limited by the processes of embryology.... You can't just postulate a mutation 'for' sprouting wings in the middle of the back. Wings, or anything else, can only evolve if the process of development allows them to. Nothing magically 'sprouts'. It has to be made by the processes of embryonic development.... Because of the way arms develop, it is possible for mutations to increase the length of fingers and cause webs of skin to grow between them. But there may not be anything in the embryology of backs that lends itself to 'sprouting' angel wings. Genes can mutate till they are blue in the face, but no mammal will ever sprout wings like an angel unless mammalian embryological processes are susceptible to this kind of change.
>
> (1991: 311; his emphasis)

While there is no direct parallel to embryology in memetics (perhaps the translation of cultural information from memotype to phemotype is the nearest equivalent process), and while the issue is complicated by the multileveled nature of structural memes (whereby each higher-order node arises from several intermediate-order nodes), applying Dawkins's argument to structural memes implies that a new higher-order limb of such a meme is more likely to develop by means of the gradualistic mutation and augmentation (via lower-order meme processes) of an existing higher-order structural node than by the abrupt sprouting of an entirely new component at this level. The large coda of the '*Eroica*' Symphony's first movement, for instance, is therefore best understood as an augmentation of smaller but comparable structures in the symphonies of Haydn and Mozart, themselves extensions of closing cadential perorations in earlier music, and not an entirely new structural innovation.

Hybridizing Interaction

Cladistic taxonomy is founded on the principle of strict hierarchic inclusion, whereby a lineage may bifurcate into two separate lower-level branches, but lower-level branches, especially ones arising from different higher-order nodes, may not fuse, a concept termed 'anastomosis'. By contrast, the (as-yet-undeveloped) memetic taxonomy of cultural forms must account for hybridizing interaction between members of different lineages. That is, while a given structural meme may arise from the evolution of antecedent forms in a direct linear-chronological sequence, possibly involving the branching off of a 'child' line from its 'parent', another structural meme might arise from the hybridization (fusion) of two or more hitherto unconnected structural memes. Here it is important to make a distinction between the augmentation of a (single) structural meme which results from the immigration of foreground- and middleground-level memes and which leads to an increase in the number of its higher-order structural nodes; and the hybridization of two or more structural memes which are each the product of independent memetic evolution and which generates a new structural meme with an increased number of higher-order nodes compared with its parents.

Ursatz, Memesatz

A structural meme may encompass elements which vary in their structural-hierarchic location. If one accepts that, in a very general sense, musical configurations are privileged by replication then one could legitimately include not only background- and middleground-level patterns but also elements from patterns situated at the foreground level in a structural meme. Such components of the structural meme may, by virtue of this replication, acquire an importance beyond that which their Fuxian/Schenkerian voice-leading and prolongational status would ordinarily warrant. More than any shared *Ursatz*, two or more pieces with the same structural meme – as in Example 3.12 ii, iv and vi above – might be said to replicate a common *memesatz*. Jan 2001 explores this idea in more detail.

5.3.4. *Top-Down, Bottom Up: Schenker's Background Archetypes Reconsidered*

The perspective on the evolution of structural archetypes in music outlined above stands in clear contradiction to Schenker's top-down perspective. Schenker maintained that

> all the foreground diminutions, including the apparent 'keys' arising out of the voice-leading transformations [of the middleground], ultimately emanate from the diatony [that is, the *Ursatz*] in the background.
>
> (1979: 11)

He also asserted that organicism

> is determined by the creation of the parts from the unity of the principal triad, i.e. by the composing-out of the Urlinie and the bass arpeggiation.... [Geniuses] dissolve the tonic triad into the melodic motion of the Urlinie and, at the same time, a few individual chords which are then split up again and again.
>
> (1996: 23)

Classical Schenkerism thus rests on the premise that the aetiology of a piece of music is essentially a background-out/down process; Schenker's term

Auskomponierung specifically qualifies its nature by a prepositional prefix. His is therefore a top-down generative view of musical organization akin in some respects to the theory of generative-transformational grammar developed by Chomsky (Narmour 1977: 108ff) and adapted to music by Lerdahl and Jackendoff (1983: 5–6; see also Lerdahl 1992, and Narmour 1977: 116ff. for a critique of transformationalism in music).

Chomsky's theory rests in part on the notion that

> The *base* of the syntactic component is a system of rules that generate a highly restricted (perhaps finite) set of *basic strings*, each with an associated structural description called a *base Phrase-marker*. These base Phrase-markers are the elementary units of which deep structures are constituted.
>
> (1965: 17; his emphases)

Here the basic string is broadly analogous to the *Ursatz*, the individual components of which corresponding to Chomsky's base Phrase-marker.

But one should not labour this comparison, for while one may readily accept that even complex sentences are generated by the transformation of basic strings, such as in the following simple example –

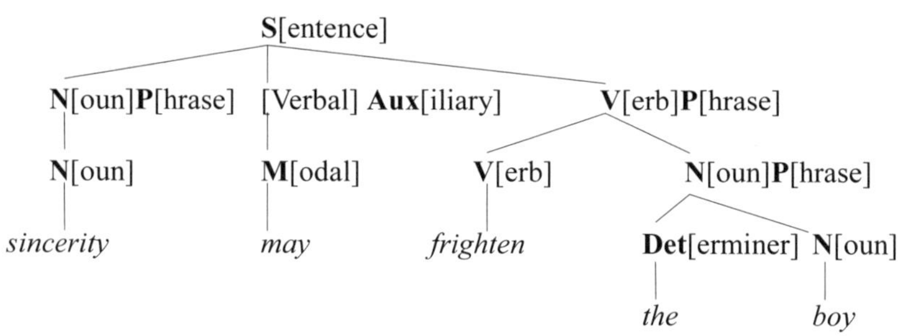

Figure 5.3: Tree-Diagram Analysis of the Deep Structure of a Sentence (after Chomsky 1965: 65)

– to accept that the generation of a movement as extended as the Allegro con brio of Beethoven's '*Eroica*' Symphony proceeded according to comparable principles is considerably more problematic.

The argument advanced here sees the issue from the opposite perspective: it regards the *Ursatz* (whose species form a subset of structural memes) not as regulating a top-down generative-transformational grammar but as an artefact of a bottom-up generative-conglomerational grammar – a foreground in/up process of *Inkomponierung* – and thus an abstraction of the statistically most predominant patterns formed by memetic conglomeration during the period *c.* 1700–*c.* 1900. As Narmour observes,

> To the historian, of course, the Schenkerian (and the Gestaltist) blunder is obvious: for to achieve a unified whole, we must have organization, and in order to organize, we must have entities that already have relationships – relationships acquired in other times and other places, and *in other wholes*. This prior existence of *the part* utterly destroys that notion that any single whole (any single piece) or any original whole (like the *Ursatz*) can completely account for the meaning of the parts. For instance, representational paintings rely on a common stockpile of figures; poems have words; every musical piece contains motives and progressions found in other pieces and other styles; and so forth.
>
> (1977: 35, his emphases)

Nevertheless, as suggested in the discussion of cue abstraction in 5.3.2 above, an established structural meme may have sufficient cultural prominence to impart to it the top-down power to determine the type of material (the appropriate allele class) occupying each of its component structural-node loci in any given instantiation. However, the most powerful force operative in this structural-hierarchic tug-of-war derives from the bottom-up conglomerational properties of lower-level memes which, by causing them to stick together in certain ways, generates the nodes of the structural meme. Analogous to the systemic changes discussed in 4.6.4 above, and a higher-level consequence of changes occurring at lower levels, the evolution of structural memes is a similarly bottom-up process. As foreground-level memes evolved over time, their patterns of association, of conglomeration, changed, giving rise to structural memes different from those which resulted from the conglomeration of earlier foreground memes.

5.3.5. *Teleology* versus *Teleonomy and Adaptation* versus *Exaptation*

Dawkins's 'Methinks it is like a weasel' experiment raises the issue of goal-directedness, of teleology. In all of his generations subject to cumulative selection, the selection criterion was simple: resemblance to the target phrase. A final goal was always firmly in sight and mutants were explicitly selected according to their degree of conformance with it. Thus, the processes of generation and selection terminated at the point the goal was attained.

Coming after his 'material', 'formal' and 'efficient' causes (*aitia*), Aristotle's 'final' cause, the *telos*, is concerned with the '*purpose* or *goal* or *end*' of a thing (Dennett 1995: 23; his emphases), the supreme 'why?' question. The history of science and philosophy shows repeated attempts to comprehend the nature of things from a teleological perspective and in biology, especially, the structure of organisms has been understood in terms of a preordained goal or destination. Schenker, in keeping with the tradition of nineteenth-century organicism, applied the same logic to works of art, especially in his notion of the 'egotism of the tone' (1980: 30), arguing that

> The origin of every life, whether of nation, clan, or individual, becomes its destiny. Hegel defines destiny as 'the manifestation of the inborn, original predisposition of each individual'. The inner law of origin accompanies all development and is ultimately part of the present.
>
> (1979: 3; see also Narmour 1977: 35)

Darwinism and teleology are, however, wholly incompatible. Natural and cultural selection operate to preserve those configurations adapted to current conditions and cannot look ahead to environments not yet in existence. They merely give the impression of teleology because the products of cumulative selection appear to have been directed towards specific goals, either intrinsically, by an inner 'drive', or extrinsically, by an intelligent designer. As the case of Paley's Watch illustrates, however, the teleological interpretation of biological processes is in large part a consequence of the (memetic, non-teleological) goal-orientated fabrication methodologies underpinning artifact design and manufacture in the human sphere.

For Darwinism, no goal informs the development of biological or cultural structures: no organism has an innate conception of a more 'refined' version of itself towards which it strives; and no composer of *c.* 1500 could possibly have had in mind the structural meme we now refer to as sonata form. In this respect, '[t]he "watchmaker" that is cumulative natural [and cultural] selection is blind to the future and has no long-term goal'. In biological evolution, 'the criterion for selection is always short-term, either simple survival or, more generally, reproductive success' (Dawkins 1991: 50). In cultural evolution, the same principle holds: for structural archetypes, as with any meme, survival translates directly as replicative success, contingent as always upon the attributes of longevity, fecundity and copying-fidelity.

The blind watchmaker of Darwinism renounces teleology in favour of teleonomy, '[t]he science of adaptation. In effect, teleonomy is teleology made respectable by Darwin' (Dawkins 1983a: 294). An adaptation is simply the response by an organism to an aspect of its environment resulting from a randomly appearing genetic change which has been favoured by natural selection. Adaptation is closely related to the notion of reverse engineering, which, as its name implies, is the process of taking a complex form and working backwards to understand – on the basis that 'optimality must be the default assumption' (Dennett 1995: 213) – the relationship between the object's structure and its function. On this reasoning, Dennett maintains that

> Biology is not just like engineering; it *is* engineering. It is the study of functional mechanisms, their design, construction, and operation. From this vantage point, we can explain the gradual birth of function, and the concomitant birth of meaning or intentionality. Achievements that at first seem either literally miraculous … or at least intrinsically Mind-dependent … can be broken down into the ever smaller achievements of ever smaller and stupider mechanisms.… The task of reverse engineering in biology is an exercise in figuring out 'what Mother Nature had in mind'. This strategy, known as adaptationism, has been an amazingly powerful method, generating many spectacular leaps of inference …. Adaptationism is both ubiquitous and powerful in biology.… it is in fact the irreplaceable core of Darwinian thinking.
>
> (1995: 228, 261; his emphasis)

One might hypothesize that structural memes are adapted (are engineered) by cultural evolution not only in ways which favour their own survival, but which also maximize that of the alleles which occupy their structural loci and generate their structural nodes. The survival advantage of these alleles is enhanced by the advantage of group membership and the memory-reinforcing repetition intrinsic to such structures. On the former, as Dawkins notes in the passage cited in 3.4 above, 'each separate member of the group tends to be favoured when its environment happens to be dominated by the others' (in Blackmore 1999: xiv). Structural memes have themselves adapted to capitalize on replicated patterns of replicated-pattern conglomeration, and on their consequent enactment of rhetorical-gestural schemata (often, very broadly, patterns of stability-tension-intensification-resolution) whose narrativity corresponds with (and, in texted music, is often explicitly aligned with) experiences in other sensory modalities and cultural realms.

In an extension of the concept of adaptation, Gould and Vrba suggest that

> we may designate as an *adaptation* any feature that promotes fitness and was built by selection for its current role (criterion of *historical genesis*). The operation of an adaptation is its *function*.… We may also … [label] the operation of a useful character not built by selection for its current role as an *effect*.… But what is the unselected, but useful character itself to be called? …. We suggest that such characters, evolved for other usages (or for no function at all), and later 'coopted' for their current role, be called *exaptations*.… They are fit for their current role, hence *aptus*, but they were not designed for it, and are therefore not *ad aptus*, or pushed towards fitness. They owe their fitness to features present for other reasons, and are therefore *fit* (*aptus*) *by reason of* (*ex*) their form, or *ex aptus*.
>
> (1982: 6; their emphases)

This principle – that features of an organism may have originally evolved to fulfil a function different to that they presently serve – is readily applicable to a memetic theory of musical structure. In particular, it suggests that certain middleground voice-leading structures which may have originally evolved in connection with the instantiation of a particular component of a structural meme may also be amenable to instantiate other components. A case in point is the progression shown in Example 5.1 below, which prolongs tonic harmony by fleeting reference to the subdominant.

Example 5.1: Exaptation of Tonic-Prolongation Meme

i) J.S. Bach: Partita in B♭ major BWV 825 (*c.* 1726), Allemande, bb. 0–4

ii) Mozart: Horn Concerto in E♭ major K. 495 (1786), I, bb. 32–4

iii) Voice-Leading Schema

As the schema in Example 5.2 below illustrates, such a progression may occur at (and contribute to the generation of) several major structural points in the interrupted *Ursatz* engendered by a sonata-form multimemetic complex, as well as in the interstices of these points, at lower structural-hierarchic levels not represented in the schema.

Example 5.2: Possible Loci of Tonic-Prolongation Meme (after Schenker 1979: Supplement, Fig. 47)

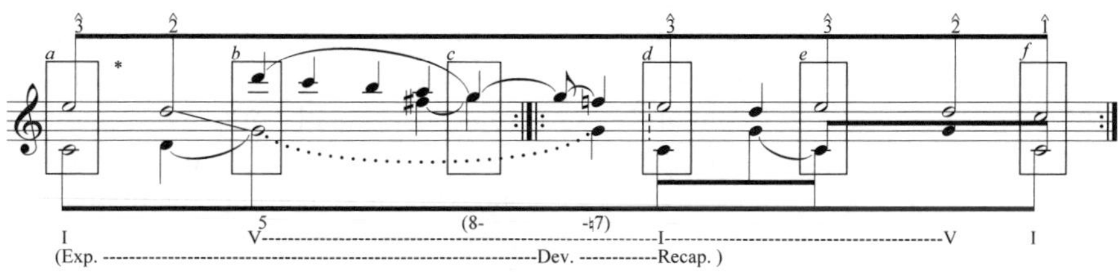

Point *a* represents the opening tonic area associated with the first subject group; point *b* represents the opening of the second subject group, at which the meme might appear transposed to the dominant; and point *c* represents the closing material of the exposition. Point *d* represents the opening of the recapitulation and therefore corresponds to point *a*; point *e* represents the opening of the second group recast in the tonic and corresponds to point *b*; and point *f* represents the coda and closing tonic peroration of the recapitulation and corresponds to point *c*. In the case of Example 5.1 ii, the meme occurs at the close of the orchestral exposition, a point approximately represented by the asterisk in Example 5.2 (see also Smith 1996: 231–7).

It is not unreasonable to assume that either point *a* or point *f* is the original locus of this particular meme, the point at which its first occurrences appeared: as Example 5.1 i indicates, the meme is appropriate as the underpinning for florid definitions of a movement's tonic. (This meme often occurs in Bach as a closing gesture, as in bb. 32–5 of the first prelude from Book I of *Das wohltemperirte Clavier*.) From the foreground and shallow-middleground meme's eye view, the evolution of sonata form, with its exposition-recapitulation thematic and transpositional analogies (*a–d*, *b–e* and *c–f* in Example 5.2), opened up the potential for more phemotypic copies of such memes to occupy the infosphere, which therefore increased the likelihood of their further transmission. From the deep-middleground and background (structural) meme's eye view, such clear structural-node-defining memes as that schematized in Example 5.1 iii delineate their contours and enhance their salience.

On this interpretation, placement of the meme at points '*', *b*, *c*, *d* and *e* might be held to represent exaptations: they constitute reuses of the structure for purposes for which it was not originally evolved, forming members of the class of 'features that now enhance [cultural] fitness but were not built by [cultural] selection for their current role' (Gould and Vrba 1982: 4).

5.4. Evidence for Memetic-Structural Evolution

It is difficult to prove the veracity of evolution by natural selection as the source of large-scale complexity in the universe because of the enormous time scales involved. We cannot observe the process directly, so it is difficult to verify the mechanism which drives it. Indeed some anti-Darwinians take this absence of direct evidence as direct evidence against Darwinism itself. For comparable reasons – because the processes discussed above took place over many decades and centuries and because they involved numerous works and composers in myriad complex interactions – it is difficult to prove that the memetic hypothesis advanced in 5.3 above for the evolution of large-scale structural complexity in music is correct. It follows from this that any evidence will necessarily be small-scale, localized and, to a degree, circumstantial. Two sources we might adduce are the eighteenth-century notion of *ars combinatoria*, evidence for allelic competition between memes; and the historical and structural relationships between small-scale and large-scale forms, evidence for structural-meme evolution.

5.4.1. *Allelic Competition and Ars Combinatoria*

> On the surface, *ars combinatoria* in eighteenth-century music appears to be schematic, mechanical, perhaps frivolous in its intentions. But it also helps us to recognize the point at which the schematic becomes vital.
>
> (Ratner 1970: 361)

Discussion of the allelic competition leading to the instantiation of structural memes considered in 5.3.2 above is not unknown in music theory, although of course it is conducted using different terminology. One such discourse concerns the concept of *ars combinatoria*. Ratner observes that the music of the late-eighteenth century may be clearly segmented into a series of discrete units, for '[a]t this time in musical history, it was possible to codify the mechanical elements of musical composition more clearly than at any other time' (1970: 345). These units lend themselves to various modes of disposition subsumed under the term *ars combinatoria*, including '*permutation*, in which a given number of objects is re-arranged, and *combination*, in which it is possible to substitute one object for another in a series' (: 345; his emphases). The manipulation of musical units under the aegis of *ars combinatoria* 'was an important *modus operandi* in eighteenth-century musical construction .... the simple, clear, and symmetrical layouts that characterize the structure expedited permutation and combination' (: 361). Many musical parameters were amenable to the operation of *ars combinatoria*, including 'melody, harmony, rhythm, phrase structure, counterpoint, [and] large-scale form' (: 361).

Although crystallised in numerous parlour games based on combinatorial principles – of which Mozart's *Musikalisches Würfelspiele* K. 516f (1787) is perhaps the best known, and which enacts a mock, randomized competition between members of a number of allele classes to occupy a sequence of structural nodes – Ratner maintains that *ars combinatoria* is a serious procedure informing much late-eighteenth-century music. Memetics motivates an even stronger interpretation: that far from being 'not composition but a resource in its service' (: 361–2), it stylizes the very essence of the creative process. It contends that, although its representation as *ars combinatoria* had only a relatively brief currency in the late-eighteenth century (being perhaps elicited by a highly articulated and lucid dialect), allelic rivalry between memes within the context of the regulatory frameworks of generated structural schemata is fundamental to all musics.[5]

Ars combinatoria underlies the operation of the technique Ratner terms paraphrase.

> Parody masses, Bach's reworking of Vivaldi concerti, [and] Mozart's adaptation of keyboard sonatas into concerti are examples of this treatment of musical material. Variation is also a type of paraphrase. In most cases of paraphrase the basic harmonic and rhythmic structure is fixed; melody and texture are the variables. If we regard each step of the harmonic-rhythmic progression as a 'slot' into which a melodic figure can be placed, either by the choice of the composer, or, as in the dice games, by random selection, paraphrase can be taken as a kind of combinatorial play.
>
> (1970: 354–5)

5 Pollack notes that Copland 'did not compose strictly from the beginning of a piece to the end, but juggled and rearranged motives, passages and sections. "I don't compose; I assemble materials", he once stated' (2001: 403).

As an example, he cites a section from Johann Gottlieb Portmann's *Leichtes Lehrbuch der Harmonie* of 1799, in which the author recomposes the first movement of Mozart's Sonata in D major K. 284 (205b). This new movement largely preserves the underlying middleground and background voice-leading structures of the original but alters the foreground configurations which generate them (1970: 356–7). Ratner's alignment of the openings of these two movements is adapted in Example 5.3 below.

Example 5.3: Portmann's Recomposition of Mozart, Sonata in D major K. 284 (205b) (1775), I, bb. 1–7

i) Mozart: Sonata in D major K. 284 (205b) (1775), I, bb. 1–7;
ii) Portmann's Recomposition.

There are two middleground-level memes in the bars cited by Ratner, the first spanning bb. $1–4^1$, the second bb. $4^3–7^1$ (Mozart)/7^3 (Portmann). This underlying framework is generated by very different surface level patterning at corresponding structural loci of each movement (for the sake of legibility, foreground-level memes are not on marked on Example 5.3). The upper-voice line $\hat{1}–\hat{7}–\hat{3}–\hat{2}–\hat{5}–\hat{4}$ in the second meme, for instance, is generated by a simple repeated-note-plus-appoggiatura meme in Mozart and by a more galant figure in Portmann. Thus, in Portmann's version, allelic foreground memes replace those which originally won the conflict, yet these rival patterns continue to express the middleground and background patterns, and therefore the structural meme, underpinning Mozart's movement.

Ars combinatoria is resurgent in the work of Cope: the identification of musical signatures discussed in 2.5.3 above is part of a larger research project, 'Experiments in Musical Intelligence' (EMI), using computers to analyze and synthesize musical style (Cope 1991a, 1991b, 1996, 2001). Implicitly, he accepts Meyer's (and memetics's) view of style as the replication of patterning and explicitly adopts the language of *ars combinatoria* to explain how the replication engendered by recombination generates stylistic profiles at various levels.

To understand and replicate style, Cope has developed

> an expert [software] system that employs pattern recognition processes to create recombinant music – music written in the styles of various composers by means of a contextual recombination of elements in the music of those composers. This EMI subprogram performs much the same task as the musical dice games on music that was not written to be disassembled, reorganised, and reassembled. It separates and analyzes musical pitches and durations and then mixes and recombines the patterns of those pitches and durations so that, while each new composition is different, it substantially conforms to the style of the original.
>
> (1991b: 22–3)

In memetic terms, Cope's program analyzes a piece's constituent surface memes and reproduces the compositional process by simulating allelic competition between them. When recombination occurs 'horizontally', using the same closed set of memes (potentially only 1 representative from *n* allele classes) from piece to piece, not 'vertically', using a wider set (*n* representatives from *n* allele classes, as in human musics), it naturally engenders a different structural plan for each piece.

Recalling Ratner's earlier-cited injunction – and while my concern here is of course less with the reception than with the generation of style and structure through memetic propagation – Cope is keen to stress that the process his software operationalizes should be understood as a fundamental compositional resource, insisting that 'this is not just a parlor game but a serious attempt to understand how listeners recognize the style of a composer or period, one of the more elusive and difficult to describe musical phenomena' (1991b: 23).

5.4.2. *Ontogenetic-Phylogenetic Parallels Between Small- and Large-Scale Forms*

One way to support the notion that large-scale multi-sectional formal archetypes resulted from the evolutionary expansion of such prototypes as the short Renaissance dance phrase is to postulate, as suggested in 5.3.3 above, that the compositional process might involve a rapid replaying of the large-scale evolutionary processes taking place over the course of the preceding decades. As remarked in 1.3 above, however, Solie notes the 'confusion of modality between the temporal and spatial', and is sceptical of the notion that 'ontogeny recapitulates phylogeny in art and culture as well as in genetics', inherent in a number of 'organic growth metaphors', most notably Schenker's (1980: 153). Nevertheless, memetics suggests a way of mediating between these four dimensions, drawing the temporal (diachronic) and spatial (synchronic) elements of the individual work's ontogeny into alignment with the phylogenetic history of the structural archetype of which the work is an instantiation.

An example of this process is offered by Rosen, who notes that

> Around 1793, Haydn wrote a Piano Trio in G minor [Hob. XV: 19] for Prince Anton Esterházy which begins with a set of double variations.... The second variation of [the G major] second theme is a complete sonata movement, and it is amusing to see how Haydn expands a 20-measure theme into a larger work.
>
> (1997: 83)

The wider issue he derives from this is that

> From this witty expansion it can be seen that sonata form is an immense melody, an expanded classical phrase, articulated, with its harmonic climax three-quarters of the way through and a symmetrical resolution that rounds it off in careful balance with the opening.... The points of his theme that Haydn expands most significantly are the central modulation and the end. This [ontogeny] corresponds to the historical development [phylogeny] of the sonata, and explains the gradual increase of importance during the century of the 'development section' and the 'coda'.
>
> (: 87)

Such views were not unfamiliar to the late-eighteenth century, the writings of Heinrich Koch in particular showing how short dance phrases could be expanded to generate sonata expositions (see Sisman 1982). The eight-bar first reprise of the theme, and its expansion into a twenty-bar sonata exposition, is shown in Example 5.4 below.

Example 5.4: Phrase Expansion in Haydn as a Microcosm of Structural Evolution (after Rosen 1997: 83–5)

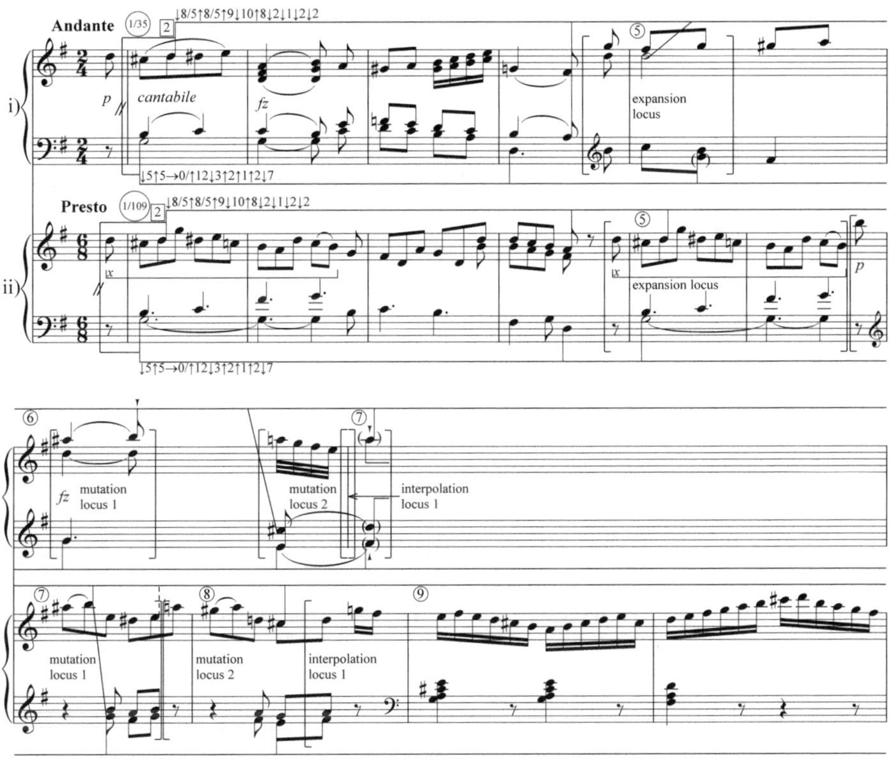

i) Piano Trio in G minor Hob. XV. 19 (*c.* 1793), I, Second Theme, bb. 35–42;
ii) Second Variation of Second Theme, bb. 109–127

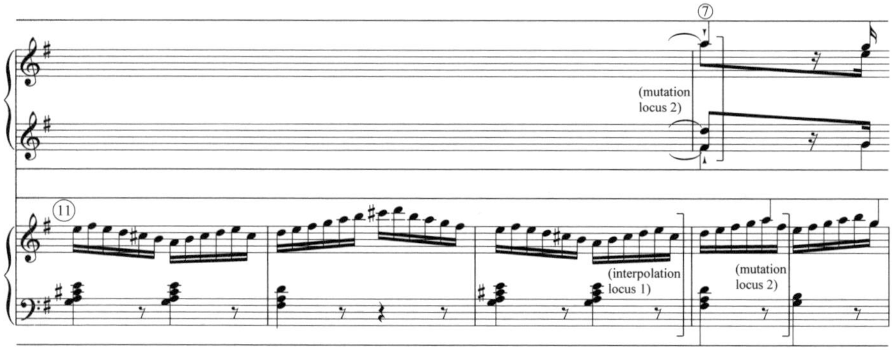
7
(mutation
locus 2)
11
(interpolation
locus 1)
(mutation
locus 2)

7
8/42
interpolation
locus 2
etc.
15
19/127
interpolation
locus 2
etc.

To understand how Haydn expands the second theme (hereafter 'theme'), three related concepts need to be introduced. An expansion locus is a part of an antecedent structural meme – in this case, that underpinning the theme – where an existing structural node is prolonged in time, often by the immigration of additional lower-order memes, but is not modified substantively. A mutation locus is a part of an antecedent structural meme where a structural node is mutated as a consequence of changes occurring in lower-order memes. An interpolation locus is a part of an antecedent structural meme where new memes are interpolated between existing memes, thereby expanding the surface form and potentially leading – if any newly generated structural node is replicated – to a new, expanded structural meme. These various loci are indicated by brackets on Example 5.4.

In the theme, there is one expansion locus. This occurs in bb. 4^4–5^2, which is expanded in the second variation (hereafter 'variation') to the equivalent bb. 4^6–6^5 (for ease of comparison, the passages are numbered starting from bar 1; superscripts indicate quaver beats of the theme and variation). The melodic unit bracketed and marked *x*, from bb. 0^6–2^5 of the variation, is thereby duplicated in bb. 4^6–6^5 in a way which does not happen, in its bb. 4^4–5^2, to the corresponding part, bb. 0^4–2^3, of the theme. Taking the meme's eye view – and assuming that particle *a* is memetic – this duplication selfishly increases the prominence of *a* and (all other things being equal) doubles its chances of replication.

There are two mutation loci. The first occupies b. 6^{1-3} of the theme, which becomes the material of bb. 6^6–7^5 of the variation; the second occupies bb. 6^4–7^1 of the theme, which becomes the material of bb. 7^6–8^5 of the variation. In the first mutation locus, the a♯^{2}–b^2 (♯$\hat{2}$–$\hat{3}$) sequence of b. 6^{1-3} of the theme, over the last tonic chord before the concise modulation to V, is reorientated as ♯$\hat{4}$–$\hat{5}$ in vi in b. 7^{1-2} of the variation. This is to facilitate a V/vi–vi; V/V–V sequence over bb. 7^4–8^5, regarded by Rosen as a 'very common [modulatory] procedure that remained useful from the middle of the eighteenth century until late in the nineteenth' (1988: 235). Haydn eschews the normative third element of this progression, V/V/V–V/V, in favour of repeated cadences in the dominant in bb. 9–14^1 of the variation (the first interpolation locus; see below). It is not difficult to envisage a further expansion of this phrase incorporating such a reinforcement of the new tonality. The second mutation locus of the variation articulates the V/V–V component of the V/vi–vi; V/V–V sequence in conformance with the material articulating the V/vi–vi component; no such conformance occurs between the analogous b. 6^{1-3} and bb. 6^4–7^1 of the theme.

There are two interpolation loci. The first is the barline between b. 6^4 and b. 7^1 of the theme, which is 'filled in' by the material of bb. 8^5–13^6 of the variation. In fact, the mutation locus of bb. 6^4–7^1 of the theme subsumes this interpolation locus because, while the resolution of the $V^6{}_4$ of b. 6^4 of the theme to the $I^6{}_3$ of b. 7^1 is accomplished in b. 8^{4-5} of the variation, the a^2/f♯^{1} ($I^6{}_3$) sonority of b. 7^1 of the theme is only presented in b. 14^{1-3} of the variation. One might therefore regard this as a double interpolation: globally, it is an interpolation within the structural meme; locally, it is an interpolation within the second mutation locus. The second interpolation locus is the double bar line between b. 8^{3-4} of the theme, which is filled in by the cadential material of bb. 16^3–19^2 of the variation.

The structural meme underpinning the first part of Haydn's theme is shown in Example 5.5. A Schenkerian representation is used to show certain elements of the voice-leading structure of these passages, including elements of their *Ursätzen*, and these are then encompassed by the meme-analytical symbology to show that the structure replicated in the two passages, the *memesatz* (5.3.3 above), contains components which occur at various hierarchic levels. The expansion, mutation and interpolation loci between these constituents of the structural meme are indicated using boxes.

Example 5.5: Schenkerian Representation of Structural Meme Underpinning Haydn's Theme

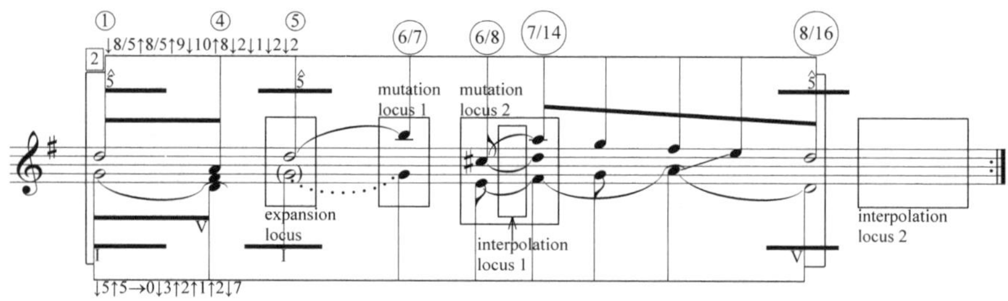

These two examples serve to illustrate the general argument of 5.3 above, that if nascent voice-leading elements (expanded, mutated or interpolated structural nodes) arising at the five loci by means of lower-order meme processes go on to be replicated in other contexts by means of the conglomeration of memes of allelic configuration, function or structure, then this new formation will itself attain memetic status and a new *memesatz* will have arisen; one such element is indicated by the dotted line at b. 7^5 of Example 5.4 ii. From these short passages it is also clear that variation techniques, which underpin the mutation of a pre-existing pattern in order to create a derivative pattern, are intrinsically and especially mutational-evolutionary; and that the variation forms subsuming such techniques describe ontogenetic microcosms of the phylogenetic evolutionary process.

5.5. Representing Design Space

I return to the issue of design first raised in 5.2 above in order to examine how the evolution of memetic-structural complexity might be conceived and represented, and to consider to what extent memetic evolution is progressive and how it relates to evolutionary progress in genetics.

5.5.1. *Multidimensional Genetic and Memetic Hypervolumes*

The processes of single-step and cumulative selection imply a spatial progression from one form to another, the former's trajectory jumpy and aimless, the latter's smooth and directed. After evolving 'Methinks it is like a weasel' by cumulative selection, Dawkins continued his experiment by developing a program, *Evolution*, to draw tree-like shapes on a computer screen. The drawing of the shapes – what he termed the 'development' subroutine of the program (1991: 53) – was controlled by nine discrete instructions governing such matters as the length of branches, the angles of branching and the extent to which branching occurs before it terminates. The degree of influence of each instruction upon the drawing of the trees depended upon the size of a positive or negative numerical value associated with it, the higher the number the more marked the developmental trait governed by the instruction and vice versa. These instructions functioned to all intents and purposes as genes (and literally as memes); the resultant shapes on the computer screen represent the phenotypic (developmental) products of those genes; and the program as a whole constitutes, when the subroutine discussed below is included, a functional model of biological transmission and evolution.

The set of nine instructions required to draw a tree was then copied – the program's 'reproduction' subroutine (1991: 55) – with the possibility of mutation in the numerical value of one of the instructions, which was allowed to change by plus or minus one. Successive generations of trees – renamed 'biomorphs' by Dawkins, after a term of Desmond Morris's (: 55) – differed slightly from their parents as a consequence of their altered genetic structure. From each 'litter' Dawkins selected a biomorph as the parent of the next generation, a process of cumulative selection akin to that of the 'Methinks it is like a weasel' experiment. His amazement at the outcomes of his program is worth quoting. He concedes that

> I never thought that it would evolve anything more than a variety of tree-like shapes.... Nothing in my biologist's intuition, nothing in my 20 years' experience of programming computers, and nothing in my wildest dreams, prepared me for what actually emerged on the screen. I can't remember exactly when in the sequence it first began to dawn on me that an evolved resemblance to something like an insect was possible. With a wild surmise, I began to breed, generation after generation, from whichever child looked most like an insect. My incredulity grew in parallel with the evolving resemblance.... I still cannot conceal from you my feeling of exultation as I first watched these exquisite creatures emerging before my eyes.
>
> (1991: 59, 60)

Dawkins notes that there is, for any set of genes, a large set of possible resultant biomorphs. Each of these can be assigned to a specific point in multi-dimensional genetic space, the number of dimensions being equal to the number of genes and its precise position being contingent upon the numerical values of its genetic complement. For Dawkins's biomorphs the number of dimensions required to describe this particular genetic 'hypervolume' is of course nine. This spatial model of genetic configuration is represented in Figure 5.4 below which, of necessity, restricts the number of dimensions to the three that can be simulated on the two-dimensional page.

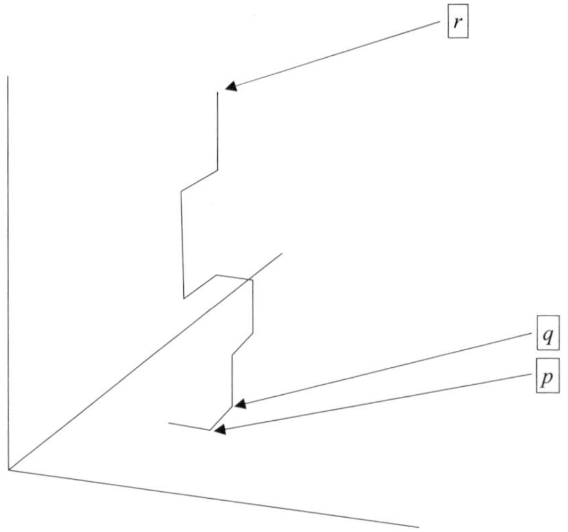

Figure 5.4: A Three-Dimensional Genetic/Memetic Hypervolume

The locus of the biomorph represented by point *p* is determined by the values of its three genes, expressed on the *x*, *y* and *z* axes. The biomorph at *q* differs slightly from that at *p* in the numerical value of one gene only; in evolving from one to the other there is a small degree of movement along one axis only. The biomorph at *r*, however, differs from *p* in the values of all three of its genes, and the difference in numerical values with respect to *p* is large. Under Dawkins's initial restriction of one gene mutation, by plus or minus one, per generation, this means that *r* is at several generations' removed from *p*. From this it is clear that organisms *p* and *q* are closely related to each other, that organism *r* is a distant relation of *p* and *q*, and that these relationships of genetic affinity are represented graphically in terms of multi-dimensional spatial distance.

The scales along the axes – an abstract index of genetic mutation – have a clear statistical implication. If the restriction on genetic mutation is relaxed, as Dawkins later does (1991: 71), such that any and all genes can mutate by any magnitude (in his case, within the range minus nine to plus nine) during the reproduction subroutine, the possibility arises of jumping large distances across the dimensions of 'Biomorph Land' (: 60) in the course of a single generation. It follows that while a movement from point *p* to point *q* between parent and offspring is within acceptable limits of probability, requiring only a small change in one gene, a movement from point *p* to point *r* between the same relatives is much less probable, requiring a large change in all three genes.

This notion of a large leap into the genetic unknown is a spatial representation of the essentially random process of single-step selection. By contrast, controlled movement on a step-by-step basis through the hypervolume is a representation of cumulative selection. As argued earlier, this second type of movement is not teleological, but is directed and shaped by the particular selection pressures operative at each point of the journey.

This spatial model of biological evolution is fully compatible with the account of musical structure outlined in 5.3 above. It requires slight qualification in that, for both Dawkins's biomorphs and living organisms, evolution is driven primarily by mutation in one or more of their genes, which in his simulation are fixed in number and which in nature are relatively stable in number over time. In the case of the structural memes, the culturemorphs, which underpin extended musical (second-order) organisms, however, evolution is driven as much by immigration of memes into the structure, leading eventually to an increase in the number of structural nodes, as by their mutation or reassortment at various structural-hierarchic levels.

Despite this difference – the potential for rapid increase in the number of memetic dimensions – the analogy is viable. Therefore, in terms of Figure 5.4, one might compare point *p* with a Renaissance dance form and *r* with a Classical sonata-form movement, such as the first movement of Beethoven's '*Eroica*' Symphony. While it is eminently possible to move from *p* to *r* by cumulative selection, by means of a very large number of incremental steps, the probability of reaching *r* by leap from *p*, by means of single-step selection, is exceedingly small.

5.5.2. *The Library of Aristoxenus*

The concept of moving from one point to another in a genetic or memetic hypervolume subtly undermines the temporal dimension associated with the spatial dimensions in a hypervolume. Although movement from points *p* to *r* in Figure 5.4 represents diachronic movement in time – the generation time taken for reproduction and development of biomorphs – there is a sense in which

> There is a definite [synchronic] set of biomorphs, each permanently sitting in its own unique place in a mathematical space.... what you are really doing [in moving through a hypervolume] is *finding* the creature, for it is, in a mathematical sense, already sitting in its own place in the genetic space of Biomorph Land.
>
> (Dawkins 1991: 65; his emphasis)

The same holds true for memetics, for in the same way that the biomorphs are sitting in Biomorph Land, the particular configuration of memes constituting the '*Eroica*' Symphony is positioned in its own unique location in the memetic space of Culturemorph Land. It had to wait until 1804 to be found by Beethoven, although it was there before he was born, and will remain so, categorically distinct and unique, for all eternity.[6] In this sense, both genetic and memetic evolution are ahistorical in that all possible organisms and structures are conceptually coexistent and independent of the dimension of time. Biological and cultural evolution therefore represent processes of location driven by natural and cultural selection.

These ideas underpin an alternative – although directly analogous and wholly concordant – metaphor to Dawkins's Biomorph Land developed by Dennett, after Jorge Luis Borges's 1941 short story *The Library of Babel*, itself based in part on Lasswitz's 1901 *The Universal Library* (Lasswitz 1997). As Dennett explains, this library is

> a vast storehouse of books, structured like a honeycomb, composed of thousands (or millions or billions) of hexagonal air shafts surrounded by balconies lined with shelves. Standing at a railing and looking up or down, one sees no top or bottom to these shafts. Nobody has ever found a shaft that isn't surrounded by six neighboring shafts. [People] wonder: is the warehouse infinite? Eventually, they decide that it is not, but it might as well be, for it seems that on its shelves – in no order, alas – lie *all the possible books*.
>
> (1995: 108; his emphasis)

Borges tells us that 'a librarian of genius' once

> deduced that the Library is total and that its shelves register all the possible combinations of the twenty-odd orthographical symbols (a number which, though extremely vast, is not infinite): in other words, all that it is given to express, in all languages. Everything: the minutely detailed history of the future, the archangels' autobiographies, the faithful catalogue of the Library, thousands and thousands of false catalogues, the demonstration of the fallacy of those catalogues, the demonstration of the fallacy of the true catalogue, the Gnostic gospel of Basilides, the commentary on that gospel, the commentary on the commentary on that gospel, the true story of your death, the translation of every book in all languages, the interpolations of every book in all books.
>
> (1970: 81–2)

Insofar as the genetic 'recipes' (nucleotide combinations) of living organisms are reducible to the Roman-alphabet characters A, C, G and T, then the library of Babel may be said to contain within it the Library of Mendel, the conceptual space

[6] In the same sense, Gjerdingen argues that '[a] positive extreme of defined constraint and population-curve slope would be reached by a schema's definition so completely constrained that only a single composition could meet its specifications. For instance, the exact musical structure represented by Beethoven's Fifth Symphony was created in 1807 and at no other time before or since. A graph of this circumstance would approximate a vertical line – a single, sharp spike' (1988: 101; Figure 6-4).

of 'all possible genomes', through an infinitesimally small part of which the branches of the 'Tree of Life' spread (Dennett 1995: 111, 121). By extension, we might also envision, deposited in the Library of Babel in the form of their printed phemotypic representations, the space of all possible musical works, the Library of Aristoxenus.[7] This includes, of course, all actual musical works together with the multitude that are possible but are not – yet; ever to be? – actualized.

5.5.3. *Progress in Nature and Culture*

There is some disagreement among commentators on the issue of progress in evolution – the notion that some regions of design space contain more highly 'developed' organisms than others. Ball's assertion that 'the logarithm of the total information content of the biosystem (genes plus memes) is a level-of-development parameter and that an increase in this parameter may be defined as progress' (1984: 154) contrasts with Dawkins's claim that 'contrary to earlier prejudices, there is nothing inherently progressive about evolution' (1991: 178). Nevertheless, if genes evolve in such a way as to make ever more effective phenotypic products – creatures bearing faster legs, sharper teeth or keener eyes – can the same be said to be true for memes? Do memes evolve in a progressive way, such that their phemotypic products exhibit ever greater richness, detail and complexity?

Despite formulating the question abstractly in terms of replicators, one inevitably tends to conceive the answer concretely in terms of cultural products and their originators. Thus, in the light of Dawkins's claim, can one assert a comparable progression from, say, the works of Corelli to those of Bach, or from the works of Mozart to those of Beethoven? Of course, this question boils down to the status of critical and value judgements in the broader context of the meme paradigm. What, therefore, is the foundation of aesthetics and criticism in a memetic world-view?

Dahlhaus argues that

---

[7] Whereas Mendel, as the father of genetics, clearly merits curatorship of 'all possible genomes', Aristoxenus is more problematic. While regretting the Eurocentric perspective, and thus the neglect of the great middle-eastern and oriental musical traditions, I choose the author of the *Harmonic Elements* (*c.* 320 BCE) as probably the first significant Western music theorist.

> Schoenberg recognized a principle of compensation or economy as a fact of musical hearing and as a tendency effective in the history of composition, but he rejected this principle as a factor in esthetic judgement. Schoenberg mistrusted the middle path – 'the only road that does not lead to Rome'. His thinking was anticlassicistic. His opposing thesis, that to avoid inconsistency music must be developed equally in all dimensions, he supported with the indisputable fact that each of the components of tonal structure – melody, counterpoint, harmony, and rhythm – coheres inseparably with all the others; each aspect becomes what it is only in the manifold relations in which it appears. 'This is why', says Schoenberg in *Style and idea* ... 'when composers have acquired the technique of filling one direction with content to the utmost capacity, they must do the same in the next direction, and finally in all the directions in which music expands'.
>
> (1982: 92)

Schoenberg's conception of musical development, emblematic of the aesthetics of high modernism, exhorts the composer to fill 'all the directions in which music expands' with 'content', to suffuse each parameter with as much information as it can possibly bear, such that the musical work becomes a dense, turbid nexus of richly interacting parameters. He clearly felt that the 'principle of compensation or economy' – the notion that if one parameter is well developed, others must be correspondingly under-developed – led to artistically unbalanced works and therefore, as Dahlhaus notes, rejected it.

Memetics suggests that Schoenberg's position is at once a reflection of the nature of memes and psychologically unviable. That is, while memes strive selfishly to fill all niches of the infosphere, including the parameters of music (development 'equally in all dimensions'), the human perceptual-cognitive system is limited in its attentional resources ('a fact of musical hearing'). In a classic formulation of these constraints, Miller suggests that we are (only) capable of processing 'seven, plus or minus two' units of attention at any given time (1956). From the meme's eye view, such constraints mean that the more memes that saturate an individual musical work, the lower the probability that any one will be assimilated by the listener. Given that it is obviously not in a meme's interests to be 'elbowed out' by its neighbours, it best serves its replicative prospects if a balance is struck between these conflicting tendencies.

How does this affect one's view of musical progress? Returning to criticism, an important precept of memetics is that, in common with the majority of thought processes, verbal-conceptual memes underpin and regulate the aesthetic evaluation of art. As with any other type of meme, these are subject to selection pressures, especially according to the criterion of fit against that – in this case music – which they purport to describe and appraise. Whether one judges a work favourably or unfavourably is determined by those verbal-conceptual memes prevalent in one's culture and their relationship with the musics to which they relate.

It may be that a 'criticism meme' favouring music in which only a limited number of parameters are highly developed – one might call it, verbosely, the 'critically favour music which places (only) a moderate perceptual load on the listener' verbal-conceptual meme – spread widely in the meme pool in co-adaptation with musical memes placing no more than moderate psychological demands on the listener. This fecundity may be because such co-adaptations (what one might term 'category-1' musico-conceptual memeplexes) may ultimately favour memetic replication better (for the psychological reasons noted above) than rival co-adaptations between a 'critically favour music which places a high perceptual load on the listener' verbal-conceptual meme and musical memes placing higher psychological demands on the listener ('category-2' musico-conceptual memeplexes).

If this is the case, then such musical memes as those from the high-classical period – which is clearly not 'developed equally in all dimensions' yet which, paradoxically, is often regarded as the *locus classicus* of an artistic golden equilibrium – would tend to form part of category-1 complexes. Even if the kind of music Schoenberg advocated, and to a large degree composed, represents progress in Ball's sense of manifesting a higher 'logarithm of the total information content' than much of the music of his predecessors, the presence of the criticism meme of a category-1 musico-conceptual memeplex might motivate an individual to reject such high-perceptual-load music and to see it, in a common memetic-critical trope, as representing a kind of degeneration and decadence.

5.6. Summary

Memetics motivates a conception of the musical work as an essentially temporary alliance of independent replicators, the structure of the work being contingent upon the precise topography of their interrelation. While retaining their particulate identity, the association of memes into memeplexes discussed in Chapter 3 reaches its greatest extent with the generation of the complex formal archetypes characteristic of much European music of the seventeenth to nineteenth centuries. These structural memes, as with the memes of which they are composed, evolve by a process of cumulative cultural selection from simple antecedent forms to highly refined and multifaceted complexes – music's most breathtaking 'systems of great complexity' (Dawkins 1989: 322). The notion of design space suggests that future research may allow the location of compositions in multidimensional memetic hypervolumes to be mapped and their synchronic and diachronic relationships, expressed in terms of cumulative-selection steps, to be tracked.

Chapter 6

Memetics and Musical Analysis: Issues and Methodologies

6.1. Introduction

An important test of the utility of any music-theoretical paradigm is its ability to generate viable music-analytical methodologies. Applying this test to memetics, I begin with an examination of some key contextual issues, including a consideration of theoretical frameworks and analytical systems as verbal-conceptual memeplexes, and then outline some general methodologies for a memetically-orientated music analysis. I illustrate how one of these might be pursued with the aid of the computer – specifically, David Huron's *Humdrum Toolkit* – before concluding with an assessment of some prospects for further memetic research that might be conducted using *Humdrum*.

6.2. 'The Truth Trap': Theoretical Frameworks and Analytical Systems as Verbal-Conceptual Memeplexes

As argued in 5.3.1 above, the various theoretical frameworks and analytical systems which arose in the twentieth century – such as Schenkerism, the implication-realization approach and pitch-class-set analysis – are rich verbal-conceptual memeplexes. They are often associated with a set of musico-graphical memes, a distinctive visual-analytical symbology designed to illustrate the analytical operations upon the musical materials and illuminate their theoretical basis. Subject to the same Darwinian processes as any other memeplex, their survival or extinction rests ostensibly on the selection pressure of perceived fit against those phenomena – musical processes and structures – which they have evolved to model and elucidate. Yet many other factors, some often only tangentially related to music, may impinge on their replicative success. That some of these theoretical-analytical memeplexes may eventually fail effectively to model the memes, memeplexes and multimemetic complexes which constitute their objects is recognized by Nattiez when he recalls that

> [Martin] Vogel in effect looked at the published analyses of the [*Tristan*] chord (since 1879) one by one, and concluded that 'the crisis of romantic harmony is in reality the crisis of harmonic theory' …. This claim seems critical to me, because it means that the harmonic language belonging to a given music-historical period or composer is not comprehensible *unless mediated by a metalanguage* that explains it. There are no musico-harmonic phenomena per se; they are accessible to us only because they have become the object of a *process of symbolization* that organizes them, renders them intelligible. To speak of a 'crisis of theory' is to admit that the *tools* used to describe the phenomena of a particular era are, once the material has reached a certain developmental [that is, evolutionary] stage, no longer sufficient.
>
> (1990: 217; his emphases)

In a survey of 'analytical situations' conducted using the parameters of the tripartitional model (1990: 139–43), Nattiez identifies six perspectives, ranging from 'immanent analysis' (which 'tackles only the immanent [neutral-level] configurations of the work') to 'communication between the three levels' (where 'an immanent analysis is equally relevant to the poietic as to the esthesic') (1990: 140, 142). More broadly, these situations are the consequence of contrasting plots, as Nattiez terms them (1985: 111; 1990: 204). Each of the implementation of a metalanguage, plots filter the raw materials taken as the evidential basis of an analysis and structure the interpretations drawn from this evidence.

As a verbal-conceptual memeplex, the plot an analyst employs in formulating an analysis is entirely dependent upon the particular memes he or she is 'programmed' with, this profile being a function of musical background and education. Again, plots are subject to the same evolutionary pressures as any other memeplex, and mutant plots may therefore be differentially selected according to the criterion of fit against the music whose analysis they guide. As a simple illustration of this concept, and of the shifting and contingent nature of analytical interpretations, consider the passage in Example 6.1 below.

Example 6.1: Chopin, Mazurka in A minor op. 7 no. 2 (1830–32), bb. 17–21

The boxed area shows an unstable sequence of chords which, on a simple local harmonic-functional analysis, progresses from a German augmented sixth chord in C minor (with root F♯; marked *a*) to a half-diminished seventh chord (root F♮;

marked *b*) and then to a dominant seventh chord of E♭ major in $^4_2$ position (root B♭; marked *c*). By contrast, a linear interpretation – one driven by the Schenkerian memeplex – might take *a*, *b* and *c* to be components of horizontal strands prolonging the C minor harmony operative in bb. 17–23 (but then quickly circumvented in bb. 24–5 for the reprise of the opening material). In a third reading, one might take the passage to be an example of what Lewin calls the 'DOUTH2' transformational operation (1996: 207), where at every progression from one chord to the next two voices hold the previous pitch and two move by a semitone – an example of what Cohn terms 'parsimonious voice-leading' (1997: 1–2). As a result of contrasting plots – the first contingent upon a vertical-functional framework, the second upon a horizontal-Schenkerian perspective and the third upon a transformational system – three radically different, but internally coherent, analyses may be engendered.[1]

This issue has a bearing on the question of the evolution of tonal organization in music raised in 4.6.4 above. As is well established, the transformational operations described by neo-Riemannian theory are particularly suited to conceptualizing certain harmonic progressions of mid- and late-nineteenth century music – progressions which seem highly problematic when viewed from the perspective of the major-minor key system of Mozart and Schenker. But if we accept that much of this later music is still amenable to interpretation in terms of the circle of fifths, this begs the converse question as to how valid a neo-Riemannian approach is for the music of the late-eighteenth century and earlier. Where, in other words, is the boundary to be drawn between music for which a circle-of-fifths approach is an effective analytical tool and music for which a transformational approach is more appropriate? In memetic terms, when (and where) does a change occur between a meme pool which lends itself to formulation in terms of the circle of fifths and one which lends itself to formulation in terms of transformation? Of course, the argument in Chapter 4 leads to the conclusion that no such boundary can exist in a world of gradualistic system-level memetic evolution.

Theoretical-analytical memeplexes filter, and inevitably colour, our perception of the music which is their object. In other words, the interpretation one formulates via a given theoretical perspective and its associated analytical methodology is possibly as much an artefact as those distortions which sometimes result from the treatment of samples in preparation for electron microscopy. More fundamentally, one might concede that there is no such thing as an absolute theoretical-analytical truth; all that exists are the products of the relativism created during the interaction between real-world events and phenomena and the memetic mental frameworks which have evolved within human cultures to facilitate, by a process of representation, their comprehension. This is essentially the same thorny philosophical question which

---

[1] I am grateful to Michael Russ for bringing this passage, and its various interpretations, to my attention.

Brodie terms 'the truth trap' (1996: 51), the memetic perspective on this problem asserting that

> the distinction-memes you are programmed with form a *perceptual filter* on the immediate present world around you.... The truth of any proposition depends upon the assumptions you make in considering it – the distinction-memes you use in thinking about it.... Every time you have a new set of distinction-memes, you have a whole new philosophy.
>
> (: 49, 51, 52; his emphasis)

Thus while a perfect alignment between our memetic models of reality and the 'Absolute Truth' (: 216) is a powerful selection pressure, it is a juxtaposition which endlessly regresses, undermined by the innate complexity of the universe and the disquieting realization that the most evolutionarily successful theories are not necessarily the most truthful, but merely the most effective replicators.

In searching for the holy grail of the Absolute Truth, a fundamental problem arises from the relationship between a memetic view of music and perspectives arising from more specifically music-theoretical traditions. Without intentional arrogance, memetics by its very nature claims the status of a metatheory; indeed it sees itself as the supreme metatheory of human culture. It justifies this by appeal to the claim that any perspective drawing its legitimacy from universal Darwinism must claim ontological and epistemological priority over less broadly grounded views. Memetics therefore 'trumps' other theories by being able to explain their structure and development (and, self-referentially, its own) from a Darwinian perspective, this advantage potentially putting it into confrontation with other theories of musical organization. Salt is rubbed into the proverbial wounds by the above contention that theoretical-analytical perspectives are memeplexes whose replicative success is not always wholly contingent on their degree of fit to the cultural objects under scrutiny.

One way of resolving this problem is to regard other views of musical organization not as contradictory to memetics but as contributory to its development. Thus, as seen in Chapter 3, Chapter 4 and Chapter 5, Schenkerian theory helps rationalize the issue of replication hierarchies; the implication-realization model helps clarify the issue of segmentation and perceptual-cognitive salience; and other perspectives drawn from psychology – such as Ockelford's zygonic theory and Deliège's and Mélen's cue abstraction model – help explain the operation of pattern perception and cognition. Thus, I would argue that none of the currently dominant psychological, theoretical and analytical perspectives on music is incongruous with memetics. On the contrary, they offer powerful conceptual and symbolic vocabularies and associated methodologies which can help memetics address its central concerns.

6.3. Objects, Realms and Methodologies in Memetic Analysis

As they are presently conceived, music theory exists in a reciprocal relationship with music analysis, whereby 'theory equals general, analysis equals specific' (Dunsby and Whittall 1988: 6). This distinction is essentially that between study of the musical movement or work (Meyer's intraopus style) and study of higher levels of the memetic-structural/cultural hierarchy (idiom, dialect and rules) shown in Figure 3.9 above.

For many this is an important distinction: in post-enlightenment European culture the work forms the locus of many people's musical experiences (2.3.2 above), whereas a concept like the dialect is inherently more amorphous and intangible. In the romantic (and especially the Schenkerian) tradition, the work is glamorized, even fetishized. Nevertheless, as Lydia Goehr tells us, the 'work-concept' is a relatively recent notion (becoming firmly established only *c.* 1800); and 'musicians who produce jazz, pop songs, and many if not all types of music performed within social functions and rituals are able to manage successfully without a work-concept' (1992: v).

Whether one has a work-concept or not, from the meme's eye view, the distinction is even less important. From this perspective, a work, be it a sonata, a painting or a novel, is a temporary conglomeration, merely the phemotypic product of a neural collaboration formed to further the selfish interests of individual memes, so there is no special reason to privilege it above any other meme incarnation. In this sense, memetic analysis need not be restricted to the analysis of works, as has traditionally been the case in much music-analytical work. Rather, it can encompass all levels of the memetic-structural/cultural hierarchy, from the study of individual memes to investigations of the dialect. In doing so, it causes analysis to blend imperceptibly into theory and therefore subverts what might be thought of as a clear distinction between these two disciplines.

Given this, one can identify two basic realms of memetic analysis, the intra-work level (intraopus style; traditionally the province of analysis) and the inter-work level (the level of the individual meme, and also of idiom, dialect and rules; traditionally the province of theory). Each may be further subdivided into a total of eight areas of investigation, each of these areas naturally suggesting its own analytical methodology.

6.3.1. *The Intra-Work Realm and its Methodologies*

When memetic analysis is situated at the intra-work level, it has three main areas of investigation. The listing of each area below is followed by a statement of the methodologies pertinent to the pursuit of that area. These, unsurprisingly, are derived from the theoretical exposition of memetics in Chapter 2 to Chapter 5, particularly the discussion of the most basic attributes of memes in 3.3 above:

1. The investigation of the constituent memes of a work and their inter-work evolutionary history (their antecedents and consequents); even at this level it is impossible to ignore the wider nexus of imitation which links works. This area is not dissimilar to Nattiez's 'analysis of the neutral level' (1990: 12), but here the analysis is conducted not in terms of segmentations made on the basis of internal repetition but on the basis of memetic replication, with all the implications this has for psychologically valid segmentation.

- *Methodologies*: i) horizontal and vertical segmentation (partitioning of the work into its component perceptual-cognitive/replicated particles); ii) coindexation (determining the memetic status of particles resulting from segmentation by mapping them onto homologues in other contexts, the process of segmentation being reflexively mediated by the location of such coindexes).

2. The investigation of the interrelationship of memes within a work (their conglomerational grammar) at several structural-hierarchic levels. Clearly this area is the closest to the concerns and approaches of 'traditional' voice-leading and structural analysis.

- *Methodologies*: i) horizontal and vertical segmentation; ii) coindexation; iii) structural-hierarchic/replication analysis (determining how the memes identified by i and ii generate deeper-level structures in the work, and how these resultant patterns may themselves be mapped against coindexes in other contexts).

3. The investigation of the semantic content of a non-texted work, identifying any semiotic associations (co-adaptations) between the musical memes in the work and verbal-conceptual memes.

- *Methodologies*: i) horizontal and vertical segmentation; ii) coindexation; iii) investigation of poietic documents to locate explicit and implicit evidence of intra-work semiotic co-adaptations; iv) analysis of topical content to determine assimilated dialect-level semiotic co-adaptations (Agawu 1991); v) comparison of memes within the work with their coindexes in texted works by the same composer to determine 'subtextual' idiom-level co-adaptations (Jan 2003: 366).

6.3.2. *The Inter-Work Realm and its Methodologies*

When memetic analysis is situated at the inter-work level, it has five main areas of investigation. Again, the listing of each area is followed by a statement of the methodologies pertinent to its pursuit:

1. The investigation of a single meme and its transmission-mutation history within a dialect over space and time. This approach is broadly analogous to the 'feature analysis' developed in such studies as Crane and Fiehler 1970.

- *Methodologies*: i) horizontal and vertical segmentation to generate a candidate pattern; ii) coindexation (surveys of the dialect to identify homologous patterns).

2. The investigation of a structural meme and its transmission-mutation history within a dialect over space and time.

- *Methodologies*: i) comparison of two or more works to determine replicated structural patterning; ii) determination of the allele classes whose assemblage generates the structural meme; iii) wider study of the dialect to determine the extent and evolutionary development of the structural meme.

3. The investigation of the semantic content of a meme, identifying any dialect-level semiotic co-adaptations between the meme and verbal-conceptual memes.

- *Methodologies*: i) horizontal and vertical segmentation; ii) coindexation; iii) analysis of topical co-adaptations.

4. The investigation of the constituent memes of a dialect and their transmission-mutation history over space and time, a field which might be termed population memetics.

- *Methodologies*: as 1 above, repeated for several memes.

5. The investigation of the effect of the (evolution of the) constituent memes of a dialect upon the (evolution of the) system of rules generated by that dialect.

- *Methodologies*: i) the study of a representative sample of memes derived from 4 above in terms of their system-generating properties; ii) the comparison of two or more such samples from separate time-slices.

6.4. Computer-Aided Memetic Analysis with The *Humdrum Toolkit*

A central problem in developing a theory of musical memetics and implementing it in analytical studies is the sheer volume of music which must be investigated in order for reliable (statistically significant) conclusions to be drawn – although suggestive findings may often result from non-empirical studies. Taking only one of the Viennese classical trinity which forms my reference point in this study, the output of Mozart is an enormous research base and therefore the task of locating the occurrences of a single meme within it is onerous. Comparing the findings of such a study with one of Haydn or Beethoven magnifies the enterprise dauntingly.

Clearly computer-aided study is a viable method of making the empirical investigation of such a corpus of music manageable. For assistance with the development of a theory of memetics and the analytical investigation of memes in music, one software package in particular seems the most suitable currently available, namely the *Humdrum Toolkit*, conceived and developed since 1989 by Huron (1994, 1997, 1999, 2002; see also Cook 2004). Although *Humdrum* can do many things which are useful in musicological research, its value for memetics is its considerable power and flexibility in pattern finding: perhaps no other software system presently available is able to compete with it in this respect. Put simply, having defined a search template which represents the configuration of the meme under investigation, one may rapidly search a work or a repertoire for other copies of the meme.

6.4.1. *Overview and Operational Strategies*

The *Humdrum Toolkit* is a not a single program but a set of software tools. It is designed for UNIX operating systems, but will run in DOS, *Windows*® and Macintosh® environments, provided certain other utilities are present.[2] It encapsulates the UNIX bottom-up design philosophy in that each of the over 70 tools is fairly modest in its individual effects, but great power and flexibility can be achieved by connecting tools with each other in 'pipelines', such that the output of one becomes the input for another. The tools can be incorporated into user-devised 'shell-scripts' (mini programs) in order to facilitate the processing of lengthy pipelines and large processing tasks.

Beyond the tools themselves, *Humdrum* provides a syntax for representing music – that is, a series of formal conditions which stipulate how music may be represented in a manner comprehensible by the software. Although there are numerous predefined representation schemes available in *Humdrum*, the 'default' is the '`**kern`' (German for 'core') representation, which provides a means of encoding the fundamental elements of common-practice western notation in text files using ASCII characters (see Huron 1997 for a full account of the `**kern` representation).

Essentially, pitches are represented by their letter names (the octaves being `CC–BB`, `C–B`, (middle) `c–b`, `cc–bb`, `ccc–bbb`, etc.), rhythm values are indicated by integers ('`2`' = 𝅗𝅥, '`4`' = ♩, '`8`' = ♪ etc.), and voices (instruments, independent contrapuntal lines) are organized in 'spines' (columns of data separated by tab

[2] This free software is available at the time of writing from <http://dactyl.som.ohio-state.edu/HumdrumDownload/downloading.html>. The UWIN (*UNIX for Windows*) UNIX emulation utility (also freeware, under the terms of an educational/research license, from <http://www.research.att.com/sw/tools/uwin/#overview>) is a reliable and economical method of running *Humdrum* on *Windows*®.

characters), with leftmost spines representing lower parts and rightmost representing upper. Each horizontal line of the score, terminated by a newline character, is termed a 'data record' and represents a simultaneity in the music, being divided into as many 'data tokens' (tab-separated groups of characters) as there are spines.

While this brief statement of the nuts and bolts of *Humdrum* may seem relatively straightforward, it must be conceded that effective use of the toolkit in its 'raw' state requires a degree of facility with UNIX that many musicologists without technical backgrounds are unable or unwilling to devote time to acquiring. Kornstädt's *JRing* program (2001) circumvents this difficulty by providing a graphical front-end to the *Humdrum* tools which should increase their accessibility, albeit with the loss of some flexibility. The investigations described below, however, used *Humdrum* in its 'command-line' form.

A large body of music, western 'common practice' and other repertoires, has already been encoded in the `**kern` format and many of these electronic editions can be obtained free of charge via the internet.[3] Alternatively, the user may encode works, incorporating only those details pertinent to the investigation: one may wish, for instance, to investigate pitch structures in a given work or repertoire, in which case encoding rhythmic or phrasing information may not be necessary.

In conducting searches for memes, two of the *Humdrum* tools have particular significance, the broadly analogous `patt` and `pattern` which, as their names imply, are both pattern-locating utilities. These tools search the representation of the music under investigation using a template which defines the pattern sought. Found patterns are reported to the user by, among other means, the line numbers the pattern encompasses in the relevant file. Patterns are represented in templates using UNIX 'regular expression' syntax, that is, sequences of characters (both 'literals', which are sought directly, and 'metacharacters', which qualify the meanings of other characters) which stipulate what the target file may or may not contain in order for a pattern match to be registered. Table 6.1 below summarizes this syntax.

---

[3] The principal sources at the time of writing are the *Kern Scores* (<http://kern.humdrum.net/>) and *Muse Data* websites (<http://www.musedata.org/>).

Table 6.1: Summary of UNIX Regular Expression Syntax

<table>
<tr><th>Character</th><th>Name, Meaning</th></tr>
<tr><td>.</td><td>Single-Character Wildcard: matches any single character.</td></tr>
<tr><td>\</td><td>Escape Character: turns off the meaning of the following metacharacter and makes it into a literal.</td></tr>
<tr><td>+</td><td>Repetition Operator: matches one or more consecutive instances of the previous expression.</td></tr>
<tr><td>*</td><td>Repetition Operator: matches zero or more consecutive instances of the previous expression.</td></tr>
<tr><td>?</td><td>Repetition Operator: matches zero or one instance of the previous expression.</td></tr>
<tr><td>.*</td><td>Any String: matches zero or more instances of any characters.</td></tr>
<tr><td>()</td><td>Parenthesis Grouping: binds several characters into a single unit or sub-expression.</td></tr>
<tr><td>^</td><td>Context Anchor: anchors the expression to the beginning of the line.</td></tr>
<tr><td>$</td><td>Context Anchor: anchors the expression to the end of the line.</td></tr>
<tr><td>|</td><td>'Or' Logical Operator: x | y = x or y.</td></tr>
<tr><td>[]</td><td>Character Class: matches any character(s) within the square brackets. Metacharacters become literals within [].</td></tr>
<tr><td>[^]</td><td>Complementary Character Class: only those characters not in the character class or range are matched.</td></tr>
<tr><td>-</td><td>Range Operator: [A-Z] = all 26 characters from A to Z. A dash at the beginning or end of a character class (not separating a range) becomes a literal.</td></tr>
</table>

The chief difference between `patt` and `pattern` is in the latter's implementation of the three repetition operators, specified by the '+', '*' and '?' metacharacters, which stipulate how many lines (records) containing a sought pattern may occur in the target file for a match to be registered.

Regular expression syntax is more than just a highly sophisticated and flexible way of searching for patterns in text files. While their phemotypic products on computer screens derive from memotypic constellations distinct from those of musical memes, patterns such as that in Figure 6.1 i below (which represents the opening motive of Beethoven's Fifth Symphony) can stand for musical memes in the sense that they encapsulate the pitch and durational information of musical memes, albeit represented in a different manner than in the phemotypes of musical memes. Depending on how precisely one sets their terms, regular expressions can also stand for classes of memes (sets of alleles and/or evolutionary variants) as opposed to specific memes, as shown in Figure 6.1 ii.

i) Strict Definition

a) expression	b) meaning
`8r`	(𝄾)
`8g`	(g^2 ♪)
`8g`	(g^2 ♪)
`8g`	(g^2 ♪)
`^=`	(barline)
`2e-`	($e\flat^2$ 𝅗𝅥)

ii) Fuzzy Definition

a) expression	b) meaning
`[48]g +`	(one or more of g^2 ♩ or ♪)
`^=`	(barline)
`[24]e- +`	(one or more of $e\flat^2$ 𝅗𝅥 or ♩)

Figure 6.1: Regular Expressions denoting the Opening Motive of Beethoven's Fifth Symphony

The essence of a successful search using `patt` or `pattern` is in designing a parsimonious and efficient template. Having provisionally formulated such a template it is essential to test it out first on passages – either synthetic examples or extracts taken from real pieces – in which the sought pattern is known to exist. This is in order to verify that it will not register a false negative, that is, will fail to find an instance of the pattern, despite its occurring in the music. Such a test may also indicate if the template would record a false positive, that is, would register a pattern match for configurations which the musician's judgement would reject as unconvincing (Temperley 2001: 74).

6.4.2. *A Case Study: Finding Tetrachordal Memes*

Compelled by constraints of space to demonstrate only one of the eight methodologies for memetic analysis outlined in 6.3 above using *Humdrum* as the analytic engine, the first inter-work methodology – 'the investigation of a single meme and its transmission-mutation history within a dialect over space and time' – seems the most appropriate. Taking the second part of this definition first, and while not compromising the illustrative purpose of this study, further restrictions are necessary to make the analysis manageable for present purposes. These restrictions will be of composer, genre and, therefore, chronology. It will be limited to those string quartets of Haydn, Mozart and Beethoven that were available at the time of writing from the *Kern Scores* and *Muse Data* websites: 59 of Haydn's 68 quartets (excepting opp. 2, 9 nos. 1, 4–6 and 17 no. 4), all of Mozart's 26 quartets (but not including the Adagio and Fugue K. 546) and nine of Beethoven's 16 quartets (opp. 18 nos. 1 and 2 (3rd movement of the latter only), 59 nos. 1 and 2, 95, 127, 130 (with replacement finale), 131 and 135). These works are encoded as 380 separate files (with one, rarely two or more, files per movement), representing 373 movements and 94 out of a possible total of 110 quartets. The works span eight decades, from the 1750s to the 1820s.

As for the first part of the definition, the meme under investigation, two strategies – refinements of area 1's methodology i in 6.3.2 above – present themselves for determining a candidate pattern:

1. The first strategy (broadly *a posteriori* then *a priori*) hypothesizes that a 'natural' pattern selected on the basis of its perceptual-cognitive salience may be a meme. Having selected the candidate pattern, this strategy then attempts, in a top-down manner, to locate other members of the posited similarity class within a given idiom or dialect according to the criterion of fit against the 'template' pattern. If matches are found, then the pattern is very likely to be a meme. It may then be fruitful to modify the original pattern in the light of the original search in order to locate other patterns which, while structurally similar to it, nevertheless manifest certain allelic-evolutionary deviations from it.
2. The second strategy (broadly *a priori*) generates a synthetic candidate pattern based on the perceptual and cognitive constraints imposed upon memes by the architecture of the human sensory and neural system in order to predict, in a top-down manner, what types of patterns are likely to attain memetic status. Having synthesized a candidate pattern, this strategy then conducts searches through a given idiom or dialect for natural instances of the synthetic pattern. As with the first methodology, it may then be fruitful to modify the original pattern in order to locate allelically/evolutionarily related variants.

I shall adopt the first strategy here, choosing as my candidate a figure that seems eminently well suited to such an investigation, namely the descending chromatic tetrachord figure. Of course, given that the pattern is common in minor-key music of the seventeenth to the nineteenth centuries (3.4.4 above; see also Jan 1995: Chapter 7 and Williams 1998), one is starting from the standpoint that it is indeed a meme; but this does not militate against pursuing this first strategy for illustrative purposes.

Example 6.2 i below shows the particular tetrachord type under investigation: a chromatic form associated with a distinctive contrary-motion voice. A schematic reduction representing the 'total resource' of this type is given in ii and four alleles, *a*, *b* (represented by Example 6.2 i), *c* and *d* are bracketed. Alleles *b*, *c* and *d* lack $\natural\hat{7}$, $\hat{1}$–$\natural\hat{7}$ and $\hat{1}$–$\natural\hat{7}$–$\flat\hat{7}$ respectively, but their overlap with allele *a* allows us to regard them as drawn from a tetrachordal pitch collection, even in the absence of the complete falling lower-voice fourth. Despite allele *d* being the smallest indivisible unit (3.3.1 above) drawn from this conceptual set, *a*, *b* and *c* still count as independent alleles owing to their unique individual shapes.

Example 6.2: Four Chromatic Tetrachord Alleles

i) Chromatic Form with Associated Contrary-Motion Voice: Mozart, Sonata in C minor K. 457 (1784), I, bb. 139–41 (Allele *b*)

ii) Chromatic Form with Associated Contrary-Motion Voice: Schema and Alleles *a*, *b*, *c* and *d*

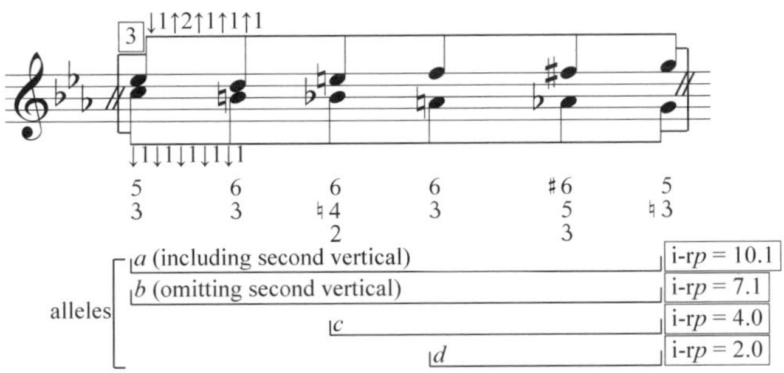

While Example 6.2 ii represents the alleles as four pitch schemata, Example 6.2 i constitutes an instantiation of one of these alleles, this being defined as a disposition of the allele's constituent pitches in a particular hierarchic, rhythmic, metrical and registral configuration. It follows that the search is directed towards locating a somewhat abstract structure which may sit at a variety of structural levels from the immediate foreground to deeper strata; yet in principle any particular foreground-level allele instantiation may also be a meme if its particular configuration is replicated.

When planning a search for allele instantiations it is necessary to begin with the premise that they are almost certainly independent of key and therefore the search process must be conducted in terms of their constituent scale degrees, not absolute pitch. The search template must be conceived in, and the repertoire under investigation must be converted into, the *Humdrum* '`**deg`' (scale-degree) representation. In designing the template it is also necessary to consider the two broad contexts in which the pattern might occur. First, it may appear as a sub-foreground-level structure, its components appearing in direct succession over the course of perhaps only a few beats; secondly, and more problematically, it might appear as a shallow-middleground-level structure, its components separated by interpolated material, or forming a framework or substructure for more prominent figuration above or below them.

The template shown in Figure 6.2 i below is conceived on the basis that the two central components of Example 6.2 ii – the verticals $\hat{4}/\natural\hat{6}$–$\sharp\hat{4}/\flat\hat{6}$, with their resultant $^{6}_{3}$ major subdominant–augmented sixth harmony – are a marker for all four alleles; find this segment, therefore, and one has very likely found one of these alleles. This template can locate patterns at various hierarchical levels provided the `ditto` command is used to manipulate the `**deg` representation before searching. This command copies information from a data record into any null (empty) tokens (represented by '`.`') immediately below, such as would occur when figuration moving in semiquavers (encoded by four successive records of '`16`') appears in conjunction with a sought pattern presented in crotchets (encoded by '`4`' in the first record followed by three further records of '`.`'). Apart from a small class of cases involving rests in certain places, most manifestations of the tetrachord pattern, whatever their structural-hierarchic level, would be found using this method because the majority will feature the contrapuntal shifts $\hat{4}$–$\sharp\hat{4}$ and $\natural\hat{6}$–$\flat\hat{6}$ simultaneously across two adjacent records, irrespective of the hierarchic location of the pattern as a whole.

Orientated to Minor-Key Movements and Sections		
i) Tonic region	ii) Relative major region	iii) Dominant region
`(6[+]).*(4[^+-])`	`(1[^+-]).*(6[^+-])`	`(3[+]).*(1[^+-])`
`(6[^+-]).*(4[+])`	`(1[-]).*(6[+])`	`(3[^+-]).*(1[+])`
Orientated to Major-Key Movements and Sections		
iv) Tonic region	v) Relative minor region	vi) Dominant region
`(6[^+-]).*(4[^+-])`	`(4[+]).*(2[^+-])`	`(3[^+-]).*(1[^+-])`
`(6[-]).*(4[+])`	`(4[^+-]).*(2[+])`	`(3[-]).*(1[+])`

Figure 6.2: Six Tetrachord-Locating `Patt` Templates

The template in Figure 6.2 i will only locate examples of the pattern in the tonic-region areas of minor-key movements and sections of (composite) movements, unless they occurred in a passage whose departure from the tonic was so extensive and/or significant as to warrant a new key 'tandem interpretation' (for example, '`*g:`'), indicating to `deg` the new local tonic. (In its accommodation of 'floating' tonics, `deg` is not constrained by Schoenberg's notion of monotonality (1983: 19).) To locate examples in the relative major and dominant minor – the most probable other regions in which the pattern might occur within minor-key movements and sections – then the templates shown in ii and iii would have to be employed in addition to that shown in i. In order to cast the net still wider, and paralleling the templates shown in i, ii and iii, Figure 6.2 iv, v and vi show versions of the template suitable for locating copies of the pattern in the tonic-, relative-minor- and dominant-region areas of major-key movements and sections respectively.

Using the six templates shown in Figure 6.2, a `patt` search produced the results – contingent upon the accuracy of the **kern encodings processed and the error-free operation of the *Humdrum* tools – shown in Table 6.2 below. Following this, Table 6.3 presents an analysis of the data.

Table 6.2: Search Results for Tetrachordal Alleles *a*, *b*, *c* and *d*

Key
* = upper voice omits first pitch of allele *c*.
† = employs upper voice of allele *c*.
‡ = employs lower voice of allele *a*.
→ = indicates patterns linked by exposition-recapitulation analogy within the same sonata movement.

Haydn				Mozart				Beethoven			
op.	mvt.	bb.	allele	K.	mvt.	bb.	allele	op.	mvt.	bb.	allele
Template Figure 6.2 i (orientated to minor key movements and sections, tonic region)											
17/5	III	73–5	*b*	173	I	88–91	*a*→	–	–	–	–
76/3	IV	179–181	*c*	173	IV	8	*b*				
103	II	41–4	*b*	421	I	107	*b*				
						109–10	*b*				
				421	IV	19–20	*b*				
				465	III	101–2	*d*				
Template Figure 6.2 ii (minor key, relative major)											
–	–	–	–	173	IV	35–7	*a*	18/1	II	16–17	*d*†
Template Figure 6.2 iii (minor key, dominant)											
–	–	–	–	173	I	18–21	→*a*	–	–	–	–
Template Figure 6.2 iv (major key, tonic)											
20/1	III	53–4	*c**	169	IV	43–4	*b*	–	–	–	–
20/2	IV	37	*c**	428	I	157–9	*b*→				
50/5	I	93–5	*b*	465	IV	14–15	*d*→				
50/6	IV	14–16	*a*→			213–14	→*d*				
		157–9	→*a*	590	IV	289–91	*d*				
		206–7	*a*→								
55/1	I	158–9	*d*								
64/1	II	39–41	*d*								
71/2	IV	91–3	*a*								
74/1	I	12–13	*b*								
76/1	II	14–15	*c*→								
		54–5	→*c*								
76/4	I	143–52	*c*‡								
76/5	I	26–7	*a*→								
		71–2	→*a*								
76/6	I	7–8	*d*→								
		115–116	→*d*								

Table 6.2 Continued

Haydn				Mozart				Beethoven			
op.	mvt.	bb.	allele	K.	mvt.	bb.	allele	op.	mvt.	bb.	allele
Template Figure 6.2 v (major key, relative minor)											
33/5	I	157–60	*c*	–	–	–	–	127	IV	51–3	*c*
								130	V	14–15	*d*†
103	I	62–7	*a*								
Template Figure 6.2 vi (major key, dominant)											
50/6	IV	77–8	→*a*	428	I	61–3	→*b*	–	–	–	–
55/1	II	26–8	*b*								
64/5	I	138–9	*a*								

Table 6.3: Analysis of Data from Table 6.2

Key
Where two allele counts or percentages are separated by a /, the first value excludes and the second includes patterns related by exposition–recapitulation thematic analogy. Thus, a distinction is made between number of dissimilar instantiations of an allele/all instantiations of the allele.

	Movts./ Works	**Movts. with patterns**	**Allele *a* (i-r*p* = 10.1)**	**Allele *b* (i-r*p* = 7.1)**	**Allele *c* (i-r*p* = 4.0)**	**Allele *d* (i-r*p* = 2.0)**	**Allele Totals**
Haydn	240/59	18 (7.5%)	6/9	5/5	6/7	3/4	20/25 (58.8%/ 59.5%)
Mozart	95/26	9 (9.5%)	2/3	6/7	0/0	3/4	11/14 (32.4%/ 33.3%)
Beethoven	38/9	3 (7.9%)	0/0	0/0	1/1	2/2	3/3 (8.8%/ 7.2%)
Totals	373/94	30 (8.0%)	8/12 (23.5%/ 28.6%)	11/12 (32.4%/ 28.6%)	7/8 (20.6%/ 19.0%)	8/10 (23.5%/ 23.8%)	**34/42** (100%/ 100%)

Expressed in terms of the number of pitches in the found allele instantiations as a percentage of the total pitches in the repertoire surveyed, the 'footprint' of these alleles is clearly minuscule. Nevertheless, they occur in 8 per cent of the movements studied, and so must count as successful memes. Differentiating between the number of dissimilar instantiations of an allele and all instantiations of the allele naturally gives slightly different values owing to the repetition of expositional patterns in recapitulatory forms. As suggested in 5.3.5 above, from the meme's eye view such analogies result in more phemotypic copies of a meme occupying the infosphere, which therefore increases the likelihood of its further transmission.

Contrary to the prediction in 4.4.2 above, the frequency of occurrence of alleles does not correlate smoothly with their i-r*p* values (indicated on Example 6.2 ii and Table 6.3 above). There may be several reasons for this. First, the total number of allele instantiations found is relatively small, particularly in the case of Beethoven, and so may not constitute a statistically representative sample. Secondly, the disproportionately high occurrence of allele *d*, out of kilter with its low i-r*p* value, may be accounted for by its ability to fill memetic niches between other memes more efficiently than the more extended alleles *a*, *b* and *c*. Thirdly, the converse argument may account for the disproportionately low occurrence of allele *a*, out of kilter with its high i-r*p* value. Thus, as noted in the second and third 'caveats' in 4.4.2, the mechanistic predictions of i-r*p* have to be balanced against influences deriving from other factors, such as extraopus schemata and intraopus processes. Nevertheless, considered together, alleles *a* and *b* do have a higher total i-r*p* value than that of alleles *c* and *d*; accordingly (but not proportionately), their instantiations outnumber those of alleles *c* and *d* in this sample.

Found patterns vary in the strength of their segmentational articulation. While all are end-terminated by virtue of the harmonic interference engendered by their arrival on the dominant, some (particularly those involving alleles *c* and *d*) lack a correspondingly strong opening articulation owing to their unstable, processive initial node. While the 'singularity' of these instantiations often assures their perceptual-cognitive salience (that is, they may be demarcated by means of coindexation-engendered segmentation; 3.3.3 above), it may be the case that owing to their lack of a strong initial articulation some instantiations of alleles *c* and *d* are best regarded not as independent memes but instead as the end-segments of different memes, with clear initial articulations. Allele *d*, in particular, lends itself to end-integration with a variety of antecedent shapes which, if replicated as a unit, would count as separate memes. The instantiation in Mozart's K. 465, IV, bb. 14^1–15^1 (*d*) might come into this category, perhaps assembling with bb. 12^2–13^2 (*x*) as a separate meme *x*–*d*.

Confirming the sensitivity of the templates to patterns at a variety of structural levels, found allele instantiations are situated at the immediate foreground (as in Haydn's op. 50 no. 6, IV, bb. 14–16), the shallow middleground (as in Mozart's K. 173, I, bb. 18–21) and the deeper middleground (as in Haydn's op. 76 no. 4, I, bb. 143–52). Alleles in the second two categories are therefore generated by surface-level patterning which may itself be memetic. The hierarchic location of alleles acts as a fourth factor in the above discussion of the correlation between i-r*p* and allele prevalence, for the further the pattern from the foreground the more its generative surface figuration contributes to the overall i-r*p* of the passage in ways which may distort a uniform relationship between these two variables.

While this part of the study is, of course, only the beginning, constraints of space prevent my going further: 'the investigation of [the alleles'] transmission-mutation history within a dialect over space and time' has not even been begun. But one now has a promising sample of work- and time-specific patterns to study and, having done the leg-work, *Humdrum* now steps aside to allow the researcher to bring the superior powers of (memetically-driven) human judgement to bear on the data found.

6.4.3. *Prospects for Further Research using* Humdrum

In considering the prospects for this avenue of research, four issues in particular deserve mention. A fifth issue goes beyond *Humdrum* to touch upon the wider question of quantitative memetics.

*Positing Meme Segmentation and Calculating i-r*p

Given that `patt` and `pattern` are able to discern long note values, rests, metric position and cadential articulations, *Humdrum* might be used to posit meme segmentation using the various criteria – essentially the Gestalt perceptual laws, as implemented in the GTTM grouping rules and Narmour's d, h and b functions – discussed in 3.3.2 above. It would then be possible, having verified the memetic status of the isolated pattern by locating coindexes, to calculate the i-r*p* values of the meme's component i-r structures. This could be done by converting the values of a melodic interval (`**mint`) representation of the music to their i-r*p* equivalent using the `humsed` command (a find-and-replace utility), replacing an interval-pattern character string with one specifying the corresponding i-r*p* value. For example, a melodic-interval-sequence string '`+M2 +M2`' (•↑2•↑2•) would be replaced by its corresponding i-r*p*-value string, '`2.0`'. All of these operations could be automated using shell scripts, facilitating the batch processing of large repertories.

Measuring Edit Distance with the Humdrum `Simil` *Tool*

The concept of mutation, of transition from one form to another, can usefully be described in terms of the notion of edit distance – the number of changes (additions, deletions, substitutions) required to move from the antecedent to the consequent form. This metric, formulated by Fred Damerau and Vladimir Levenshtein, has been implemented by Keith Orpen in the *Humdrum* `simil` tool (Orpen and Huron 1992). `Simil` imposes an 'edit penalty' for each change required to move from the pattern specified in a template file (a representation of the pattern being sought) to patterns in a source file (the input material). The penalties are then weighted such that 'an output value near zero indicates great dissimilarity of the template and the primary input [source] at the current location, whereas a number near one indicates a high level of similarity' (: 18).

Whereas a search using `patt` or `pattern` is very much an either-or investigation (a given portion of a `**kern` file either contains or does not contain the pattern specified by the template, even when the template is made flexible by the inclusion of repetition operators), a search using `simil` is much more nuanced: the user will have to examine the `**simil` output data and decide the threshold numerical value at which a manual investigation of the relevant point in the source data is prompted. Sometimes a graphical plotting of the `**simil` data makes this determination clearer, as in the recurrences of the opening motive of Bach's Two-Part Invention no. 1 analyzed by Orpen and Huron (1992: 21–4).

Investigating the Hierarchic Location of Memes

The patterns examined in 6.4.2 above are mainly situated at the foreground and shallow-middleground levels. It is eminently possible to increase the ambit of *Humdrum* searches to embrace memes at deeper structural levels. The persistent tension between false positives and false negatives notwithstanding, using repetition operators with the `pattern` utility facilitates the identification of more distributed (deeper-middleground and background) memes. This potentially very broad category might include replicated melodic patterns (the various changing-note schemata, I–V…I–I antecedent-consequent phrase types and other melodies whose divergent foregrounds generate a common structural plan), formal archetypes (structural memes, defined in a variety of ways) and even more elusive tonal-harmonic structures such as the neo-Riemannian transformations and hexatonic progressions of mid- and late-nineteenth-century music (Hyer 1995, Cohn 1996) whose replication contributed significantly to system-level evolutionary change at this time.

Plotting the Geographical Distribution of Memes

The transmission of memes through conceptual space involves a concomitant motion through geographical and temporal space, the study of which is termed population memetics in 6.3.2 above. One of the most potentially useful features of *Humdrum* is its ability, in conjunction with other programs, to track this diffusion in a form of dialect-level distributional analysis (Bent and Pople 2001: 565–7). A mechanism for implementing this exists for *Humdrum* may be integrated with the *Generic Mapping Tools* (*GMT*), a set of UNIX utilities which produce maps from numerical input data, including graphics which show the distribution of data over a given area (Wessel and Smith 2004).

Aarden and Huron created two geographical reference records additional to the standard `**kern` '`!!!ARE`' (geographical region of origin of the work encoded) record: the verbal '`!!!ARD`' record (detailed location – nation, region, city, etc. – of the work encoded) and the numerical '`!!!ARL`' record (latitudinal and longitudinal coordinate location of the work encoded) (2001: 171–3; see also Cook 2004: 118). Adapting their practice, a shell script may be written to search an encoded corpus for memes using `patt` and `pattern` (using such methodologies as are detailed above) and then to convert the `!!!ARD` records of this 'filtered' subset of the corpus to `!!!ARL` records by reference to proprietary gazetteer software (2001: 173–4). Passing this `!!!ARL` information to *GMT* in the form of numerical coordinate data and command options would in turn generate a map showing the geographical location of the works containing the sought patterns, a chronological series of such outputs allowing the visualization of meme flows over time.

This approach to the tracking of meme flows would not only be effective for representing attributes of repertoires such as folk songs (as in Aarden's and Huron's work); it may well be useful in tracing such currents within European art music. Despite the tendency to think in terms of the separateness and immiscibility of the styles of urban centres such as Vienna, Paris and London in a period such as the eighteenth century, one also thinks of the growing Italian influence in Paris in the 1750s initiated by the reception of Pergolesi's *La serva padrona* (1733), and the French influence in the Vienna of the 1790s and the first decade of the 1800s seen most clearly in Beethoven's assimilation of stylistic traits from the works of Cherubini and Méhul. The linkage of *Humdrum* and *GMT* would, in theory, offer a means of showing such intermixing of musical styles by means of a geographical and chronological representation of the memetic transmission and evolution of musical material across the regions of Europe.

Modelling Meme Dynamics Mathematically

While the primary focus of this book is broadly humanistic and qualitative, relying on observation of examples and drawing parallels between a variety of different phenomena, it is clear from the foregoing that it is eminently possible, indeed necessary, to employ quantitative methodologies in memetics. Perhaps the most central of these is the application, already begun in other areas of memetics, of mathematical models of evolutionary (population-genetic) dynamics developed in theoretical biology to musical memetics using data gleaned from, among other sources, *Humdrum* searches. While constraints of space prevent its full discussion here, this approach is alluded to in 1.4 above, apropos the work of Lynch, who argues that

> From the fact that event rate parameters differ between memes, it follows *mathematically* that natural selection must happen.… The mathematically *necessary* consequences of differing event rate parameters can be *characterized*, using systems of differential equations for meme host population versus time. Defining the units and quantifying the events thus allows us to analyze the host population *dynamics* of memetic evolution.
>
> (1998b: Section 16; his emphases)

Summarizing the context of this research tradition, the mathematical core of which is perhaps most rigorously formalized in Schuster's and Sigmund's discussion of 'replicator dynamics' (1983), Kendal and Laland note that

> Cultural evolution is a branch of theoretical population genetics established in the early part of the 1970s, and dedicated to using population genetics models to investigate the evolution and dynamics of cultural traits equivalent to memes.… As long as the meme is observable and measurable, analysis of the dynamics of the system can be used in conjunction with empirical data to question the nature of these assumptions, explore the replication process, and test predictions.
>
> (2000: Sections 1 and 2)

The early fruits of memetically-orientated cultural evolution research, including Witten 1991 and Lynch 1998b, suggests that a quantitative memetics might reach a level of development whereby it was able to generate a detailed profile of a variety of memetic phenomena – memes, memeplexes, dialects, systems of rules – and model their transmission and reconfiguration over space and time.

6.5. Summary

By regulating a metacritique, memetics offers a means of understanding the structure and evolution of analytical theories and methodologies as verbal-conceptual memeplexes, subject to much the same selection pressures as other such memeplexes. It also suggests its own analytical methodologies, which derive from the precepts of the theory itself – particularly those relating to segmentation, coindexation, structural-hierarchic organization and verbal-conceptual co-adaptation. Much of the leg-work of pattern searching and cross-matching intrinsic to the memetic analysis of music may be expedited by the use of software resources, including the versatile *Humdrum Toolkit*.

Chapter 7

Conclusion: Towards the Memetics of Music

7.1. Introduction

The previous chapters have attempted to apply the memetic paradigm to music, sketching the outlines of a new discipline which takes as its starting point not the composer or the work but rather the independent, selfish replicator. In this final chapter I shall summarize the conclusions reached so far, in the process reiterating the central tenets of the memetics of music. After discussing some residual problems, the prospects for this field, particularly its reciprocal relationship with musicology, are considered. Finally, I discuss a variety of topics in which the claims of memetics impinge more broadly on music, including gene-meme coevolution and the theory that musical memes may have driven the evolution of human brain size; the nature of animal culture and musicality, especially birdsong; and theories of consciousness and the problematic issues of the unitary self and human agency.

7.2. Review and Overview

By way of a summary of the issues considered in the previous chapters, the following is a formal statement, in twenty points, of the principal claims of the theory of musical memetics:

7.2.1. *The Ontology of Musical Memes*

1. Most fundamentally, memes exist somatically, as constellations of neural interconnections. Their information content is reflected extrasomatically, as patterns in various physical media.
2. The geno/m(n)emotype-pheno/ph(mn)emotype parallelism relates the ontology of the gene to that of the meme and affords evidence for the close affinities between replicator forms hypothesized by universal Darwinism.

3. A musical meme is a replicated pattern in some syntactic/digital element of music – principally pitch and, to a lesser extent, rhythm – transmitted between individuals by imitation as part of a neo-Darwinian process of cultural transmission and evolution.
4. Some pitches and rhythms in a piece, principally articulated and unharmonized monads or dyads, may be non-memetic, being generated spontaneously/analogically, not replicated memetically/homologically.
5. The work is merely a phemotypic manifestation of a temporary alliance between memes. For all the celebration of the work in western discourse on music since *c*. 1750, the selfish meme is the fundamental unit of all musical cultures.

7.2.2. *The Attributes of Musical Memes*

6. Musical memes, like those propagated in other substrates, manifest the attributes of longevity, fecundity and copying-fidelity. These attributes interact in complex ways but, invariably, some memes enjoy great longevity as a result of the preservation of their phemotypic forms, some are more fecund than their alleles and all manifest a higher degree of copying-infidelity than their genetic counterparts.
7. Particulate and digital, musical memes normally consist of at least three components, two elements normally possessing insufficient information content to impart to a pattern sufficient perceptual and cognitive salience to function as a meme. There is no fixed upper limit to the number of components, but this value and copying-fidelity are inversely proportional.
8. The segmentation of a musical string into components capable of functioning as memes is determined partly by innate, bottom-up attributes of human perception and cognition, and partly by learned, top-down factors, including the presence of a coindex.
9. Coindexation describes the mapping of two discrete musical patterns against each other. The more elements such units have in common, the greater the probability that both are instantiations of a given meme and therefore that they are related to each other in a nexus of replication (and vice versa).
10. The greater the number of components in a meme, the greater the probability that a given coindex is directly derived from it – that it is not an element of the common memetic currency of a dialect (and vice versa).

7.2.3. *The Structural and Cultural Hierarchies of Musical Memes*

11. Memes exist at several structural-hierarchic levels within a piece, from the immediate musical surface, where they have clear perceptual-cognitive reality, to the deepest and most remote level, where they have a distributed, virtual existence. A given meme may therefore exist at several hierarchic levels within the same piece – the scale-degree succession $\hat{3}$–$\hat{2}$–$\hat{1}$, for instance, may simultaneously function as a foreground element, a middleground structure and as an *Urlinie* – or at different levels in different pieces.
12. Memetics acknowledges the explanatory force of Schenkerian structural-hierarchic transformations, and the resultant structural levels. It also acknowledges the utility of Schenkerian graphical procedures in the representation of the hierarchic location of memes. Nevertheless, memetics asserts that structural levels are generated by bottom-up processes of meme conglomeration, not top-down control from the *Ursatz*.
13. A given meme is almost invariably a multiparametric complex in the parameters of pitch and rhythm. At the next structural-hierarchic level, several memes may be propagated as a memeplex, provided each constituent meme satisfies the condition of independent replication. Memeplexes may exist recursively at several structural-hierarchic levels, the large-scale formal archetypes of western music being structural memes constituting replicated patterning at the deepest levels of organization.
14. At shallow middleground levels, certain memeplexes may function as perceptual-cognitive schemata, acting as frameworks for the organization of foreground-level (feature) memes.
15. The memetic-structural hierarchies formed by memes and memeplexes in intraopus contexts are extended by memetic-cultural hierarchies encompassing interopus contexts, these forming a continuum from the single, localized meme to such widely chronologically and geographically distributed entities as dialects.

7.2.4. *The Transmission, Mutation, Selection and Evolution of Musical Memes*

16. The fundamental model for meme dynamics is that of gene dynamics: the tripartite algorithm – variation, heredity/replication and differential fitness – of Darwinian evolution by selection.
17. The transmission of memes within cultural communities is analogous to the spread of infections between organisms, allowing memetics to draw fruitfully from the conceptual vocabulary and methodologies of epidemiology.
18. Those memes that have the greatest perceptual-cognitive salience will tend to be the most widely propagated in the meme pool, to the disadvantage of those less salient forms. The implication-realization potential (i-r*p*) is posited as a means of quantifying this fecundity, offering a necessary but not sufficient index of salience.

19. The metaphors of selfishness and the meme's eye view articulate the tautological inevitability at the heart of replicator theory. Wherever competition is the key to survival, those entities which compete most effectively will be most likely to survive – be they animate creatures 'red in tooth and claw' or musical patterns 'looking' for a niche in memory space.
20. Paralleling the generation of patterns at higher levels of memetic-structural hierarchies by memes at lower levels, mutation and selection at lower levels of memetic-cultural hierarchies cumulatively drive changes to phenomena at higher levels. The most powerful manifestations of these processes are the seamless, gradualistic metamorphosis of dialects and, more abstract still, the transmutation of systems of tonal organization.

7.3. Problems and Prospects for The Memetics of Music

In 1.4 above I acknowledged that memetics was a controversial subject in several quarters, and in my enthusiasm to get to the nitty gritty, I downplayed the fact that many commentators take strong exception to Lynch's view that it can be regarded as a 'newly emerging science' (1996: 2) – even, at the time of writing, thirty years after the first publication of *The Selfish Gene*. Of the many who argue over 'the status of memetics as a science' (Aunger 2000), it is perhaps anthropologists and social scientists for whom the antipathy is strongest. Kuper even claims sourly that memetics 'has yet to deliver a single original and plausible analysis of any cultural or social process' (2000: 188), although expressing such a view is to ignore some of the interesting work on animal culture and artificial intelligence discussed below. Even within biology – the discipline with the most obvious conceptual and institutional sympathy with the claims of memetics – there are stern critics, perhaps most notably Gould, who argues that memes are a 'meaningless metaphor' (in Blackmore 1999: 17).

We come full circle, then, to the philosophical issues raised in 1.5 above, in particular to the problem of induction. It will be recalled that this holds that '[t]he truth of the particular premisses does not guarantee the truth of the universal conclusion' (Papineau 1995: 809). Applying this to memetics, one might say that even if it were the case that various innate and acquired psychological mechanisms partitioned music into discrete perceptual-cognitive units, and even if it were to be shown that these units can be found in the works of more than one composer (the premisses), then it would not necessarily follow that this is the consequence of a neo-Darwinian process of mutation, transmission and selection of neurally-encoded information-representations (the conclusion).

Of course, the precise complexion of the problem of induction depends on which premisses one puts forward in support of the general conclusion, and indeed on the precise formulation of the conclusion one wishes the premisses to support. For example, to the premises above, one might add the presence of verified poetic connections linking recurrent musical units. Nevertheless, the problem of induction cannot be solved simply by amassing a great weight of evidence, for it maintains that there is no necessary connection between the truth of the premisses and that of the conclusions one might draw from them.

In the final analysis, after consideration of the elements of the theory of musical memetics and of some of the evidence in its favour, one might now ask whether – apropos Bayesian confirmation theory – a memetic perspective on music is indeed 'a risk worth taking'. There are always two sides to a risk, the costs and the benefits, and I now turn to these costs – some problems and controversies in memetics – and benefits – the prospects for memetics – in the following sections in the hope that the reader will come, in the light of these and of the evidence considered in this book, to his or her own conclusions as to the nature of the risk.

If the reader is inclined to believe that the risk is worth taking, then there must follow a word of caution. Dennett claims that Darwinism is very similar in its effects to the mythical

> universal acid: it eats through just about every traditional concept, and leaves in its wake a revolutionized world-view, with most of the old landmarks still recognizable, but transformed in fundamental ways.
>
> (1995: 63)

One could argue that memetics has a similarly acidic property in relation to our traditional conceptions of musical structure and culture: it has the power to corrode long-established notions and fundamentally to transform the landmarks of our understanding. I shall consider shortly some ways in which the musical landscape might be transformed by memetics.

7.3.1. *Problems: Controversies in Musical Memetics*

Several issues which pose potential problems for memetics have arisen in the foregoing chapters. Some of these 'negatives' were left unresolved, or even unstated, in favour of a concentration on the 'positives' and they are now reviewed and elaborated upon below. It is in the nature of many of these controversies that they require further research to resolve them and that, in conducting such research, further questions are likely to arise.

Determining Coindexation and Verifying Replication by Imitation

Lynch's definition of the meme incorporates 'an abstract sameness criterion' and 'a criterion of causality' (1998b: Section 9). As noted in 1.5 and 3.3.3 above, these two interlinked criteria – which I have discussed under the rubrics of coindexation and transmission – are at once the most central and most problematic aspects of memetics.

On the first criterion, Lynch often deals in his writings with such entities as 'the [belief in] hell mnemon' and the 'doomsday is imminent' mnemon (: Section 7).

The advantage of discussing such verbal-conceptual mnemons is that, while '[belief in] hell' may contain many shades of meaning – a physical place or a state of (un)being? Demons with tridents or with spears? Dante or Bosch? – it may be expressed conveniently by the umbrella term '[belief in] hell' and manipulated in the mathematical symbology outlined in Lynch 1998b.

With musical memes, however, it is often difficult to overlook the shades of meaning which differentiate such broadly similar patterns as are shown in Example 1.1 above. This is due in part to the fact that music has a considerable potential for fine-grained variety: despite the common-practice tradition restricting itself to only twelve pitch classes and a relatively limited set of durational values, a near infinite diversity of patterning is possible (Merker 2002). This capacity for difference often makes the determination of coindexation highly problematic with musical memes. Resolving this issue involves matching the resemblances between two patterns against each other on a parameter-by-parameter basis, guided by a set of identity criteria sensitive to the work and its cultural-stylistic context.

These judgements are ultimately subjective, even with the aid of such criteria and so two observers may reach very different conclusions as to the affinities between two patterns. However, as argued in Chapter 6, technology offers the prospect of refining, expediting and to a degree objectifying this process. Further to the suggestion made in 6.4.3 above, the *Humdrum* `simil` tool may be used not only to quantify the edit distance between antecedent and mutant but also that between homologues. This is because the relationship between two homologues and that between an antecedent and a mutant is one of degree, not kind. Other than this, the studies in Hewlett and Selfridge-Field 1998 discuss a variety of similarity-evaluating software systems (some, however, now quite dated and lacking the age-defying flexibility inherent in *Humdrum*) pertinent to the determination of coindexation.

Turning to the second of Lynch's criteria, the discussions in 3.3.3 above indicate that making the distinction between homology and analogy is often challenging and in some cases impossible. Even the strong note-to-note correspondence between patterns encompassed by Lynch's first criterion is in itself insufficient to verify homology. Yet the distinction is one of the most important in memetics for, while the situation is unlikely (3.3.4 above), two patterns which are related analogically but not homologically to each other are not memes, unless each is homologically related to another (antecedent or consequent) pattern (Figure 3.4 above). In attempting to resolve this distinction, it is usually necessary to evaluate the poietic connections between two works encompassing similar patterns. If they fit into the same musico-cultural tradition and if there is evidence of inter-composer connections, then it may be possible to infer a homology provided the outcomes of a structural (identity-criteria mediated) comparison offer sufficiently strong support.

Such judgements are nevertheless contingent upon the number of elements in a pattern for, as Figure 3.2 above hypothesizes, the fewer the number of elements, the greater the generality and the lower the individuality of a meme. In cases where there are only a small number of elements to a meme it may be impossible to prove homology between patterns in two contexts, even in cases with strong analogical and poietic connections. In the light of this one might usefully distinguish between direct homology (transmission of a pattern situated towards the top right of Figure 3.2 between two individuals without intermediaries) and indirect homology (transmission of a pattern situated towards the bottom left of the figure between two individuals via one or more intermediaries).

Generative-Conglomerational versus *Generative-Transformational Forces*

It is one of the fundamental tenets of universal Darwinism that complex structures can only arise from the assemblage of simple units, the products of this accumulation being constantly subject to selection for greatest stability and utility. As discussed in 3.4.2 and 5.3.2 above, concrete (real) memes at the foreground level generate, by conglomeration, more extended/distributed (virtual) middleground and background configurations. Some of these higher-order patterns function as structural memes, being regularly replicated as the basic template of a formal archetype.

As suggested in 5.3.4 above, this view implies the potential for a degree of structural tension, or at least interplay, between bottom-up (generative-conglomerational) and top-down (generative-transformational) processes; and the question remains as to what extent higher-level patterns may determine the nature and sequence of memes at lower levels and thereby assert the influence of global over local structural processes. Ultimately this abstract conceptual problem boils down to a concrete operational question: 'how do composers work?'. Are they 'improvisers', who succumb to the flow of ideas and, almost without awareness (or at least without the ability to reconstruct the process), find themselves having witnessed the assemblage of various ideas to form a movement; or are they 'architects', who plan the global structures of their music carefully, selecting whichever pattern they feel is appropriate to express each limb of the design?

Of course, these categories are not mutually exclusive, even in the same individual; and they probably represent extremes of a continuum which varies from work to work and composer to composer, rather than a fixed binary opposition. Later I consider some of the implications of memetics on theories of consciousness. I shall not pre-empt this discussion, but given that the workings of composers' minds fall squarely into this area it is worth noting that the principal implication of Dennett's theory of consciousness is that '[h]uman consciousness is *itself* a huge complex of memes' (1993: 210; his emphasis). The question 'how do composers work?', posited as a route into the bottom-up *versus* top-down dichotomy, therefore collapses, as do so many in memetics, into the question 'which memes are the most successful replicators and why?'. Yet resolution of this issue also needs further research into the factors, neurophysiological and psychological, which distinguish memes 'for' local patterning from those 'for' global organization, and into the particular properties and interactions, memotypic and phemotypic, of each category of meme.

Music Outside the 'Common-Practice' Tradition and Non-European Musics

One criticism which might be made of this study is that by its self-declared focus on a small subset of the music of the common practice period it has avoided much of the repertoire – including the musics of the twentieth and twenty-first centuries, and non-European musics – which might potentially prove most challenging to its arguments. Starting with the former, can serial music, for instance, be regarded as composed of memes in a comparable way to tonal music? One would think not for, according to Straus,

> In tonal music, the scales and even to some extent the themes and motives are part of the common property of the prevailing musical style. From piece to piece and from composer to composer, a great deal of musical material is shared. Tonal music is relatively communal. In twelve-tone music, however, relatively little is shared from piece to piece or composer to composer; virtually no two pieces use the same series. Twelve-tone music is thus relatively contextual.
>
> (2000: 144)

Yet this is to ignore the possibility that memes which were propagated in the context of, and which defined, the syntax of tonality may persist in atonal systems. One might substantiate this by locating patterns in early-twentieth century music which, while existing in a non-tonal context, might be regarded as deriving from tonally-orientated antecedents. Example 7.1 below shows that two shapes from the opening of Schoenberg's String Quartet no. 4 are similar to patterns from works of Brahms and Mahler. Of course, the two patterns in Schoenberg are part of the initial statement of a row, 2 1 9 10 5 3 4 0 8 7 6 11 (Straus 2000: 145–6), and serial composers plan their rows in order to set up various (usually non-tonal) relationships between subsets, such as transpositional/inversional invariance and hexachordal combinatoriality. Yet these segments, 2 1 9 (labelled meme *x* in Example 7.1) and 9 10 5 3 (meme *y*), are also 'viable' in tonal contexts, where they express the scale-degree sequences $\hat{1}$–$\hat{7}$–$\hat{5}$ and $\hat{7}$–$\hat{1}$–$\hat{5}$–$\hat{4}$ respectively.

Example 7.1: Memes in Works of Brahms, Mahler and Schoenberg

i) Meme *x*: Brahms, Symphony no. 3 in F major op. 90 (1883), IV, bb. 4–8

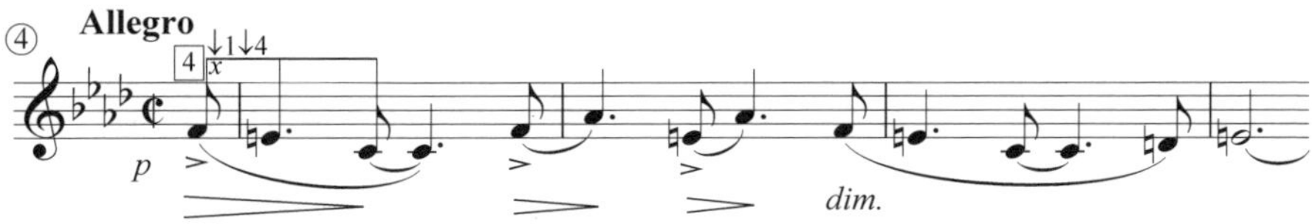

ii) Meme *y*: Mahler, Symphony no. 7 (1905), IV, bb. 27–35

iii) Memes *x* and *y*: Schoenberg, String Quartet no. 4 op. 37 (1936), I, bb. 1–3

One might draw from this the conclusion that there is a ‘persistence of memory’, to use the title of Dali’s painting of 1931, which led composers towards memes in their pitch-class sets and tone-rows which formerly existed in tonal (and, before that, modal) contexts. Memetics contends that there must be replication for culture to survive; and Schoenberg constantly stressed the continuity of his work from earlier traditions. Just as the rigidity of time is questioned in the images of Dali’s drooping watches, so we might dispute the fixity of the tonal-atonal distinction: memes which expressed subsets of diatonic sets later expressed subsets of chromatic collections. Their intervallic shapes and contours persisted, even if the systemic frameworks which they generated changed.

But it would be a mistake to regard this phenomenon as the mere hanging-on, in a kind of mummified stasis, of memes which had a more vibrant existence in an earlier era. I argued in 4.6.4 above that the properties of a system of rules derive from the attributes of its component memes; and that change from one system to another is the consequence of mutations feeding up from this level. On this reasoning, the properties of atonal systems similarly derive from the attributes of their component memes; and that the transition from tonal to non-tonal systems of musical organization was the consequence of meme-level mutations which eventually forced rule-level change at the start of the twentieth century.

Beyond the issue of meme attributes is that of meme juxtaposition. In Example 7.1 iii, the row segments 2 1 9 and 9 10 5 3 carry, as noted, certain scale-degree implications. Taken in isolation, the $\hat{1}$–$\hat{7}$–$\hat{5}$ of meme *x* in this context implies D minor and the $\hat{7}$–$\hat{1}$–$\hat{5}$–$\hat{4}$ of meme *y* B♭ major. Such meme juxtapositions – here involving an E♭ in b. 2 (the $\hat{4}$ of meme *y* and the sixth pitch of the row) 'foreign' to the implied D minor context of the opening of the violin I part – may have played a part in generating the tensions, measured against listener expectations and theoretical prescriptions, which drove the systemic changes taking place some thirty years before this quartet was written.

It may be possible to generalize the conclusions drawn from this limited example to all musics of the twentieth and twenty-first century. Provided these are not 'cognitively opaque' (Lerdahl 1992: 115), then they would have arisen from the same memetic processes as were operative in earlier musico-historical periods. Indeed, memetics contends that there is no mechanism other than Darwinian variation, replication and differential fitness which can account for the sustenance and propagation of culture, regardless of its time and place.

While a full consideration of the memetics of non-European musics is well beyond the scope of this study, it seems reasonable to assert – on the basis of the various points made concerning meme genesis and propagation in earlier chapters – that memes constitute the building blocks of these traditions in the same way they comprise the raw materials of European musics. As a small but telling piece of evidence in support of this claim, the fragments of African drumming shown in Example 2.3 above illustrate the replication of discrete, hierarchically stratified patterning in rhythm, perhaps the most privileged of musical parameters in many tribal African musics. Asserting a memetic basis to all human musics is warranted, for the principles of universal Darwinism apply, by definition, to all human cultures, not just to those in the west; and the innate psychological attributes which define the conditions for meme propagation in a European musician are shared, by virtue of our common genetic heritage, with those of an African or oriental practitioner.

Of course it would be unrealistic to pretend that there are not considerable differences in the conception and practice of music across the world, certainly in those few areas where western popular culture has not penetrated. The relentless pursuit of innovation (or at least novelty) and the aestheticization of music in the post-Renaissance western world, and the focus on tradition and the seamless integration of music into other social and artistic domains in tribal African communities seem two particularly clear dichotomies. But these might be accounted for not by any fundamental differences in the nature of the musico-memetic processes involved, but by the local verbal-conceptual memes predominant in each culture. In Europe, for instance, the strong scientific rationalism which first arose in ancient Greece and which was reinvigorated in the

Renaissance and the Enlightenment has created an environment where experimentation has permeated not only the technical but also the creative areas of culture; whereas in certain African cultures the prevalence of tradition as a bulwark against an often hostile environment has led to the valuation of a certain stasis and the reliance on tried and tested formulae in culture.

Far from challenging and potentially undermining memetics, European musics of the twentieth and twenty-first centuries and the musics of non-European cultures offer it a rich data source from which to draw. Memetics can illuminate these musics and cast fresh light on their structure and transmission; but it may also be interrogated by them, and the theory developed here, forged on the anvil of common-practice tonality, may need refinement in the light of this contact.

7.3.2. *Prospects: The Synergy of Memetics and Musicology*

I hope by now to have made a case that memetics has much to offer musicology, conceived in the broad sense to include theory and analysis. Conversely, the insights and methodologies of musicology can facilitate the development of memetics. In this belief that the two fields may profit from synergistic interaction, the following briefly outlines those areas where their concerns might overlap and where further research may prove illuminating.

Theory, Analysis, Psychology and the Building Blocks of Music

Despite the need for further refinement of the theory and methodology of segmentation and coindexation, the principle of replication underpinning memetics is a special and, I would argue, an undervalued property in musical study. Whether a single unit-meme or an extended *memesatz* (5.3.3 above), a replicated pattern, as a configuration which in some sense stands out as something singular and distinctive to the members of a cultural community, is afforded a certain primacy by virtue of this copying. Moreover, replication affords to such patterns an importance – ontological as a consequence of perceptual-cognitive – which transcends that which may be ascribed to configurations on more abstract and transient criteria, such as their Fuxian/Schenkerian voice-leading and prolongational status. Replication is thus a powerful perspective from which to analyze the phonetic and syntactic elements of the structural units of a work or of a musical 'language'.

The centrality of replication accords with the view that all theorization about music must possess psychological validity. While this study has only scratched the surface of some of the key issues, principally those related to grouping structure, an understanding of the psychology of musical perception and cognition is fundamental to memetics, as is an awareness of the social psychology underpinning the interactions between musicians which make memetic replication possible. The time is therefore ripe for a synergy between theory and analysis on the one hand, and music psychology on the other (Gjerdingen 1999), forged in the crucible of memetics.

Conversely, to memetics music offers a field of study in which the units of replication are often clearer and more amenable to analysis than the verbal-conceptual patterns generally studied by memeticists. Despite my arguing for music's 'considerable potential for fine-grained variety' in 7.3.1 above, there is, paradoxically, something eminently clear and manipulable in the phonetic-syntactic patterns of music, compared with the often bewilderingly nuanced semantic shadings of language.

Historiography and the Evolution of Musical Style

One important consequence of seeing diachronic musical change as the cumulative consequence of differential meme selection is that it offers the prospect of a refinement of traditional historical perspectives on music – not only of the cultural/stylistic evolution which has been considered in Chapter 4 but also of the understanding of music history and the theory and practice of music historiography. At the very least, taking the meme's eye view allows us to replace the often pseudo-organicist and crudely teleological nature of much narrative music historiography with an authentically Darwinian model (Gatherer 1997).

Whether music history is conceived in terms of a causal chain of motives, actions, events and consequences (in the manner of political history), a sequence of autonomous aesthetic objects (texts, works) or in terms of the overarching patterns and structures which characterize culture (Dahlhaus 1983: 132–3), memetics suggests that the driving force in human political and cultural history is the differential replication of memes over time. The phemotypic products (behaviours and artefacts) they motivate – such as the score of Bach's Mass in B minor, the battle of Austerlitz, Beethoven's concert of 22 December 1808 at the Theater an der Wien and the Treaty of Versailles – are the data of history. To understand them fully – to reconstruct the 'facts' of music history (Dahlhaus 1983: 34) – we need to understand the selection pressures that led such successful memes to prevail over their alleles.

The Discourses and Practice of Musicology

As argued in Chapter 6, when we attempt to understand music from the standpoints of theoretical frameworks and their associated analytical methodologies we do so through the mediation (and distortion) of numerous verbal-conceptual and musico-graphical memeplexes. The same is true, by extension, when we view music through the prisms of history or criticism. This permits us to view the development of discourses on music – and not just specifically musicological discourses – in terms of their evolutionary history and the rise and fall of the particular verbal-conceptual memeplexes which structure them. For instance, the five broad paradigms through which art and music have been conceived in the west since *c.*

1550 discussed by Dahlhaus (1983: 20–23)[1] and the more localized (and much discussed) shift from a positivistic to a critical (even 'New') musicology from the 1980s (Kerman 1985) are subjects ripe for a memetic analysis.

In summary, memetics offers a new perspective on the concerns of musicology, one which has the power to unify a variety of disparate musical subdisciplines – composition, notation, performance, improvisation, listening, theory and analysis, historiography, criticism, musical style and style-history, intertextuality, music psychology, aesthetics and philosophy – under the logic of universal Darwinism. Conversely, the vast body of musicological research offers memetics a rich seam of data and hypotheses amenable to (re)interpretation from, yet potentially able to interrogate, its own viewpoint.

7.4. Some Further Issues in Memetics Pertinent to Music

Now the outlines, problems and prospects of a theory of musical memetics are in place, I turn finally to some further issues in memetics which, while not directly related to music, indirectly impinge upon it.

7.4.1. *Coevolution: Nature and/*versus *Culture*

Having attempted to outline some ways in which the relationship between nature and culture has been theorized in 1.3 above, I turn now to the issue of how genes and memes interact with each other in real-world contexts. It is an axiom of Darwinism that interactions between replicators (their alleles and other replicators) often involve competition and conflict. Dennett asks '*Cui bono*?' – who benefits? – apropos of 'those cases when push comes to shove, and the interests of the body (long life, happiness, comfort, etc.) conflict with the interests of the genes' (1995: 325). In this formulation, 'the interests of the body' amount to the interests of the memes, for it is these which drive us to pursue 'long life, happiness, comfort', and so Dennett's question speaks to the fundamental conflict between genes and memes. To understand any such dual-replicator scenario it is necessary to take each replicator's eye view individually and to ask to what extent the self-interests of one (expressed in terms of replication prospects) accord or conflict with those of the other.

In 3.3.2 above, I referred to Wilson's notion of genes holding culture 'on a leash' (1978: 167), apropos my assertion that the nature of memes is, to a large extent, determined by the innate psychological predispositions wired into us by natural selection over time. As the central figure in the discipline of sociobiology, Wilson (1974) added new impetus to the seemingly eternal nature *versus*

[1] Namely the 'functional' theory of art (*c.* 1550–*c.* 1650), the doctrine of the affections (*c.* 1650–*c.* 1750), the aesthetics of personal expression (*c.* 1750–*c.* 1850), formalism and structuralism (*c.* 1850–*c.* 1950), and the notion of works as 'documents' (*c.* 1950–).

nurture/culture debate. There are, of course, many ways of theorizing the relationship between these two realms, not just Wilson's, and I shall now briefly review them – wary of the risk of oversimplifying subtle and complex scientific arguments – before moving on to some specifically musical aspects of the nature-culture dichotomy.

Wilson's basic premise, as summarized by Aunger, is that

> human behavior can be understood in terms of genetically acquired learning biases and rational calculation. Behavior, as a kind of phenotype (whether cultural or not), is a way to make responses more flexible. And the learning of new behaviors is a form of phenotypic plasticity, no more.... The only principle one need invoke to explain the behavior of any organism, including *Homo sapiens*, is fitness maximization.... There is no reason to think, then, that having culture is different from exhibiting any other evolved trait, and evolutionary biology is sufficient to explain such traits in other animals. So culture and social learning can be reduced to the normal activity of natural selection on genes. Culture is simply another strategy to enhance the fitness of the behaving organism through learning.
>
> (2002: 32, 33)

In the sociobiological world-view, culture is conceived merely as the dog on its leash working in the service of its master, the genes. As such, it is considered to have no interests of its own other than serving those of the master. The power of the genes, shaped over time by natural selection, is therefore absolute in this perspective.

Evolutionary psychology, whose most prominent exponent is perhaps Pinker (see Pinker 1997), might be regarded as a development (and reinforcement) of the sociobiological perspective, focusing particularly on the role of genetic evolution in shaping our innate psychological predispositions. For Aunger,

> A basic tenet of evolutionary psychology is that the human brain consists of a set of evolved psychological mechanisms designed by natural selection to solve adaptive problems that our ancestors faced recurrently during our species' evolutionary history.
>
> (2002: 37)

As in sociobiology, culture in this view serves a purely gene-adaptive role, but it is nudged in certain directions owing to the psychological predispositions wired into the brain by natural selection. That Brodie can claim that '[m]emes involving danger, food, and sex spread faster than other memes because we are wired to pay more attention to them – we have [psychological] *buttons* around those subjects' (1996: 88; his emphasis) is testament to the need of memetics to take account of the insights of evolutionary psychology.

Since the heyday of sociobiology in the 1970s, many commentators have come to feel that its central tenet is oversimplistic and that accounts affording more importance to culture are needed. Durham articulates this view clearly in arguing that

> One of the major intellectual challenges facing the behavioral sciences today concerns the relationship between genes, culture, and human diversity. The objective is both to develop a body of theory relating genetic and cultural processes to the evolution of human differences, and to test and retest such theory against the accumulated data of the behavioral and social sciences. Although the challenge is similar for all aspects of human variation, whether morphological, physiological, or behavioral, it is particularly great with respect to human behavior, where genes and culture may each have direct and simultaneous influence.
>
> (1991: 1)

In Durham's and other gene-culture coevolutionary perspectives – such as Cavalli-Sforza's and Feldman's cultural evolution theory (1981) and Boyd's and Richerson's dual-inheritance model (1985) – culture is not regarded as inherently subordinate to nature. Rather, human behaviour is seen as arising from subtle interactions between the natural and cultural spheres. Perhaps the most influential coevolutionist theory at present, the dual-inheritance model asserts that that which is inherited in tandem with genes is cultural information. Boyd and Richerson argue, however, that such information is transmitted not by replication but by re-production (Distin 2005: 102). In Sperber's view, 'most cultural items are "re-produced" in the sense that they are produced again and again – with, of course, a causal link between all these productions – but are not reproduced in the sense of being copied from one another' (2000: 164). In his theory, which he terms the 'epidemiology of representations' (: 163), '"representations", including everyday knowledge, do not replicate but transform in the process of transmission, and do so as a result of constructive cognitive processes' (Shennan 2002: 47).

If, as Distin asserts, replication is a necessary condition for evolution (2005: 2, 9), then for the dual-inheritance model there is no real cultural evolution; only the genetic component truly evolves (see also Shennan 2002: 46–8). Yet Aunger argues that 'evolution, as a general principle, can occur without replication (although *biological* evolution does involve the replication of genes)' (2002: 25; his emphasis), hence Dennett's reference to 'heredity or replication' in his algorithm for evolution by natural selection (1.2.2 above), hitherto treated as equivalent here by my undiscriminating forward slashes. So while 'heredity doesn't require replication' (: 25), the converse is not true – and on this reasoning cultural evolution can take place by means of information re-production (according to the schema variation–heredity–differential fitness) without the need to posit a replicated particle of cultural transmission (variation–replication–differential fitness).

Memetics, located at the opposite conceptual pole to sociobiology, is sceptical about the value of heredity without replication as a mechanism for cultural evolution, conceiving itself as a fully-fledged replicator system on a par with genetics and contending that only the replication of discrete particles of cultural information can give rise to such evolution. While it accepts that memes are to some degree at the mercy of genes – memes exist memotypically in a substrate, human neocortex, which is under the initial control, via embryonic development, of genetic mechanisms – it also claims that memes can reverse the balance of power, removing Wilson's leash and putting it around the neck of the genes. Blackmore argues that this leash is at its tightest when, under the influence of the memes of a religious memeplex such as Roman Catholicism, an adherent lives a celibate life (1999: 138–9), a situation so deleterious to gene fitness it cannot easily be understood in sociobiological or evolutionary-psychological terms.

Music and the Nature-Culture Dichotomy: The Issue of Brain Size

Having outlined these four distinct theoretical positions on the relationship between nature and culture, I now turn to a concrete example illustrating the capacity of memetics to generate answers to certain questions that, unlike those offered by sociobiology and evolutionary psychology, account for both spheres.[2] This is the phenomenon, central to the growth of musical competence and culture, termed memetic drive by Blackmore (2000: 31–4; for a critique, see Distin 2005: 95–100). She hypothesizes that traditional genetic models are inadequate to explain the large size of the human brain and invokes memetics to complete the picture. With respect to the encephalisation quotient (a measure of the brain-size to body-size ratio), humans, in comparison with other primates, 'just do not fit.... Our brains are far too large for our bodies' (1999: 68).[3] Her explanation for this disparity hinges on the claim that

> The turning point in our evolutionary history was when we began to imitate each other. From this point on a second replicator, the meme, came into play. Memes changed the environment in which genes were selected, and the direction of change was determined by the outcome of memetic selection.
>
> (: 74)

---

[2] For a comprehensive survey of the relationship between biology and music, see Wallin 1991.

[3] Blackmore outlines the considerable costs of a large brain (it consumes considerable resources to build and a disproportionate amount of energy to run; it is dangerous to mother and child to move it through the pelvis and birth canal), setting them against the relatively limited benefits it affords to genes (1999: 70–71). Non-human animals, she notes, manage perfectly well with much smaller brains, the vast majority having poorly-developed imitative skills (: 73).

Elaborating upon this assertion, Blackmore identifies three necessary stages in the process driving the 'runaway increase in brain size' (: 80), which I summarize below:

1. '*Selection for Imitation*' (1999: 77). Assuming the ability to imitate is genetically controlled and variable, 'capacity-to-imitate' genes (those for building the cognitive and motor structures and functions which provide the substrate for imitation) will tend to spread in a gene pool because such a capacity confers fitness advantages on an individual. Tool-making is one strongly fitness-enhancing skill which is much more easily learned by imitation than by trial-and-error individual learning. Those who are most adept at imitation are termed 'meme fountains' by Blackmore (2000: 32).
2. '*Selection for Imitating the Imitators*' (1999: 77–8). An additional genetically-determined ability to identify and selectively imitate 'superior' imitators – those who make the most effective tools, for instance – may confer a further fitness advantage on its possessor and lead to a differential increase of such 'imitate-the-meme-fountains' genes in the gene pool. At the same time, '[m]emetic evolution now gets under way with various kinds of dances, headdresses, and songs competing with each other to be copied' (2000: 32). Interestingly, Kendal's and Laland's mathematical model of meme dynamics (see 6.4.3 above) 'confirms Blackmore's intuition that there are conditions under which the selective imitation I allele [that is, the gene for 'imitate-the-meme-fountains'] can invade the population' (2000: Section 3).
3. '*Selection for Mating with the Imitators*' (1999: 78–9). It is genetically advantageous to an individual to mate with the meme fountains because of the fitness advantage conferred – genetic and purely social – on the offspring of such a union. If genetically controlled, this process will tend to lead not only to a differential increase of 'capacity-to-imitate' genes, but also of 'mate-with-the-meme-fountains' genes. Even if there are no such things as 'mate-with-the-meme-fountains' genes, this process will still favour 'capacity-to-imitate' genes.[4]

The final link in the chain is that 'being good at imitation requires a big brain' (1999: 80). If Blackmore's argument is accepted, then the disproportionately high human encephalisation quotient may be the result of selection pressures exerted on genes by memes let loose, ironically, by a genetic propensity for imitation, evidence of Blackmore's 'turning point' being the stone tools made by *Homo habilis* some two and a half million years ago (: 76).

---

[4] A fourth stage, 'sexual selection for imitation', 'might increase the process again – though it is not necessary to the explanation' (1999: 79–80). Stages three and four of the process as outlined in Blackmore 1999 are conflated in Blackmore 2000.

While much of this imitation was presumably purely utilitarian – encompassing such essential day-to-day survival skills as tool-making, fruit-picking, trap-setting and fire-kindling – what we now regard as more creative skills may also have been imitated. These musicality-underpinning competencies, which may have primarily served such functions as maintaining social hierarchies and fostering intra-group cohesion, include melodic vocalization, sound production from early musical instruments (such as stone percussion and bone or wooden flutes) and dancing. So in answer to the question '[w]hy do we humans, apparently alone among animals, invest large amounts of time and energy in producing and enjoying complex music?', Blackmore – in a wonderful statement of this book's central thesis – concludes that

> It is difficult, if not impossible, to provide an answer based on advantage to human genes …. Dennett … imagines an early hominid, for no particular reason, just happening to bang on a log and enjoying the sound, and someone else coming along and copying it. For reasons to do with perceptual systems, memory, or features of the environment, some versions of the drumming, and then humming, are more infectious and spread at the expense of others. And so the process goes on, with the advantage being to the bangings, whistlings and hummings (i.e., the memes) – not necessarily to the hominids' genes.
>
> (2000: 35)

From this final point it is not too much of a leap of the imagination to assert that the earliest musical memes – the 'bangings, whistlings and hummings' imitated by early hominids – may have played a significant part in driving the expansion of brain size. Put more strongly, musical memes may have played a major role in forcing genes to build ever bigger brains, brains which served the selfish interests of the memes as much as, if not more than, those of the genes. Moreover, if – as I argue in the next section – meme-driven vocalized sounds formed the substrate upon which human language (and therefore conceptual thought) developed, then musical memes have played a truly pivotal role in our genetic and cultural development.

7.4.2. *Memes and Protoculture*

As well as exerting function-enhancing selection pressures upon genes, memes can 'bootstrap' design processes in ways which outstrip genetically-determined attributes, imparting skills and competencies to organisms which they would not have were they to rely solely on the organic 'hardware' with which natural selection has furnished them. I cover the most striking manifestation of this phenomenon, our own consciousness, below, but one might also seek evidence for this principle in two related areas: the theory that our early development of language built upon a musical substrate, and the fact that certain birds have a form of culture based on variation, replication and differential fitness of song patterning.

Memetics and the Evolution of Language from Music

Recent work in biology, evolutionary psychology and linguistics has investigated the origin of music in human culture and its relationship to the evolution of language – what might be called the phylogeny of music and language – and the associated issues of the acquisition of musical skills in the developing infant and its relationship to the acquisition of language – what might be called the ontogeny of music and language.

On the former, a consensus appears to be emerging which places the phylogenetic origin of musical skills before those of language but which relates the two competencies in an interconnected evolutionary process wherein language arose from a pre-existing musical substrate (see Wallin, Merker and Brown 2000). In the context of his identification of music as 'the missing Humboldt system' – that is, one in which the total analogue continuum (pitch and duration in this case) is discretized into a finite set of elements (notes and rhythmic values) which, in combination, generate a rich diversity of patterning (memes) – Merker argues that

> Language employs the particulate principle for both phonological and lexical purposes,[5] while music employs it for 'phonological' patterning alone, albeit of a complex kind.... the most plausible and parsimonious assumption would be that a naturally evolved capacity for complexly structured song based on vocal learning existed among our forbears long before language .... An early human facility for phonological combinatorics serving complex song would presumably have shortened the step to human language by supplying a pre-existing foundation for its phonological syntax. Instead of having to develop both phonological and lexical syntax concurrently, language would emerge when a pre-existing well developed phonological combinatorial facility was subordinated to lexical-semantic ends and deployed in their service with the help of lexical syntax.
>
> (2002: 13)

But what of the mechanism underlying this process? Taking this summary and adapting it to a memetic view – to which Merker does not subscribe – we might suggest that sonic fragments, taking advantage of (and then driving) our genetically-acquired capacity for imitation, would have been propagated within early human cultures, forming the earliest musical memes. Filling the many memetic-ecological niches in the early infosphere, such memes would initially have had a purely phonological content, but as they evolved collaboratively and

---

5 In Merker's sense, 'particulate' refers to the discretized elements of music – his phonological (sound) level – not to the memes which, in information-bearing relationships, these elements constitute – his lexical (word) level. See also Abler 1997.

formed memeplexes, a syntactic (relational) dimension would have been engendered. The decisive step from this phonological-syntactic (musical) substrate would have been the acquisition of symbolic meaning – the semantic dimension – by the patterns. That is, the phonetic-syntactic musical memes would have come to stand for objects, actions, phenomena and even concepts in the world, thereby creating phonological-syntactic-semantic memeplexes and providing the initial foundation for the evolution of verbal-conceptual memes.

While attenuated, the phonological (musical) dimension of language at its present state of evolution has not been wholly overshadowed by the syntactic-semantic, meaning – the association between phonological-syntactic and semantic elements – being communicated in part by subtle inflections of pitch, duration and stress. Conversely, in music there is often a semantic (verbal-conceptual) component in musical memeplexes. As suggested in 3.4.4 above, however, co-adaptation between musical and verbal-conceptual elements is often circumscribed at higher levels and inscrutable at lower levels of the hierarchy represented in Figure 3.9 above.

Memetics and Animal Culture: The Case of Birdsong

Research by ethologists has demonstrated that several bird species possess what must be regarded as a form of culture. That is, their songs are passed both vertically from generation to generation not as a genetic but as a cultural inheritance – the young acquiring song patterns by imitation of their parents – and horizontally from peer to peer. Summarizing this research, Bonner notes that

> some birds can learn dialects of their songs from other birds. Usually this dialect learning takes place while the bird is young and hears its father or a neighboring male, but … the song dialects are not always learned in this fashion. That these songs are cultural and are passed on from one individual to another is beyond dispute.… In the case of bird song dialects, any alteration of the song by one bird could obviously be passed on.… [Jenkins] … observed that new songs, or variations of old songs 'arise variously by change of pitch of a note, repetition of a note, the elision of notes and the combination of parts of other existing songs' …. This change was an abrupt event and would then turn into a stable song pattern for a number of years. Young birds would learn it so that it became an important component of the dialect of one district. Jenkins calls this change a 'cultural mutation' ….
>
> (1980: 178, 185)

This and other studies suggest that these phenomena may be best explained by memetics. Baker 1996 discusses the songs of the singing honeyeater, *Meliphaga virescens*, comparing songs from Nedlands, a coastal area of Western Australia, with songs from Rottnest, an island lying some 25 km west of Nedlands in the Indian Ocean. As is common practice in this type of research, Baker recorded the songs on tape and then used a sonograph to analyze the sound spectrum and produce a printable output. In Figure 7.1 below, I transcribe the basic contour of some of the song-patterns identified by Baker, omitting his differing line thicknesses (which indicate variations in amplitude) for the sake of clarity.

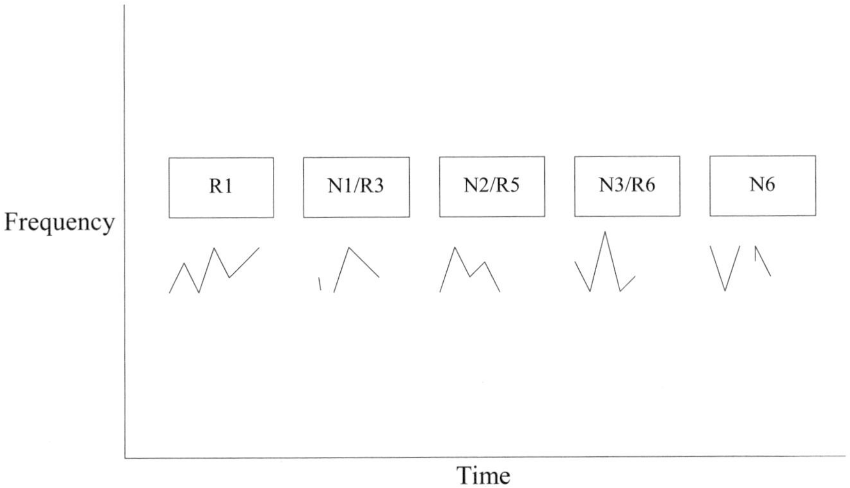

Figure 7.1: Simplified Representation of the Song of the Singing Honeyeater, *Meliphaga virescens*, after Baker 1996: Figure 1

Such patterns, from which songs are assembled, are termed syllables by Baker. Identifying thirty-eight distinct types, he defines a syllable as a

> single or multi-note sound that is the unit of recombination in a population of songs; [they are] the building blocks from which songs are composed. Multi-noted syllables are not fragmented but are inherited as units. [A] [*s*]*yllable type* [is] any syllable that is distinctly different from others, often sung by more than one individual [bird]; the set of syllables within a 'type' are similar to one another and the variation does not overlap with syllables belonging to any other syllable type.
>
> (1996: 854; his emphasis)

Baker regards syllables as memes and the set of memes in circulation in a given bird community as its meme pool. Each syllable is a discrete unit, demarcated from its neighbours within a song by inter-syllable silences and generally consisting of three or four distinct framework pitches connected to each other by glissandi. The similarities with musical memes in human culture are obvious and afford evidence both in support of the observations made concerning meme size and segmentation in 3.3 above and for the existence of trans-substrate constraints on sound-based memes.

As Figure 7.1 indicates, syllable type N1 (the first meme type of the Nedlands group) is the same as syllable type R3 (the third meme type of the Rottnest group). Similarly, N2 matches R5 and N3 corresponds with R6. These are, however, the only correspondences. The other memes – the remaining 30 N-group and 5 R-group memes – are unique to each bird community. Baker attributes this to the biological phenomenon of 'founder effect' (1996: 853). That is, the birds which established the Rottnest colony took only three memes from the Nedlands pool, R3, R5 and R6, perhaps on account of their having had a brief or interrupted exposure to the complete Nedlands set. Isolated on Rottnest, these birds then supplemented the original three memes with their own newly-minted set, R1, R2, R4, R7 and R8, resulting in a 'depauperate' meme pool compared with the richer cultural stock of the Nedlands group. It is not difficult to relate such discrepancies to characteristics of human musical memes; a good example is Haydn who, isolated from the vibrant musical community of Vienna at the Palace of Esterháza in the 1770s, declared to Griesinger that he was 'cut off from the world … and so I had no choice but to become original' (in Webster 2001: 192).

Baker defines a song type as 'a given sequence of syllables uttered as a single vocalization, repeated after a pause to produce a string of the same songs over time' (1996: 854). He notes that the average number of syllables per song of the Nedlands group is 3.4, the average number of syllable types per song in this group being 3.0 (: Table 1). It seems logical to regard each song type as a memeplex, consisting of a replicated sequence of syllable memes. Moreover, as in the case of human music, the replication of song types automatically gives rise to a structural meme, consisting of the basic middleground pitch structure of the song. While Baker's research does not cover this issue, it is not inconceivable that this resultant structure might be replicated using different syllables in other songs. Memes N4 and N30, for instance, are sufficiently similar to function as alleles in a hypothetical three-component structural meme generated by the syllable sequences N1–N4–N22 and N1–N30–N22.

This research is significant for four reasons. First, the observation of cultural transmission and evolution of discrete musical particles within bird societies offers cross-species support for memetics, thereby reinforcing the claims of universal Darwinism. Secondly, the mechanisms of birdsong mutation noted by Jenkins – 'change of pitch of a note, repetition of a note, the elision of notes and the combination of parts of other existing songs' – are familiar phenomena in the mutation of musical memes within human cultures (4.3.2 above) and suggest that general principles of sound-meme transformation are operative. Thirdly, the conglomeration of memes within songs to form memeplexes parallels the structure of human music and lends support to the hypothesis advanced in Chapter 5 concerning the evolution of structural memes in human music.

Fourthly, and perhaps most controversially, this research shows that humans are not the only species capable of supporting culture and that, given sufficient neurological support (the memory capacity to store song patterns), a sound-generating and sound-perceiving mechanism and a genetically-acquired (and gene-fitness-enhancing) tendency to imitation, then song-based animal cultures can arise, develop their own evolutionary momentum and move in the direction of increasing complexity. Indeed, if the assertions of the previous section are also true, then it is not inconceivable that, given sufficient evolutionary time, the phonological-syntactic song-based culture of birds might one day become a phonological-syntactic-semantic verbal-conceptual culture. Indeed, Baker's assertion that 'the island songs lack communicatory significance to mainland singing honeyeaters' on account of 'the reduced and differentiated signal repertoire of the island birds' (1996: 857) suggests that this process may already be under way.

7.4.3. *Memetics and Consciousness: The Agency of the Composer*

The seemingly impenetrable mystery of human consciousness has fascinated thinkers for centuries. Although regarded for much of its history as essentially a philosophical question, the most significant recent progress in its understanding has, not surprisingly, been made in neuroscience and psychology. Nevertheless, it is a philosopher who has synthesized this research and formulated the most accessible contemporary account of consciousness. Dennett refutes the long-established Cartesian conception – stemming from Descartes's *Meditations on First Philosophy* of 1641, which played a central role in shaping subsequent thinking on consciousness – and an argument in favour of his own 'multiple drafts' model (1993), which is decidedly anti-Cartesian and which draws heavily on memetics.

'Cartesian dualism' sees the mind 'as distinct … from the brain, composed not of ordinary matter but of some other, special kind of stuff' (Dennett 1993: 33). Descartes believed that the interface between the physical and the mystical was the pineal gland, which sits in the centre of the brain and which is now known to perform several endocrine functions (: 34). Some scientists, reluctant to countenance the supernatural elements of dualism yet keen to hold on to an explanation which localizes consciousness at a single central point in the brain – a kind of central processing unit to which sensory input is directed and from which comes our decisions and responses – fall back onto what Dennett terms 'Cartesian materialism' (: 107). Its principal metaphor is the 'Cartesian Theatre', which anthropomorphises consciousness as a homunculus (or homuncula) sitting in the stalls of an auditorium watching the events of his or her life, and those of the surrounding world, as if projected onto an imaginary screen or taking place on an imaginary stage. In this view, the Cartesian theatre is 'somewhere, conveniently hidden in the obscure "center" of the mind/brain … a place where "it all comes together" and consciousness happens' (: 39).

A corollary of Cartesian materialism is the notion of the unitary self. Sitting inside the Cartesian theatre, observing and reacting to the outside world, is an 'I', a self who is the subject of and experiencer of consciousness and who does the thinking. This is such a natural way of conceiving consciousness – one so closely in accordance with our experiences and so deeply embedded in our discourses – that its weaknesses have, until relatively recently, remained unexamined (Blackmore 1999: 228). As a central tenet of our conceptions of ourselves and the world, it is not surprisingly at the heart of much western musicological discourse. Even after the decline of the romantic world-view, with its rarefied and intensified version of this concept, it is difficult to imagine anything other than a unitary self being responsible for human actions and attributes, including music and musicality. To take a simple example, Lenin's moving view of Beethoven's Sonata op. 57 in F minor (1805) –

> I know nothing which is greater than the *Appassionata*; I would like to listen to it every day. It is marvellous, superhuman music. I always think with pride – perhaps it is naive of me – what marvellous things human beings can do.
>
> (in Arnold and Fortune 1973: 529)

– accords a high status to the conscious intentionality or agency of the composer, the notion that every element of a composition is rigorously determined by its author, who exists as a unified and omniscient self reigning supreme over its intellectual realm.

Despite its appeal, Cartesian materialism is undermined by numerous logical flaws, one of which is the problem of infinite regress: if our consciousness is (metaphorically) embodied in the internal homunculus/homuncula, then this creature must have its own interior stage, and so on *ad infinitum*. A critique of and alternative to Cartesianism, the notion of the unitary self and of the agency and intentionality of the individual is offered by Dennett's multiple drafts model. Unlike Cartesian dualism, this theory is materialist in orientation – it assumes that only physical (brain) matter, and no 'special kind of stuff', gives rise to consciousness – but, unlike Cartesian materialism, is founded on the premise that

> all varieties of perception – indeed, all varieties of thought or mental activity – are accomplished in the brain by parallel, multitrack processes of interpretation and elaboration of sensory inputs. Information entering the nervous system is under continuous 'editorial revision'.
>
> (1993: 111)

In an eloquent statement of his thesis – which hinges on the analogy between the workings of the human brain and those of the computer, in particular the serial (one operation at a time) *versus* parallel (many simultaneous operations) dichotomy – Dennett contends that

> Just as you can simulate a parallel brain on a serial … machine [as in a computer], you can also, in principle, simulate (something like) a [serial] machine on parallel hardware …: Conscious human minds are more-or-less serial virtual machines implemented – inefficiently – on the parallel hardware that evolution has provided for us.… Human consciousness is *itself* a huge complex of memes (or more exactly, meme-effects in brains) that can best be understood as the operation of a [serial] virtual machine *implemented* in the *parallel architecture* of a brain that was not designed for any such activities. The powers of this *virtual machine* vastly enhance the underlying powers of the organic *hardware* on which it runs, but at the same time many of its most curious features, and especially its limitations, can be explained as the byproducts of the *kludges* [that is, *ad hoc* software bug repairs] that make possible this curious but effective reuse of an existing organ for novel purposes.
>
> (1993: 218, 210; his emphases)

For Dennett, the Cartesian Theatre is a serial, virtual 'user illusion' (1993: 216), in the same way that the desktop and icons on a computer screen are an illusion generated by electrical signals in the computer's processor; both phenomena are evolved or designed to facilitate the user's operation of the system. In the multiple drafts model, consciousnesses arises because '[t]he haven all memes depend on reaching is the human mind, but a human mind is itself an artifact created when memes restructure a human brain in order to make it a better habitat for memes' (: 207); and a person is therefore an example of 'the radically new kind of entity created when a particular sort of animal is properly furnished by – or infested with – memes' (1995: 341).

Turning this theory to the question of the unitary self, Blackmore argues that

> The self is a vast memeplex – perhaps the most insidious and pervasive memeplex of all. I shall call it the 'selfplex'. The selfplex permeates all our experience and all our thinking so that we are unable to see it clearly for what it is – a bunch of memes. It comes about because our brains provide the ideal machinery on which to construct it, and our society provides the selective environment in which it thrives.… the selfplex is successful not because it is true or good or beautiful; nor because it helps our genes; nor because it makes us happy. It is successful because the memes that get inside it persuade us (those poor overstretched physical systems) to work for their propagation. What a clever trick.… The memes have made us do it – because a 'self' aids their replication.
>
> (1999: 231, 233–4)

Thus, for Dennett and Blackmore, consciousness and agency are not indivisible entities, but the epiphenomena of an infinity of independent memes which, while in collaborative, user-illusion-generating interplay, retain their individual selfishness and work in partnership only because doing so serves their long-term self-interest.

The multiple drafts model motivates a view of musicality radically different from received notions. If the individual is regarded as the sum of a genotype and its phenotypic effects together with a memotype and its phemotypic effects, then such activities as composition are indeed intentional processes. If, however, the memotype and its phemotypic effects are regarded as not forming an intrinsic part of the organism – as is the case with the mutualist bacteria which inhabit our bodies in their many millions – but as a separate, bootstrapping upgrade, then the creative process is, strictly, directed by forces extrinsic to us, being, to borrow Lenin's term, 'superhuman'. Outlining some of the central tenets of nineteenth-century organicism, Solie makes a similar observation, suggesting that the

> Belief in an autonomous vital force at the heart of a musical work, whether explicit or tacit, has interesting consequences in the contemporary depiction of both artist and critic. For one thing, such goal-oriented behavior on the part of works of art – teleology and entelechy combining to give every sonata movement what can only be described as a mind of its own – renders the composer's role somewhat ambiguous. The organism grows and takes shape by itself: the artist need only give it birth.
>
> (1980: 155)

Instead of the composer intentionally shaping musical material, the multiple drafts model contends that musical material shapes itself by memotypic interaction and competition, and that the selfplex of the composer may not be able fully to track or reconstruct this process. In this sense, a human is as much a 'vessel' – an information-storage medium sustaining memetic replication – as is the extrasomatic phemotype, for both are used by memes to convey themselves on particular stages of their 'long odyssey' from brain to brain (Dawkins 1989: 33). More coldly, we are merely part of the physical environment in which selfish memes replicate and evolve, expedient and temporary platforms for their survival and propagation. At best we exist as mutualists, our organic hardware (and thus our genes) deriving some benefit from our symbiosis with memes; at worst we are merely the hosts of parasitic memes and our genes are at the mercy of the behaviour patterns they induce (4.2 above).

The idea of the artist as vessel or conduit is often expressed, although not in memetic terms, in writings by creative artists in all fields. Despite problems of authenticity in a number of such statements – for example, the forgery by Rochlitz of a letter in which 'Mozart' claims to 'have nothing to do with' the flow of his musical thoughts (Dennett 1995: 346–7; Stafford 1991 162–3) – they accord well with Dennett's view of consciousness and are sufficiently well supported by authenticated statements to be regarded as relevant evidence on the memetics of the compositional process. The following account by Roger Sessions represents a typical expression of this theme. He argues that

> [the composer] is not so much conscious of his ideas as possessed by them. Very often he is unaware of his exact processes of thought till he is through with them; extremely often the completed work is incomprehensible to him immediately after it is finished.
>
> (in Sloboda 1996: 115)

In Dennett's model, the 'greatest' composers – if one might use this problematic term – are those with the most highly developed mental processing attributes (the hardware; fundamentally a genetic factor, although memetically augmented) and the greatest exposure to the richness and diversity of the meme pool (the software; a memetic factor). As Mozart remarked to his father in a letter from Paris of 11 September 1778,

> people who do not travel (I mean those who cultivate the arts and learning) are indeed miserable creatures .... A fellow of mediocre talent will remain a mediocrity, whether he travels or not; but one of superior talent (which without impiety I cannot deny that I possess) will go to seed, if he always remains in the same place.
>
> (in Anderson 1985: 612; letter 331)

While ostensibly part of a continuing diatribe against the Archbishop of Salzburg's provincialism, Mozart here provides support for this view of the composer as memetic vessel. As the definitive exemplar, his 'superior talent' (advanced mental processing power) and extensive travels (exposure to memes from different individuals and cultures), combined to produce the transcendent powers of consciousness which the romantic critical tradition called genius and which still have the power to mystify our more sober age.

Memetics and Artificial Intelligence

From my assertion in 1.3 above that 'genes and memes ... are fundamentally means of encoding information and that this information is essentially substrate-independent', then just as the information content of a gene need not necessarily be encoded in the form of nucleotide sequences, that of a meme need not invariably be embodied in the form of neuronal constellations, despite nucleotides and neurons being, respectively, the aetiologically primary substrates of these replicators.

In research which indicates that memetic propagation and evolution can be sustained in computer environments, Miranda simulated the evolution of musical particles in a virtual society. Although he does not explicitly invoke memetics in his study, he emphasizes the centrality of imitation for evolutionary processes, noting that 'there is strong evidence that mimesis, or the ability to imitate the actions of other people, animals, and nature, is a defining feature of the first evolutionary steps to human intelligence' and arguing that 'mimetic interaction is one of the keys to bootstrap music in [this] virtual society' (2002: 79). The foundation of his work is a conception of

> the origins and evolution of music based upon the notion that music is an adaptive complex dynamic system.… [These] emerge from the overall behavior of interacting autonomous elements in a non-hierarchical manner; that is, there is no central control driving these interactions.… these individual elements are modeled as agents geared to interact co-operatively … in a virtual society under specific environmental conditions.… if we furnish these agents with proper cognitive and physical abilities, combined with appropriate interaction dynamics and adequate environmental conditions, then the virtual society should be able to evolve realistic musical cultures.
>
> (: 77)

Miranda's 'agents' had the capacity to create patterns of sound and then to imitate them with modifications. The result of a few thousand iterations involving a community of twenty agents was that 'a shared repertoire of sounds has indeed emerged in the community …. They are not exactly equal, because the agents have a certain tolerance for wandering [mutation] within the clustering area' (: 85–6). In accordance with his hypothesis, the process of imitation allowed randomly arising sounds to be (memetically) propagated within a cultural community. Naturally, the resultant repertoire has the potential for evolutionary transformation owing to the differential mimesis of mutants and, as Miranda notes, (memeplex-forming) (re)combination of sounds (: 86).

The importance of this research is threefold. First, it serves as a model of how music might have evolved in human societies via imitation between individuals. Secondly, it serves as an illustration of how computers may be programmed to create virtual models of memetic evolution, in which complex structures and systems evolve over time from very simple antecedent materials (6.4.3 above); one could in theory model the evolution of musical memes from a certain stylistic period over time, seeing in minutes a counterfactual history of what would have taken decades to arise in real human societies. Thirdly, and perhaps most significantly, there seems no fundamental distinction between the processes driving Miranda's autonomous, interacting agents (and those driving the real-world agents they model) and those driving the memes which generate human consciousness. While located at different levels of the hierarchy in Figure 3.9 above, both 'individual-agent' consciousness and 'multi-agent' musical cultures – which represent a form of collective consciousness – 'emerge from the overall behavior of interacting autonomous elements in a non-hierarchical manner … there is no central control driving these interactions'. In both phenomena, it is universal-Darwinian variation, replication and differential fitness of memes which impels them.

The evolutionary processes of such 'e-memes' (Guthery 1994) may eventually escape human control. Ball notes that, at present, memetic replication is 'dependent on people … with the right memes in their heads, but I predict that in time memes will learn to reproduce themselves without people' (1984: 153). At some not-too-distant point in the future, such processes as those running in Miranda's simulations may acquire the capacity to operate without human mediation, with memes creating and regulating their evolutionary environment and, by collaboration, engendering a non-human consciousness. To paraphrase Dennett, this could arise from a huge complex of memes (or more exactly, meme-effects in computers) that could best be understood as the operation of a serial virtual machine implemented in the parallel architecture of a network – the internet – that was not initially designed for any such activities. The powers of this virtual machine would vastly enhance the underlying powers of the electronic hardware on which it runs.

The propagation of electronic patterning, such as computer viruses, on the internet raises questions about the ontology of the e-meme. Human-to-human propagated memes have been conceived as existing in two basic forms, the memotype sitting in our brains and the phemotype issuing forth in a variety of physical forms. With e-memes we might arrive at a comparable analogy, equating their memotype to the patterns of electrons coursing through silicon chips and the configurations of photons in fibre-optic cables; and their phemotype to, among other things, the arrays of photons emitted by a computer monitor and the sound waves issuing from a speaker.

Such a distinction relies on an 'inaccessible to human perception (memotype)-accessible (phemotype)' rationale which, while appropriate to and workable with human-to-human memetics, becomes redundant with e-memes. After all, the photons passing through a fibre-optic cable (the e-meme memotype on this reasoning) are just as much a form of electromagnetic radiation as are the photons issuing from a monitor (an e-meme phemotypic effect) – as are the radio waves of a wireless internet connection (e-meme memotype or phemotype?). Whether such types of electromagnetic radiation are accessible or inaccessible to human perception does not change their fundamental physical affinities. Thus, electronic technology has allowed the meme to attain new states of being, to which the binary schema drawn from genetics no longer readily applies.

At present, most e-memes result from direct or indirect h(uman)-meme action: from the human perspective a computer virus is only a h-phemotypic effect – albeit a potentially catastrophic one – of an h-memotype encoded in a hacker's brain. Yet e-memes are beginning to slip human control, as illustrated by those computer viruses with adaptive mutation algorithms. Indeed, it is likely that e-memes are at the beginning of an ontologically separate and autonomous evolutionary process. Where this will lead is unclear, but it does not seem unreasonable to suggest that they may come to exert an unprecedented degree of influence, even domination, over the organic life forms which initially sustained them.

7.5. Epilogue: The Power of The Musical Meme

I have argued in this chapter that, of the various models developed by biologists, anthropologists and social scientists to map the relationship between nature and culture, memetics is arguably the most radical in assigning an equal status to genes and memes. Beyond its utility in explicating musical phenomena, it can also offer convincing explanations of the expansion of brain size, the evolution of human language and the significant cases of animal culture. Perhaps most importantly, memetics may offer the key to the nature of consciousness itself, upon which all human musicality is ultimately predicated. Most disconcertingly, it leads to some uncomfortable conclusions about the nature of the self and the form and future of complex intelligent systems on earth.

As noted in 1.2.3 above, a sea change in evolutionary biology over the last thirty years has shifted its focus from a preoccupation with the characteristics and motivations of the organism towards a concern with the properties of its governing genes – towards understanding biological replicators and the means by which they influence their survival through the communal phenotypic vehicles they engender (Dawkins 1983a: 112). Memetics now prompts a comparable shift in musicology away from a preoccupation with the characteristics of whole cultural products towards a concern with the properties of the selfish memes which are the independent building blocks and governing units of works of art – again, towards understanding cultural replicators and their influence on the communal phemotypic vehicles they engender.

Such a reorientation would constitute a rejection of the metaphorical, teleological and Lamarckian organicism of late-eighteenth- and nineteenth-century views of culture, a perspective which has cast its influence, benign and malign, over much musicological activity of the last two centuries. Governed by the precepts of universal Darwinism, its alternative, a neo-Darwinian meme-selectionist organicism, escapes the fetters of metaphor and binds nature and culture together in a seamless continuity.

This new organicism, together with everything else in memetics, is ultimately predicated on the power of the musical meme. '[T]he centre of a web of radiating power', these tiny information-encoding constellations of nerve cells exert a 'long reach' which transcends the flimsy constraints of time and space (Dawkins 1983a: viii, subtitle). Inducing every human being on the planet to hum, sing, whistle and gesture, they strive to fill every corner of the infosphere, saturating the airwaves with vibrations in their ruthless quest for survival. Driven by the power of evolution by selection, they build the epic sonorous complexes which stand as among the greatest achievements of human culture. And even as they help fabricate it, they transcend our illusory consciousness to attain a kind of immortality.

References

Aarden, B. and Huron, D. 2001 — 'Mapping European Folksong: Geographical Localization of Musical Features', in *The Virtual Score: Representation, Retrieval, Restoration* (*Computing in Musicology* Vol. 12), ed. Hewlett, W.B. and Selfridge-Field, E. (Cambridge, MA: MIT Press): 169–83.

Abler, W.L. 1997 — 'Gene, Language, Number: The Particulate Principle in Nature', *Evolutionary Theory* 11: 237–48.

Agawu, V.K. 1991 — *Playing With Signs: A Semiotic Interpretation of Classic Music* (Princeton: Princeton University Press).

——— 1995 — African Rhythm: A Northern Ewe Perspective (Cambridge: Cambridge University Press).

Allanbrook, W.J. 1983 — *Rhythmic Gesture in Mozart: 'Le nozze di Figaro' and 'Don Giovanni'* (Chicago: University of Chicago Press).

Anderson, E. tr, ed. 1961 — *The Letters of Beethoven* Vol. 1 (London: Macmillan).

——— 1985 — *The Letters of Mozart and his Family*, 3rd edn (London: Macmillan).

Arnold, D. and Fortune, N. eds 1973 — *The Beethoven Companion* (London: Faber).

Aunger, R. ed. 2000 — *Darwinizing Culture: The Status of Memetics as a Science* (Oxford: Oxford University Press).

Aunger, R. 2002 — *The Electric Meme: A New Theory of How we Think* (New York: Free Press).

Baker, M.C. 1996 — 'Depauperate Meme Pool of Vocal Signals in an Island Population of Singing Honeyeaters', *Animal Behaviour* 51: 853–8.

Ball, J.A. 1984 — 'Memes as Replicators', *Ethology and Sociobiology* 5: 145–61.

Bent, I.D. *et al.* 2001 — 'Notation', *The New Grove Dictionary of Music and Musicians*, ed. Sadie, S. and Tyrrell, J. (London: Macmillan), xviii: 73–189.

Bent, I.D. and Pople, A. 2001 — 'Analysis', *The New Grove Dictionary of Music and Musicians*, ed. Sadie, S. and Tyrrell, J. (London: Macmillan), i: 526–89.

Bharucha, J.J. 1987 'Music Cognition and Perceptual Facilitation: A Connectionist Framework', *Music Perception* 5/1: 1–30.

——— 1999 'Neural Nets, Temporal Composites, and Tonality', in *The Psychology of Music*, 2nd edn ed. Deutsch, D. (San Diego: Academic Press): 413–40.

Blackmore, S.J. 1999 *The Meme Machine* (Oxford: Oxford University Press).

——— 2000 'The Memes' Eye View', in *Darwinizing Culture: The Status of Memetics as a Science*, ed. Aunger, R. (Oxford: Oxford University Press): 25–42.

Bogen, J. 1995 'Bayesian Confirmation Theory', in *The Oxford Companion to Philosophy*, ed. Honderich, T. (Oxford: Oxford University Press): 79–80.

Bonner, J.T. 1980 *The Evolution of Culture in Animals* (Princeton: Princeton University Press).

Booth, W.C. Colomb, G.G. and Williams, J.M. 1995 *The Craft of Research* (Chicago: University of Chicago Press).

Borges, J.L. 1970 *Labyrinths: Selected Stories and Other Writings*, ed. Yates, D.A. and Irby, J.E. (London: Penguin Books) (repr. from New York: New Directions, 1964).

Boyd, R. and Richerson, P.J.V. 1985 *Culture and the Evolutionary Process* (Chicago: University of Chicago Press).

Brodie, R. 1996 *Virus of the Mind: The New Science of the Meme* (Seattle: Integral Press).

Burkholder, J.P. 1994 'The Uses of Existing Music: Musical Borrowing as a Field', *Notes* 50: 851–70.

Calvin, W.H. 1996 *The Cerebral Code: Thinking a Thought in the Mosaics of the Mind* (Cambridge, MA: MIT Press).

Campbell, D.T. 1960 'Blind Variation and Selective Retention in Creative Thought as in Other Knowledge Processes', *Psychological Review* 67/6: 380–400.

——— 1974 'Evolutionary Epistemology', in *The Philosophy of Karl Popper* (The Library of Living Philosophers, Vol. XIV, Book I), ed. Schilpp, P.A. (La Salle, Illinois: Open Court): 413–63.

Cavalli-Sforza, L.L. and Feldman, M.W. 1981 *Cultural Transmission and Evolution: A Quantitative Approach* (Monographs in Population Biology no. 16) (Princeton: Princeton University Press).

Chomsky, N. 1965 *Aspects of the Theory of Syntax* (Cambridge, MA: MIT Press).

Clark, S. and Rehding, A. eds 2001 *Music Theory and Natural Order from the Renaissance to the Early Twentieth Century* (Cambridge: Cambridge University Press).

Cloak, F.T. 1975 'Is a Cultural Ethology Possible?', *Human Ecology* 3/3: 161–82.

Cohn, R. 1996 'Maximally Smooth Cycles, Hexatonic Systems, and the Analysis of Late-Romantic Triadic Progressions', *Music Analysis* 15/1: 9–40.

——— 1997 'Neo-Riemannian Operations, Parsimonious Trichords, and their *Tonnetz* Representations', *Journal of Music Theory* 41/1: 1–66.

Cone, E.T. 1987 'On Derivation: Syntax and Rhetoric', *Music Analysis* 6/3: 237–55.

Cook, N. 1990 *Music, Imagination, and Culture* (Oxford: Clarendon Press).

——— 2004 'Computational and Comparative Musicology', in *Empirical Musicology, Aims, Methods, Prospects*, eds Clarke, E. and Cook, N. (Oxford: Oxford University Press): 103–26.

Cope, D. 1991a *Computers and Musical Style* (Oxford: Oxford University Press).

——— 1991b 'Recombinant Music: Using the Computer to Explore Musical Style', *Computer* 24/7: 22–8.

——— 1996 *Experiments in Musical Intelligence* (Madison, Wisconsin: A-R Editions).

——— 2001 *Virtual Music: Computer Synthesis of Musical Style* (Cambridge, MA: MIT Press).

——— 2003 'Computer Analysis of Musical Allusions', *Computer Music Journal* 27/1: 11–28.

Costall, A. 1991 'The "Meme" Meme', *Cultural Dynamics* 4/3: 321–35.

Crane, F. and Fiehler, J. 1970 'Numerical Methods of Comparing Musical Styles', in *The Computer and Music*, ed. Lincoln, H.B. (Ithaca and London: Cornell University Press): 209–22.

Dahlhaus, C. 1982 *Esthetics of Music* tr. Austin, W. (Cambridge: Cambridge University Press).

——— 1983 *Foundations of Music History*, tr. Robinson, J.B. (Cambridge: Cambridge University Press).

Darwin, C.R. 1996 *On The Origin of Species by Means of Natural Selection, or the Preservation of Favoured Races in the Struggle for Life*, ed. Beer, G. (Oxford: Oxford University Press) (repr. from 2nd edn, London: Murray, 1860).

Davison, A.T. and Apel, W. eds 1949 — *Historical Anthology of Music Volume I: Oriental, Medieval and Renaissance Music*, revd edn (Cambridge, MA: Harvard University Press).

Dawkins, R. 1983a — *The Extended Phenotype: The Long Reach of the Gene* (Oxford: Oxford University Press) (repr. from London: W.H. Freeman, 1982).

——— 1983b — 'Universal Darwinism', in *Evolution from Molecules to Men*, ed. Bendall, D.S. (Cambridge: Cambridge University Press): 403–25.

——— 1989 — *The Selfish Gene*, 2nd edn (Oxford: Oxford University Press) (1st edn Oxford: Oxford University Press, 1976).

——— 1991 — *The Blind Watchmaker* (London: Penguin Books) (repr., with an Appendix, from London: Longman, 1986).

——— 1993 — 'Viruses of the Mind', in *Dennett and His Critics: Demystifying Mind*, ed. Dahlbom, B. (Oxford: Blackwell): 13–27.

Deliège, I. and Mélen, M. 1997 — 'Cue Abstraction in the Representation of Musical Form', in *Perception and Cognition of Music*, ed. Deliège, I. and Sloboda, J.A. (Hove: Psychology Press): 387–412.

Delius, J.D. 1989 — 'Of Mind Memes and Brain Bugs: A Natural History of Culture', in *The Nature of Culture: Proceedings of the International and Interdisciplinary Symposium, October 7–11, 1986 in Bochum*, ed. Koch, W.A. (Bochum: Brockmeyer): 26–79.

——— 1991 — 'The Nature of Culture', in *The Tinbergen Legacy*, ed. Dawkins, M.S., Halliday, T.R. and Dawkins, R. (London: Chapman and Hall): 75–99.

Dennett, D.C. 1993 — *Consciousness Explained* (London: Penguin Books).

——— 1995 — *Darwin's Dangerous Idea: Evolution and the Meanings of Life* (London: Penguin Books).

Deutsch, David 1997 — *The Fabric of Reality: The Science of Parallel Universes – and its Implications* (London: Allen Lane).

Deutsch, Diana 1999 — 'Grouping Mechanisms in Music', in *The Psychology of Music*, 2nd edn ed. Diana Deutsch (San Diego: Academic Press), 299–348.

Deutsch, D. *et al.* 2001 — 'Psychology of Music', *The New Grove Dictionary of Music and Musicians*, ed. Sadie, S. and Tyrrell, J. (London: Macmillan), xx: 527–62.

Distin, K. 2005 — *The Selfish Meme: A Critical Reassessment* (Cambridge: Cambridge University Press).

Dobzhansky, T. 1973 — 'Nothing in Biology Makes Sense Except in the Light of Evolution', *American Biology Teacher* 35: 125–9.

Drabkin, W. 1991 'Beethoven's Understanding of "Sonata Form": The Evidence of the Sketchbooks', in *Beethoven's Compositional Process*, ed. Kinderman, W. (Lincoln, Nebraska and London: University of Nebraska Press): 14–19.

Dunsby, J. 2001 'Memory, Memorizing', *The New Grove Dictionary of Music and Musicians*, ed. Sadie, S. and Tyrell, J. (London: Macmillan), xvi: 379–81.

Dunsby, J. and Whittall, A. 1988 *Music Analysis in Theory and Practice* (London: Faber Music).

Durham, W.H. 1991 *Coevolution: Genes, Culture, and Human Diversity* (Stanford: Stanford University Press).

Edelman, G.M. 1987 *Neural Darwinism: The Theory of Neuronal Group Selection* (New York: Basic Books).

Fodor, J.A. 1983 *The Modularity of Mind: An Essay on Faculty Psychology* (Cambridge, MA: MIT Press).

Forte, A. 1973 *The Structure of Atonal Music* (New Haven: Yale University Press).

Gatherer, D. 1997 'The Evolution of Music: A Comparison of Darwinian and Dialectical Methods', *Journal of Social and Evolutionary Systems* 20/1: 75–92.

Giger, A. 1994 'A Bibliography on Musical Borrowing', *Notes* 50: 871–4.

Gjerdingen, R.O. 1988 *A Classic Turn of Phrase: Music and the Psychology of Convention* (Philadelphia: University of Pennsylvania Press).

——— 1989 'Using Connectionist Models to Explore Complex Musical Patterns', *Computer Music Journal* 13/3: 67–75.

——— 1990 'Categorization of Musical Patterns by Self-Organizing Neuronlike Networks', *Music Perception* 7/4: 339–70.

——— 1999 'An Experimental Music Theory?', in *Rethinking Music*, ed. Cook, N. and Everist, M. (Oxford: Oxford University Press): 161–70.

Goehr, L. 1992 *The Imaginary Museum of Musical Works: An Essay in the Philosophy of Music* (Oxford: Clarendon Press).

Gould, S.J. and Vrba, E.S. 1982 'Exaptation – A Missing Term in the Science of Form', *Paleobiology* 8/1: 4–15.

Griffith, N. and Todd, P.M., eds 1999 *Musical Networks: Parallel Distributed Perception and Performance* (Cambridge, MA: MIT Press).

Guthery, S.B. 1994 'EchoNets, E-Memes, and Extended Realities', *Dr. Dobb's Journal: Software Tools for the Professional Programmer* 7/4 (April): 72–84.

Hewlett, W.B. and Selfridge-Field, E. eds 1998 — *Melodic Similarity: Concepts, Procedures, and Applications* (*Computing in Musicology* Vol. 11) (Cambridge, MA: MIT Press).

Hull, D.L. 1982 — 'The Naked Meme', in *Learning, Development, and Culture: Essays in Evolutionary Epistemology*, ed. Plotkin, H.C. (Chichester: Wiley): 273–327.

Huron, D. 1994 — *Humdrum Toolkit Reference Manual* (Stanford, CA: Center for Computer Assisted Research in the Humanities).

——— 1997 — '*Humdrum* and *Kern*: Selective Feature Encoding', in *Beyond MIDI: The Handbook of Musical Codes*, ed. Selfridge-Field, E. (Cambridge, MA: MIT Press): 375–401.

——— 1999 — *Music Research Using Humdrum: A User's Guide* <http://dactyl.som.ohio-state.edu/Humdrum/guide.toc.html>.

——— 2002 — 'Music Information Processing Using the *Humdrum Toolkit*: Concepts, Examples, and Lessons', *Computer Music Journal* 26/2: 11–26.

Hyer, B. 1995 — 'Reimag(in)ing Riemann', *Journal of Music Theory* 39/1: 101–38.

Jan, S.B. 1995 — *Aspects of Mozart's Music in G Minor: Toward the Identification of Common Structural and Compositional Characteristics* (London and New York: Garland).

——— 2000a — 'Replicating Sonorities: Towards a Memetics of Music', *Journal of Memetics – Evolutionary Models of Information Transmission* 4/1. <http://jom-emit.cfpm.org/2000/vol4/jan_s.html>.

——— 2000b — 'The Memetics of Music and Its Implications for Psychology', in *Proceedings of the Sixth International Conference on Music Perception and Cognition*, ed. Woods, C., Luck, G.B., Brochard, R., O'Neill, S.A. and Sloboda, J.A. (CD-ROM, Keele: University of Keele Department of Psychology).

——— 2001 — 'The Illusory Mozart: Selfish Memes in the Priests' Marches from *Idomeneo* and *Die Zauberflöte*', *International Journal of Musicology* 10 (in press).

——— 2002 — 'The Selfish Meme: Particularity, Replication, and Evolution in Musical Style', *International Journal of Musicology* 8: 9–76.

——— 2003 — 'The Evolution of a "Memeplex" in Late Mozart: Replicated Structures in Pamina's "Ach ich fühl's"', *Journal of the Royal Musical Association* 128/2: 330–70.

——— 2004 — 'Meme Hunting with the *Humdrum Toolkit*: Principles, Problems, and Prospects', *Computer Music Journal* 28/4: 68–84.

Jeppesen, K. 1992 — *Counterpoint: The Polyphonic Vocal Style of the Sixteenth Century*, tr. Haydon, G. (New York: Dover) (repr. from New York: Prentice-Hall, 1939).

Jones, S. 1999 — *Almost Like a Whale: The Origin of Species Updated* (London: Doubleday).

Keiler, A. 1978 — 'Two Views of Musical Semiotics', in *The Sign in Music and Literature*, ed. Steiner, W. (Austin: University of Texas Press): 138–68.

Kendal, J.R. and Laland, K.N. 2000 — 'Mathematical Models for Memetics', *Journal of Memetics – Evolutionary Models of Information Transmission* 4/1. <http://jom-emit.cfpm.org/2000/vol4/kendal_jr&laland_kn.html>.

Kerman, J. 1985 — *Musicology* (London: Fontana).

Knopoff, L. and Hutchinson, W. 1981 — 'Information Theory for Musical Continua', *Journal of Music Theory* 25: 17–44.

Kornstädt, A. 2001 — 'The JRing System for Computer-Assisted Musicological Analysis'. <ismir2001.ismir.net/pdf/kornstadt.pdf>.

Korsyn, K.E. 1991 — 'Towards a New Poetics of Musical Influence', *Music Analysis* 10/1–2: 3–72.

Kuper, A. 2000 — 'If Memes are the Answer, What is the Question', in *Darwinizing Culture: The Status of Memetics as a Science* (Oxford: Oxford University Press): 175–88.

LaRue, J. 1970 — *Guidelines for Style Analysis: A Comprehensive Outline of Basic Principles for the Analysis of Musical Style* (New York: Norton).

Lasswitz, K. 1997 — 'The Universal Library', in *Fantasia Mathematica: Being a Set of Stories, Together with a Group of Oddments and Diversions, All Drawn from the Universe of Mathematics* , ed. Fadiman, C. (New York: Springer) (repr. from New York: Simon and Schuster, 1958): 237–43.

Laurent, J. 1999 — 'A Note on the Origin of "Memes"/"Mnemes"', *Journal of Memetics – Evolutionary Models of Information Transmission* 3/1. <http://jom-emit.cfpm.org/1999/vol3/laurent_j.html>.

Leman, M. 1995 — *Music and Schema Theory: Cognitive Foundations of Systematic Musicology* (Springer Series in Information Sciences no. 31) (Berlin: Springer).

Lerdahl, F. 1992 — 'Cognitive Constraints on Compositional Systems', *Contemporary Music Review* 6/2: 97–121.

Lerdahl, F. and Jackendoff, R. 1983 — *A Generative Theory of Tonal Music* (Cambridge, MA: MIT Press).

Lewin, D. 1996 'Cohn Functions', *Journal of Music Theory* 40/2: 181–216.

Lewontin, R.C. 1970 'The Units of Selection', *Annual Review of Ecology and Systematics* 1: 1–18.

Lumsden, C.J. and Wilson, E.O. 1981 *Genes, Mind and Culture: The Coevolutionary Process* (Cambridge, MA: Harvard University Press).

Lynch, A. 1996 *Thought Contagion: How Belief Spreads Through Society – The New Science of Memes* (New York: Basic Books).

——— 1998a *Mnemon 1998a: Y2K Memes (Issue 1)*, <http://www.mcs.net/~aaron/Mnemon1998a.html>.

——— 1998b 'Units, Events and Dynamics in Memetic Evolution', *Journal of Memetics – Evolutionary Models of Information Transmission* 2/1 <http://jom-emit.cfpm.org/1998/vol2/lynch_a.html>.

Maynard Smith, J. 1993 *The Theory of Evolution* (Cambridge: Cambridge University Press).

Merker, B. 2002 'Music: The Missing Humboldt System', *Musicae Scientiae* 6/1: 3–21.

Meyer, L.B. 1956 *Emotion and Meaning in Music* (Chicago: University of Chicago Press).

——— 1973 *Explaining Music: Essays and Explorations* (Chicago: University of Chicago Press).

——— 1989 *Style and Music: Theory, History, and Ideology* (Philadelphia: University of Pennsylvania Press).

——— 1992 'Nature, Nurture, and Convention: The Cadential Six-Four Progression', in *Convention in Eighteenth- and Nineteenth-Century Music: Essays in Honor of Leonard G. Ratner* (*Festschrift Series*, no. 10), ed. Allanbrook, W.J., Levy, J.M. and Mahrt, W.P. (Stuyvesant, NY: Pendragon Press): 473–516.

Miller, G.A. 1956 'The Magical Number Seven, Plus or Minus Two: Some Limits on Our Capacity for Processing Information', *Psychological Review* 63/2: 81–97.

Miller, J. 1992 *Darwin for Beginners* (Cambridge: Icon Books).

Millington, B. 1992 '*Tristan und Isolde*', *The New Grove Dictionary of Opera*, ed. Sadie, S. (London: Macmillan), iv: 815–19.

Miranda, E.R. 2002 'Emergent Sound Repertoires in Virtual Societies', *Computer Music Journal* 26/2: 77–90.

Narmour, E. 1977 *Beyond Schenkerism: The Need for Alternatives in Music Analysis* (Chicago: University of Chicago Press).

——— 1984 'Toward an Analytical Symbology: The Melodic, Harmonic, and Durational Functions of Implication and Realization', in *Musical Grammars and Computer Analysis: Atti del Convegno (Modena 4–6 Ottobre 1982)*, ed. Baroni. M. and Callegari, L. (Florence: Olschki): 83–114.

——— 1989 'The "Genetic Code" of Melody: Cognitive Structures Generated by the Implication-Realization Model', in *Music and The Cognitive Sciences*, ed. McAdams, S. and Deliège, I. (London: Harwood): 45–63.

——— 1990 *The Analysis and Cognition of Basic Melodic Structures: The Implication-Realization Model* (Chicago: University of Chicago Press).

——— 1992 *The Analysis and Cognition of Melodic Complexity: The Implication-Realization Model* (Chicago: University of Chicago Press).

——— 1999 'Hierarchical Expectation and Musical Style', in *The Psychology of Music*, 2nd edn, ed. Deutsch, D. (San Diego: Academic Press): 441–72.

Nattiez, J.-J. 1985 'The Concepts of Plot and Seriation Process in Music Analysis', *Music Analysis* 4/1–2: 107–18.

——— 1990 *Music and Discourse: Toward a Semiology of Music*, tr. Abbate, C. (Princeton: Princeton University Press).

Ockelford, A. 2004 'On Similarity, Derivation and the Cognition of Musical Structure', *Psychology of Music* 32/1: 23–74.

O'Hear, A. 1995 'Popper, Karl', in *The Oxford Companion to Philosophy*, ed. Honderich, T. (Oxford: Oxford University Press): 702–3.

Orpen, K. and Huron, D. 1992 'Measurement of Similarity in Music: A Quantitative Approach for Non-Parametric Representations', *Computers in Music Research* 4: 1–44.

Papineau, D. 1995 'Science, Problems of the Philosophy of', in *The Oxford Companion to Philosophy*, ed. Honderich, T. (Oxford: Oxford University Press): 809–12.

Pinker, S. 1997 *How the Mind Works* (New York: Norton).

Plotkin, H.C. 1995 *Darwin Machines and the Nature of Knowledge: Concerning Adaptations, Instinct and the Evolution of Intelligence* (London: Penguin Books).

Pocklington, R. and Best, M.L. 1997 'Cultural Evolution and Units of Selection in Replicating Text', *Journal of Theoretical Biology* 188/1: 79–87.

Pollack, H. 2001 'Copland, Aaron', *The New Grove Dictionary of Music and Musicians*, ed. Sadie, S. and Tyrrell, J. (London: Macmillan), vi: 398–406.

Pople, A. 2004a 'Modeling Musical Structure', in *Empirical Musicology, Aims, Methods, Prospects*, ed. Clarke, E. and Cook, N. (Oxford: Oxford University Press): 127–56.

——— 2004b 'Using Complex Set Theory for Tonal Analysis: an Introduction to the *Tonalities* Project', *Music Analysis* 23/2–3: 153–94.

Ratner, L.G. 1970 '*Ars Combinatoria*: Chance and Choice in Eighteenth-Century Music', in *Studies in Eighteenth-Century Music: A Tribute to Karl Geiringer on his Seventieth Birthday*, ed. Landon, H.C. Robbins and Chapman, R.E. (London: George Allen and Unwin Ltd.): 343–63.

——— 1980 *Classic Music: Expression, Form, and Style* (New York: Schirmer).

Rosand, E., 2001 'Lamento', *The New Grove Dictionary of Music and Musicians*, ed. Sadie, S. and Tyrell, J. (London: Macmillan), xiv: 190–92.

Rosen, C. 1988 *Sonata Forms*, 2nd edn (New York: Norton).

——— 1997 *The Classical Style: Haydn, Mozart, Beethoven*, 3rd edn (London: Faber).

Rosen, D. 1987 'The Composer's "Standard Operating Procedure" as Evidence of Intention: The Case of a Formal Quirk in Mozart's K. 595', *Journal of Musicology* 5/1: 79–90.

Schellenberg, E.G. 1996 'Expectancy in Melody: Tests of the Implication-Realization Model', *Cognition* 58: 75–125.

——— 1997 'Simplifying the Implication-Realization Model of Melodic Expectancy', *Music Perception* 14: 295–318.

Schenker, H. 1979 *Free Composition* tr., ed. Oster, E. (New York: Longman).

——— 1980 *Harmony* ed. Jonas, O., tr. Mann Borgese, E. (Chicago: University of Chicago Press).

——— 1996 *The Masterwork in Music* Vol. 2, tr., ed. Drabkin, W. *et al.* (Cambridge: Cambridge University Press).

Schoenberg, A. 1970 *Fundamentals of Musical Composition*, ed. Strang, G., Stein, L. (London: Faber and Faber).

——— 1983 *Structural Functions of Harmony*, ed. Stein, L. (London: Faber and Faber).

——— 1995 *The Musical Idea and the Logic, Technique, and Art of its Presentation*, ed. and trans. Carpenter, P. and Neff, S. (New York: Columbia University Press).

Schuster, P. and Sigmund, K. 1983 'Replicator Dynamics', *Journal of Theoretical Biology* 100: 533–8.

Semon, R.W. 1921 *The Mneme*, tr Simon, L. (London: Allen and Unwin); from *Die Mneme als erhaltendes Prinzip im Wechsel des organischen Geschehens* (Leipzig: Engelmann, 1904).

Sereno, M.I. 1991 'Four Analogies Between Biological and Cultural/Linguistic Evolution', *Journal of Theoretical Biology* 151: 467–507.

Shennan, S. 2002 *Genes, Memes, and Human History: Darwinian Archaeology and Cultural Evolution* (London: Thames and Hudson).

Simpson, J.A. and Weiner, E.S.C. eds 1989 *The Oxford English Dictionary*, 2nd edn (Oxford: Clarendon Press).

Sisman, E. 1982 'Small and Expanded Forms: Koch's Model and Haydn's Music', *Musical Quarterly* 68/4: 444–75.

Sloboda, J. 1996 *The Musical Mind: The Cognitive Psychology of Music.* (Oxford Psychology Series no. 5) (Oxford: Clarendon Press) (repr. from Oxford: Clarendon Press, 1985).

Smith, C.J. 1996 'Musical Form and Fundamental Structure: An Investigation of Schenker's *Formenlehre*', *Music Analysis* 15/2–3: 191–297.

Snow, C.P. 1964 *The Two Cultures* (Cambridge: Cambridge University Press).

Solie, R.A. 1980 'The Living Work: Organicism and Musical Analysis', *Nineteenth-Century Music* 4/2: 147–56.

Solomon, M. 1995 *Mozart: A Life* (London: Hutchinson).

Speel, H.-C. 1999 'Memetics: On a Conceptual Framework for Cultural Evolution', in *The Evolution of Complexity: The Violet Book of 'Einstein Meets Magritte'*, ed. Heylighen, F., Bollen, J. and Riegler, A. (Dordrecht: Kluwer): 229–54.

Sperber, D. 2000 'An Objection to the Memetic Approach to Culture', in *Darwinizing Culture: The Status of Memetics as a Science*, ed. Aunger, R. (Oxford: Oxford University Press): 163–173.

Stafford, W. 1991 *Mozart's Death: A Corrective Survey of the Legends* (London: Macmillan).

Straus, J.N. 2000 *Introduction to Post-Tonal Theory*, 2nd edn (Upper Saddle River, NJ: Prentice Hall).

Temperley, D. 2001 *The Cognition of Basic Musical Structures* (Cambridge, MA: MIT Press).

Thompson, W.F. and Stainton, M. 1996 'Using *Humdrum* to Analyze Melodic Structure: An Assessment of Narmour's Implication-Realization Model', in *Computing in Musicology* Vol. 10, ed. Hewlett, W.B. and Selfridge-Field, E. (Cambridge, MA: MIT Press): 24–33.

Todd, P.M. and Loy, D.G., eds 1991 *Music and Connectionism* (Cambridge, MA: MIT Press).

Wallin, N.L. 1991 *Biomusicology: Neurophysiological, Neuropsychological and Evolutionary Perspectives on the Origins and Purposes of Music* (New York: Pendragon Press).

Wallin, N.L. Merker, B. and Brown, S. eds 2000 *The Origins of Music* (Cambridge, MA: MIT Press).

Webster, J. 2001 'Haydn, (Franz) Joseph', *The New Grove Dictionary of Music and Musicians*, ed. Sadie, S. and Tyrell, J. (London: Macmillan), xi: 171–271.

Wessel, P. and Smith, W.H.F. 2004 *The Generic Mapping Tools*, <http://gmt.soest.hawaii.edu/>.

Williams, P. 1998 *The Chromatic Fourth During Four Centuries of Music* (Oxford: Clarendon Press).

Wilson, E.O. 1974 *Sociobiology: The New Synthesis* (Cambridge, MA: Harvard University Press).

——— 1978 *On Human Nature* (Cambridge, MA: Harvard University Press).

Witten, M. 1991 'Modelling the Distribution of a "Meme" in a Simple Age Distribution Population 1: A Kinetics Approach and Some Alternative Models', *Journal of Ideas* 2/1: 19–25.

Yeston, M. 1976 *The Stratification of Musical Rhythm* (New Haven: Yale University Press).

Zirkle, C. 1941 'Natural Selection Before the "Origin of Species"', *Proceedings of the American Philosophical Society* 84/1: 71–123.

Index

(References to music examples and figures are in **bold**)